The Global Film Book

The Global Film Book is an accessible and entertaining exploration of the development of film as global industry and art form, written especially for students and introducing readers to the rich and varied cinematic landscape beyond Hollywood.

Highlighting areas of difference and similarity in film economies and audiences, as well as form, genre and narrative, this textbook considers a broad range of examples and up-to-date industry data from Europe, Africa, Asia, Australasia and Latin America.

Author Roy Stafford combines detailed studies of indigenous film and television cultures with cross-border, global and online entertainment operations, including examples from Nollywood to Korean Cinema, via *telenovelas* and Nordic crime drama.

The Global Film Book demonstrates a number of contrasting models of contemporary production, distribution and consumption of film worldwide, charting and analysing the past, present and potential futures for film throughout the world.

The book also provides students with:

- a series of exploratory pathways into film culture worldwide
- illuminating analyses and suggestions for further readings and viewing, alongside explanatory margin notes and case studies
- a user-friendly text design, featuring over 120 colour images
- a dynamic and comprehensive blog, online at www.globalfilmstudies.com, providing updates and extensions of case studies in the book and analysis of the latest developments in global film issues.

Roy Stafford has taught film in further, higher and adult education in the UK. He is now a freelance lecturer working in cinema-based film education. He is co-author of *The Media Student's Book* (5th edition, 2010) and has written widely on film, including *Understanding Audiences and the Film Industry* (2007) and study guides on *La haine* (2000) and *Seven Samurai* (2001).

Praise for this edition

'The idea of introducing undergraduate students to industry, modes of production, audience, consumption and the relationship of international films and their industries to Hollywood and other dominant film cultures is simply brilliant. Stafford goes beyond this to show how national cinemas, including the dominant industries, are producing vibrant transnational genres today.'

Negar Mottahedeh, *Associate Professor of Literature and Women's Studies, Duke University, USA*

'Impeccably researched, brilliantly structured, and most importantly, written in an accessible yet highly intelligent style, this is an essential resource for academics, students and the general reader alike ... It is a pleasure to see a book that approaches film from different cultures, offering a voice to film industries including the Middle East, India and China that are equal to, if not more, prescient than Hollywood's domination of the film landscape. *The Global Film Book* is likely to become a key resource for the classroom as it offers both teachers and students exciting approaches of looking at old and new areas of world cinema.'

Omar Ahmed, *Head of Film, Aquinas College, UK*

'Roy Stafford is clearly passionate about cinema. With *The Global Film Book* he distils that enthusiasm into a book that is dedicated to film as an art form that continues to energise artists, producers and audiences from the UK to China and beyond. Focussing on texts and the industries that produce them as well as the structures of distribution and exhibition that see them reach our screens, the clarity and depth of Stafford's work ensures that this is a title that will be on the top of many students' reading lists.'

Dr Andy Willis, *Reader in Film Studies, University of Salford, UK*

The Global Film Book

Roy Stafford

Routledge
Taylor & Francis Group

LONDON AND NEW YORK

First published 2014
by Routledge
2 Park Square, Milton Park, Abingdon, Oxon OX14 4RN

Simultaneously published in the USA and Canada
by Routledge
711 Third Avenue, New York, NY 10017

Routledge is an imprint of the Taylor & Francis Group, an informa business

British Library Cataloguing in Publication Data
A catalogue record for this book is available from the British Library

Library of Congress Cataloging-in-Publication Data
A catalog record for this book has been requested

ISBN: 978-0-415-68896-3 (hbk)
ISBN: 978-0-415-68897-0 (pbk)
ISBN: 978-0-203-13042-1 (ebk)

Typeset in 9/12 Sabon LT Pro
by Fakenham Prepress Solutions, Fakenham, Norfolk NR21 8NN
Printed by Ashford Colour Press Ltd, Gosport, Hampshire

To the memory of Manuel Alvarado, a pioneer of global film and media education.

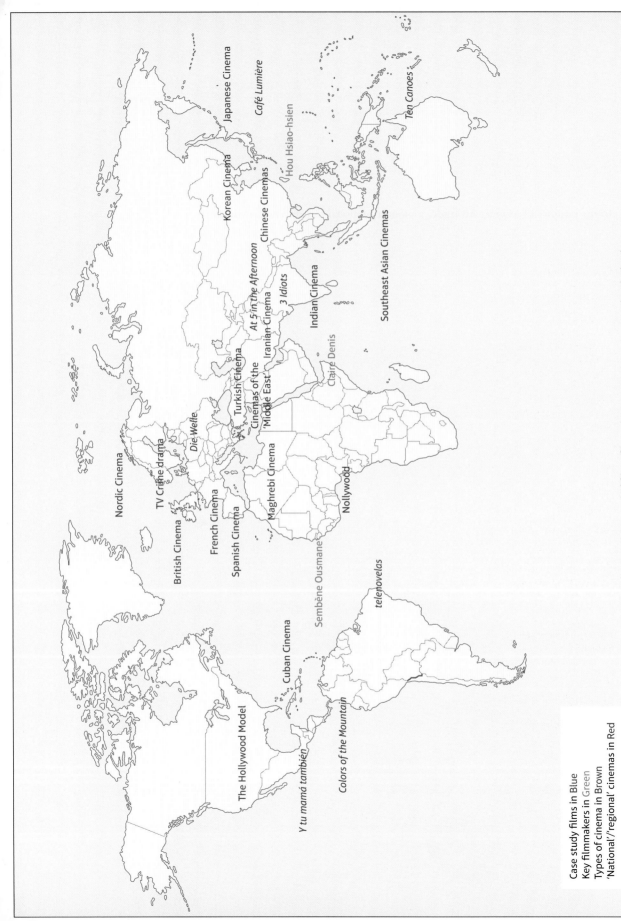

Case study films in Blue
Key filmmakers in Green
Types of cinema in Brown
'National'/'regional' cinemas in Red

Map showing the spread of films, filmmakers, territories etc. covered in the book

Nordic Cinema

TV Crime drama

British Cinema

French Cinema

Spanish Cinema

Die Welle

Japanese Cinema

Café Lumière

Hou Hsiao-hsien

Ten Canoes

Korean Cinema

Chinese Cinemas

At 5 in the Afternoon

Turkish Cinema

Cinemas of the Middle East

Iranian Cinema

3 Idiots

Indian Cinema

Southeast Asian Cinemas

Claire Denis

Maghrebi Cinema

Nollywood

Sembène Ousmane

telenovelas

The Hollywood Model

Cuban Cinema

Y tu mamá también

Colors of the Mountain

Contents

Illustrations

The images below have been reproduced with kind permission. While every effort has been made to trace copyright holders and obtain permission, this has not been possible in all cases. Any omissions brought to our attention will be remedied in future editions.

Chapter 2

Chapter 3

Chapter 4

Chapter 5

Chapter 6

Chapter 7

Chapter 8

Chapter 9

Chapter 10

Chapter 11

Chapter 12

Acknowledgements

This book has been a long time in the making and thanks are gratefully offered to my blogging colleagues Nick Lacey, Des Murphy, Rona Murray, Keith Withall and Omar Ahmed for their comments and suggestions. I would also like to thank Gill Branston, Bill Lawrence and Leung Wing-Fai for their support.

The range of films and research materials used in the book is only possible because of the help of friends and colleagues at various cinemas, film festivals and education venues, and I especially want to thank the education staff and projectionists at the National Media Museum in Bradford and Cornerhouse Cinema in Manchester. What I gained from working with students and teachers on courses and events at those venues has also been immensely valuable.

I would like to thank Natalie Foster for her faith in my original proposal and support throughout and my indefatigable editor Niall Kennedy for his major contribution in putting together what I hope is a useful and accessible book for students. Last but not least, writing would not be possible at all without the support of Marion Pencavel.

Guidance notes for readers

Pathways through the material in *The Global Film Book*

This book is not organised to fit any specification or syllabus. It makes sense to read the Introduction and Chapters 1 to 3 first, as these are designed to form the background for study of global film, but after that there are connections between the material in different chapters that could be approached in various ways. Chapter 12 offers a summary and ideas about new developments. Here are some ways in which individual topics could be approached. These are not the only topics covered, and links between the chapters are highlighted throughout. The map on page vi gives a sense of the spread of material related to film activity in different parts of the world.

Area studies

Chapter 4 on national cinemas followed by material organised by territory:

African cinema: Chapter 8.

Australia: brief analysis in Chapter 3 of *Ten Canoes* and *Toomelah*.

China: Chapter 11.

Egypt: Chapter 6 and Chapter 9 (Ramadan serials).

France: industry and diaspora filmmakers in Chapter 4 as well as discussion of Francophone cinema and French cultural policy pre- and post-colonial in Chapters 6 and 8.

Germany: analysis of *Die Welle* in Chapter 3.

India: Chapter 10.

Iran: Chapter 3 on Samira Makhmalbaf as well as Chapter 6.

Japan: Chapter 5.

Latin America : Chapter 3 on *Y tu mamá también*, Chapter 7 on *Colors of the Mountain*, Chapter 8 on Third Cinema, Chapter 9 on *telenovelas*.

Lebanon: Chapter 6.

Nordic Cinema: Chapter 4 as well as Nordic crime fiction TV in Chapter 9.

Southeast Asia: Chapter 12.

South Korea: Chapter 5.

Spain: Chapter 4.

Turkey: Chapter 6 and Chapter 9 (TV melodrama).

UK: industry and diaspora filmmakers in Chapter 4 as well as British TV in Chapter 9.

Art cinema/specialised cinema

Chapters 7 and 8 as well as discussion of specific filmmakers. Chapter 3 attempts to deal directly with some of the questions about approaching specialised cinema.

Auteur cinema

Extended case studies on Claire Denis (Chapter 7) and Hou Hsiao-hsien (Chapter 11) – linked via Ozu Yasujiro.

Ann Hui, Zhang Yimou, Jia Zhangke in Chapter 11.

Diasporic and exilic filmmakers

Chapter 4: Britain and France; Chapter 6: Iran and Israel and Palestine; Chapter 8: African diaspora; Chapter 10: Indian diaspora cinema; Chapter 11: Chinese diaspora.

Globalisation, global trade in filmed entertainment

Chapter 1 on the history of global film.

Chapter 2 on the Hollywood model.

Chapter 9 on 'global TV'.

Chapter 12 on potential future developments.

Postcolonialism/orientalism

Chapter 4 on British and French diaspora filmmaking.

Chapters 5 and 11 on orientalism.

Chapter 8 on African cinema.

Remakes and multiple versions

Aspects of Chapters 1, 2, 5 and 10.

Representation and identity

Issues are covered throughout the book but Chapters 4, 6 and 8 perhaps highlight specific issues and examples.

Women filmmakers

Samira Makhmalbaf (Chapter 3).

Gurinder Chadha (Chapter 4).

Claire Denis (Chapter 7).

Aparna Sen (Chapter 10).

Ann Hui (Chapter 11).

Names and titles

The intention throughout this book is to present film titles, where appropriate, in their original form for a specific language cinema and in the 'international English' form that may be used within the international film market. The title will be accompanied, the first time it is used in a chapter, by the year of its first release and the national designation; for example, *Pan's Labyrinth* (*El laberinto del fauno*, Spain/Mexico/US, 2006). There are a couple of issues to note here. Sometimes a film may have several titles for different territories. A judgement will be made on which title to use if the film is mentioned more than once. In the title above, the Spanish version uses the convention of not using upper case for each word. Conventions do vary. Titles in Indian cinema are often not translated into English. Chinese films are often known by their English title. If in doubt, the title presented here is the one most likely to be used in cinema listings or on DVD.

Names in the book will be given according to the conventions of the film culture in question. In East Asia, family names are given first and personal names second. For some reason the convention in the film industry has been to treat Chinese and Korean names in this manner, but not Japanese. We will follow the same convention for all three (e.g. Zhang Ziyi, Bong Joon-ho, Kitano Takeshi). Some well-used websites such as IMDb.com show all three the other way round. In South India, perhaps because of the length of names, the convention is sometimes to use either initials only for personal names or to use just a single name, so two of the best-known film composers in Indian Cinema are A.R. Rahman and Ilayaraja.

As far as possible, all names and titles will use the diacritical marks that in many language systems indicate how characters are pronounced or stressed. Where the original language does not use the Latin alphabet, names must be transliterated and this can produce a range of results. Transliteration or 'Romanisation' of Chinese script is further complicated by the use of different systems in Mainland China and (up until 2008) in Taiwan. The official Chinese system is Pinyin which replaced the earlier Wade-Giles system; hence references to Mao Zedung instead of Mao Tse-Tung. However, the Taiwanese director Hou Hsiao-hsien in Pinyin would be Hou Xiaoxian. Chinese names in Hong Kong have often been 'Anglicised' but sometimes both English and Chinese names are necessary to avoid confusion (e.g. between the two popular Hong Kong stars, Tony Leung Chiu-wai and Tony Leung Ka-fai).

Where foreign language terms are used they will usually be italicised (e.g. *kabuki* theatre in Japan).

Key terms and definitions

Some important names and terms with specialised meanings are emboldened in the text. Sometimes bold is just used for emphasis, but usually names are accompanied by a brief biography and the terms explained either in the main text or in a margin entry. Key terms are listed in the Glossary on page 346. The indices in the book include separate lists of names, key terms and film titles.

Films in distribution

As far as possible, films used as examples in this book will be available on Blu-ray/ DVD or via online streaming or digital download. Most films have been checked as available on either Region 1 (North America) or Region 2 (Europe) DVD. Other titles, especially from India, are often available as Region 0 (i.e. 'region-free').

The following suppliers carry DVDs (and VCDs) not necessarily released in Europe/ North America (check carefully re the Region code and subtitle options) but available for import:

Induna: www.induna.com/ for Hindi, Bengali, Marathi, Telugu language films from India.

Ayngaran: eshop.ayngaran.com for Tamil films (UK and Worldwide sites).

YesAsia: www.yesasia.com for Chinese (Mainland, Hong Kong, Taiwan), South Korean and Japanese films.

Tulumba: www.tulumba.com for Turkish films (and some Iranian and Arab films).

Arab Film Distribution: www.arabfilm.com/ selected films from across the Arab world (and Turkey, Iran and Pakistan).

There are numerous websites that sell DVDs (or VCDs) from Nigeria and Australia, Spain and other European film-producing nations. More information on acquiring films is included at the end of specific chapters.

Various websites offer free and legal online services which can be useful resources for finding older films. Examples include the YouTube channels run by Doordarshan, the Public Service TV Broadcaster in India (www.youtube.com/user/ DoordarshanNational1) with a range of archive material, including documentaries and parallel films. The National Film Development Corporation of India also has a channel (www.youtube.com/user/NFDCCinemasofIndia) showing clips from parallel films mentioned in Chapter 10. The Confucius Institute Online (http://video.chinese. cn/en/article/2009-09/09/content_53537.htm) offers a low resolution (but watchable) version of Zhang Yimou's *Not One Less* (with English subtitles). Other titles are also available.

Internet references

URLs of specific websites have been kept to a minimum in the book. Live links are available on the companion website at www.globalfilmstudies.com.

Select bibliography

Each chapter has full references and some suggestions for further reading and, where appropriate, further viewing. The following textbooks and collections of papers are recommended as the main sources used in preparing this book.

Dennison, Stephanie and Song Hwee Lim (eds) (2006) *Remapping World Cinema: Identity,Culture and Politics in Film*, London: Wallflower Press.

Ďurovičová, Nataša and Newman, Kathleen (eds) (2010) *World Cinemas, Transnational Perspectives*, New York and Abingdon: Routledge.

Ezra, Elizabeth and Rowden, Terry (eds) (2006) *Transnational Cinema: The Film Reader*, Abingdon: Routledge.

Hill, John and Church Gibson, Pamela (1998) *The Oxford Guide to Film Studies*, Oxford: Oxford University Press.

Nagib, Lúcia, Perriam, Chris and Dudrah, Rajinder (eds) (2012) *Theorising World Cinema*, London and New York: I.B. Tauris.

Nelmes, Jill (ed.) (2012) *Introduction to Film Studies* (5th edn), Abingdon: Routledge.

Shohat, Ella and Stam, Robert (1994) *Unthinking Eurocentrism: Multiculturalism and the Media*, London and New York: Routledge.

Vitali, Valentina and Willemen, Paul (eds) (2006) *Theorising National Cinema*, London: BFI.

Film industry information has been gathered mainly from the following:

British Film Institute
European Audio-visual Observatory
filmbiz.asia.com
Screen International/Screendaily

Introduction

Watching films – in cinemas of all kinds, on TV screens, on computers or handheld devices – is a global activity and has been for well over a hundred years. The original film technologies proved in the twentieth century to be the basis for the medium which allowed anyone, anywhere, to watch a 'film show' that as well as offering entertainment might tell them something about themselves – and, just possibly, about life in other parts of the world. Film became the art and entertainment form that could bring all the other arts into play and take them to mass audiences. Yet the production, distribution and exhibition of films have not been developed in the same way in every part of the world. There have been some 'global films' watched by audiences everywhere, but even then such films have been watched and understood in different ways by different audiences.

First thoughts

This book appears at a time when the digital 'revolution' is almost complete. The film industries are struggling with new business models and audiences are finding new ways to watch films as well as new ways to discuss them and share their experiences. The global *impact* of films and film culture seems assured for the foreseeable future. But what kinds of films will we see? How will we watch them and what will we make of them? A global film culture is more a possibility than a reality. But do we want everyone to watch the same few films? Diversity in film choice seems to be a better goal. What stands in the way of diversity and what are the options for moving towards it?

Fig 0.1
An INOX multiplex located
in Forum Mall, Kolkata.

Let us take a look at some contemporary film-viewing experiences. In our
first example we approach a large shopping mall. To get to the cinema we ride
escalators up several floors past smart fashion shops and restaurants, we buy
tickets and a snack and enter a darkened auditorium. Where are we? We could be
almost anywhere in the world in a big city with a sizeable population of people
affluent enough to enjoy a trip to the cinema. But when we entered the mall we
had to pass through a metal detector and show our bags to a security guard. The
air-conditioning in the mall is welcome – it's very hot outside. When the film begins
it is set in London but the characters are not speaking English and soon there is a
spectacular dance sequence on the streets. This narrows things down considerably.
We are probably in a big city in India, or possibly in Kenya, South Africa, Malaysia
or the Gulf where popular Hindi and Tamil films are released.

Take a different example. We wander down streets in a city that has welcomed
traders and their customers for hundreds of years. We enter an old building and
eventually find ourselves in a comfortable auditorium. We recognise the actors on
screen who are Hollywood stars. They are speaking English, but across the bottom
of the screen there are subtitles in a European language. Elsewhere in Europe we
might watch the same film but hear voices dubbed into a local language. It's a
strange experience to see a star we know but to hear a different voice. This doesn't
bother most of the audience though, since that is the voice they associate with the
star.

There are interesting film-watching experiences to be had across the world,
including outdoor screens or 'pop-up' cinemas temporarily housed in all kinds of

Fig 0.2
Grand Teatret,
Copenhagen, a cinema
since 1913 – now
six screens showing
Danish and subtitled
specialised films.

buildings. But today most films are probably seen on TV screens. We might get on a bus (or a train or a ferry) for an inter-city ride along with an assortment of students, travellers and families. The TV screens may show us a Hollywood film but equally it may be a 'local' film, possibly made for television.

These examples are not oddities – they typify the experiences of many people across the world. Films are popular everywhere and there is an enormous variety of cultural experiences associated with something that is too often reduced to the consideration of a small number of mainstream Hollywood films, a standard multiplex auditorium and a box of popcorn. Let us finish this section with an example of what global film culture can produce.

The Band's Visit (Israel/US/France, 2007) sees a police band from Alexandria (Egypt's second city and one-time cosmopolitan centre of the Eastern Mediterranean) invited to Israel to perform at the opening of a new Arab Cultural Centre. But when the eight band members exit Tel Aviv airport carrying their instruments there is nobody to welcome them. When they try to negotiate their way to their destination they end up in the wrong town in the far south of the country in the Negev desert. There is no bus back and no hotel, so they are forced to take up the offer of the owner of the local diner, an attractive 40-something single woman, to stay in her home and those of her regular customers.

This tale of a 'cross-cultural encounter' proved popular around the world. The film won prizes at festivals from Tokyo to Cannes and attracted over a million spectators on release in Europe and North America. The story 'concept' is universal, but how did writer-director Eran Kolirin come up with the idea for this specific story? One of the characters in the film gives us a clue when she talks about watching Egyptian movies. Apparently, up until the early 1980s, the then single

In some countries there may be two sets of subtitles and the same film may be playing in both subtitled and dubbed versions (see more on subtitling in Chapter 1).

Fig 0.3
This Spanish restaurant in a resort area shows films each Wednesday evening.

Israeli TV channel used to broadcast Egyptian films that were very popular with some Israeli audiences.

> Sometimes, after the Arab movie, they'd broadcast a performance of the Israeli Broadcasting Authority's orchestra. This was a classical Arab orchestra, made up almost entirely of Arab Jews from Iraq and Egypt. When you think of the IBA orchestra, maybe the custom of watching Egyptian movies sounds a little less odd.
>
> (Eran Kolirin writing in the film's Press Notes, 2007)

Perhaps if Israeli TV still broadcast Egyptian movies, there might be more opportunities for Israelis to learn about their neighbours – and perhaps there could be reciprocal showings in Egypt? (See Chapter 6 for more on Israeli and Egyptian films.)

This book is designed to help you explore some of these cinema-going scenarios and global film culture stories, and to open up the amazing diversity of global film. In some ways it is a polemical book. It argues that we should find out why films are not often studied in this global context. There are several good reasons why we should consider widening our understanding. We are constantly

Fig 0.4
The Alexandria Police Band from Egypt are stranded in an Israeli desert town in *The Band's Visit*.

being told that we live in a 'globalised' world. Film is both a global product and an agency through which ideas about global culture are mediated. Indeed, for most of us, what we know about other cultures, especially in those countries that have experienced war or natural disasters, has been gleaned from news reports and films, often made by the same organisations operating from within Anglo-American culture and following similar institutional practices. However, multichannel television and the internet have also enabled us to watch and listen to other voices as well through YouTube, Al Jazeera and news media broadcast from India, China and Russia.

This isn't an 'anti-Hollywood' book but it does refuse to look at the global picture *only* from a Hollywood perspective. The problem is that there is not just a domination of cinema screens in most countries by the Hollywood studios, but also, within film studies and possibly to a lesser extent in media studies, there has been a tendency to study any film culture outside North America via an approach which defines it as 'not Hollywood' – almost as if there were just two kinds of films. This sounds silly, but think about how films are marketed. In the dwindling number of stores still selling DVDs in the UK and on the 'virtual shelves' of online stores, film titles are organised sometimes alphabetically by title and sometimes grouped under genre labels. Most of the DVDs on display are Hollywood titles or at least films in English (with the exception, perhaps of 'Anime', 'Bollywood' or 'Martial arts'). The rest are gathered into a small section under the heading 'World Cinema'. Presumably Hollywood is not part of the world? You may be studying a course with a module entitled 'World Cinema'. What on earth does it mean? We will explain a little later why there is a marketing category for certain kinds of films that are distributed internationally under that label – much as there is a music marketing category of 'world music'.

World or global?

In *Remapping World Cinema* (2006) the editors Stephanie Dennison and Song Hwee Lim tackle this problem of naming/defining their field of study. They point out that there is a second popular approach to World Cinema and that this refers to a collection of **national cinemas**. We can find plenty of examples of this kind of approach. Sometimes film studies courses are based in university departments that deal with 'language studies' or 'area studies' so that students take courses in French cinema, Japanese cinema, or possibly wider concepts such as Arab cinema or Latin American cinema. Yet, just like the 'Hollywood problem', this neat classification works against an approach that wants to consider global film in terms of gender, sexuality or economic power, or any other criteria that cut across national boundaries. This has in turn prompted a third general approach around questions of 'cultural resistance', perhaps most clearly organised under the heading of **postcolonial studies**. A related development, concerned with the ways in which filmmakers and audiences as well as the films themselves have transcended the concept of a national cinema, is the use of the term **transnational**.

We will explore what these concepts mean in some detail below, but it will be useful at this point to explain *our* choice of title – why call this *The **Global** Film Book*? At the simplest level, 'global' is used here to refer to all forms of film culture wherever they are found. We are interested in how these different film forms produce meaning in different cultural contexts and how filmmaking is possible (or not) in different parts of the world. In doing so we will encounter all the other approaches and perhaps suggest why a single approach is likely to be lacking in some way. In *Theorizing World Cinema* (2012) Lúcia Nagib, Chris Perriam and Rajinder Dudrah extend the analysis of Dennison and Lim outlined above. One of the many interesting and useful ideas they introduce is an attempt to escape from the negative effect of **binarisms** – the concept of simple oppositions to explain complex relationships. The most obvious of these is Hollywood versus the Rest of the World, which can lead in turn to 'us' and 'them' or 'centre' and 'periphery'. As they point out:

> In multicultural, multi-ethnic societies like ours, cinematic expressions from various origins cannot be seen as 'the other', for the simple reason that they are us. More interesting than their difference is, in most cases, their interconnectedness.
>
> (Nagib *et al.*, 2012: xxiii)

This statement follows a move away from a **eurocentric** approach to films and film theory credited to the impact of the pioneering work of Ella Shohat and Robert Stam and their 1994 book *Unthinking Eurocentrism: Multiculturalism and the Media*. Shohat and Stam argued that scholars needed to think their way out of a situation in which knowledge and theoretical work had developed in the context of colonialist systems with their assumptions of control over other cultures. *The Global Film Book* endorses and hopes to contribute to a move towards what Nagib *et al.* have termed **polycentrism** in film studies. This means we will recognise that there are many starting points for discussing film culture and many different 'flows' of films between different parts of the world. We won't find it easy to try to understand how these flows operate or how films might create different kinds of meanings in different cultural contexts, but in making an attempt we will both enrich our own film culture and make ourselves more open to others.

Let us return to our decision to use the term 'global'. Like 'world' or 'transnational', global is a term that can certainly be problematic. Bhaskar Sarkar (2010: 36) makes a useful distinction in his discussion of 'global media theory' when he points out that '*global* media theory' is media theory that applies everywhere and isn't restricted to any one region. But *global media* theory is theory about a specific form of media that operates on a global basis. Although we are going to explore some theory work in this book, it will not be our prime concern. Perhaps we should describe our aim as exploring '*global* film practices'; i.e. we want to consider how films are produced, distributed and 'received' in all parts of the world. In doing so we will discover that some films remain largely '**local**' and are not exported. Other films are produced in the hope that they may well sell to overseas buyers. Some of these films may well become *global films* in the sense that they are seen in many film territories worldwide. These are the films that may also be termed 'transnational' in that it is their international rather than only local appeal that defines them.

Finally, before we leave the 'global', we should note that the term **globalisation** is problematic too. There are two traps associated with the ways in which the term has entered public discourse. First, there is the false conception that globalisation is an inherently American-led process; and second, that it is associated with the inevitable supremacy of Anglo-American forms of advanced capitalism in all the world's markets. To counteract this, we might note (as Sarkar does) that Chinese, Indian and Arab cultures began to grapple with concepts which we now understand to constitute 'modernity' several centuries before similar concepts (forms of science, international trade, arts, rational-bureaucratic systems of governance, etc.) were well developed in Europe. The financial crisis since 2008 in Europe and North America has exposed the importance of the Chinese economy in world trade and highlighted the continued growth in the economies of the **BRIC** countries (Brazil, Russia, India, China) – economies that don't necessarily conform to the same economic policy models as those in Brussels or New York.

Industry and culture

One other pair of terms that we should try sort out here is **film culture–film industry**. These are not opposed in a binarism: rather they overlap. In this book we will try to refer to **film industries** as the production bases for films and the network of organisations that buy and sell film rights for distribution and exhibition. Most film industries are nationally based, though in smaller countries there may be relatively few such organisations and much of the film industry will operate on the basis of co-production deals between two or more countries. In some larger countries there may be more than one film industry; thus, for example, in India films are produced in several languages in different parts of the country and there is a significant difference between the two largest film industries in Mumbai (the Hindi industry) and Chennai (where Tamil and some other South Indian-language films are made). We will also refer to the **international film industry** and its conventions governing how films are traded.

Film culture is a broader term used to encompass how audiences behave in cinemas, how critics write about films, how governments create film policies, etc. It

Hollywood refers to its domestic market as 'North America' but it shares that market, not only with independent US producers and importers of foreign films but also with *two* Canadian industries, one of which is a French-language industry in Quebec.

may also include aspects of how film industries approach production, distribution and exhibition. If, for example, a French film is sold internationally and is distributed in parts of Africa and parts of East Asia, its place in local film culture may vary from one territory to another – and certainly may be very different to its place in metropolitan French film culture.

What does this mean to you?

But let us turn to more practical issues. What is your concept of 'global film'? We are all likely to have different ideas depending on our personal background. If you are relatively new to film and media studies and your first language is English, you are likely to have seen mostly English-language films so far. The chances are that you won't have seen that many subtitled or even dubbed films, since these films take only a tiny percentage of the box office in Anglophone countries. Just 2 per cent of admissions were to subtitled films in the UK in 2011 (*BFI Statistical Yearbook 2012*). On the other hand, you will be part of an active film culture (English-speaking countries fare well in the cinema admissions figures in Fig 0.5 below) and those subtitled films are accessible (i.e. screened in selected cinemas) – if you know where to find them.

If English isn't your first language, you may well comprise that part of the global audience which has a more consistent relationship with films made in languages other than English. You may be part of the **diaspora** audience for your first-language cinema, seeking out cinema screenings or importing DVDs via friends or online stores or download services. In most parts of the world outside South and East Asia, your choice of films to see is likely to be dominated by Hollywood, but 'local' tastes are important and there will be films to find in your first language.

Wherever you are, you cannot see everything. Every year, the total of films produced worldwide exceeds 5,000 (perhaps as many as 7,000). In some film

Fig 0.5 doesn't show Nigeria and Ghana with estimates of up to 1,000 video films produced each year in the local video film industry but only a handful of films destined for cinemas (see Chapter 8).

Rank	Territory	Admissions (millions)	Gross B.O. ($millions)	Per capita visits p.a.	Local films produced in 2011
1	India[1]	2,700	1,500	2.1	1,300
2	US & Canada[2]	1,360	10,800	4.1	900
3	China	624	2,740	0.3	588
4	Mexico	229	845	1.9	73
5	France	204	1,650	3.2	272
6	South Korea	195	1,300	3.4	216
7	UK	172	1,880	2.7	274
8	Russia	169	1,350	1.2	64
9	Japan	155	2,150	1.1	441
10	Brazil	149	783	0.7	99

Fig 0.5 Table of the ten largest film markets ranked by the number of admissions. The table also demonstrates the disparity in box office income and the size of the local production industry. **Notes**: 1. Indian film industry statistics have not been published for 2012 or 2011. The figures here are estimates based on 2010. 2. The MPAA statistics for North America do not separate the US and Canada. Sources: *Focus 2012, Screen International, Hollywood Reporter*, MPAA, CMM Intelligence.

markets you can get access to around 500 or so films in cinemas, although outside major urban centres that falls to 200 or fewer. But several thousand titles are available via DVD and VOD and, if you are prepared to buy DVDs from online stores in another country, there is virtually no barrier (apart from the language options) to which films you can see.

Fig 0.5 gives you some idea of the extent of the world's most important film markets in 2012. It is apparent straight away that India and the US stand apart from all other countries in terms of the number of admissions and the number of films produced. But China is growing very quickly with new cinemas opening all the time and, if the cinema-going habit returns to China, we could again see audiences of well over a billion. You should find this chart useful in studying several chapters in the book.

Dealing with Hollywood

Whatever your personal experience and film tastes, you will find that in any film or media course it is essential to study Hollywood. In one sense this is inevitable. Although the six Hollywood studio majors together distribute only around 150 US films in total each year, a select group of these are the films that are most widely seen around the world and which make the most money. How these particular films are made and distributed to some extent defines what we all understand as 'contemporary cinema' and influences what happens in most other film-producing countries. Indeed, 'Hollywood films' – films part-financed or distributed by the Hollywood studios – are also made in many countries in Europe and elsewhere.

The trap for the film scholar is in the conception of Hollywood as both 'all powerful' and 'normal'. The dangers of this trap are manifested in two ways. First is the failure to see Hollywood as a dynamic institution that needs to interact with and feed off the energy created by film cultures across the world. Hollywood needs to maintain its audiences worldwide – more revenue now comes from the 'International' market (around 69 per cent) than from 'Domestic' (31 per cent from the US and Canada). It also needs to regularly re-invigorate itself with fresh blood (creative personnel, stories, genres, etc.). Second, film studies risks treating all film culture outside North America as 'other', defining it as 'non-Hollywood' rather than in its own terms.

In this book we recognise three main 'modes of production' which in turn are treated as signifying three different kinds of films to be distributed and exhibited in different ways.

The first is the '**studio** production' system of the Hollywood majors and some independent companies in North America and elsewhere in the world. This produces big budget films (US$50 million production budgets or more in Hollywood) that are distributed internationally by the six Hollywood majors (who may have had little involvement in the actual production – it is the distribution rights ownership that make the studios 'major'). These 150 or so films will be distributed to most **territories** worldwide. There were other studio systems that flourished around the world in the period from 1930 to 1970 (e.g. in Japan), but although some of the studio brands from those systems are still operating, most do not have the range of activities or the resources to compete directly with Hollywood in the international market.

A '**territory**' is a geographical region for which the rights to distribute a film to cinemas, TV, online and DVD may be traded. It is often based on a single country, but the UK territory includes Ireland, and India comprises several separate territories.

The second mode is what we might term the '**independent**' or '**specialised film**' mode of lower budget production targeting specialised audiences. These films may well be traded internationally, often on the basis of the profile and prestige of the filmmakers (directors, producers, stars) or because they belong to some recognisable artistic movement or 'school'. This mode of filmmaking is sometimes called '**artisanal**' (i.e. as if the films were 'hand-crafted' rather than 'assembly-line produced' like the studio films). Although specialised films in English probably have an advantage in the international market, the system of film festivals and arthouse distribution in many countries enables specialised films from any producer to develop the potential to enter the film markets in most territories.

The third mode is '**local** production' of popular entertainment. This is the least likely mode to produce films that are distributed globally. Hollywood films comprise a major part of the local product of the US, but they are rarely considered as such. Some of the local product of India, China, France and Japan may be widely distributed. UK production, because of the strong Hollywood connections, may find itself in any of the three categories above. It is worth remembering too that virtually all films from outside the US (including British films or other English-language films such as Australian or New Zealand titles) will usually be deemed to be 'specialised/independent' films in the US market, even if at home they are effectively **blockbusters.**

These modes/categories are not strictly defined and there will be exceptions for particular titles. The categorisations are useful because they begin to explain why some films are easily traded in the international film market and others are not. The market is not 'free' but heavily controlled by the Hollywood majors. They are able to maintain their own operations in each of the major territories – or to broker advantageous deals with local distributors. This way they can guarantee distribution and reduce costs on a global scale. All other distributors are forced to sell rights for overseas territories. *Slumdog Millionaire* (UK, 2008) is a good example of a wholly British film that was produced in the UK on the basis of selling the rights outside the UK and France to a Hollywood studio. The profits from a very successful worldwide release mostly went back to the US. Indian distributors have maintained their hold over distribution in the UK and US to mainly **diaspora** audiences, but if they wish to extend distribution beyond the current 16 to 18 territories where Non-Resident Indians (NRIs) live, they may need Hollywood partners. Indian producers have already begun to work with Hollywood studios (see Chapter 10).

You may come across different ways of describing these forms of production, and Paul Julian Smith (2012) offers a classification of three types of **transnational** films. In this context 'transnational' refers to films that involve production factors and distribution patterns that spread across more than a single territory. Genre films, Smith's first category, fit into the 'local production of popular films' above. 'Festival films' are discussed in Chapter 7 and are part of 'specialised cinema' but 'prestige pictures' offer something different. These are films that are funded and shot/ post-produced in several countries, often with an international cast and crew and intended for an international audience. Smith's examples include some of the films of Mexican director Alejandro González Iñárritu and Brazilian Fernando Meirelles. He also terms these **transnational blockbusters** – they attempt the commercial appeal of genre films but also the artistic status of festival films.

This book is organised in such a way that we will explore production, distribution and exhibition in a range of territories, and we may find that the mix of the three

The South Korean action/horror film *The Host* (2006) was released in the US as a specialised film, but in South Korea it was seen by around one-third of the population – over 13 million people – in cinemas.

modes varies considerably across that range. What we will certainly discover is that there are other factors which are important as well. For instance, in many territories there may be an important role played by **public funding** and **government cultural policies**. Filmmaking may be a political activity or it may be dependent on local cultural partnerships or legacies from previous arrangements – hence the production of films in French from Africa, supported by French cultural projects in former French colonies. In all countries we will also need to consider the importance of television in funding film production (and broadcasting local films). We will also consider whether there is a **global television** industry and if this is significantly different to global film.

If we return to the earlier reference to **world cinema**, we can see from the above that it refers in the main to specialised films from around the world as well as those examples of 'popular local production' that are seen as easily marketable to specific audiences in North America and Europe (e.g. Bollywood, *anime*, martial arts films, etc.).

How do we see the world?

On page vi of this book there is a map showing where the different film industries, films and filmmakers discussed are located. We chose our map projection – representing a three-dimensional globe as 'flat' – carefully. The 'Robinson projection' offers a compromise in terms of distorting the size and shape of different continents when 'flattening' the globe. It tries not to over- or under-emphasise different continents. Compare this with 'Mercator's projection' produced by a Flemish cartographer in the sixteenth century which was used by European navigators in their voyages of 'discovery'. The map worked well as a navigation tool but it distorted the size of the land masses, making them bigger towards the poles. If you visit http://www.petersmap.com/page2.html you will see a comparison of Mercator's projection and a controversial projection by an East German historian and filmmaker Arno Peters who in 1973 promoted a new projection which he claimed challenged the political distortions inherent in Mercator's work. (His 'new' projection was actually based on earlier, similar maps.) Peters' map aimed to represent the relative *sizes* of each land area accurately, even if it distorted their shapes. The overall effect of his new projection was to emphasise the size of Africa in particular and to diminish the visual domination of 'northern' areas such as Europe, Russia and North America.

The Peters projection created great controversy among cartographers, especially when it was used by various aid agencies and development organisations to counteract what was seen as **eurocentrism** and to stress the physical size of Africa and the tropical world, long misrepresented in comparison with Europe and North America. It is worth exploring this debate because similar issues arise when we consider the kind of profile that filmmaking has in some parts of the world and how difficult it is to break down perceptions. The Peters projection still distorted but it did its job in alerting us to the fact that all maps and texts of any kind embody the values and attitudes of their creators in the context in which they are produced and used. We will try, as far as possible, to use accurate figures for audiences, numbers of films produced, etc. in each of the film territories we discuss, but it is worth remembering that our ways of perceiving the world are still being shaped, even if only to a limited extent, by the practices of European and later

Collecting accurate data on the film industry on a global basis is very difficult. *Focus 2012*, the annual survey of 'World Film Market Trends', headlines its report 'Statistical landscape in the mist'.

	US/Canada	Europe, Middle East and Africa	Asia Pacific	Latin America
2008	9.6	9.7	6.8	1.6
2012	10.8	10.7	10.4	2.8

Fig 0.6 The 'Global Box Office' for 'all films' (in US$ billions) as seen by the Hollywood studios. Source: from MPAA Theatrical Market Statistics 2012, www.mpaa.org.

The 'triangular trade' of the eighteenth century was the basis for the wealth of European colonialists. It took slaves from West Africa to the Americas and brought back sugar, tobacco and cotton. Cheap manufactured goods were sent to Africa to barter for slaves.

American colonisers of the rest of the world. We will pick up some of these issues in later chapters.

Fig 0.6 shows how the current studio chiefs in Hollywood see the rest of the world in terms of box office returns. Three broad observations are useful. First, box office outside North America has grown faster over a four-year period. Second, 'Asia Pacific' and Latin America are growing much faster than Europe; and third, Africa and the Middle East are simply 'tagged on' to Europe. Chapters 6 and 8 attempt to redress that seeming disinterest in certain markets. Here let us focus on the growing audiences and confidence of local industries in 'Asia Pacific'. Perhaps the world map needs redrawing with its centre in the Pacific and a new triangle being drawn between Beijing, Mumbai and Los Angeles. What might the new 'triangular trade' produce?

Fig 0.7
Life of Pi. Source: The Kobal Collection/www.picture-desk.com.

Life of Pi: a global film?

The cover of this book features a still from *Life of Pi*. Book covers need arresting images to attract attention and this one seemed to fulfil that aim. But *Life of Pi* is an American film. Is it appropriate as an example of the films discussed in these pages?

In many ways *Life of Pi* embodies discussions in different chapters of the book. Here is a 'property' that is Canadian – the novel by Yann Martel that won the Booker prize for English-language fiction from the Commonwealth in 2002. Martel himself was born in Spain to Québécois parents and travelled widely before deciding to write in English. The narrative of the film starts in India and ends in Canada. Its director Ang Lee trained in the US and has made several high-profile American films, but he has also made films in the UK and China, and he decided to make *Life of Pi* primarily in his homeland of Taiwan. The production also included location shoots in India and Canada. The composer Mychael Danna is Canadian; the cinematographer Claudio Miranda was born in Chile. The three leading actors are Indian and the fourth British. The American elements of the film were crucial to its production – the persistence of Fox 2000 President Elizabeth Gabler, the studio's money (it's difficult to see a producer outside the US coming up with US$120 million), the script by David Magee (and other key heads of department) and the visual effects by Rhythm and Hues. These four elements make the film a 'Hollywood movie'.

In his insistence in making the film in 3D, Ang Lee helped to create what might be a Hollywood blockbuster, but his other decisions, including the choice of an unknown 17-year-old Indian as his leading man, undercut that description. 3D blockbusters are also produced in East Asia, but *Life of Pi* is an English-language film. When the film opened in North America on Thanksgiving Weekend it was well received but the returns were modest for such an expensive film. It settled into a consistent performance in the Top Ten over the next few weeks, never higher than No. 5, but showing 'legs' in attracting audiences beyond the first two weeks. Meanwhile, the film topped the Chinese charts in the Mainland and on Taiwan, and also performed extremely well in India. When the film opened in Europe in time for Christmas it soon became apparent that it would prove to be the international market that would not only save Fox's investment but would return significant revenues. *Pi*'s great success at the 2013 Oscar ceremonies (11 nominations, four wins) boosted its North American revenue but the international market produced four times the box office total (US$484:124 million) and more than four times the audience (with cheaper ticket prices in India and some other territories).

Life of Pi is a global film. An analysis of its box office performance suggests that it took time for its American audiences to fully respond – perhaps they saw it as a 'foreign film'. Unfortunately, separate Canadian figures aren't easily accessible but the film's box office in China and Taiwan out-grossed North America after the first few weeks. Around the world the film 'spoke' to audiences in new ways, partly through spectacle (3D and visual effects are very popular in China), partly through a universal but unusual story, and partly because the film presents itself as 'Asian' as well as 'North American'. Officially the film is 'American' but Taiwan, India and Canada should be part of its identity. In the context of this book *Life of Pi* is a 'transnational blockbuster' and an indicator of what may be a trend towards cooperation between filmmakers and funders across major film-producing territories.

Studying film

This textbook on global film cannot also be an introduction to film studies. It is assumed that you are already familiar with the basic theoretical concepts associated with reading a film and studying film production, distribution, exhibition and reception – or that you will be following a complementary film introduction course. In addition, it is assumed that you are familiar with mainstream Hollywood films and also your own local film culture if you live outside North America.

Most of the chapters include case study films and these offer the opportunity to explore a range of issues associated with theoretical ideas, film production practices, issues of film culture and, in some cases, questions about representation. This isn't a conventional textbook as it doesn't support a specific syllabus or programme. Nor does it offer a formal course structure. It does however attempt to support anyone interested in studying global film, and each chapter will carry at least one suggested activity ('Research and explore') to follow up through personal research. As far as possible the films presented in the case studies or suggested for personal research will be widely available – but of course this will depend on where you are. A multi-region DVD player is a useful piece of kit for a global film student – alongside a fast broadband connection. With these you should be able to see what you want. (See below for advice on resources.)

How the book is organised

The book comprises 12 chapters. Chapter 1 offers a historical view that introduces some of the major issues in the development of global film culture in outline form, and Chapter 12 is intended as both a form of conclusion and a look ahead to what the emerging issues may be. In between are ten chapters, some focusing on a specific national or regional cinema but also some looking more widely. These chapters are not offered as a sort of gazetteer of all the world's film cultures. Instead, they have been chosen to illustrate specific issues grounded in a detailed context. In some cases major industries are discussed because they offer different histories and possibly different approaches to similar issues (e.g. India and China). There is no hierarchy implied by the ordering of the chapters and no significance should be attached to any omissions. The book does not give much space to Hollywood production as such – only where it has a direct relationship with the issues being discussed. The 'Guidance notes for readers' on pages xix–xxiii offer ideas for 'pathways' through the book and also guidance on the presentation of names and titles, references and support material.

Information and resources

The Global Film Book is fully referenced with suggested further reading/viewing at the end of each chapter. It also offers advice on the accessibility of DVDs and references indicate the sources of statistical information. Long lists of URLs for websites, blogs, etc. are not appropriate in a textbook like this so it is recommended that you make full use of the companion blog to this book, **globalfilmstudies.com**. The blog will be the means of updating the material in the book and extending discussion to include examples of film practice from other cinemas.

References and further reading

British Film Institute (2012) *Statistical Yearbook*. Available online or as a downloadable pdf at http://www.bfi.org.uk/education-research/film-industry-statistics-research/statistical-yearbook.

Dennison, Stephanie and Song Hwee Lim (eds) (2006) *Remapping World Cinema: Identity,Culture and Politics in Film*, London: Wallflower Press.

Ezra, Elizabeth and Rowden, Terry (eds) (2006) *Transnational Cinema: The Film Reader*, Abingdon: Routledge.

Nagib, Lúcia, Perriam, Chris and Dudrah, Rajinder (eds) (2012) *Theorising World Cinema*, London and New York: I.B. Tauris.

Sarkar, Bhaskar (2010) 'Tracking Global Media in the Outposts of Globalisation', in Nataša Ďurovičová and Kathleen Newman (eds) *World Cinemas, Transnational Perspectives*, New York and Abingdon: Routledge.

Shohat, Ella and Stam, Robert (1994) *Unthinking Eurocentrism: Multiculturalism and the Media*, London and New York: Routledge.

Smith, Paul Julian (2012) in Nagib, Perriam and Dudrah (eds) (op. cit.).

CHAPTER 1

The development of global film

- ■ The story begins
- ■ The first studios
- ■ Before 'language cinema'
- ■ European war and the rise of Hollywood
- ■ Changes with sound
- ■ Dubbing and subtitling in global film
- □ Case study 1.1: Subtitling and *La haine*
- ■ The context for Hollywood's hegemony
- ■ The international film market today
- ■ International art cinema
- ■ It's not all feature films ...
- ■ Summary
- ■ References and further reading

The story begins

Within a few months of the first public demonstration of their new technology for presenting moving images (the *cinématographe*) to a public audience in late December 1895 in Paris, the **Lumière Brothers** were able exploit their invention on a global scale. These highly astute technological innovators had compiled a short programme of one-minute films in advance of the event. They had also ordered more of their *cinématographes* to be made and had set up training for a force of *opérateurs*. In 1896 their films were being shown throughout Europe, as well as in the US, India and Australia and many other places around the world.

The Lumières' preparation had two important features. First, the *cinématographe* itself was portable (weighing around 5.5 kilos) and it acted as combined film camera, printer and projector. Today's tablet with a camera is an equivalent. The *cinématographe* could be carried in a small suitcase and trained *opérateurs* could put on a screening in any form of public arena. The Lumières controlled the production, distribution and exhibition of their own films. Not only that, but an *opérateur* could also shoot footage of local events or scenes from everyday life and screen the footage the following day. A film programme in Bombay or Buenos Aires could include both the original French films and something local. These two factors – control over the whole process (**vertical integration** of film production, distribution and exhibition)

Auguste (1862-1954) and **Louis** (1864-1948) **Lumière** were the first 'global' filmmakers. A Lumière film programme ran in Bombay in July 1896.

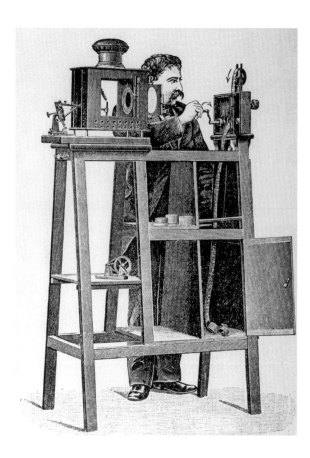

Fig 1.1
A *cinématographe* as used
by Lumière *opérateurs*.
Source: Time Life Pictures/
Mansell/Time Life
Pictures/Getty Images.

and the mixing of **international** and **local** product – are key to the success enjoyed by the major Hollywood studios in a global film context today.

But the Lumières could not hold on to their position as sole purveyors of this new entertainment, 'cinema', for long. They did have some advantages over potential competitors from overseas given the large French imperial market, but the same was true for competitors in the UK and the US (which 'acquired' overseas territories during the Spanish-American War of 1898). For the next 20 years or so, the new form of entertainment, and in a broad sense 'secondary knowledge' about how things were done differently elsewhere, developed on a global scale. This period of **early cinema** has been compared to the development of **new media** a century later. It takes time for a new commercial medium to become institutionalised. Early cinema was the site for several different developments between 1895 and 1914:

- standardising technologies and **film formats** so that films could be shown anywhere with the same standard facilities (screen shape, physical film format – size of projected image, projection speed, etc.);
- purpose-built cinemas rather than converted public buildings;
- the length of films moved towards a standard for a feature as opposed to a **short;**
- the make-up of film programmes (which included live performances among **short films** in some countries);
- expectations of audience behaviour during screenings (which did vary from one country to another);

There are different definitions of what is understood as a 'feature film'. In France a feature is now at least 60 minutes. A short film could be any length from 1 minute to 59 minutes.

- film genres – some based on popular theatre or literature;
- a **business model** which enabled film producers to earn a profit;
- the emergence of different sectors in the cinema business – producers, exhibitors and eventually distributors operating 'film exchanges' that enabled a rental system for exhibition;
- the emergence of **stars** – celebrities who became known through their appearances in films and who subsequently influenced the ways in which cinema would be marketed to audiences.

The first studios

Although cinema began as an enterprise that offered a new experience for audiences anywhere in the world, the development of cinema varied in different regions. In France some of the first film companies developed quickly and the names of their founders have remained important brands in the film industry. Léon **Gaumont** (1864–1946), an engineer-inventor, established his company in 1895 and had opened a studio by 1905. Gaumont also established a British company which opened the Lime Grove Studio in London in 1915 and acquired cinemas in the UK. The **Pathé** Brothers established their business in 1896 and developed it alongside their existing music business. Like Gaumont they established a British operation but this was alongside interests across Europe, Japan and Australia as well as the US. Pathé also acquired the Lumière Brothers' patents in 1902.

'Cinema' was 'new' in the 1890s but audiences of wealthy people had already enjoyed 'magic lantern' shows (slideshows) that had been developing in sophistication for a century before the first Lumière Brothers film screenings.

Fig 1.2
A poster depicting the Pathé Brothers by Adrien Barrère.

In the US, the early cinema pioneers included Thomas Edison (1847–1931), the original rival to the Lumières. Edison, probably the most successful inventor of modern times, had many other interests but his role in developing cinema was central. His kinetoscope was a device that offered a small screen for an individual viewer and it was suited to the concept of the amusement arcade (perhaps looking forward to the electronic arcade games of much later). But Edison's most important business decision was based on recognising the importance of copyright for films. In 1908 he was the leading figure in the establishment of the Motion Picture Patents Company (MPPC). This brought together the leading American film producers of the time as well as Eastman Kodak, the main supplier of technologies. It followed a period when Edison's attempts to protect his own patents had forced smaller companies to import films from Europe. At this time in the US, films were sold outright to an exhibitor who screened them until they wore out. The MPPC helped set up a rental exchange system, the basis for modern distribution practices.

The MPPC members were mostly based in the Northeast US and when some of the smaller independent companies decided to challenge the new order they found Los Angeles to be not only sunnier (so allowing less expensive daylight shooting) but also a long way away from Edison's lawyers. The development of the Hollywood studios began around 1912 with smaller companies merging to create both Paramount and Universal. By the early 1910s, American film distributors had fought off the 'invasion' of European companies that had come into the US market when it expanded quickly with the boom in shop-front cinemas or nickelodeons. From now on, North America would be a 'closed market' with US companies clamouring for import tariffs on foreign films.

The earliest film studios in Japan had a rather different genesis. The oldest, formed in 1912 with the coming together of several small producers and theatre chains, is Nikkatsu. However, although it began film production only in 1921, Shochiku had been founded in 1895 as a production company in the popular *kabuki* theatre industry. It also ventured into other forms of theatre production such as the more classical *noh* before embracing cinema. Japanese cinema has seen **studio production** and industry domination in similar ways to Hollywood but in a different cultural context (see Chapter 5).

Before 'language cinema'

Early cinema was enjoyed without synchronous dialogue. This doesn't mean it was 'silent'. Different forms of sound accompaniment were offered in cinemas, ranging from a single pianist to a full-scale orchestra or a 'mighty organ' in the picture palaces of the 1920s. Recorded music on discs also began to appear regularly in the 1920s. The audience made their own accompaniment as well but in some cultures a narrator provided a commentary on the action and sometimes lines of dialogue. In Japan the narrator was known as a *benshi*, deriving from theatre practices. Something similar was introduced into Japanese overseas possessions, including Korea and Formosa (Taiwan). 'Sound cinema' arrived later in Japan than in North America or Europe, partly perhaps because of the popularity of the *benshi*.

One advantage of the lack of dialogue in films was that films were easily exported across language divisions. The provision of intertitles or title cards developed as films became longer with more complex narratives in the 1910s. These sometimes became quite elaborate graphics in themselves, allowing distributors of imported films to localise the presentation in visual terms as they translated the titles. This created some extra cost but was not prohibitive. As a result, some smaller producing countries became major exporters of films. In Europe, Denmark was a major producer, exporting to the much larger German market as well as Sweden and other neighbouring countries in the years between 1909 and 1914. Asta Nielsen, who starred in the Danish film *Afgrunden* (*The Abyss*, 1910), an 'erotic melodrama', was able to develop her career in Germany and become Europe's biggest film star. Italian producers were also able to export films successfully, especially spectacular historical epics and bourgeois melodramas. By 1914 Italy was regarded, alongside France, as one of the major national exporters of films.

European war and the rise of Hollywood

Up until 1914 the global exchange of films was quite extensive. Films made in different European countries were seen across Europe and in the US to a certain extent. Equally, American films could be seen in many parts of the world – but did not dominate markets to the extent that they would in later years. Kristin Thompson (1985) points out that Britain and Australia/New Zealand were already effectively American territories, and American films held the largest share in other Northern European territories. But in Southern Europe and most of the rest of the world, France and Italy dominated. The American films that were sold to Asia or Latin America often arrived via London, which controlled the American overseas film trade. When war in Europe began in 1914 it had several immediate effects on the film business:

- European production was disrupted and the import/export of films became more difficult in some territories;
- there is a paucity of easily accessible research on how audiences changed in wartime but it seems likely that cinema attendances were affected in several different ways: for instance, films could be offered to audiences of soldiers or women working in munitions factories;
- the possibilities of propaganda cinema began to be explored – film began to be recognised as a national resource helping the war effort (something that would be totally understood by 1939).

Meanwhile, the development of Hollywood was unhindered by the conflict. The constituent companies of three of the later Hollywood studio 'majors' – MGM, Warner Bros. and Fox – were all founded or consolidated during this period, and the three major stars of Hollywood – Charles Chaplin, Mary Pickford and Douglas Fairbanks – joined with the leading director D.W. Griffith to form United Artists in 1919. During the post-war period, the three stars travelled to meet fans in many parts of the world as the first *global* film stars.

By 1916 American film exporters had realised their opportunity to replace French and Italian exporters – and to switch the centre for the organisation of overseas distribution of American films away from London to New York.

During the post-war period, the German film industry attempted to match Hollywood through a process of consolidation. Ufa, founded in 1917 as a publicly funded studio, merged in 1921 with Decla-Bioscop, the other major film company in Germany, establishing almost a monopoly position in a country producing

Fig 1.3
(From left) Douglas Fairbanks, Mary Pickford and Charles Chaplin promoting Liberty bonds in a 'celebrity endorsement' tour of the US in 1919. Source: British Film Institute Stills Collection.

around 600 films per year in the 1920s. This was the period of high-profile 'artistic filmmaking' (some of which became known as German Expressionism). Some films, such as the horror titles *The Cabinet of Dr. Caligari* (1919) and *Nosferatu* (1922), were widely seen abroad and proved influential on Hollywood producers. Thompson points out that in the 1920s currency devaluations in Europe made American films expensive for a period and allowed German films into the US more cheaply.

Towards the end of the 1920s, sound technologies began to appear for cinemas, and a duopoly was set up with cinemas choosing between American systems or Tobis Klangfilm from Germany. Sound had a profound effect on the film industry and on the audience experience in cinemas. However, we should not also forget that from the mid-1910s onwards the quality of acting, camerawork, set design – all the elements of film production, including direction – had been improving all the time. Before 1914, films had been sold 'by the foot'; they were commodities even if audiences were beginning to show their preferences. By 1927, some films had become highly sophisticated art and entertainment and, with the emergence of the studio production system in Hollywood, American films were beginning to look and now sound like a quality product. A new wave of cinema building in the 1920s introduced much more glamorous 'picture palaces' that attracted more middle-class audiences in the major urban areas of many countries.

Research and Explore 1.1

Gaumont, Pathé and Ufa were three of the most important film 'brands' before the advent of sound. All three brands still exist – what do they stand for now and who owns them?

Changes with sound

Sound created problems for producers in countries with a smaller language base – films for export now encountered an obstacle that was expensive to overcome. If films were not exportable, this in turn meant that local production might not be sustainable on any scale given the relative size of the local language market. A second important factor was the cost of the new technologies, both in producing sound films and equipping cinemas. New technology requirements strengthened the hold of manufacturers and patent-holders, most of whom were based in the US or in the major European territories. Competing technologies also meant that for several years the international industry was in turmoil as standards had to be renegotiated.

In Europe, which had the most diverse range of languages and local production opportunities in the early 1930s, one of the first responses to the new conditions was the development of simultaneous **multiple-version productions** in different languages. The same company might make a German-language version of a film on sound stages and then repeat the production in English or French with different actors using the same sets.

Charles O'Brien (2005) suggests that during the period 1930 to 1932 one-third of all German film production was multiple version. O'Brien also quotes the German producer Erich Pommer on the importance of deciding in advance of a film's production whether or not it was intended for export. The requirements of the new sound production techniques meant that meticulous planning was needed if multiple versions were to be produced effectively – and economically.

Multiple-version production held the promise of a film that could satisfy popular audiences in different language markets, but it was a relatively expensive and cumbersome process. It is still in operation today in isolated instances; for example, in the work of Indian director Mani Ratnam who has produced separate Tamil- and Hindi-language versions of *Ayitha Ezhuthu/Yuva* in 2004 and *Raavanan/Raavan* in 2010 using different actors (see Chapter 10 on Indian cinemas).

The long-term solution to the language problem was found in the choice between **subtitling** and **dubbing**. The first subtitled sound film *The Jazz Singer* (US, 1927) was screened in Paris in January 1929. A French company also opened one of the first dubbing studios. It became apparent relatively quickly that the choice between the two processes depended on the size of the language market and the relative costs associated with each method. Subtitling is considerably cheaper and, for smaller language territories like the Nordic countries, it was really the only option. But in France, Italy, Germany and Spain the language market was able to sustain a large-scale dubbing operation with specialist studios and dubbing artists organised to dub all foreign-language imports. The decisions taken in the late 1920s and 1930s tended to cement the options for audiences in many territories over the next 80 years.

Since this topic is so central to the exchange of films across language barriers we shall deal with it in detail here, interrupting our chronology of the development of global film.

One of the famous titles produced in two languages was Joseph von Sternberg's *Das blaue Engel* (*The Blue Angel*, Germany, 1931) made for Ufa with both Marlene Dietrich and Emil Jannings repeating their roles in English and German.

Dubbing and subtitling in global film

In the 1930s the routine dubbing of Hollywood films into the four major European languages as well as Mandarin for the Chinese market enabled the new sound films to reach most parts of the world (i.e. including into Spanish-speaking Latin

America and across the French Empire). One of the effects of dubbing was to enable censorship – something which the Nazis in Germany and the fascists in Italy institutionalised and which became possible for the Spanish fascists in the 1940s.

Both dubbing and subtitling involve extra expense for distributors, so decisions to release a foreign-language film with one or the other form of translation require careful consideration of potential box office. In a mass-market scenario, distributors have tended to assume that popular genre films are acceptable as dubbed but that **specialised films** which attract a more critical audience need to be subtitled.

The 'FIGS' countries (France, Italy, Germany, Spain) routinely dub all foreign-language imports for popular film and television, although with the increasingly blurred boundaries between **mainstream** and specialised films it is now possible in France to find the same film showing in both dubbed and subtitled versions in different cinemas in the same town – or even on different screens in the same cinema. While some audiences complain about 'reading' subtitles, other audiences object to the mismatched lip movements of dubbed films and the inappropriate voices (but this partly depends on the care taken in dubbing: some dubbed soundtracks are extremely effective). French cinemas helpfully list foreign-language films as being 'VF' (*version française*: dubbed into French) or 'VO' (*version originale*: subtitled in French) so that audiences can choose. In India, Hollywood imports are now often dubbed into local languages (Hindi, Tamil and Telugu) as well as being shown in English.

Subtitling is seen as a less expensive option for smaller language groups. Often, audiences in, for instance, Scandinavian countries will in any case be competent in English, German and/or other languages. The willingness to dub and the acceptability of subtitling varies across European countries (and elsewhere in the world). The situation in the UK perhaps exemplifies the kinds of issues raised. When cinema in the UK was still a mass market (up until the early 1970s), dubbed films were relatively common in UK cinemas. But as cinemas closed and audiences dwindled, distributors and exhibitors became reluctant to book popular genre films that required dubbing. At the same time, the number of subtitled films on release has risen to supply what has been the relative success of specialised cinema exhibition. European producers have sometimes complained that the reluctance to dub in

Fig 1.4
Film listings at a multi-screen cinema in Malmö, Sweden. English-language films are presented with Swedish subtitles except the animations in Screens 6 and 8 which are dubbed into Swedish (*sv tal*). *Call Girl* is unusual as a Swedish-language film showing with Swedish subtitles (*textad*) because the dialogue may be difficult for some audiences to follow.

Fig 1.5
UGC Ciné Cité multi-
screen cinema in Lille,
Northern France, shows
films in French (VF) and
in original languages
with subtitles (VOST).
Some popular Hollywood
films and children's films
are also dubbed into
French.

the UK – compared to the FIGS countries – has reduced the possibility of a wider
distribution of popular European films such as French crime films and Italian horror
films. The same arguments occur with Hong Kong martial arts films.

The debates about subtitling and dubbing were re-invigorated in the 1950s as
television broadcasting spread worldwide. The split followed similar lines so that
filmed TV series from American studios were again routinely dubbed into the
four main European languages. In the English-speaking world, where the number
of foreign-language film and television imports has been historically quite small,
dubbing has never been routine except in the case of animation (and some Hong
Kong films). The argument has been that animated features are unlikely to suffer
from lip-synch problems and subtitles are not suitable for younger audiences (i.e.
under 10s). Subtitling was preferred for films intended for an adult audience,
especially when the films imported tended to be art films that were assumed to
appeal only to a minority audience.

The UK is the second
largest European market
(after France) and other
European producers
should have advantages
in entering it, but the UK
is a notoriously difficult
market for foreign-
language films.

Case study 1.1: Subtitling and *La haine* (France, 1995)

The French youth picture *La haine* and its celebrated young writer-director Mathieu Kassovitz makes an interesting case study for the subtitling/dubbing debate. The film's title translates simply as 'Hate' (but the French title is usually used in the UK) and the narrative concerns 20 hours in the lives of three young men from one of the large housing estates built for workers' families some way out of Paris. The economic recession and the treatment of migrant communities in France have created antagonism between youths on the estates and the police, and this forms the basis of the film's dramatic conflict – following a protest demonstration, one of the youths from the estate is in hospital after being shot by the police, and angry youths want to avenge him. The film made a big impact in France and Kassovitz was called '*l'enfant terrible*' of French cinema. It was clear that the film would have export possibilities, but also that translating the dialogue of the youths in the film would be difficult. The three central characters are '*blanc, beur et noir*' (white Jewish, North African and West African), and they speak a mixture of contemporary French slang and *verlan* (French 'back' slang) with various references to contemporary global youth culture.

English subtitles are invariably designed for the North American market, and in this case some subtitlers decided to substitute the French slang with phrases and references derived from the Hollywood cycle of urban crime thrillers, especially those featuring African-American youth such as *Boyz n the Hood* (US, 1991). In many ways this made sense and fitted aspects of the story, since the youths in the film are seen discussing Hollywood films and listening to French hip-hop and rap. Director Kassovitz also made clear his interest in and respect for certain Hollywood directors, including the New York directors Jim Jarmusch and Spike Lee. Yet, other aspects of the film fared less well. The three central characters at one point discuss the comics they read as children. The subtitles suggest they are discussing the US cartoon strip 'Peanuts' instead of the French 'Pif et Hercule' which featured in the communist newspaper *L'Humanité*. When *La haine* was broadcast on BBC2 in the UK, a new set of subtitles, in British English, was used, and

Fig 1.6
UK subtitles show the three central characters in *La haine* discussing the comic book heroes of their childhood. Pif the dog and Hercule the cat also appeared in TV animations. This is the type of cultural reference that subtitles can bring out – or cut out – for different language audiences.

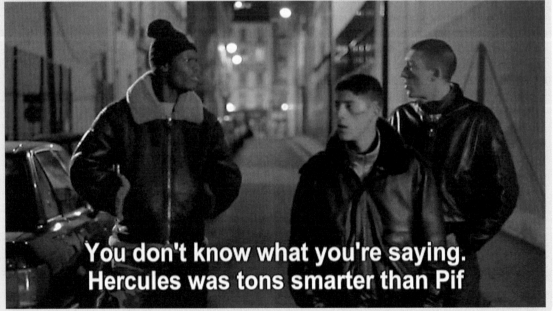

You don't know what you're saying. Hercules was tons smarter than Pif

though these had the same problems translating the *verlan*, they did at least give a much more distinctive representation of a specific aspect of French culture. The European Blu-ray release of 2009 took this even further in substituting British references, so the local purveyor of stolen goods on the estate who is known as 'Darty' (a French electrical goods chain) becomes 'Dixons' (a British chainstore).

La haine was successful in the UK and the US as a specialised film, with strong interest in the DVD release and later cinema re-release. The next Kassovitz film to receive a UK release was *Les rivières pourpres* (*The Crimson Rivers*, France, 2000). Based on a popular novel, this is a similarly popular film in the form of an action thriller. As indicated in several parts of this book, films like this challenge overseas distributors. The specialised cinema audience that took to *La haine* may find this film 'too Hollywood' with its plot about a police search for a serial killer featuring chase scenes in the French Alps, but similar ingredients work effectively in Hollywood thrillers for the multiplex. Could the film work in a multiplex and would it need to be dubbed? This was a real question in 2000, since the French film company UGC then operated a number of mainstream UK multiplex cinemas that could potentially take the film. The distributor Columbia-Tri-Star had the UK rights and registered both a dubbed and subtitled version with the BBFC (the UK's film classification board, the British Board of Film Classification). In the event neither version was given a significant release, suggesting that the distributor couldn't decide, and the film failed at the UK box office. Elsewhere in Europe, and especially in East Asian markets, dubbed versions of the film were very successful.

Ironically, a year later in 2001 Mathieu Kassovitz featured as a lead actor in *Amélie* (*Le fabuleux destin d'Amélie Poulain*) which became one of the biggest-ever box office successes for a subtitled film in the UK market. Kassovitz went on to direct films in English and, like his one-time production partner Luc Besson, he remains interested in making popular genre films in Europe in English. After *Les rivières pourpres* there has been little interest in dubbing French films for cinema release in the UK – although examples of very effective dubbing into English may be found on certain DVD releases, for example, *36* (*36 Quai des Orfèvres*, France, 2004).

In North America, dubbing has fared as badly as in the UK. Arguments have been put forward to blame the very poor-quality dubbing of Hong Kong martial arts films for setting up negative expectations for audiences. But there is no reason why the careful selection of voice actors and close attention to remixing soundtracks shouldn't work for most audiences. The *La haine* example points to crucial differences between British and American English. This is apparent in the export of UK films to North America – not just in the use of different words for common terms but also in the use of dialect and regional accents. Several British films, including *Trainspotting* (UK, 1996), have either had dubbed soundtracks or subtitles for a US release. It is much more difficult to come up with examples of American speech proving a problem in the UK (but there have been suggestions that some British films need subtitles when shown within the UK itself).

Momentum released *The Girl With the Dragon Tattoo* (Sweden/Denmark, 2010) in the UK as both a subtitled and a dubbed print. Audiences were offered a choice in some cities which research suggests was appreciated (see http://industry.bfi.org.uk/audiences).

Graham Roberts (2003) offers an interesting investigation into assumptions about dubbing and subtitling in the UK, with some (student) audience survey material.

Research and Explore 1.2

Find a DVD with a choice of language soundtracks and different language subtitles.

Watch the same few scenes with dubbed voices and then with the original soundtrack and subtitles.

- List the pros and cons of dubbing and subtitling from your perspective.
- Try and persuade a small sample of people to carry out the same task.

What conclusions do you draw?

Is there anything that could improve the experience of watching dubbed or subtitled films?

A related issue to the subtitling/dubbing debate is the casting of actors in international productions and how this works with audiences. In *The Eagle* (UK/US, 2011), (British) director Kevin McDonald decided to give all the Roman soldiers, in this story about Britain in the fourth century, American accents – some of the actors playing Romans were American but others were British. The actors playing the (local) Picts were required to use regional British accents (one of these actors was the Maghrebi-French actor Tahar Rahim).

Slumdog Millionaire (UK, 2008) provides an example of a part-subtitled film that confounded expectations in several ways. As a film set in India, where English is sometimes used for film productions and often mixed with Hindi or other Indian languages, it was not surprising that subtitles would be necessary for part of the film. However, it did mean that the producers had to persuade normally conservative US TV networks to accept it as a mainstream 'Hollywood-style' movie. Perhaps the wide acceptance of the film is partly explained by the creative use of graphics in the presentation of the subtitles – different colours and different positioning around the screen all work to integrate them into the visual look of the film. The amount of English-language dialogue in the film did, however, mean that for a wide release in India two versions of the film were made available: English for the upmarket screens and a Hindi dub for cinemas outside the major cities. The English version seems to have been more successful at the Indian box office (see Branston with Stafford 2010: 163–171).

The following is a valuable observation about subtitling from South India which summarises some of the preceding discussion and adds some further thoughts:

> The advent of the age of DVDs and global television has made the use of subtitles more widespread and also popular. Most of the channels that broadcast films now show them with subtitles, even for English films. The wide and prevalent use of subtitles has in fact globalised our viewing experiences in such a way that the very notion of 'foreignness' has become problematic. As Atom Egoyan and Ian Balfour put it, 'Globalisation has left its prints on how cinema is made, circulated, and received. [...] We need to make sense of the foreign on our own terms. We have to define what is foreign to our individual experience, before we can hope to understand the roots of collective misunderstanding. Subtitles offer a way into worlds outside of ourselves. They are a unique and complex formal apparatus that allows the viewer an astonishing degree of access and interaction. Subtitles embed us.'
>
> Obviously, the act of subtitling involves 'universalising' the 'particular' which brings the 'local/regional' in dialogue with the 'national/global'. It raises a lot of questions, similar to the ones confronted by a translator. This also poses troublesome questions about 'regional' identities and 'locality' of a film and the film viewing experience.
>
> Should one 'translate out' all the regional and culture-specific nuances to make the dialogues accessible to the global audience? Or, should one maintain the local flavour? If so, how? But the problem with subtitles is that they do not offer any scope for footnotes or explanations. So, subtitling is an act of balancing between the pressure to be concise yet cogent, true yet communicative, local yet global.
>
> (from the blog of Malayalam subtitler 'venkiteswaran' http://venkiteswaran. blogspot.com/2010/11/watching-movies-reading-subtitles.html)

The context for Hollywood's hegemony

Let us return to our chronology of the overall development of global cinema. By the early 1930s, the Hollywood **studio system** had been established and, although the studios saw their prime activity as maximising revenue in the North American market, they also opened offices and sometimes their own studio facilities in key film territories overseas. With their competitors for the export of films having fallen away for the reasons outlined earlier in this chapter, the studios could systematically build and service an overseas audience with films that were in accountants' terms already amortised (i.e. had covered production costs with the revenues in their domestic market). Gradually the studios secured what later theorists would describe as **hegemony** – the domination of markets largely through the consent of audiences more than willing to place the pleasures of American cinema before those of local or regional productions (Hollywood studios were also prepared to twist the arms of local distributors and exhibitors as well via pressure from trade bodies).

The Hollywood studio system: a classical system?

The 'Hollywood studio system' refers to the domination of the American film industry in the early 1930s by large **vertically integrated** film companies. The five major studios (MGM, Warner Bros., Paramount, RKO and 20th Century Fox) that developed in the 1910s and 1920s owned production facilities, distribution companies and chains of cinemas – often the biggest and most profitable cinemas in prime locations in major cities. Columbia and Universal were major producers and distributors but suffered from not owning their own cinema chains. United Artists was primarily a distributor of independently produced films. Disney and the leading 'independents' like Samuel Goldwyn and Selznick International also worked within the studio system, enjoying relationships that saw their titles being distributed by the majors. Outside the system, smaller producers (of westerns, crime films, etc.) were forced into distributing their films in **second- and third-run** cinemas.

Similar forms of studio operation involving integrated production, distribution and exhibition did develop in other film industries, especially in the UK and Japan and on a smaller scale in Hong Kong and elsewhere. However, nowhere else was there a home market so large and profitable, enabling the financing of overseas operations for the export of studio product in quite the same way.

In film studies the formulation of Classical Hollywood as an aesthetic approach to production alongside the economic model has been crucially important. Often associated with the work of David Bordwell, Janet Staiger and Kristin Thompson (see below), this approach is associated with the following:

- a form of 'Hollywood **realism**';
- the importance of continuity editing which serves the function of '**transparency**' in narrative flow;
- an emphasis on developing technologies (sound, colour, widescreen, etc.);
- the use of contracted **stars** in both structuring the film narrative and promoting the film.

Most film studies courses aim to define Classical Hollywood in order to secure understanding of a mode of production against which other forms may be measured. There are many excellent reasons for doing this and the idea of what a Hollywood

Hegemony is a concept that in film and media studies derives from the writings of **Antonio Gramsci**. Originally it referred to the power/leadership of governments over other countries. Today, hegemonic Hollywood may be seen as one example of US **soft power** on a global scale.

Antonio Gramsci (1891-1937) was a Marxist thinker whose ideas influenced many later theorists in film, media and cultural studies.

The hegemonic power of Hollywood is often seen displayed by the **MPAA**, the Motion Picture Association of America, first formed in 1922 and now comprising the six major studios. See the website at www.mpaa.org.

Fig 1.7
How to Read Donald Duck.
Source: International
General Books.

film might be did become ingrained into the cinema-going experiences of audiences across the world. But as we will discover in the rest of this book, it has also caused problems of understanding.

As well as an economic model for the organisation of film production – involving a form of global operation – the Hollywood studio system has also been seen as a defining cultural model. It enabled a form of **cultural imperialism** so that global audiences shared and sometimes adopted various aspects of social behaviour they had seen in Hollywood films. The effects of this on individuals would of course vary enormously, as would the impact in different countries.

One of the earliest sustained analyses of the cultural imperialist tendency was offered by Ariel Dorfman and Armand Mattelart in *How to Read Donald Duck*, first published in Chile in 1971 and translated into English in 1972. Dorfman and Mattelart were actually concerned with the ideologies that underpinned the cartoon strips published by Disney but their study was indicative of the way in which sociologists and cultural theorists focused on iconic American characters and brands – all circulated on a global basis via Hollywood films and their associated products or 'tie-ins'. Any Disney character is a good example of a hegemonic Hollywood icon – seemingly purely an entertainment construction. Another would be Coca Cola as a brand. The French director Jean-Luc Godard summed up the power of the brand in

LES ENFANTS DE MARX ET DE COCA-COLA

Fig 1.8
An 'intertitle' card from
Masculin féminin – a
possible title for a film
about young people in
France.

a famous slogan he created for one of his political films of the mid-1960s, *Masculin féminin* (France, 1966), when he referred to 'The Children of Marx and Coca Cola'. Like many of Godard's quotes at this time, the phrase seems both glib *and* analytical. During the 1960s radical politics and the new consumerism did indeed seem to be uneasy bedfellows.

As well as the cultural imperialist argument, film scholars have also explored the ways in which Hollywood costume design has influenced high street fashions and how **product placement** in Hollywood films has developed over time. The impact of these **externalities** however was largely confined to North America until American consumer products became more widely available in overseas markets (which began to occur post-1941 with the presence of American military bases in many territories). Externalities are possible benefits (or disbenefits) from economic activity not easily measured by economists but useful in considering the overall worth of that activity to society. The studios began to recognise that charging for product placement was an additional income stream and this became more important when certain products began to generate global advertising. The more general point, however, is that Hollywood 'sold' an American lifestyle which then helped American corporations gain influence overseas.

In 1982 Coca Cola actually bought a Hollywood studio, Columbia Pictures, subsequently selling it to Sony in 1989.

If Hollywood was a prime agent in the 'Coca-Colonisation' of most of the world and this was deemed to be cultural imperialism, it was also seen as a potential agent of modernisation in many cultures. The argument here is that in countries where traditional social structures constrained social behaviour, exposure to Hollywood films could have the effect of persuading young women, for example, to go against parental wishes in terms of marriage partners or employment prospects.

The sense of Hollywood in the studio period as a business model, a mode of industrial organisation, a system of work practices and aesthetic approaches and a cultural agency – all with a global influence – has been summed up in the concept of the **Classical Hollywood Cinema**. This was the title of a large and well-researched book by David Bordwell, Janet Staiger and Kristin Thompson, first published in 1985. At the end of the book there is a short section on 'Alternative Modes of Film Practice' that includes this assertion as part of its summary:

Fig 1.9
A production still from
Mad Love (US, 1935), an
MGM film directed by the
German cinematographer
Karl Freund and starring
the Hungarian actor Peter
Lorre, newly arrived from
the German film industry.
The film is a version of
The Hands of Orlac, a
French novel previously
adapted as a film in
Germany in 1924. Source:
The Kobal Collection/
www.picture-desk.com.

> Finally, in constructing alternatives to Hollywood, we must recognise that the
> historical centrality of that mode creates a constant and complex interchange
> with other modes. No absolute, pure alternative to Hollywood exists.
>
> (Bordwell *et al.*, 1988: 384)

In other words, all modes of filmmaking have engaged with 'Classical Hollywood
Cinema' in some way since the 1920s. In one sense that sounds indisputable. It is
difficult to conceive of a filmmaker who has never seen a Hollywood film. A problem
arises when we move to the next stage of the argument that creates the **binarism** – any
'alternative' mode is, by definition, 'not Hollywood'. It cannot create its own 'classical
system'; it can only be defined by what it isn't in Hollywood terms. The term 'classical'
implies that this was a system which reached a form of perfection or which reached
a standard that all others would refer to. This creation of a status for Hollywood is
much more problematic and, as we shall see in other chapters, there are plenty of
challenges to this position. We might also note that there is an implied Hollywood
arrogance here. Hollywood studio practices were just as likely to absorb influences
from other industries via the personnel recruited, especially from Europe, as vice versa.

This American domination took place in an international context that has
changed dramatically since the 1930s. It is useful to distinguish four phases of
international activity since 1930.

The 1930s

Cinema was developing as a medium of mass entertainment across the world. Most
of Africa and Asia was still controlled by European colonial powers, and Latin
America was culturally and economically influenced by both European and American

activity. In many of the smaller colonial territories, cinema drew audiences of mainly European colonial administrators, traders and settlers but significant commercial industries catering for a local language market developed in, for instance, Egypt, India and Shanghai, as well as in Mexico, Brazil and Argentina. Japan was itself a colonial power in Korea, Taiwan and Manchuria, and during the 1930s rivalled Hollywood in the number of films produced (though not in the spread of film exports). The local production in all these industries both borrowed from Hollywood and Europe but also developed new forms of cinema derived from local forms of storytelling, both traditional and popular. During the period 1939 to 1941 when Hollywood was arguably at its creative peak, all the other major producers were engaged in a war effort (or coping with occupation). Hollywood joined the war directly in 1942.

1945 onwards through the 1950s and 1960s

Most of Africa and Asia achieved political independence during this period. In Latin America, revolutionary struggles produced a new economic and cultural climate, and this was mirrored in different ways in some of the newly independent states in Africa, as well as in India and parts of the Middle East (see Chapter 6). Although it wasn't a term used at the time, scholars now recognise the need to discuss what happened to film culture in these countries under the heading of anti-colonialism and then **post-colonialism** and **neo-colonialism** (see Chapter 8 for a detailed discussion of these issues).

This long period saw two contradictory changes in audiences. In North America and the UK, audiences began to fall from the late 1940s, partly (but not completely) because of competition from the new medium of television. In the rest of Europe and Japan film industries took time to recover from wartime disruption and reached their peak audience numbers much later in the 1960s before following the US and UK into relative decline. Hollywood's revenues didn't decline in the same way as those in the UK, partly because the overseas markets for its exports held firm for longer. Hollywood also made conscious attempts to produce films in Europe (especially in Rome and London). In China, Russia and Eastern Europe film culture during this period developed in the context of communist systems with control over local film industries during the Cold War (and barriers to the import of Hollywood material).

The Hollywood studio system declined during the 1950s and is often seen to have ended in the late 1960s after several expensive flops – and several low-budget hits. The withdrawal by Hollywood producers from London and Rome contributed to the eventual further decline of the UK and Italian industries.

The 1970s and 1980s

As first video and later multi-channel TV began to cut into the cinema market, popular cinema as a 'theatrical' experience began to decline in most markets, though not always at the same rate. Again the North American market saw developments that maintained industry profits. The studios eventually realised that video, rather than threatening the industry, offered ancillary profits to compensate for lost ticket sales, and network television proved to be a lucrative source of revenue via film libraries as well as relatively recent films airing for the first time – in both domestic and overseas markets.

In the meantime some of the biggest markets, including Japan and Germany alongside the UK, saw further serious falls in admissions while France, which had

Films like *Jaws* (1975) and *Star Wars* (1977) changed film distribution, first in the US and then in other territories, with simultaneous releases across the country. Previously, film openings had taken several weeks to cross the country.

never previously been the biggest European market, held on to more of its audiences. China and the Soviet Union held on to very large audiences under their systems of state control over popular culture until the 1980s. After the Cold War ended, Russian cinemas closed at an alarming rate and they have only begun to recover strongly in the 2000s. Something similar happened in China where the spread of pirate video copies in the 1990s had a big impact but the market is now also recovering strongly. Elsewhere we have seen the rise of Indian cinema since the 1970s and periods when Hong Kong has been very strong (prior to the 'return' to China). There are references in several chapters of this book to the changing fortunes of popular cinema in different countries at different times throughout the 1960s to the 1980s.

The 1990s onwards

Tentpole movies literally 'hold up' the tent – they offer a 'safe bet' to underpin the slate of films for distribution by a studio each year. The concept is now also visibly in operation in Japan, China and South Korea.

A **multiplex** is a cinema with three screens or more. In practice most multi-cinemas have between six and 20 screens. The largest are sometimes referred to as megaplexes and the smallest as miniplexes.

Hollywood renewed itself in the 1980s on the back of technological changes, including the development of visual effects and later CGI, and the continued shift towards youth-orientated action pictures that began in the 1950s. Building on the 'wide' distribution patterns introduced in the 1970s, the studio distributors began to focus on a smaller number of mainstream blockbusters with several **tentpole** titles designed to create interest during the holiday seasons. Many of these big-budget films sold well overseas, but perhaps the most important Hollywood export was not the films themselves but the concept of the **multiplex** and its offering of several films in comfortable auditoria with new sound and projection facilities, often located in a food and retail complex of some kind.

The multiplex as it is known today has its origins in the innovative practices of cinema exhibitors in the US and Canada in the 1960s and 1970s (see the account of the development of the Canadian company Cineplex and its subsequent American expansion in Gomery (1992: 104–114)). But it wasn't until the late 1980s that multiplexes began to be built in large numbers in Europe, Australia and East Asia. Ironically, some of the Hollywood studios that had lost their cinema chains in the US following the 1949 Paramount decree were instrumental in this new development.

Fig 1.10
The Warner Village nine-screen Multiplex opened in Kirkstall, Leeds, in 1998 – and became a Vue cinema in 2006.

Warner Bros. in conjunction with the Australian company Village Roadshow began to build multiplexes in parts of Europe and East Asia in the 1990s. Paramount and Universal were joint operators of UCI cinemas founded in 1989 and responsible for building multiplexes in Europe and South America. Paramount was also acquired by (and made part of the Viacom group) by Sumner Redstone, whose private company National Amusements operated the Showcase chain of cinemas in the US. The company built multiplexes in the UK, Latin America and Russia.

Although Warner Bros., Paramount and Universal eventually withdrew from some of their overseas ventures, their support for the 'multiplex revolution' was important. They helped to sell the American experience of cinema-going and guaranteed the flow of American product to territories where the fabric of traditional cinemas was in dire need of replenishment. Local chains of multiplexes soon developed alongside the American operators and, though the multiplex building boom has slowed in Western Europe, the building frenzy has not abated in South Asia and East Asia. In July 2011 the first 'multi-screen' cinema opened in Cambodia showing mainstream Hollywood films (http://www.filmbiz.asia/news/legend-is-cambodian-multiplex-first).

The growth of 'multiplex culture' worldwide from the 1990s onwards signalled a shift in the sources of Hollywood's revenues. On the one hand, DVD began to develop as an extremely profitable ancillary market. If titles failed to match costs in

'The Paramount decree' was the final act in 1949 of a long legal process that led to the major studios 'divorcing' themselves from their cinema circuits under pressure from independent producers and anti-trust interests in the US government.

Fig 1.11
The Amazing Spider-Man scheduled to arrive at a multiplex in Belgium one day after its UK and US release in 2012.

the theatrical market they could still potentially move into profit through DVD sales. Overseas, however, the theatrical market for Hollywood was expanding with the multiplexes attracting audiences to special effects action pictures in particular. As we noted earlier, Hollywood once saw the 'international market' as a bonus – the bulk of revenues were made in the domestic market. By the late 1990s 'international' was moving ahead and by 2011 was twice the size of the domestic North American market.

Both theatrical and DVD sales were badly affected by piracy in the 1990s and into the 2000s. Partly as a response, but also because the new multiplex screens made it more possible, the studios began to develop 'day and date' releases for major films. Tentpole releases are released 'simultaneously' across thousands of screens worldwide (in practice, owing to time zones, the launch may be spread over a couple of days). This lessens the impact of pirated DVDs and builds on the promotional possibilities of internet campaigns, etc. The practice has significantly altered distribution patterns for major films and has encouraged other film industries to think differently about distribution. The major Indian distributors now release big-budget Hindi and Tamil films in 18 territories on the same day. It is worth noting that in China, one of the territories most affected by pirate DVDs, a massive multiplex building programme has enticed audiences back into cinemas (though not necessarily to see all the Hollywood releases, since the Chinese government still controls the import of foreign film titles).

In 2012, as if to prove that the industry is still dynamic, some studios began to stagger releases again, releasing first in international markets and then in North America in the case of *Prometheus*. The year 2012 also saw major territories moving towards digital film as the main form of commercial distribution and exhibition (see Chapter 12 for discussion of what this might mean).

> Box office figures are collected on a territory basis but also on a national and sometimes a regional basis. Internal film industry data often quotes **domestic** (i.e. North America: Canada and US), **international** (everywhere else) and **worldwide** (domestic plus international).

Local and international

Throughout this book you will come across the terms 'local' and 'international' to describe productions. The use of **local** here refers to the 'ownership' of a film production in the sense of where the film is made, the participation of local production companies, and in many cases the official recognition of the nationality of the production – often necessary for a production to qualify for forms of public funding.

Local production usually implies that a film is being made in the local language. However, a local identity does not necessarily preclude Hollywood involvement in the production. Hollywood may see advantages in being part of local production or 'picking up' local films for distribution in the territory. This happens most frequently in the UK but there are examples of this kind of activity in most major film territories.

International productions are intended to be distributed internationally. For this reason they are usually made in English. Although there are some exceptions to this rule, the other convention is that they must not be too 'local' in their audience appeal – and this is commercially dangerous to ignore. Most international films have Hollywood backing (or at least US investment), but it isn't essential.

A film may be counted as both local and international usually when Hollywood studios make films in countries with a strong local industry. Thus the *Harry Potter* films that grossed US$9 billion worldwide were officially UK/US productions. The profits went back to Warner Bros. but the prestige (and the employment and industrial development opportunities) remained within the UK. Some other major Hollywood productions based in the UK are, however, considered as American in identity terms (see Chapter 4).

UK-US productions are often 'seamless' in terms of their joint identity, but other **transnational** productions have more easily distinguishable features. *Blindness* (2008) is a film mostly in English directed by a Brazilian, adapted from a Portuguese novel and shot mainly in Canada and Uruguay with a multinational cast. Officially it is a Brazilian-Canadian-Japanese production.

The Fox studio in Australia produces films that again can be both 'local' and 'international' (e.g. *Moulin Rouge* (US/Australia, 2001)).

The international film market today

The contemporary international film market is surveyed, not without difficulty, by film industry monitors each week. In practice, this is the film market that complies more or less with the industrial practices of 'Global Hollywood' and ignores any box office returns from parts of Africa and the Middle East, parts of South Asia and smaller territories of limited commercial importance for the studios (and which actually may be impossible to collect with any guarantee of accuracy). The weekly chart published by *Screendaily* is our guide here. *Screendaily* is the online edition (www.screendaily.com) of *Screen International,* a UK publication. London is in some ways still the base for the *international* film industry – where Hollywood, Bollywood and European interests meet. It is less important for East Asian markets, and for contacts in Africa and the Middle East and Latin America.

Fig 1.12 represents an analysis of the international box office chart over a 26-week period from November 2011 until May 2012. The bars represent entries in the Top 20 chart based on 20 points for No. 1, 19 for No. 2, etc. It is immediately clear that Hollywood hegemony still holds. The films that are seen everywhere and which attract the most box office revenue are American – both 'studio pictures' (made by **MPAA** members and affiliates) and independents. Two aspects of this domination are worth noting. First, Hollywood films are distributed widely – sometimes up to 62 territories simultaneously. Second, those 62 territories include all the countries with high ticket prices such as Japan and Europe. Titles from India or Turkey will have most admissions in territories where ticket prices are lower. The chart does not necessarily show which films have the largest audiences, since it is based on box office revenue, not admissions.

The rest of the chart represents 'local' productions in the other major film-producing countries. In several cases this might mean a co-production, often with an American company, and sometimes a film made in English even though the main partners may be France or Germany, Italy, etc. In most weeks the chart will include at least one title from France, UK, Japan, China, South Korea and India. In all other cases only a small number of titles across the year are likely to register. Since the data in Fig 1.12 were collected the number of Chinese titles featuring in the chart each week has risen significantly – though they are still restricted to a small number of territories.

In Fig 1.12 Australia is represented by *Happy Feet Two* (Aus/US) and the UK figure is boosted by the inclusion of *Sherlock Holmes: A Game of Shadows* (UK/US)

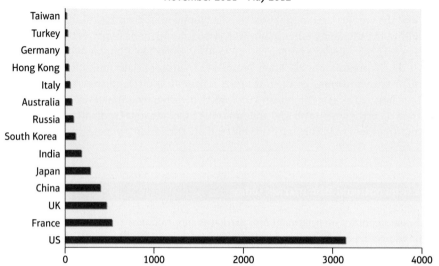

Share of International Box Office Top 20
November 2011 – May 2012

Fig 1.12
Comparative performance
of local titles in the
International Box Office
Chart. Each bar represents
the number and ranking
of locally produced film
titles for each of the
major film-producing
countries as they appeared
in the International Top
Twenty Box Office Chart
between November 2011
and May 2012. Source:
*Screen International/
Screendaily.*

Intouchables
(*Untouchable*, France,
2011) attracted
enormous audiences,
not just in France but
elsewhere in Europe, Asia
and Latin America. Its
UK/US box office was
only US$13.4 million out
of a global box office of
US$426 million by 2013.

– co-productions have been assigned to whichever seems the appropriate production base (i.e. the major partner). Any film that registers in the chart will usually have generated around a minimum US$2 million at the box office over that week. Apart from Hollywood, only Indian films (mostly in Hindi) regularly appear on the chart with multiple territory releases and then many fewer than the Hollywood norm. In a typical week, a Hollywood film showing in 40-plus territories may be in the chart next to a Japanese film only being seen in its own domestic territory and a Hindi film being shown in perhaps 18 territories. In practice, the chart tends to underestimate the export of Hindi films, partly because some of the territories may not report figures and partly because successful Hindi films often take many months to reach some territories. If we looked at the box office totals for individual films over this period, we would see several Hollywood films earning more than US$200 million, but also the French production *Intouchables* with US$332 million.

One conclusion that may be drawn from the chart is that as far as popular cinema is concerned, only Hollywood has a global reach. The chart is intended to illustrate market share in a visual way and it suggests that around 60 per cent of official international box office is for Hollywood films. If we added in 'domestic' (i.e. North America), the Hollywood share of **worldwide** box office would be much higher. Some academics suggest that 90 per cent of all revenues go to American films (Miller *et al.* 2005). This seems a little too high – though the release of a 'monster' blockbuster like *The Avengers* (US, 2012) can skew figures based solely on chart positions as it opened on US$100 million from the first three days in the international market. Another way to gauge the dominance of Hollywood is to consider the total value of the global cinema box office. MPAA figures for 2012 (mpaa.org) show a global box office total of US$34.7 billion, with the North American market contributing US$10.8 billion. The international figures do not mean that all the box office receipts return to the US of course. Distribution deals vary from one territory to another but an industry rule-of-thumb figure suggests that a 30 to 40 per cent share goes to the distributor. At various times Hollywood has had to face **blocking** strategies in some territories, restricting the return of profits to the US.

Fig 1.12 does not give the whole picture, but currently it does suggest that the globalising thrust of popular cinema still has more to do with changing the nature of Hollywood releases than with any other film industries mounting a sustained challenge to Hollywood's leading position. Changes are coming via the links between Hollywood studios and major film producers in India and China, and a desire by Hollywood to be involved in local productions.

Some scholars have also argued that Hollywood mainstream pictures, especially the action films and some of the fantasy-driven 'family films'/animations, style themselves as dealing with 'universal themes' in settings that are non-specific in cultural terms. This enables producers to move productions overseas, to adapt non-American material and also to cast 'local' stars in lead roles. Audiences probably don't notice the large number of British, Canadian or Australian actors in Hollywood films – or the number of British cultural properties. Other North Europeans can also be relatively easily smuggled into Hollywood productions (e.g. Noomi Rapace from Sweden, Diane Kruger from Germany). More visible are the Spanish and Latin American stars such as Penelope Cruz, Antonio Banderas, Javier Bardem and Salma Hayek – valuable both for their appeal in Hispanic markets overseas but also for the growing Hispanic audience in the American domestic market. Hollywood has had mixed success in using major stars from Hong Kong cinema such as Jackie Chan, Jet Li, Chow Yun-fat, Michelle Yeoh, etc. but casting of these and similar names is set to increase as Hollywood moves to retain and expand audiences in East Asia.

International art cinema

In Chapter 7 we look specifically at concepts of art cinema and the ways in which institutions like the international film festival circuit and its associated systems of production and distribution have developed since 1945. At this point it is important in our overview to recognise the ways in which more specialised cinema has circulated since 1945 and in particular to recognise the impact that 'foreign film' has made both with audiences and with cultural policy-makers as well as with filmmakers and the studios – an impact far beyond what might be expected from the relatively small audience numbers involved.

We should also acknowledge that film scholarship and the way in which it has developed into an academic discipline of film studies, screen studies or even media studies/cultural studies has created certain kinds of distinctions between 'popular' and 'art' cinema. Film academics and industry personnel have sometimes used different terminology to describe similar distinctions, so we need to be careful in labelling films.

When we consider the relationship between the Hollywood mainstream and popular cinemas in the other major film-producing countries, we are often looking at similar industrial practices, including similar uses of stars, genres, etc. This is discussed in Chapter 2. Hollywood also produces specialised films, 'Hollywood art films' perhaps, and in some ways these are no different from the specialised films produced in France or Turkey or South Korea which might all be selected 'in competition' at the Cannes or Venice film festivals. However, the similarities are sometimes lost because of the insularity of English-speaking markets in which all

'**Blocking**' of returns was once an element of film distribution in territories such as India. This strategy forbids a foreign distributor from taking profits out of the country and therefore encourages further productions in that country using the blocked funds. China still restricts the activities of Hollywood distributors in various ways, though the MPAA, working through the World Trade Organisation, managed to negotiate an increased quota for foreign films in 2012.

foreign-language films are effectively treated as specialised, even if at home they are popular blockbusters.

It's not all feature films ...

Our study of global film will be primarily concerned with 'the feature film', still expected after 100 years of theatrical exhibition to be a fiction narrative film of around 100 minutes in length. This is the most recognisable product to be found in every film territory and it remains the main focus for the global film industry. We will also refer to the **filmed entertainment business** which includes films on television (see Chapter 9), and on DVD and online (for streaming or download). One of the important differences between the film industries of the US, UK and Japan and those of, for instance, China and India is that the reliance of producers on the theatrical exhibition market is much greater in the latter two cases. If Indian production companies want to emulate Hollywood it is primarily in terms of developing the ancillary markets for their products and reducing the risks of relying on the cinema box office. Fig 1.13 shows the comparison of filmed entertainment revenues in selected territories.

Territory	Value (US$ millions) 2011	Percentage of global total 2011	Projected Value (US$ millions) 2016	Projected percentage of global total 2016
US	29,953	35.1	30,933	31.00
Japan	8,175	9.6	8,667	8.7
UK	6,022	7.0	6,199	6.2
France	4,407	5.2	5,445	5.5
China	2,719	3.2	7,374	7.4
India	1,658	1.9	2,668	2.7

Fig 1.13 Filmed entertainment in the six major international film markets by value in 2011 and 2016 (estimated). Source: Compiled from data presented in the *British Film Institute Statistical Yearbook 2012*.

Summary

This overview has been mostly historical, and that is important. We want to start the book with a realisation that Hollywood does have an extensive global reach and a hegemonic hold over the international film market. We have discovered that the reasons for Hollywood's prominent position are several and varied. We have noted:

- the size of the North American domestic market (and what this means for exports);
- the control over the development of film technologies;
- the 'accident' of history in restricting the operations of competitors during 1914 to 1920;
- the development of an efficient studio system;
- the use of English as a language once dialogue arrived with synchronous sound;
- the value of library titles to provide revenue streams to underwrite new ventures.

Hollywood grew dynamically due to a combination of factors and its progress has not been without setbacks. There is nothing 'natural' about Hollywood's position and Hollywood films aren't 'simply the best'. They are however likely to do the best business – partly because Hollywood recruits the best talent from other film industries and attempts to respond to new ideas. In the past ten years, Hollywood's global status has changed and the studios have become more reliant on what happens outside North America, as the shift in box office data indicates. See Chapter 12 for ideas about what might happen next.

Research and Explore 1.3

Go to the Box Office Mojo website and select 'International' (http://boxofficemojo.com/intl/). The data are not foolproof but they give a good indication of which films are distributed internationally. Check the top non-Hollywood title in the charts for Japan, Sweden, Brazil, Australia and Poland. See if you can find out anything about that film's genre or narrative content. Is it playing in any other countries? (Just click on the film title.) What conclusions do you draw from this kind of box office data?

References and further reading

Bordwell, David, Staiger, Janet and Thompson, Kristin (1988) *The Classical Hollywood Cinema: Film Style and Mode of Production to 1960*, London and New York: Routledge.

Branston, Gill with Stafford, Roy (2010) *The Media Student's Book* (5th edn), Abingdon: Routledge.

Dorfman, Ariel and Mattelart, Armand (1972/1991) *How to Read Donald Duck: Imperialist Ideology in the Disney Comic*, trans. and updated introduction by David Kunzle, New York: International General.

Egoyan, Atom and Balfour, Ian (eds) (2004) *Subtitles – On the Foreignness of Film*, Cambridge, MA: Alphabet Media Book, MIT Press.

Gomery, Douglas (1986) *The Hollywood Studio System*, Basingstoke: Macmillan/BFI.

Gomery, Douglas (1992) *Shared Pleasures: A History of Movie Presentation in the United States*, London: BFI.

Gottlieb, Henrik (2002) 'Titles on Subtitling 1929–1999', in Annamaria Caimi (ed.) *Cinema: Paradiso delle lingue. I sottotitoli nell'apprendimento linguistico* (Rassegna Italiana di Linguistica Applicata, Anno XXXIV, 1/2-2002), Rome: Bulzoni Editore.

Ivarsson, Jan (2004) 'A Short Technical History of Subtitling in Europe'. Available at http://www.transedit.se/history.htm.

Kramer, Peter (2011) 'Hollywood and its Global Audiences: A Comparative Study of the Biggest Box Office Hits in the United States and Outside the United States Since the 1970s', in Richard Maltby, Daniël Biltereyst and Philippe Meers (eds) *Explorations in New Cinema History: Approaches and Case Studies*, Chichester: Wiley-Blackwell.

Miller, Toby, Govil, Nitin, McMurria, John, Maxwell, Richard and Wang, Ting (2005) *Global Hollywood 2*, London: BFI/Palgrave Macmillan.

Nowell-Smith, Geoffrey and Ricci, Steven (1998) *Hollywood and Europe: Economics, Culture, National Identity 1945–95*, London: BFI.

O'Brien, Charles (2005) 'Multiple Language Versions and National Films,

1930–1933; Statistical Analysis, Part I', in *Cinema & Cie: International Film Studies Journal*, no. 6 (winter). Available at http://www.cinemetrics.lv/obrien.php.

Roberts, Graham (2003) 'Subtitling, Dubbing and the Future of the International Film'. Available at http://ics.leeds.ac.uk/papers/vp01.cfm?outfit=ifilm&folder=17&paper=23.

Thompson, Kristin (1985) *Exporting Entertainment: America in the World Film Market 1907–34*, London: British Film Institute.

UNESCO (2012) 'From International Blockbusters to National Hits 2010', UNESCO Institute for Statistics. Available at http://www.uis.unesco.org/culture/Documents/ib8-analysis-cinema-production-2012-en2.pdf.

The Hollywood studio model

Hollywood dominates global cinema in terms of box office revenues – that seems conclusive, as we discovered in Chapter 1 – but only around 200 out of a total of more than 5,000 films produced globally each year fit the description 'Global Hollywood'. Our aim is to present a perspective on global film that is not created solely from within Hollywood's conception of cinema – in which other film cultures are defined as simply 'other' or 'not Hollywood'. Even so, we cannot simply ignore Hollywood. We need instead to explore how Hollywood engages with the rest of the world's film industries and cultures, how it operates in a **hegemonic** way and how other industries respond – but also create their own perspectives, perhaps using Hollywood's ideas as appropriate for their purposes.

UNESCO figures suggest that more than 7,000 films were produced globally in 2009 (UNESCO 2012: 8).

Across the whole book we are investigating a dynamic set of relationships in which film industries learn from each other and change their practices over time. Later, in various chapters, we will look at what some theorists have called **contra-flows** (see Thussu 2007) or exchanges of films between countries that don't involve Hollywood at all, but in this chapter we look at the idea of Hollywood as the dominant **mode** of entertainment cinema and the different ways in which it has been influential.

The hegemony of Hollywood in global cinema manifests itself not just in the presence of films distributed by the major studios being on offer to audiences in most of the world's film markets, but also in the way that Hollywood seems to define what an entertainment film should be no matter where it is made. Various arguments are suggested as to why Hollywood films are so successful in the global marketplace:

- in a nation built on migration (especially during the early twentieth century when film industries were developing), American filmmakers have learned how to appeal to the universal aspirational values which drive economic migration;
- by attracting talent and acquiring original properties from other film cultures, Hollywood itself has become a form of supranational cinema;
- Hollywood has developed storytelling techniques that are highly efficient, perfected through commercially organised industrial processes;
- Hollywood popular genres tend towards action, and the ultra-high budgets promise spectacle and/or stars and celebrities;
- like Bollywood, Hollywood entertainment refers to an idealised world into which audiences can escape from everyday reality.

Many filmmakers around the world openly admire Hollywood and hope to emulate American films, and it's equally true that audiences respond to American stories, often preferring them to local films. But there is also resistance to the glamour and economic power of Hollywood, and with it attempts by filmmakers around the world to compete on a local, regional and global level.

Global Hollywood

The North American market is the world's biggest market by value for **filmed entertainment**. With over 300 million potential customers paying a relatively high price for a cinema ticket (or for a cable subscription, Pay Per View, download or DVD/Blu-ray), the size of this market has had two distinct effects:

The film territory that Hollywood terms **domestic** covers the US and Canada – with a population of 350 million. Unfortunately it isn't always clear whether statistics are for North America or just the US.

Box office totals for *Hero* are US$53.7 million in North America and US$123.7 million in the international market.

1 Historically it has been large enough to sustain domestic production based on the **studio model**. Since the mid-1990s revenue from the international box office has grown to become the major source of the studios' theatrical income, but strength at home remains important (see Chapter 1).

2 Because North America is the biggest market, any film title from another territory must seek an American release if it is to gain a global profile and the possibility of further sales around the world. In 2014 the blockbuster titles from India, China, South Korea, etc. don't yet have that global presence – their audience is limited to at best a regional level (e.g. within East and South East Asia) or, in the case of Indian exports, to a largely separate **diasporic** market. Because it was so successful at the North American box office, Zhang Yimou's film *Hero* (China, 2002) is arguably better known internationally than any of his other films.

The Hollywood studios themselves have had an impact on global film in several different ways:

Admiral is a biopic about Admiral Kolchak, one of the leaders of the White Russian forces who fought against the Red Army in the Russian Civil War of 1918 to 1920.

1 They are dominant because of their power as **distributors**. With offices in most major film territories, the Hollywood studios distribute not only their own films (or those of other **MPAA** members) but also some of the most important local films. This isn't so noticeable when they produce a film in the UK perhaps, but it may seem odd that a 'patriotic' Russian historical film such as *Admiral* (Russia, 2008) should be released in Russia by 20th Century Fox.

2   This distribution presence in other territories also extends into production deals
    so that the studios become players in other industries as well as in their own.
    This activity has been described as an aspect of 'Global Hollywood' but it is
    important to distinguish between films that are made by American producers
    using locations in, say, Slovakia or Morocco and productions by local companies
    such as *A Very Long Engagement* (France, 2003). This major production from
    Warner Bros. France and its co-producing partners Tapioca Films and TF1
    Productions caused problems in both the US and France in terms of its eligibility
    for awards and cultural subsidy because it was not clearly American *or* French.
    The activities of Hollywood studios in co-production deals in other major
    territories are always likely to create these kinds of problems because of national
    cultural policies on film – in China especially (see Chapter 4 on definitions of
    national cinema).

3   Hollywood's global outlook includes a desire to draw on talent and creative
    ideas from wherever these are spotted. It is relatively easy for Hollywood to
    attract directors and actors (or any other creative personnel) with the promise of
    higher remuneration, bigger budgets, more exposure, etc. Similarly, Hollywood
    money can be used to buy remake rights for local hit films. There are arguments
    for and against this seemingly one-way flow of talent and creative ideas, and
    the concept of remakes is explored below. What do you make of the box office
    returns for the Hollywood version of the Japanese film *Ringu/Ring* in Japan?
    Although the Japanese version was a hit at home in 1998, the Hollywood
    remake was a much bigger hit everywhere in the world, including in Japan in
    2002.

4   The US and Canada are often seen as attractive destinations for film students
    seeking training, or perhaps for dissident directors to find more amenable
    working conditions. A number of notable diaspora filmmakers now make films
    about their own cultures from a North American base. Although this does not
    necessarily involve a direct Hollywood connection, it does mean that the work
    of directors such as Mira Nair and Deepa Mehta from India or Shirin Neshat
    from Iran is more likely to achieve exposure via North American distribution.
    In turn, the experience of training in American film schools means that some of
    these directors take American approaches into other industries.

There have been periods
when the talent flow
has been reversed. In
the 1950s Hollywood
creative personnel fleeing
persecution during the
McCarthy hearings on
'Un-American Activities'
joined the British film
industry.

In 2012 Mira Nair
with *The Reluctant
Fundamentalist* and
Deepa Mehta with
Midnight's Children both
premiered major films
with South Asian content
at major international
festivals.

Mira Nair is now based
in New York but it is
noticeable that some
of her films set in
India have received
significant support from
the UK public service
broadcaster Channel 4.

It is worth noting that the overall impact of American involvement/influence on
filmmaking elsewhere is sometimes different to that involving European or East Asian
partners. In Europe and East Asia there are cultural agencies (including public service
broadcasters) and film festivals that will support exilic and diasporic filmmakers
working in Asia and Africa (see Chapters 4 and 7).

Genre production and the studio model

The academic film studies that is now recognised internationally first developed in
Europe and North America. It perhaps isn't surprising that when film academics
turned to the film *industry* as a study focus, they would use Hollywood as their
prime case study (but we should also note that scholars were studying aspects of
film industry and culture in many different countries by the 1920s and 1930s –
they just hadn't recognised that what they were doing was part of 'film studies').
The introduction of **genre** as a critical tool in scholarly work was seen as partly

concerned with legitimising the study of Hollywood's industrial output. Up until the 1960s, film studies had tended to deal mainly with prestige or 'quality' pictures – films with either a serious social theme or an origin in another art form. These might be studio pictures or they might be made by acknowledged film artists (who would later be labelled **auteurs** – see Chapter 7). Genre study was intended to open up for study the full range of films, not just the prestige films.

The pioneers of this approach in the 1940s and 1950s were Robert Warshow, Laurence Alloway and André Bazin among others. The first genres to be studied in detail included the western and the gangster picture. Besides their popularity (at that time) these two genres seemed to offer most in terms of the approaches adopted by the early scholars. The western dealt with the myths of the American frontier, and the **gangster film** to some extent offered a contrast by focusing on an industrialised urban America and the social issues that partly contributed to the rise of organised crime. Genre study was in some ways concerned with 'American' genres.

'Genre' is a concept understood by film producers and distributors/marketeers, used extensively by film reviewers and critics and also by audiences as one of the criteria for choosing a film to watch. This 'common-sense' understanding, based on everyday experience of the cinema, means that genre is an attractive 'way in' to studying films, but, as Tom Ryall points out, this 'ordinary usage carries with it the implication that the concept of genre is clear and well-defined, non-problematic' (Ryall 1975: 27). Ryall goes on to argue that there are several problems with the application of genre as a critical tool, including the differences between how the concept is viewed in film studies compared to its use in, for example, literary studies. Films are produced in a range of different industrial modes which themselves contribute to what constitutes a genre definition; therefore, in this book we distinguish between 'studio films' and forms of 'artisanal' filmmaking (see Chapter 7).

Ryall also refers to a crucial development in genre study when it became apparent that the interesting question is not necessarily what constitutes a 'western' (i.e. how to classify a film) but what constitutes a 'genre film'. The latter question implies that beyond the recognition of certain 'elements' (locations, characters, stylistic features, etc.) that signify a specific genre, industry professionals, critics and audiences bring other expectations into play in thinking about genre films more generally – and other conventions related to budget, stars, 'entertainment value', etc. become important. Work on genre began to be linked to work on other aspects of film study. In particular, studies of the actual working practices of Hollywood studios identified ways in which ideas about genre underpinned the organisation of the industrial process. Thus, for instance, the unit production system in some Hollywood studios was developed around specific genres. This enabled a specialised division of labour (actors and creative teams working mainly on the same types of films) and economies of scale (the reuse of studio sets, costumes and other props, etc.).

More recent genre study has suggested that in reality production decisions by Hollywood executives were and are based on much broader concepts of genre, and most films have always drawn on several genres, defined in different ways (including by budget, use of animation, documentary, different modes of realism, etc.). Genre is a fluid concept that may be applied in many different ways and it should be useful in studying film production in many different countries. But we would have to recognise that, for many international audiences, Hollywood genre films are the ones they are most likely to see and local genre films will be measured against them.

Genre in a global context

Genre in the study of film cultures outside Hollywood has been contentious, tied up as it has been with concepts of **national cinema** and **auteurism**. Genre films outside of Hollywood are by definition the kinds of popular film that are not usually traded internationally (with a few notable exceptions). This means that it has been quite difficult for scholars to look across the same genre in different film cultures – someone researching a national or regional cinema in an 'area studies' department of a university may have access to a wide range of films from that region, but not necessarily the same depth of knowledge about other regions. Even so there are some possibilities for genre study on a global scale.

If we look at the popular cinema of all the major film-producing countries (i.e. where a regular output of films has been watched by a mass local audience) we find that there is a limited range of what might be termed **universal genres**. It is these universal genres that prompt the unequal comparison with the 'Hollywood model'. It is possible to see the concept of the 'universal' as a trap in which a distinctive group of films from one culture are studied from a Hollywood perspective simply because that is how Anglo-American scholarship has defined a specific genre. Thus, for instance, the study of horror as a genre makes extensive use of the concept of the Gothic, a term first used to describe a Scandinavian tribe who appeared in the Roman world in the third century AD. In the eighteenth century it was applied to the dark romantic fiction that would in time produce novels such as *Frankenstein* (1818) and *The Vampyre* (1819), and in the 'Gothic revival' at the end of the nineteenth century during which *Dracula* (1897) appeared. This literary Gothic has become the source of one of the definitions of the term – as pertaining to 'gloomy and sinister environments'. It developed a related but slightly different tone in the work of different writers in Germany, France and the UK – and it also included the work of the American writer Edgar Allan Poe whose stories, written in the 1840s, were often set in a recognisably European Gothic milieu.

In the twentieth century this Northern European sense of the Gothic infiltrated Hollywood in the form of adaptations of well-known Gothic novels. The films made at Universal in Hollywood in the 1930s were by British, German and other European directors and actors, and were influenced by the German expressionist films of the 1920s. Gradually the style and tone of these films seeped into other Hollywood genres. In the 1960s a distinctive American Gothic began to emerge in Hollywood horror films. Ironically, just as films like *Psycho* (US, 1960) began to develop American Gothic, Victorian Gothic was revived in the UK by Hammer Studios with films that became popular in the US, and by the American director Roger Corman who adapted Edgar Allan Poe's stories, including *The Tomb of Ligeia* (UK-US, 1964) shot in the UK.

Outside the major producing countries genre production of any kind is not really an option, since there will not be enough films produced to enable generic conventions to develop – although filmmakers can still refer to conventions from more universal genres.

'Southern Gothic' is a distinctive genre repertoire in American literature referring to stories set in the Southern states by writers such as William Faulkner or Tennessee Williams.

Genre in film studies

Most recent work on genre assumes the fluidity of genre as a concept related to classification or categorisation. The methodology used in this book will refer to **genre repertoires** – loose collections of genre elements which overlap and which absorb other elements over time (see Branston with Stafford 2010: 83–86)

All this seemed straightforward until scholars began to consider how they might approach similar horror films that came from different cultural traditions. Horror films from Mexico and Spain certainly shared something of the Gothic sensibility of their North European counterparts – but they also carried the influence of a peculiarly Spanish Catholicism. Japan too had its own strong horror traditions developed through the centuries in *noh* and *kabuki* theatre traditions. Philip Brophy suggests that in Japan the Northern European Gothic was not absorbed as it was in the US. Instead it was 'injected' into Japanese traditions producing 'micro-terrains of cultural mutation' (Brophy 2005: 150). Brophy's comments are in a paper discussing the music score in a Japanese film declaring itself to be based on Emily Brontë's *Wuthering Heights*, a 'romantic-Gothic' novel.

It may be argued that audiences themselves make genre connections when they watch films, based on what they know rather than what might be intentionally constructed by filmmakers. For instance, the worldwide success of *Ringu/The Ring* and other J-horror films may have influenced audience readings of *KM 31* (*Kilómetro 31*, Mexico, 2007). This Mexican film is based on local stories about a roadside ghost and involves flashbacks to the Spanish conquest of Amerindian peoples in Central America. We would expect elements of Spanish horror to appear in a Mexican film but here we may also be seeing something that draws on Japanese horror filtered through Hollywood. Mexican audiences wouldn't necessarily have seen any J-horror, but they are likely to have seen an American remake or a Hollywood film influenced by J-horror (the writer-director Rigoberto Castañeda claims he wrote the script before he saw the Japanese film – see Wilkinson 2007).

Although we need to be wary about how we approach similar stories and modes of storytelling in different film cultures, it would be strange if, at the simplest emotional level, audiences in any part of the world did not respond to similar genre elements in much the same way. The following is a list of genre categories we might find being referenced in most major film industries.

Fig 2.1
Nuño (Adrià Collado) and Catalina (Iliana Fox) approach the 'house in the woods' not far from the site of her twin sister Agata's car accident in *KM 31*.

'Universal' genres

- comedy
- horror
- crime

- romance
- action adventure
- war
- historical drama
- social drama

These genres are all on one level universal but they also refer to local history and cultural norms. This means that although many titles will get some form of international distribution, it will often be restricted owing to the assumptions held by sales agents and distributors. Certain kinds of comedy are deemed 'not likely to travel' because their appeal relies on dialogue and specific cultural references. The top films at the box office in Italy, Spain or Germany will often be local comedies and none of them will travel far outside their domestic territory. Even Hollywood comedies that rely on verbal gags will struggle in international distribution. The winners are comedies with a high proportion of physical comedy such as the *Mr Bean* films with relatively few dialogue scenes. One of the cultural differences that makes comedy films difficult to sell is the broad nature of much slapstick comedy in, for example, Chinese New Year films such as the *All's Well, Ends Well* films from Hong Kong that have seen several outings since 1992, each featuring the comic adventures of an array of different characters. Indian popular films also feature traditional comic characters. Although the visual slapstick in these films appeals universally, the underlying cultural mores are unfamiliar and the overall effect is unpredictable for a global audience.

Comedy has been seen as an acceptable element in Hong Kong action films such as those featuring Jackie Chan or Stephen Chow (e.g. *Shaolin Soccer*, *Kung Fu Hustle*) in which the familiarity of the action sequences hooks audiences for whom the comedy is not necessarily the main attraction. Action is perhaps the most exportable genre. Plots are not necessarily driven by complex dialogue, and **dubbing** has always seemed more acceptable in this particular genre. Cultural difference may also be a positive if it offers attitudes towards violence that go 'outside' the norms of Hollywood. However, this can also lead into the ghetto of the **extreme film** – something that plagued Italian westerns in the 1970s and more recently Japanese and Korean horror/martial arts films marketed as 'Asia Extreme' (see Chapter 5).

By 2012 there were six sequels to the first *All's Well, Ends Well* which starred Stephen Chow, Leslie Cheung and Maggie Cheung in 1992.

Fig 2.2
From the trailer for *All's Well, Ends Well* (Hong Kong, 2012) released in two UK cinemas in Manchester and London during Chinese New Year.

When one popular genre proves exportable there is a danger that the whole range of cinema from that film culture is 'reduced' in the eyes of overseas audiences to that single genre identity.

The relationship between **national cinemas** and specific genres is quite complex. In Chapter 4 we look at some specific examples of national cinemas and discuss genres that are closely associated with particular film cultures (i.e. genres that don't occur anywhere else in the same way). We will just note here that some genres such as the biopic or the historical/war drama have been used in several different countries to create popular films that work to celebrate or revise aspects of national history. In the early twenty-first century there have been a number of 'new histories' of aspects of the Second World War, especially from smaller film industries telling unique stories that have not previously been told within Anglo-American film culture. Examples include *Max Manus* (Norway, 2008), *Flame & Citron* (*Flammen & Citronen*, Denmark, 2008) and *Katyn* (Poland, 2007). *Indigènes* and similar Maghrebi-French films are discussed in Chapter 4. China and Russia have produced similar films about periods of their national history – both under communism and in the post-communist (Russia) and 'market-orientated' (China) systems of the past few years. Sometimes these are films that transcend genre as such and become prestige films associated with the idea of the **national-popular** or films that represent national myths through forms of popular entertainment.

The **national-popular** is a concept derived from the work of Antonio Gramsci and used by scholars writing about concepts of national cinema (see Chapter 4).

Research and Explore 2.1: *Crime films*

Crime films have always been popular across the world and there are many examples of successful crime films that have influenced filmmakers in other countries.

- *The Godfather* and *The Godfather 2* (US, 1971/1972) have formed the basis for many successful Indian films (e.g. *Sarkar*, 2005, *Gangs of Wasseypur I* and *II*, 2012). Why does the original Italian-American story work in a country like India?
- John Woo is an acknowledged fan of Jean-Pierre Melville. What is the connection between the films of the two directors, and between Hong Kong and French crime films?

The western was based on mythology rather than historical events. How much global audiences understood this is open to question. The 'admittance' of African-Americans and Chinese migrant workers into western narratives from the 1970s onwards challenged the Hollywood myth.

We don't have space here to explore all the universal genres or to argue in detail why others aren't included in the list. Instead we will focus on two contrasting (but actually related) genres: **the western** and **melodrama**. We will find examples of both in a range of different film cultures. The western may be seen as transnational in its appeal but with melodramas, though we find the genre everywhere, individual titles are not so easily exported/remade (except in the form of television serials – see Chapter 9).

The western

Westerns are inextricably linked to Hollywood. *The Great Train Robbery* (US, 1903) is often quoted as the first western (but Rick Altman has questioned that assumption and others, suggesting instead that it was a film combining the successful 'railroad story' and the violent crime film). Later, some similar films were described as 'cowboy pictures' and sometimes as 'historical dramas' (see Altman 1999: 34–38). The western as we know it now has been retrospectively constructed as a genre so that we see it as being developed from novels and newspaper reports, from paintings of frontier life and from live events such as Buffalo Bill's travelling show. When Hollywood began to produce western films in great numbers in the 1920s, some of the historical characters of the 1880s and 1890s were able to act as advisers. For the early critics and theorists the western was a genre about American history. It was defined by geography and history – the 'frontier' of American society in the West and Southwest mainly between the end of the Civil War in the late 1860s and the closing of the frontier at the end of the nineteenth century. This was the 'American genre'. But it was popular across Europe and it had an impact and an influence on filmmakers across Asia, Africa and Latin America. How do we explain this – and how did the western become transnational?

The European interest in westerns is partly explained by elements of a shared history. The West was partly settled by first- or second-generation migrants from Northern Europe. The history of the American West is coterminous with the European scramble for Africa and the final establishment of European empires. If this is the historical context, the similar geography of plains, deserts and mountains may be found in parts of Africa, Australia, Canada, Central and South America and Central Asia where settlers on horseback encounter indigenous people and establish new communities and forms of 'frontier justice'.

The appeal of the western is based on fundamental emotional responses. Visual beauty – horse and rider in photogenic landscapes – is matched by dramatic action. The violent action of western narratives can be reduced to seemingly simple confrontations between 'good' and 'bad' characters, and audiences are able to identify with characters facing stark choices about survival. All of these attractions suggest a universal genre. But the relationship of the western to American history, both in representing the past and struggling over meanings in the present, makes it a very interesting case study. The western mythologised American history in the nineteenth century, reaffirming an identity imbued with the 'frontier spirit' that gave the country a sense of vitality and 'progress'. In the 1960s and 1970s, perhaps the last years of producing westerns on a large scale in Hollywood, scholars began to refer to the 'revisionist western'. This was the period when significant directors such as Sam Peckinpah (*The Wild Bunch*, 1969), Arthur Penn (*Little Big Man*, 1970), Robert Aldrich (*Ulzana's Raid*, 1972) and Robert Altman (*McCabe & Mrs Miller*, 1971, *Buffalo Bill and the Indians*, 1976) were making films that questioned the values inherent in the traditions of the genre. They also appeared to engage with the counter-culture of resistance to the war in Vietnam and support for the Civil Rights struggle in the US through the use of allegory. The most striking example perhaps was Ralph Nelson's *Soldier Blue* (US, 1970) which showed, in graphic detail, the slaughter of Cheyenne women and children by the US Cavalry. The film was released soon after the 'exposure' of the My Lai massacre in Vietnam by US troops. Like the film itself, the title song by Buffy Sainte-Marie was a hit in Europe and Japan but neither film nor song was successful in America.

The dissident Hollywood directors of westerns also found themselves working in a genre that was being changed by the success of European directors making westerns in Spain and then in the US itself (e.g. Sergio Leone's *Once Upon a Time in the West*, Italy/US, 1968).

The Hollywood directors who 'revised' the western were themselves influenced by directors from other cultures – Sam Peckinpah by Kurosawa Akira (see Chapter 5), Robert Altman by Federico Fellini, Arthur Penn by the French New Wave, etc. By the early 1970s it was evident that the western had become completely global as a genre

'The Western is a universal frame within which it is possible to comment on today. [...] There are a great many people who are disturbed because they feel something is going wrong. I am one of them' (Sam Peckinpah quoted in Weddle 1996: 317).

Fig 2.3
The killers in their long
'duster coats' in *Once
Upon a Time in the West*
are led by Henry Fonda
playing against his star
image as a 'liberal'
heroic figure. Here he
is about to kill the
boy – wiping out the
entire family in Leone's
'revisionist western'.

Fig 2.4
A promo image from
Sholay suggests the
possible influence of
Sergio Leone's Italian
westerns and their stories
of cruelty and revenge.
Source: British Film
Institute Stills Collection.

repertoire to be plundered by any filmmaker. *Sholay* (India, 1975), the film that in many ways revived the Hindi film industry and helped to usher in 'Bollywood', is an action adventure film that uses western conventions in its narrative involving bandits, mercenaries and personal feuds in the hills of South Central India. These conventions had by then been developed through films such as Leone's *A Fistful of Dollars* (Italy, 1964), itself a version of Kurosawa's *Yojimbo* (Japan, 1961).

See Figs 2.3 and 2.4 opposite.

Westerns in East Germany

During the Cold War, film industries in Eastern Europe and the Soviet Union produced a range of popular films, some remarkably similar in generic form to Hollywood genres. Because of the long German interest in the popular western stories by German writer Karl May (1842–1912), western films became an important part of the production schedule of DEFA, the nationalised film studio in East Germany. Rarely seen in Western Europe or North America at the time, these westerns now startle viewers with their reversal of Hollywood norms. In narratives dealing with confrontations between 'cowboys' and 'Indians' it is the cowboys who are the bad guys (embodying American values) and the Indians who are the heroes.

The phenomenon of the East German western is explored on the following web pages:

http://www.nysun.com/arts/when-westerns-made-their-way-east/42479/
http://www.progress-film.de/en/filme/feature.php#western
http://indianerfilm.narod.ru/english/index.html

You don't have to look too far to find examples of films made outside the US that appear to be in some form of 'dialogue' with the Hollywood western. In Chapter 5 there is a brief discussion of the relationship between the western and the *chanbara* or East Asian swordfight film. In Chapter 8 the ideological status of the western in somehow representing American military/political power is explored in oppositional

The Good the Bad and the Weird (South Korea, 2008) is a comedy action film with an English-language title directly referencing Sergio Leone.

Fig 2.5
Tears of the Black Tiger.

films from Latin America and Africa. The Argentinian nomination for Best Foreign Language Film at the 2012 Oscars was *Aballay*, a *gaucho* western that resembles Peckinpah and Leone on one level, but also uses a folkloric/mythological theme and a metaphor for Argentinian political history. The western is a very adaptable form.

Research and Explore 2.2: *Tears of the Black Tiger (Fai Thalai Chon, Thailand, 2000)*

Find out what you can about this Thai film which featured at Cannes in 2001 and was subsequently released in Europe and (eventually) North America. The US distributors Magnolia Pictures have posted detailed production notes on http://www.magpictures.com.

The director, Wisit Sasanatieng, says that the film's unique approach is rooted in Thai film history. Reviews and comments on IMDB, etc. discuss the film as a western. How would you explain the relationship between Thai culture and the western genre?

Melodramas

The term **melodrama** is used quite differently in contemporary public discourse and contemporary forms of academic writing. This confusion can get in the way of useful studies of the genre across national categorisations. If you wish to study popular cinema traditions in Europe, Latin America and Asia, an understanding of what melodrama might mean in different circumstances is essential.

In common usage (i.e. in general film reviews and media commentaries) in the US and UK 'melodrama/melodramatic' tends to be used pejoratively to describe performances and dramatic scenes that are 'over the top' with a sense of filmmakers having 'lost control' of the subject matter. It may also mean something old-fashioned or highly formulaic – either way it is definitely seen as a 'bad thing'. However, the term is used by film scholars in much more defined ways and it is this usage that is important in considering popular films in several major territories.

Melodrama (*melos* – music) was originally used to describe forms of popular theatre in eighteenth-century Europe, especially in France and England. The 'official theatre' of the period, confined to a few theatres awarded royal patents in the capital city, performed classical dramas that were mainly dialogue-based. Theatrical entertainment for the broader audience in the 'illegitimate theatre' drew instead upon traditional forms that used music, gesture and mime, since the performance of plays was not allowed without a patent.

Les enfants du paradis (France, 1945) is a much-loved film that uses as its setting the Paris theatre district in the 1820s with its two kinds of theatres. The history of melodrama is woven into the plot of the film.

Melodrama became the mainstay of popular theatre in the nineteenth century and European melodrama easily made the crossing to North America. By the end of the century melodrama had become both spectacular and sensational, with some shows featuring live animals and even steam engines on stage. Such spectacular theatre coincided with the early days of cinema, so it is not surprising that in Hollywood from the 1910s until the 1960s the term 'melodrama' was often applied to films that provided fast and violent action, horror or suspense. The slang term 'meller' was added to other genre descriptors to produce 'gangster meller', 'action meller', etc. (Neale 2000: 180–181). Early western films were sometimes referred to as melodramas.

While this use of 'meller' has now almost disappeared, a second, equally long-established but seemingly contradictory usage was revived and legitimated in the 1970s, especially by feminist scholars. In the collection of essays *Where the*

Heart Is (1987) edited by Christine Gledhill, a seminal work in placing melodrama back on the film studies agenda, Gledhill herself offers an introduction in which she explains that the collection is concerned primarily with Hollywood as the place where 'European melodramatic traditions were re-moulded in such a way that they could return in the twentieth century – their Victorian, national and class specificities transformed – to found both international and local popular film and televisual cultures' (Gledhill 1987: 1–2). She recognises that work had already started on the analysis of Brazilian *telenovelas* (see Chapter 9) but argues that it is too early even to be certain that melodrama is a legitimate categorisation that may be discussed as having a parallel development in, for example, South Asian or East Asian forms.

Much more scholarship has emerged since the early 1990s that has investigated melodrama as a useful concept in relation to Indian, Chinese and Japanese film cultures. Some of that work will be alluded to in this book, but at this point we need to clarify a number of issues about melodrama as a **mode** rather than as a genre as such. It is possible to define certain specific film genres related to Hollywood melodrama such as the 1930s/1940s 'woman's film', and the 1950s family melodrama and feminist scholarship was moved to investigate these genres owing to their low status in film criticism as formulaic and addressed to primarily female audiences. However, one way to validate these studies was to conceptualise melodrama as something more extensive than a set of specific subgenres but instead a pervasive aesthetic mode that could be applied to a range of very different genres. While 'crime melodrama' became an alternative term for many *films noirs*, westerns and combat pictures could be addressed as male action melodramas. What the melodrama mode brought was attention to style – to camerawork, *mise en scène*, performance, use of music – to the expressionist aesthetic in which emotions are expressed through the excessive expression of the elements of style. Famously in the 1970s it was this kind of approach to the family melodramas of 1950s Hollywood, directed by Douglas Sirk in particular, which introduced a new way of thinking about genre.

The argument around Sirk was that he was a highly cultured director who had first worked on European melodramas in Germany in the 1930s, developing formal strategies to code the meanings of his films in a period when the Nazis took over the German film industry. Faced with the melodramas of domestic affluence in Eisenhower's complacent America of the 1950s, he similarly critiqued American society through his displays of visual excess. Later this approach too would be re-evaluated but the interest in excessive style remained and came to encompass genres rather than just one auteur. As Gledhill points out, it also turned attention towards the real pleasures audiences derived from engaging with these excessive forms.

Let us summarise some of the findings of melodrama scholarship:

- Narratives focusing on family and community relationships allow for the exploration of changing social mores and the problems of a modernising society. We can see this in the family melodrama when economic and social changes have an impact on how children are brought up, who sons and daughters should marry, what kind of work/play is suitable for men or women.
- Focus on visual display and use of music.
- Narratives are gendered in some way – they may deal with the social roles of women and men.

Excessive symbolism in *mise en scène*

Fig 2.6 a, b and c
All That Heaven Allows.

Fig 2.7 a, b and c
Fear Eats the Soul.

A striking example of Sirk's critique comes in *All That Heaven Allows* (US, 1955). The narrative focuses on a widowed middle-class woman played by Jane Wyman. Her two children are now grown-up and they apparently have no understanding of how a woman in her forties might feel. They buy her a TV set for Christmas, imagining that she will spend her days in domestic isolation (Fig 2.6a). Sirk shows her staring at the blank screen which reflects her unhappy face back at her (Fig 2.6b). She is sitting alongside her daughter. Mother is dressed in black. Daughter wears scarlet, complete with a hat featuring an erect little 'nipple' – the inference is clear: the daughter is announcing her sexual activity (she is getting married) and the mother is signified as if still in mourning (Fig 2.6c). The mother had wanted to marry again but the children thought that the younger man she chose was unsuitable.

The German director Rainer Werner Fassbinder developed ideas from *All That Heaven Allows* in *Fear Eats the Soul* (*Angst essen Seele auf*, West Germany, 1974). This dealt with Emmi, a widow in her sixties who marries Ali, a much younger *gastarbeiter* (migrant worker) from North Africa. When she announces the marriage to her grown-up children (Fig 2.7a), one of her sons expresses his anger by kicking in the TV screen in her flat (Fig 2.7b). Fig 2.7c shows the aftermath of this family row in a careful composition that emphasises the open door through which the widow's children have left. The wrecked TV set and the empty chair represent the 'broken' family. Behind Ali and Emmi, on the wall, are medals for wartime service and some African *objets d'art* – (over-)representing her two husbands.

- Gendering may also affect the audience composition with women sometimes seen as the main audience.

Associated with melodrama's role in 'changing societies' are assumptions about realism. Melodramas in the nineteenth century were often criticised because they were not like the realist novels that were validated in literary culture. They simplified stories and encouraged stock characters, easily recognised as 'good' or 'evil', and they relied on contrivance and coincidence in narratives. When it seemed that realism in cinema was again being validated at the expense of melodrama, it was sometimes assumed that the two were opposites. However, we will see in various examples across global cinema that 'realist melodramas' are distinctly possible whether it is a realist narrative that sometimes uses melodrama elements to heighten its emotional appeal or a melodrama that uses realism as part of its aesthetic approach – the absence of obvious excess perhaps.

Cinematic forms that resemble European melodrama also developed in the major Asian film cultures of India, China and Japan – and the European mode of melodrama not only developed in North America but also in Latin America. In Asian cultures, what some film scholars have described as melodramas have their roots in indigenous forms of theatre and music performance, but they have also been influenced by European and American imports at different times, for example, the *shinpa* and later *shingeki* theatrical forms in Japan (see Chapter 5).

Melodramas are central to popular cinema and this may be partly because the excessive use of colour and music combined with familiar social types and exaggerated narrative devices makes stories easy to follow. However, just as some melodramas are populist in their appeal, many others target educated middle-class audiences with nuanced characters, meticulous performances, very precise *mise en scène* and highly sophisticated narrative development. Melodrama is the main cinematic form adopted by celebrated filmmakers such as Ozu, Mizoguchi and Naruse in Japan, Guru Dutt and Raj Kapoor in India, Zhang Yimou and Stanley Kwan in China/Hong Kong, Fassbinder in Germany, Luchino Visconti in Italy, Pedro Almodóvar in Spain, etc. Only Almodóvar and Zhang are still making films but the legacy of the others is still influencing contemporary filmmakers in different ways.

Star systems

Film stars emerged in the 1910s in the US and in Europe. The earliest included Asta Nielsen from Denmark who became famous in Germany and the Canadian-born Mary Pickford in the US (see also Chapter 1). There had been stars before in both legitimate theatre/opera and popular theatre/music hall in the nineteenth century, but those stars had depended on personal appearances and the circulation of images, drawn or photographic (sometimes on postcards). They would be celebrated locally and their fame would spread but new audiences had to wait to see them 'in the flesh'. The new stars of cinema could be seen by audiences of millions at roughly the same time, and their live appearances and newspaper coverage extended and consolidated their fame. One of the earliest indications of the power of the star image came with the visits to Europe by Mary Pickford and Douglas Fairbanks in the 1920s. Enormous crowds turned out for these trips and for the funeral of the Italian actor Rudolph Valentino who died in 1926 aged 31 at the peak of his film career in Hollywood. Nielsen, Pickford and Valentino became stars outside their

Todd Haynes made a third version of *All That Heaven Allows* as *Far From Heaven* (US, 2002) in which the 'taboo' relationship is doubled in 1950s America. A married man has a homosexual affair and his wife then turns towards their African-American gardener. Haynes consciously referenced Sirk and Fassbinder.

Fig 2.8
Asta Nielsen as *Hamlet*
(Germany, 1920
– produced by the
star's own company).
Source: The Kobal
Collection/www.
picture-desk.com.

native countries, something easily possible before the arrival of 'talking pictures'. The
stars who emerged from the 1930s depended on their speaking voice and language
skills as well as their appearance.

The Hollywood studio system from the 1930s onwards treated actors with
specific skills and physical characteristics as commodities that could be constructed,
moulded and shaped into stars to be used by particular production units. Some
were associated with specific genres or social types. Others represented glamour. All
were restricted in what they could do by means of tight contracts and the practices
of the studio publicity machine. When the studio contract system ended the stars
became free agents – or rather their agents became free agents. Some of them became
independent producers and all of them tried to maintain their status. The business
practices of Hollywood meant that stars remained as important elements in the
'production packages' offered to the studio distributors. In many ways, Hollywood
A List stars (the top stars, able to attract audiences – to 'open' a new film and
drive box office to US$100 million and more) are, alongside the studio logos, a
prominently visible sign of Hollywood glamour and quality. The recent emphasis
on 3D and CGI spectaculars has been argued as a sign of the diminishing role
of stars. However, Hollywood films still routinely use stars and the industry as a
whole looks for new stars. The high salaries paid to stars have long been a means of
keeping Hollywood budgets higher than they need to be and thus deterring potential
competitors.

Because stars are 'constructed', they do not have to be 'authentic' – they only
have to appear authentic. In 2012 the three American comic-book heroes Batman,
Superman and Spider-Man were all being portrayed by 'British' actors. Since the
1930s, Hollywood has accepted recent immigrants to America or young actors from

overseas as potential stars and helped them to develop a star image. The glamour of stardom has come from Hollywood and, in many film territories where local stars have had space to build careers, the work practices and techniques of star construction and promotion have been copied from Hollywood. But this doesn't mean that all star systems are the same. Those of India and China/Hong Kong/ Taiwan are different in ways that we explore later in the book.

Modern, modernity and modernism

These terms litter much of the theoretical work concerned with global film. What do they mean and why do we use them? **Modern** is an adjective that is applied to the environment with which we surround ourselves. We live in the 'modern' world, characterised by material goods, our built environment, the provision of certain services and the prevalence of certain ideas about social behaviour. We experience the social condition of **modernity**. By contrast, **modernism** is a philosophical position or a movement in art and culture that aims to refute the traditional or **classical**. The modernist movement has also been defined historically, being seen to run from about the end of the nineteenth century up to the 1960s or 1970s. After modernism comes **postmodernism** – though most theorists see quite a large overlap so that much of the artistic output of the 1960s is claimed as both modernist and postmodernist.

Modernism has been associated with literature, art, architecture, music and other forms. It should therefore be possible to designate a **modernist** period of cinema. But this is difficult for several reasons. Cinema was born as modernism was being recognised. Although it draws upon traditional modes of literature and theatre, cinema itself is inherently modern. As it develops as an entertainment form, it strives to remain modern through the application of new technologies and new modes of spectatorship as well as the creation of new types of stories. Yet theorists have argued for a designation of certain types of cinema as classical – as if they have reached a standard of perfection and cannot be improved. **Modernist cinema** then becomes a reaction against classical cinema.

A second problem is that modernist cinema is by definition a minority cinema – one which challenges audiences and asks difficult questions about the world. This is part of its reaction against classical forms: it refuses to tell a simple story with conventional characters. Such a cinema cannot replace classical cinema, so modernist cinema instead runs in parallel with the mainstream. But this assumes that classical cinema cannot be modern – and we have already argued that it is almost modern by definition. These knotty problems are part of the fascination with the New Wave movements of the late 1950s/early 1960s. A film like *A bout de souffle* (France, 1960) by the 'critic-turned-director' Jean-Luc Godard is both consciously 'modern' in its focus on young Parisians as well as 'modernist' in its play with familiar story conventions and its commentary on Hollywood (and French) crime films.

Hollywood is then the conflicted art form that is presented as modern but not modernist – although during the 1970s some Hollywood directors were seen to be influenced by European modernist cinema. In its global reach, Hollywood is potentially progressive because it introduces audiences to modernity and the benefits of changes in social behaviour, new business practices, new technologies, etc. But it achieves this by using a **transparent** approach that doesn't encourage those audiences to question what they are watching. In this sense it is conservative. In addition, it doesn't necessarily engage with or negotiate the traditional cultures to which

'Parallel cinema' is also the name given to a certain kind of cinema in India, mainly in the 1970s and 1980s (see Chapter 10).

French films since 1960 have often approached 'modernity' through an interrogation of the impact of American popular culture in France.

some audiences outside North America adhere. This 'promise' of modernity that Hollywood brings is therefore questionable and perhaps contributes to the charge of 'cultural imperialism' so often made against American popular culture.

The transparency of Hollywood cinema is sometimes referred to as **Hollywood realism**. Mainstream Hollywood employs various techniques to disguise its ideological intentions and present its narratives in such a way that the audience suspends disbelief. 'Invisible editing' (another way of describing continuity editing) is designed to drive the narrative forward without drawing attention to its construction. Stars have become an integral part of the experience of watching films so that we accept that leading men are usually handsome and women are beautiful – but both are 'special' in some way. Narratives are usually set not in 'real locations' but in a world only recognisable from other Hollywood films. This becomes more noticeable when a Hollywood film adopts some of the elements of a **neo-realist** or **social realist** film. *Erin Brockovich* (US, 2000) was in some ways a surprise hit film. Director Steven Soderbergh, a fan of aspects of British 1960s/1970s cinema, presented a 'based on real events' story with locations and casting decisions that suggested social realism – against which Julia Roberts 'negotiated' her star image in order to play the titular heroine (who mounts a legal campaign against a polluting gas company). Roberts at the time was the biggest female star in Hollywood but somehow audiences accepted her performance, even though it could be seen as working against the other 'social realist' elements.

Part of the 'realism' in *Erin Brockovich* derives from the 'ordinary-looking' people who work alongside Erin in the legal office.

Social realism is a very broad term that has come to be associated with certain directors, especially in Europe, in order to distinguish their work from entertainment films that follow the Hollywood model. **Neo-realism** (discussed in detail in Chapter 3) may be seen as the basis for most social realist approaches but attempts to represent the 'real world' on screen are evident in the 1930s and earlier. The crucial aims are to represent the social lives of 'ordinary people' in specific communities and to explore social problems. This will involve representing the social environment in terms of 'authentic detail' and considering the relationship between the characters and the conditions under which they live. Many of the filmmakers who attempt this have some kind of political or 'progressive' project in mind. We should note also that social realism may be used in conjunction with various genre repertoires (social comedies, realist melodramas, crime stories, etc.). 'Social documentary' is a term used in some European film cultures as well as a tradition within photography. (See Lay (2002) for an account of social realism in a British context.)

What then of the **postmodern**? The 'p' word was very much at the centre of debates in film studies from the mid-1980s through to relatively recently. Partly that was because the theoretical project of film studies was being reassessed and postmodernism seemed to offer a way of approaching change. One of the difficulties of dealing with postmodernism is that it is understood to mean at least three different things. First, it signals a change in culture generally. The world we live in, at least in the West, is 'post-industrial', it's post the Cold War, it's a world of 'portfolio employment' rather than a 'job for life', etc. Second, there has been a change in art forms themselves so that architecture, art, music, literature, film, etc. all now exhibit signs of 'post-modernity'. Third, we can describe the new aesthetics by means of its key features – the mixing of styles from different periods or cultures (*bricolage*, hybridity), the lack of any direct connection to concepts of the 'real world' and the increasing intertextuality between art objects, the 'playfulness' of new forms and the use of parody. Underpinning this is the sense that we have moved into a period of uncertainty in which there are no 'grand narratives' such as Marxism that can explain how and why the world is changing. Transnational films sometimes pose questions for different audiences because what is understood as postmodernism in one culture may be read completely differently in another.

Hollywood strategies: adaptations, remakes, re-workings

One of Hollywood's strengths as an industrial producer is the set of strategies that have been devised in order to ensure a flow of profitable films for distribution. The same strategies may be found in other studio systems but the fact that the Hollywood majors have the resources to put several different strategies into operation at the same time and to pursue them with vigour has marked out the Hollywood way of doing things.

The basic premise is that Hollywood producers are in many ways risk-averse – they prefer to deal in films they understand and that they know have attracted audiences in the past. This does mean that they will actually risk a large budget on something similar but different – spending more to minimise risk. The key to Hollywood's hegemony is that there are enough hits (and enough revenues from '**back catalogue**') to cover the misses. The flow of mainstream Hollywood releases (the annual 'slate' of 20 to 30 titles available for release from each studio) ensures that the studios always have something out in front of audiences in both North America and the international market. That flow of product also blocks out any foreign competitors who will struggle to win a slot in the multiplex programme.

The establishment of this system means that the foreign buyers/distributors and exhibitors in the international market know what to expect and they ask for something similar from their own domestic producers. There is a pressure to make Hollywood-style films to fit the system. That's impossible of course on the scale on which Hollywood operates. How does Hollywood get so many new titles developed and produced?

The starting point for any film production is the 'property'. Often this will be a pre-existing idea, a story that has in some way already been written. It could be:

- a folk tale
- a ballad
- a play
- a novel

or

- a news report
- a historical 'document'
- a biography.

All of these sources of material offer an important advantage to filmmakers. They have already passed an audience test – someone, somewhere has thought the story worth recording/reproducing and in turn audiences have enabled it to continue in some form of circulation. It has become a *known* property. Re-presenting the story to an audience is likely to provoke signs of recognition. Films are expensive to make

Back catalogue has become increasingly important to both the film and music industries. As the number of media platforms expands, 'carriers' need more 'product' and the studios' libraries have increased in value.

Even if a multiplex has 14 screens, independent distributors will still struggle to find a slot, since each of the majors, as well as the large independents like Lionsgate, will have a film in its second or third week and one coming out this week or next.

and if some of the risk is removed by using a story that is known, raising finance may become easier.

Producers will have to decide whether known characters are in fact *too* well known or whether it is worth paying large sums to secure the production **rights** of best-selling novels, etc. Rights are crucial for the business practices of commercial cinema. Large-scale Hollywood production is dependent on the process of developing **franchises** – the creation of a film package of story, setting and characters that can be exploited over a series of big-budget pictures. As far as possible a franchise will have an international profile with changing settings and personnel (e.g. *Mission Impossible*, the *Bourne* films, *Pirates of the Caribbean*, etc.) or be based on a literary phenomenon with an international readership (*Harry Potter*, *Lord of the Rings/The Hobbit*, *Twilight*).

The simplest form of acquiring a known property is simply to buy the remake rights of a film that has already been successful. In film history up until the 1960s, with studio production in Hollywood and other major markets, it was commonplace for a studio to remake its own films every ten years or so for a new audience. Sometimes, to make sure that the new version had a clear run, the studio would destroy the prints of the older version. This has changed with recognition of the value of library titles and the possibilities of further revenues from DVD, cable/satellite TV reruns, etc.

In India, certain popular stories have seen many outings. *Devdas* by Sarat Chandra Chattopadhyay was published in Bengali in 1917 as a romance about a boy and girl growing up in the same village but with different caste and class backgrounds. The first film adaptation was released in 1927 and a further 13 versions in several different South Asian languages have been made since. Five versions have been released since 2002, including a **blockbuster** starring Shahrukh Khan and Aishwarya Rai, and a 'modern-day' version, *Dev.D* (2009) directed by Anurag Kashyap, one of the more experimental Bollywood directors (see Chapter 10).

The Hollywood practice of remaking foreign-language hits appears to be based on the assumption that because the vast majority of North American filmgoers don't want to watch subtitles (or dubbed films) the remake is effectively a 'new' film, even if the original was on a limited release only a year or so earlier. The producers are quite happy to dismiss the complaints of a small number of fans who insist that the American remake is inferior to the original (e.g. *The Girl With the Dragon Tattoo* (US, 2011) vs. *The Men Who Hate Women* (Sweden/Denmark/Germany/Norway, 2009), *Let Me In* (US, 2010) vs. *Let the Right One In* (Sweden, 2008) and *The Next Three Days* (US, 2010) vs. *Pour elle* (France, 2008)).

This current practice is only one of several different modes of re-working properties in a global context. We might describe this mode as an:

1   Official, licensed, **remake** of a specific film title in a different language/cultural setting. This implies that the original filmmakers have agreed to the remake and may even be involved in the production (as was the case with *The Girl With the Dragon Tattoo*).

Other modes are:

2   **Multiple versions** – the same script produced in more than one language version

simultaneously or close together (i.e. with different actors rather than simply dubbing a new soundtrack) (see Chapter 1).

3   Adaptations of the same novel/play in different language/cultural settings. This can create arguments about whether a film is a different version of the book as distinct from a remake of the first film. The Coen Brothers' version of *True Grit* in 2010 was promoted not as a remake of the 1969 film but as a new adaptation of the novel. The distinction was contestable. However, the two versions of Patricia Highsmith's novel *Ripley's Game* as *Der amerikanische Freund* (*The American Friend*, West Germany/France, 1977) and *Ripley's Game* (Italy/UK/US, 2002) are clearly different approaches.

4   Multiple uses of the same historical/mythical/fictional figure in different contexts – including 'borrowing' narrative elements for new characters.

5   Unofficial, copies or 'borrowings' of hit titles and characters. This is perhaps more common than audiences realise. A successful international Hollywood film, especially an action film, is always likely to provoke an imitator in Indian cinema and other commercially driven popular cinema film industries. How much of an idea needs to be borrowed before the film becomes a copy? The Hindi film *Tezz* (India, 2012) borrows a central plot point from *Speed* (US, 1994) but the bomb is aboard a train in the UK rather than a bus in Los Angeles.

Fig 2.9
The two lovers representing Heathcliff and Cathy in Luis Buñuel's version of *Wuthering Heights* (*Abismos de pasión*, Mexico, 1954).

Research and Explore 2.3: *Wuthering Heights*

One of the most adapted novels, Emily Brontë's story about Cathy and Heathcliff has been the basis of film and TV productions in at least eight different countries since the first British film in 1920.
Search for details of different versions and suggest some reasons why this might be seen as a 'universal story'. Which countries have produced versions of the story? Do you think all the elements of the story are likely to be of equal interest in each case?

Hollywood and transnational genre production

At the end of the 1990s Hollywood seemed to sense the need to re-invigorate itself by looking east (or rather west across the Pacific). In 1996 Disney signed an agreement to distribute the films of Studio Ghibli, the Japanese *anime* producer, in English-language versions. In 1997 *Princess Mononoke* became the most successful film of the year in Japan and in 2002 *Spirited Away* was a major success in the international market for Disney as well as at home in Japan. The strength of the deal was partly based on the mutual admiration of the animators themselves in the two companies.

Director Quentin Tarantino, a long-time admirer of East Asian action pictures, made his own homage in the form of the two-part *Kill Bill* (US-Japan, 2003/2004). But Hollywood has had a long history of drawing upon East Asian cinema for new stars and action genre ideas from *Godzilla* and Kurosawa Akira's *Seven Samurai* in the 1950s through Bruce Lee in the 1970s and Jackie Chan in the late 1980s. In 2002, *The Ring*, a remake of a low-budget (by US standards) Japanese horror film, made nearly US$250 million worldwide (Branston and Stafford 2006: 94–102). With a production budget of US$40–50 million, the remake was clearly profitable for Dreamworks, and Roy Lee, the Korean-American agent responsible for setting up the remake deal, became a 'player' in Hollywood with his company Vertigo Entertainment. Over the next few years Lee became involved in several other successful remakes, including *The Grudge* (2004) and *The Departed* (2006) (a version of *Infernal Affairs* from Hong Kong – see Chapter 11). Given Hollywood production and marketing costs, only a few of these remakes were as profitable as *The Ring* – but most of them provided the studios with properties at a low price that could be developed within the Hollywood system.

Box Office Mojo offers a Top 20 list of Asian remakes (http://www.boxofficemojo.com/genres/chart/?id=asianremake.htm).

The final chapter of Gary G. Xu's book on *Contemporary Chinese Cinema* (2007) (updated in 2008) offers an analysis of 'East Asian remakes' with some useful findings. He argues that what the remakes represent is a Hollywood process whereby the successful East Asian product is stripped of its ethnicity and its links to specific local cultures – and always made in English with English-language stars. As Xu points out, the most ironic example is *The Grudge* in which the Japanese director of the original film presented Sarah Michelle Gellar as an American in Tokyo in the remake. In conversation with Roy Lee, Xu discovers that production costs for genre films such as horror, crime and romance/romantic comedy are so low in East Asia that local filmmakers will accept a low Hollywood price for remake rights because it will still cover the production costs of the original. In fact, Lee maintains, East Asian filmmakers now regularly send him videos and even scripts before their films have been made.

Xu concludes that this process is analogous to 'outsourcing' by American corporations whereby Apple's computers are manufactured in China but the brand remains American. We can support this by noting that the films which prompted the successful remakes in the early 2000s were mostly made by East Asian filmmakers who themselves had absorbed or responded to Hollywood films of the 1970s. In turn this reminds us that in the 1950s certain Japanese manufacturing industries such as motor vehicles production would import vehicles from the West, 'backwards engineer' them and eventually produce their own superior models. Could this happen with film? Has the one-way flow of film exports from Hollywood to the East been turned into a two-way process? Xu suggests that since Hollywood remains in ownership of the final 'global film', the transnational development of these films has in fact strengthened Hollywood's hegemonic position. The economic basis of this is explained by the lengthy and expensive process of Hollywood script development, and later audience previews and re-edits. In this context, studios often prefer making sequels to producing from original scripts because, although they usually gross less, they are much easier to produce. Similarly, East Asian hit films are easier and less expensive to produce because they have already 'proved' the value of the script.

At the end of his argument Xu does recognise that it is also possible that cooperation and 'flows' of product between East Asian producers could interrupt this process; but what of his central argument? There is much more in Gary G. Xu's piece than we can cover here, though other aspects of it are addressed in Chapters 5 and 11. Let us just note that there have probably been as many failed or uncompleted remakes as successful ones. Some of those failures may be put down to the common attrition rate of Hollywood production failures, but others question the extent to which popular hits in East Asia are all equally available for remaking on the model outlined above. We will conclude this chapter with a case study of a film that prompted several remakes.

Case study 2.1: Remaking romantic comedy: *My Sassy Girl (That Bizarre Girl, South Korea, 2001)*

This romantic comedy was released in South Korea during the early period of the resurgence of the local film industry (see Chapter 5). At the time it was deemed the most successful local comedy release and it proved to be a valuable export, selling very well throughout East and Southeast Asia, and winning festival prizes for its writer-director Kwak Jae-yong and its female lead **Jun Ji-hyun**. It was subsequently remade in both India and the US. In Japan it became a TV series, and a 'sequel' (actually a similar story by the same Korean writers) was made in China, making it a good example of a regional and international property. The initial property was a novel by Kim Ho-sik based on a series of blog postings – widely seen as a form of 'internet novel' (see Kang 2008).

Jun Ji-hyun, a model with a high visibility through advertising contracts, became a celebrity figure throughout East Asia via *My Sassy Girl*. Her film career then declined but was revived by the blockbuster success of *The Thieves* (S. Korea, 2012)

Plot outline

The initial meeting of 'boy and girl' is on a commuter train platform. The girl is beautiful but clearly drunk. The boy, 25-year-old engineering student Gyeon-woo, attempts to help her as she stumbles, and when she vomits violently over another passenger he feels obliged to apologise and clean her up since the other passengers assume she is his girlfriend. From this point on she will abuse him – and he will accept the abuse. The 24-year-old girl (never named) is suffering from a trauma and behaving in a bizarre way. Gyeon-woo is mild-mannered, polite – and feminised to some extent by his mother's treatment of him as a young child. The romance that develops between him and the girl has mildly sadomasochistic edges: she hits him on occasions when he is not responding as she wants and she writes film scripts that are acted out – often in ways which humiliate Gyeon-woo.

The original film is in three parts – like a baseball game with 'Part 1', 'Part 2' and 'Overtime'. Part 1 is the longest, detailing the first meeting and the subsequent dates and adventures for the couple. Part 2 brings Gyeon-woo into contact with the girl's wealthy family and their attempts to find her a suitable young man, and ends with a parting scene in which the couple bury a time capsule containing a sealed letter to each other. They vow to return to the same spot two years later. 'Overtime' takes place when they finally meet again.

Fig 2.10a
My Sassy Girl
(South Korea, 2001).

Fig 2.10b
My Sassy Girl
(USA, 2008).

Fig 2. 10c
Ugly Aur Pagli
(India – Hindi, 2008).

Remakes

The film has been remade twice in India. A Telugu version entitled *Maa Iddari Madhya* was released in 2006 but this version is difficult to find. The Hindi remake *Ugly Aur Pagli* (*Ugly and Crazy*, India, 2008) repeats many of the original scenes in detail. For the first 20 minutes it seems like a departure from mainstream Bollywood, but then a music-and-dance sequence is inserted with the leads performing in a fairground. Apart from this there appears to be an interesting match between the middle-class lives of characters in Seoul and Mumbai. Higher education colleges, the suburban railway system and modern cafés for young people are all similar in the two cities. Mumbai has the more striking visual attractions with rooftop views across the city and along the seafront from Nariman Point.

Nowhere in the press pack (http://www.uglyaurpagli.com/homepage.html) from Pritish Nandy Communications, the producers of the film, is there any mention of *My Sassy Girl*, although Bollywood Hungama's reviewer refers to the Korean film (http://www.bollywoodhungama.com/moviemicro/userreview/type/view/userid/3003/id/55713) and the IMDb users mostly seem to know the original. We are obliged to see this as an unofficial 'borrowing' of Korean property. The director of the Indian film, Sachin Khot, had previously directed TV serials in Indonesia – perhaps he was familiar with the Korean property in that context. Or perhaps the Hindi version is simply a remake of the Telugu film. This seems more likely. There is no official mention of the original Korean script for the Telugu version either.

The leads in the Hindi film are well-known actors (Ranvir Shorey and Mallika Sherawat). Both actors are around ten years older than the Koreans in the same roles. The film suffers from a music score that was not received as well as the Korean soundtrack with its hit song 'I Believe'. But perhaps the major reason for the failure of the Hindi version is the cultural difference. The Indian script seems to back away from the more outrageous aspects of the story – but still manages to offend audiences. The importance of the drinking subtext may be a problem in terms of different attitudes. Nevertheless, the IMDb user comments that compare versions all opt for the Korean version.

The American remake (with Roy Lee involved) was eventually released 'straight to video' in the US in 2008. IMDb also suggests it was released in South East Asia in 2008. It was made by a group of American independents with Korean major CJ Entertainment on board (CJ Entertainment was not the original Korean producer). Starring Canadian actress Elisha Cuthbert with Jesse Bradford as the male lead, the film was the first American outing for French director Yann Samuel. Why Samuel? He had only one previous credit – for *Jeux d'enfants* (*Love Me if You Dare*, France, 2003), a romantic comedy starring Marion Cotillard and Guillaume Canet. That film had been a hit in France, praised for its invention, and it does have a plot with some similar elements to *My Sassy Girl,* including a boy and girl who make a childhood pact and then play quite dangerous games that continue into their adult lives. There is a sense of 'quirkiness' about *My Sassy Girl* and Samuels directs sequences that might be influenced by *Amélie* (dir. Jean-Pierre Jeunet, France, 2001) or by the films of Michel Gondry, who had a big US independent hit with *Eternal Sunshine of the Spotless Mind* (US, 2004). In one fantasy sequence, the couple in the American *My Sassy Girl* act out a scene from *Titanic* on a stage with wooden props forming the waves. But this still seems a gamble – adding a French perspective on romantic comedy to Korean material for a Hollywood audience? *My Sassy Girl* is not a bad film and in many ways it is quite enjoyable. But like the Indian versions it seems unable to use the Korean script 'as is' and attempts to tone it down and to add Hollywood conventions such as the young man's 'best (male) friend' who is there to explain to him what is going on. Ironically perhaps, the spirit of the Korean original is arguably closer to 1930s screwball Hollywood comedies such as *Bringing Up Baby* with Katherine Hepburn as the dominant/aggressive female character.

The Japanese TV series (11x55-min. episodes) and the Chinese 'sequel' *My Sassy Girl II* (China, 2010) don't face the same problems of cultural difference and they are made for markets where the first film is well known. This doesn't mean that they are simply copies. The Japanese TV series is a different format and has to find more narrative material – or treat it in different ways. The Chinese film has a Hong Kong director and actors from Singapore, Hong Kong, Taiwan and China.

> *My Sassy Girl 2* has much more in common with Hong Kong styled wacky romantic comedies than it does with the original. On the plus side, this means that there is far less of a focus on angsty melodrama than in most Korean genre outings, with the film aiming mainly for laughs and never quite falling prey to the usual final act dive into tears and staring into the rain.
>
> (James Mudge on BeyondHollywood.com (3 May 2011))

What does this case study tell us? It would probably have made more sense to release the original film with subtitles in North America – and possibly in India, where the market for foreign-language (i.e. not English) titles is growing. But such a release in cinemas would face the problem of the specialised cinema/popular genre film assumptions. This film in its Korean version may have fared better as a subtitled DVD release in the US.

Our comments about possible cultural differences between East Asia and the US run the risk of **orientalism,** as suggested by Xu in his analysis (see Chapter 5). The perceived differences between the Korean and Indian versions need some other explanation. They raise questions about Pan-Asian film exchanges that are seen as possibilities in Chapters 5 and 12.

Research and Explore 2.4: *Remakes*

■ If you are able to find a copy of the original Korean *My Sassy Girl*, try to make a list of the reasons why the film was so successful in East Asia and therefore what an American producer should have considered as essential for a remake. Is there anything in the original that you don't think would work in an American context?

Remakes are not only an East to West phenomenon.

■ Zhang Yimou's *A Woman, A Gun and a Noodle Shop* (Hong Kong/China, 2009) is an (acknowledged) remake of the first Coen Brothers' film *Blood Simple* (US, 1984). What do you think Zhang hoped to do with the remake? What is the effect of the change in location and genre repertoires?

Summary

This chapter has attempted to explore some of the reasons why 'the way Hollywood does things' has been taken as a model by other film industries around the world. At the same time we want to query the assertion by Bordwell, Staiger and Thompson (quoted in Chapter 1) to the effect that 'No absolute, pure alternative to Hollywood exists'. Our final discussion in this chapter suggests that just as Hollywood needs the international market as the most important outlet for its products, it also needs other film industries to provide at least some of its resources. Perhaps we need to rethink what defining the Hollywood model means for film studies. It is certainly the most frequently used model of production, distribution and exhibition. Other film cultures may use the model and exclude Hollywood, but in terms of global film all the film industries, including Hollywood, are interdependent.

References and further reading

Altman, Rick (1999) *Film/Genre*, London: BFI.

Branston, Gill and Stafford, Roy (2006) *The Media Student's Book* (4th edn), Abingdon: Routledge.

Branston, Gill with Stafford, Roy (2010) *The Media Student's Book* (5th edn), Abingdon: Routledge.

Brophy, Philip (2005) 'Arashi ga oka (Onimaru): The Sound of the World Turned Inside Out', in Jay McRoy (ed.) *Japanese Horror Cinema*, Edinburgh: Edinburgh University Press.

Choi, Jinhee (2010) *The South Korean Film Renaissance, Local Hitmakers/Global Provocateurs*, Middleton, CT: Wesleyan University Press.

Gledhill, Christine (ed.) (1987) *Where the Heart Is*, London: BFI.

Hunt, Leon and Leung Wing-Fai (eds) (2008) *East Asian Cinemas*, London and New York: I.B. Tauris.

Kang Kyoung-lae, 'Novel Genres or Generic Novels: Considering Korean Movies Adapted from Amateur Internet Novels' (2008) *Masters Theses*, Paper 96. Available at http://scholarworks.umass.edu/theses/96.

Lay, Samantha (2002) *British Social Realism: From Documentary to Brit Grit*, London: Wallflower.

Neale, Steve (2000) *Genre and Hollywood*, London: Routledge.

Ryall, Tom (1975) 'Teaching Through Genre', *Screen Education* No. 17, winter 1975/1976.

Thomas, Brian (2003) *VideoHound's Dragon Asian Action & Cult Flicks*, Canton, MI: Visible Ink Press.

Thussu, Daya Kishan (ed.) (2007) *Media on the Move: Global Flow and Contra-flow*, Abingdon: Routledge.

UNESCO Institute of Statistics (2012) *From International Blockbusters to National Hits: Analysis of the 2010 UIS Survey on Feature Film Statistics*, Montreal: UIS Information Bulletin No. 8. Downloadable from http://www.uis.unesco.org.

Weddle, David (1996) *Sam Peckinpah: 'If They Move … Kill 'Em'*, London: Faber and Faber.

Wilkinson, Amber (2007) http://www.eyeforfilm.co.uk/feature/2007-12-06-rigoberto-castaneda-on-km-31-feature-story-by-amber-wilkinson.

Xu, Gary G. (2007) *Sinascape: Contemporary Chinese Cinema*, Lanham, MD: Rowman & Littlefield.

Xu, Gary G. (2008) 'Remaking East Asia, Outsourcing Hollywood', in Hunt and Leung (op. cit.).

CHAPTER 3

Approaching films from different cultures

Enjoyment in watching films

Can you remember when you watched your first film? Probably not – we learn how to read stories from a very young age and we aren't usually conscious of struggling to make sense of what we see. But if your first exposure to films from different film cultures is not until you are in your teens, the sense of having to learn new codes and conventions and/or explore new cultural environments can be surprising. Some people find it an exciting challenge and plunge straight in, some back away, but most of us try to deal with what at first seems like an absence of some familiar pleasures of narrative and identification with characters and ideas. Can we really enjoy films from other cultures?

It is worth thinking about this notion of enjoyment. We all tend to think of films first as entertainment, although we all have our own tastes and some audiences enjoy a serious documentary as entertainment because it also offers to inform or to educate us. Others prefer a romantic comedy or an action film with well-known stars. Either way we don't expect to have to *work* at understanding and enjoying an entertainment film. This leads us towards the concept of **specialised** or **art cinema** (see Chapter 7). There *are* films screening in cinemas that demand work from the audience, and the difficulty that audiences find with such films has been an element in the distinction between mainstream and specialised labels. But these definitions are not fixed and often they are completely arbitrary. Think carefully. Have you ever watched a film, perhaps on DVD or on television or online, enjoyed it and then been surprised to find that the film is obscure and barely received a release in cinemas?

The degree of difficulty in watching a film may be to do with the subject matter or the values underpinning the filmmakers' approach. It may be narrative complexity or the style of camerawork or acting that creates problems. Some of these factors will involve cultural questions and assumptions about audiences. How much do we feel peer-group pressure when we are told (or when promotional materials suggest) that a film is 'not for us' – because we are too old, too young, the wrong gender or perhaps not from the culture that has produced the film?

Whatever the reason, we tend to enjoy the films with which we are most comfortable. Film studies asks us to consider a diverse range of films and so we need strategies to approach very different films. In the context of global film we will encounter films in other languages and from other cultures – and films made for different purposes and for different audiences in different contexts. Watching these films will require some work – but that work should eventually produce a great deal of enjoyment. It is also important to remember that many of the films from other cultures that we are asked to study are actually popular entertainment films. They just happen to be presented in a language that is unfamiliar. (You are going to be asked to watch films that require subtitling or dubbing, and if you want to explore the issues associated with the choice between the two, see the appropriate section in Chapter 1.)

Everybody watches films differently and there is no 'correct' way to approach unfamiliar types of films. However, it is probably best to avoid the common practice of some audiences as revealed in comments by viewers on social media. This involves a kind of guessing game with a film narrative, with viewers attempting to predict what will happen. If they turn out to guess correctly the film is then dismissed as predictable, but if the film doesn't 'deliver' what they are expecting this is equally disappointing. Trying to predict what will happen in many of the films discussed in this book will not be particularly helpful. It is far better to simply make yourself open to whatever the filmmaker offers you. This doesn't mean just sitting back and passively watching. It is better to engage the narrative as closely as possible without making too many assumptions. In this chapter we will consider four titles from different film industries and explore ways of reading them closely.

Case study 3.1: *Die Welle* (*The Wave*, Germany, 2008)

This seems a good place to start, since the narrative is centred on a high school classroom and features the interrelationships both between the students and with their teacher. It is a familiar genre with a narrative featuring a thematic and plot twist associated with the politics of authority and control. *Die Welle* is definitely a 'popular film' and rare to find outside its domestic habitat, since German popular cinema is usually only shown in German-speaking territories (Germany, Switzerland and Austria). But school experience is universal, and this film found a significant audience in France, Spain and Italy as well.

Die Welle recorded 3.7 million admissions across Europe in 2008/2009 but was not released in the US until 2011. In the US and the UK it played mainly on arthouse screens – arguably missing its target audience.

The film opens much as any Hollywood teen film. Someone is driving to school and, though some of the housing stock by the roadside is distinctively German, the music on the car radio is the Ramones' 'Rock and Roll High School'. But this is a teacher rather than a student, a man in his late thirties dressed in black in a Ramones T-shirt, jeans and a leather jacket. The school is modern and open plan, and the camerawork involves low angles and sweeping tracking shots. This is not a 'slow' art film. After affectionately greeting a colleague (who we will later learn is his wife) the man finds himself summoned to see the school principal, at which point he seems more like a student being told that he's got to do something he doesn't want to do. He still thinks that he is a rebel and he is shocked that instead of a summer project on 'anarchy' he is being told to teach about 'autocracy' – especially when it becomes clear that the teacher who has been given anarchy as a subject won't swap. This dialogue exchange presents our first hurdle. Apart from the subtitles and getting used to the sound of German spoken quite quickly, the viewer is also offered a cultural reference – the man 'squatted in Kreuzberg'. What does this mean? Does it matter if we don't know where Kreuzberg is?

In the next sequence, a familiar scenario in which students are rehearsing a play and a spat develops between the lead actors, we discover that the play is by Dürrenmatt. Again, do we know this reference? There are two points here. First, we can still understand the narrative without the specific cultural knowledge of these two names – but if we do know them, the meaning is emphasised and given nuances that will enrich our overall appreciation. Second, there is a danger that if we don't get the references we may assume that this film is targeting an élite audience (i.e. trying to appear as a specialised film by making obscure references). This would be a mistake, since the two names are both well known in a German context. Kreuzberg is a district of Berlin known for its ethnic mix and for its counter-cultural politics, sending a Green Party MP to the Bundestag (German Parliament). Friedrich Dürrenmatt (1921–1990) was a Swiss-German playwright and one of the most important dramatists of the 1950s and 1960s worldwide as well as in the German-speaking world. His plays deal with general political questions about guilt and responsibility.

These two references underline the central theme of the film that will emerge over the next few scenes. The first time you watch it you will probably want to keep going, following the narrative of what is a well-paced film. If you are studying the film and therefore watching it for a second or third time it is worth looking up such references through a quick online search. Subtitles actually make this easier, since with accented English or poor dubbing it is often difficult to catch the references in spoken dialogue.

In the first classroom scenes it is clear that the students are being presented as generic types, recognisable from mainstream international cinema. There is a 'jock' (even if the school sport this term is water polo rather than football). His girlfriend is the most academic student (and the lead in the play). There are three 'bad boys', a very

If you are studying films on DVD it's worth checking out all the subtitle options, since, even if you know the language, the subtitles may confirm names, brands, places, etc. In the UK, around six million TV viewers have turned on subtitles for English-language programmes, even though they have no hearing impairment (Ofcom Research).

The director Dennis Gansel said in an interview that he chose water polo (popular in Germany) because football/soccer is used all the time in German films and he wanted something visually more unusual. See: http://www.movieweb.com/news/exclusive-dennis-gansel-talks-the-wave-and-we-are-the-night (*We Are the Night* is a vampire movie.)

Fig 3.1
The classroom in *Die Welle* before the project begins.

political young woman, a class clown, etc. Some of these are German variations on the Hollywood type but overall the first classroom scene is similar to the classroom scene at the beginning of *10 Things I Hate About You* (US, 1999). Genre is a good way in to studying foreign-language films because genres use 'social types' extensively and these are more likely to reference global culture – especially global youth culture. In a sense we don't need spoken language to understand the dynamics of the classroom because we quickly read the types through their dress, facial gestures, body posture, voice, etc.

The classroom dynamics are carried over into the nightclub scene and other locations, including the various home situations. But what happens in these 'out-of-school' scenes develops the political theme and a commentary on German social values as well as pursuing some of the usual teen concerns such as romance, peer-group pressure, gang rivalry, etc. Most of these narrative sequences are quite accessible for a non-German audience but again, understanding is deepened by some cultural knowledge. One of the students picks up a slur on East Germans. He is himself an 'Ossi' (i.e. 'from the East') and one of his mates is second-generation German-Turkish. The Turkish migrant community is the largest in Germany (3 to 4 million first and second generation). Is this character included simply to be representative of a 'normal' German student body – or does he represent the Turkish community in a film about political ideas in contemporary Germany?

The central narrative line in the film involves the teacher's attempt to teach the meaning of autocracy through a kind of simulation project whereby his students create for themselves a youth movement that they decide to call 'The Wave'. For all viewers this inevitably becomes linked to ideas about the Nazi Party in Germany. This raises a potential problem for audiences outside Germany. We may think we know a great deal about the Nazis, but what else do we know about German history and contemporary German social life and politics? What do we know about how Germans feel about their own history? The film actually deals with these questions and some of those dealing with contemporary Neo-Nazism quite carefully. It is also worth noting that there have been several important German films over the past few years dealing with aspects of the Nazi period, including *Der Untergang* (*Downfall*, Germany, 2004) and *Sophie Scholl – Die letzten Tage* (*The Last Days*, Germany, 2005).

Downfall, about Hitler's last days in his Berlin bunker, became something of an international hit, but *Sophie Scholl* is less well known outside Germany. Sophie was an 18-year-old student who with her brother and others organised a leaflet campaign urging an end to the war in 1943. She was arrested and the film deals with her interrogation (in which she bravely sticks to her principles) during her 'last days'. The importance of her stand against the Nazi state is evident in the three other films about her and the fact that the 2005 film was circulated free to German schools. Thus, when we see the students' reaction in *Die Welle* to the possibility that a project on autocracy might involve learning more about Nazi ideologies, we might reflect on what they already know and how they might respond based on that knowledge (i.e. some will have been deeply moved by stories like that of Sophie Scholl, while others may have reacted by ignoring them). As with the cultural references to Kreuzberg and Dürrenmatt, you will still be able to follow the narrative without this knowledge but being aware of it will enhance your reading.

Die Welle plays out much as we might expect from this kind of genre film. The film is based on a German novel that in turn drew on a real high school project conducted in California in the 1960s. There is therefore the possibility that the film will draw on

German 'Reunification' took place in 1990 after the fall of East German communist state. Although West Germans strongly supported the move, it had to be subsidised and economic differences helped perpetuate the social type of the Ossi, even though young people in Germany in 2008 knew little about life in the East before 1990.

See the blog entry for 'Sophie Scholl' on globalfilmstudies.com.

another subgenre, namely the psychological thriller dealing with social experiments – which we expect to go wrong in some way, especially when the romances and gang violence of the teen picture are mixed in.

The other interesting aspect of this film concerns the classification into mainstream or specialised for films like this – particularly important for the prospects of foreign-language genre films. In the UK, the film was released as a specialised film and then dismissed by some critics because its genre form and style made it 'simplistic' and 'naïve' in its handling of ideas about fascism. But for the high school students in the film and a younger audience exploring how fascism works in practice for the first time, the film is provocative in a useful way. The introduction of a uniform into a liberal German high school and therefore a group identity for the Wave members is revealing of the inclusiveness that the students then feel, especially those who have previously felt excluded owing to wealth differences, abilities in specific school subjects, etc.

Research and Explore 3.1

The high school film is a feature of popular cinema in several major film cultures.

- What is different and what is similar in the ways in which the different social types in the school classroom interact in *Die Welle* compared to a Hollywood teen film?
- *Die Welle* is based on an American high school experiment – how might an American version of the same story be different?
- Japanese and South Korean high school films tend towards different genre mixes – how would you compare the classroom relationships between students and with their teacher in *Die Welle* and *Battle Royale* (Japan, 2000), *Confessions* (Japan, 2011) or *Whispering Corridors* (South Korea, 1998)?

If *Die Welle* is a relatively straightforward introduction to a genre film from another culture, the next case study film offers a little more of a challenge, even if it is partly based around the same Hollywood type of teen picture.

Case study 3.2: *Y tu mamá también* (Mexico/US, 2001)

This film received more critical attention than *Die Welle*. It found a North American (and UK) audience as well as a Mexican and Spanish audience. Overall it attracted over 1 million admissions in Europe and 2.3 million in the US (many of these may have been Spanish speakers). However, in some ways this is a more difficult film to read than a more mainstream film like *Die Welle*.

The film was written by Carlos Cuarón and directed by his brother Alfonso. These two, as well as the two young leads Gael García Bernal and Diego Luna, and two other directors Guillermo del Toro and Alejandro González Iñárritu, became collectively known as the 'Amigos' and identified as **transnational** filmmakers. In the late 1990s and early 2000s they were able to work on a variety of their own projects in Mexico *or* Hollywood *or* Europe. Few other filmmakers have been able to straddle different filmmaking traditions in this way. Thus, although *Y tu mamá también* is a Mexican story, set in Mexico and made by Mexicans, it has a Spanish female lead and sometimes an American sensibility. Much of this latter comes from the deployment of familiar Hollywood genre conventions

See Chapter 2 on ideas about melodrama.

Alfonso Cuarón is probably best known for directing *Harry Potter and the Prisoner of Azkaban* (UK/US, 2004) and *Children of Men* (UK/US, 2006).

from the road movie and the 'coming-of-age' youth picture as well as social comedy and melodrama. The film has tended to keep its Mexican title, even in the US and UK. The literal translation is 'And Your Mother Too' – a riposte suggesting bravado that doesn't really work in English.

Outline story

(NB: If you haven't seen the film yet, be warned that the next few paragraphs give away important plot details.)

Julio and Tenoch are young men in Mexico City about to see off their girlfriends who are travelling in Europe. Stuck for something to do for this last summer before they start university, they decide on a road trip to find the mythical 'magic beach' known as 'Heaven's Mouth'. At a family wedding they meet Luisa, an older woman from Spain who is married to Tenoch's cousin – and seemingly unhappy with her lot. To their great surprise, she agrees to accompany them on their trip. The boys compete to seduce Luisa, who is far more experienced than either of them. After a series of adventures, they arrive at the coast and become friendly with a local fisherman and his family. There is a twist at the end of the tale and an epilogue when the boys meet again after the first year of their degree courses.

Reading the film

This all sounds very straightforward – and it is. On one level the film may be enjoyed simply as a 'romp' with familiar incidents on a road trip. But at various times there are whispered voiceovers that seem to comment on the narrative, and at the end there is quite a sharp change of tone. It is probably fairly obvious that the Cuaróns intend some kind of social commentary to go alongside the fun, but to fully appreciate this you need some knowledge of art cinema and some insights into Mexican politics and culture.

Alfonso Cuarón recalls seeing the films of Jean-Luc Godard in *ciné* clubs in Mexico when he was a teenager (see Chapter 7 on the impact of New Wave cinema in France) and he suggests that this is where the idea of the voiceover commentary comes from. He makes specific reference to *Masculin féminin* (France, 1966) (Basoli 2002: 27) and in other interviews he mentions *Bande à part* (France, 1964) – one of Quentin Tarantino's favourite films (and the name of his production company) with a plot featuring two men and one woman.

Godard, one of the most important directors associated with the French New Wave, made films that were avant-garde in terms of both aesthetics (how they used sound and image) and, increasingly in the 1960s, revolutionary politics.

The voiceovers in *Y tu mamá también*, as Edward Lawrenson (2002) suggests, tend to give an air of melancholy to the film, often commenting on death – something unconsidered by the teenagers but an important element of the narrative. But it is another aspect of the voiceovers and the general aesthetic of the film that reveals its political subtext. Cuarón takes care with his camera to reveal to the audience the 'other Mexico' through which the boys travel and which most of the time they fail to see properly.

Tenoch and Julio are both, by Mexican standards, very well off. Mexico has a large population (115 million), most of whom live in urban areas. This means that many parts of what is a large country are sparsely populated – by poor families. The per capita income in Mexico is something like a quarter of that in the US. Mexico has a small, wealthy middle class and a large working class, many of whom have moved to Mexico City to look for work. This is the subject of the 'commentary' near the beginning of the film about the worker who is killed crossing the road in order to save time getting to work. The division by social class is mirrored by an ethnic divide. The largest ethnic group in

Mexico (around 60 per cent) is classified as *mestizo* or 'mixed'. These are the descendants of intermarriage between Europeans (predominantly Spanish) and the local Amerindian peoples of Central America. The Amerindians themselves make up some 30 per cent of the Mexican population. Europeans make up 9 per cent, leaving 1 per cent to cover all other groups. The 9 per cent of Europeans constitute the Mexican middle class. The decision by his parents to name Tenoch after an Aztec chieftain who founded what is now Mexico City is a calculated attempt to assert 'Mexican-ness'. The Aztecs were from North Mexico and they dominated the Southern Maya people before the arrival of the Spanish. A name like Tenoch could be provocative for the people of Southern Mexico (especially in Chiapas, the state that is home to the Zapatistas).

Julio and Tenoch are themselves separated by a class division. Julio lives with his mother and sister, who both work. Tenoch has a father who is an important politician and he lives in a grand house with a maid (who was also Tenoch's nanny). This distinction between the boys is central to the narrative.

The journey undertaken by the boys is from cosmopolitan Mexico City southwest towards the Pacific coast of Oaxaca. This is a movement from urban to rural, from sophisticated to 'simple', from rich to poor and from European to Amerindian. The film shows the two boys to be almost oblivious to the changing environment, but the camera and the voiceovers mean that the audience is constantly invited to notice the discrepancy between the rich boys' internal world and the realities outside.

David Heuser (see website reference) offers a fascinating analysis of the film which he reads as a commentary on the impossibility of Mexico getting the kind of government he thinks it deserves. In this analysis, Tenoch and Julio are representative of the two main political forces in Mexico (the upper class and the lower middle class). Their obsession with selfish (sexual) demands prevents them from recognising what they could achieve through cooperation. For Heuser, the car represents Mexico, and Luisa (Maribel Verdú), the Spanish migrant, represents the possibilities of European-style government. Once she takes over, the goal of the journey, Heaven's Mouth, becomes real, not a myth – just as

Zapatistas are 'libertarian socialist revolutionaries' defending local communities in Chiapas. They are named after Emiliano Zapata, one of the heroes of the Mexican Revolution of 1910.

Fig 3.2
Luisa buys a soft toy bearing her name from a roadside stall in *Y tu mamá también*.

the political goals of the country could become achievable. However, when the boys leave their tent, the pigs (i.e. the peasants) run amok, 'proving' to the boys that the peasantry cannot be trusted. When they wake up in bed together after a heavy night's drinking the boys are horrified – they cannot face the prospect of being together. The ending of the film confirms that the experiment too has ended. This is a detailed and quite convincing reading.

In an interview on the Region 2 DVD, director Cuarón says the film is about 'identity': for Luisa, for the boys and for the country – Mexico is a 'teenage country' that still needs to find its identity. He also confirms that the names of the characters refer directly to Mexican history. Luisa is a 'Cortés' – the name of the original Spanish conqueror (*conquistador*) of Mexico. Tenoch is an 'Iturbide' – the name of one of the early political leaders of revolutionary Mexico who wanted to become President. Julio is named Zapata – the name of the great revolutionary fighter (from whom the contemporary Zapatistas take their name).

Cuarón argues that dealing in this kind of detail in his Hollywood films proved impossible, but here it adds a great deal to our understanding. The voiceover commentary reveals to the audience things Julio and Tenoch do not know about each other and also shows aspects of Luisa's behaviour that the boys don't notice. A good example of this is when the car breaks down and Luisa buys a soft toy from a local woman because it has her name. The voiceover later tells us the story behind the toy and that Luisa is thinking about it when she passes a funeral procession for a child. This links to later scenes by the beach when she plays with the fisherman's children. Finally the voiceover tells us that she left the toy to the fisherman's daughter. Throughout the film Luisa is much more aware of the lives of people around her – in contrast to the boys, who are interested only in themselves. Another good example is when the car is stopped by a group from a small village and the boys are asked for money for the village festival queen. Only Luisa looks at the young woman. (Yet a little while earlier they have passed the village where Tenoch's nanny was born.)

The voiceover also tells us about characters who are either peripheral to the story (like Chuy, the fisherman) or completely outside the boys' story. These are comments on the lives of Mexico's rural/migrant poor and the voiceover also reminds us of the political changes in Mexico. This stealthy political comment is also taken up in the cinematography and *mise en scène*.

Camera and *mise en scène*

The camerawork is an integral part of the overall 'feel' of the film. It is fluid but not overly expressive. Much of the time scenes are shown in relative long shot (e.g. in the two scenes when Luisa seduces the boys). The central three characters are in the frame together inside the car for long periods. Organising this when they are travelling in the car is quite difficult and sometimes requires a distorting wide-angle lens. If it is not peering into the car, the camera is often showing the car in long shot, from in front or behind on the road itself, or at an angle from the road. Alternatively, the camera looks out of the car windows at the countryside passing by. It is the shifting balance between these kinds of shots that slowly begins to show the audience more about the conditions of the local people.

In the early part of the journey the camera is largely focusing on the trio, but there are several instances, often in conjunction with the voiceover, when it manages to capture what is happening at the edges of the frame, or just out of the frame in which the boys

Fig 3.3a
The three characters in the car in *Y tu mamá también*, seemingly oblivious to the world around them.

Fig 3.3b
The boys drive past soldiers questioning a motorist in *Y tu mamá también*.

are appearing. The best example of this is in the scene when the trio arrive for their first overnight stay in a country hotel. As they are about to order food, the camera leaves the party and follows one of the family in the hotel into a back room and then on into the kitchen where the family are eating and getting on with their busy lives. There are also examples of the repression carried out by police at roadblocks, etc., all passed without a sideways glance by the boys in the car.

Popular culture

The political commentary in the film is not recognised by every audience (in fact, it is probably recognised by a small minority in audiences outside Mexico). Some critics have lambasted the film because it panders to American teen culture. It has been described as mirroring *American Pie* (US, 1999) or *Dude, Where's My Car?* (US, 2000). Although there are some obvious similarities with these films, both the tone and the look of the Mexican film are quite different.

The interaction with American culture is also more complicated than simple acceptance of the dominance of American forms. Xan Brooks (2002) quotes Paul Julian Smith on the way that the language used by the boys – *chilango*, a kind of Mexican 'youth speak' – is quite distinctive. As is the music, much of which is a form of Mexican-style Anglo-American music – performed either by Mexican bands or Hispanic bands in the US. Other tracks are drawn from European rock or more traditional Mexican music.

A complete soundtrack listing is available at www.imdb.com/title/ tt0245574/soundtrack.

An example of how music codes the changing world through which the car travels comes at the point where the portable tape player runs down because its batteries are fading. The boys have been playing American or Mexican rock but now, as the political struggles in the world outside the car become more apparent, the music on the soundtrack becomes more local or more 'roots' as it must be derived from local radio stations. As the soundtrack switches to this rootsier music of accordions, the world outside becomes more alien – the boys' car is hemmed in by cattle and they react angrily. Later they have to be towed to a garage behind an ox cart.

The stars

The success of the film is partly down to its young stars, especially Gael García Bernal. Bernal (born 1978) had already featured in *Amores Perros* (Mexico, 2000), an international hit for director Alejandro González Iñárritu, when he began work on *Y tu mamá también*. A child actor in a soap on Mexican TV, he went to London to study acting at the Central School of Speech and Drama. In 2004 he became known as one of the hottest young stars in international cinema when he featured in Pedro Almodóvar's *Bad Education* (Spain) and *The Motorcycle Diaries* (Argentina/US/Chile/Peru/Brazil/UK/Germany/France), in which he played a young Che Guevara for the Brazilian director Walter Salles. Diego Luna (born 1979) has a similar background as a child star on Mexican television. In 2004 he started to appear in Hollywood films, notably in the lead for *Dirty Dancing: Havana Nights* and as a supporting player in Spielberg's *The Terminal*. In 2008 the two stars were together again in *Rudo y cursi* (2008), this time directed by Carlos Cuarón. They repeated their pairing in the Hollywood 'comedy' (it isn't quite what it seems) *Casa de mi Padre* (US, 2012) with Will Ferrell.

Toby Miller (2010: 144–154) details the distribution of *Y tu mamá también* in the US and argues forcibly that film studies has failed to understand how films like this are received by audiences. He provides evidence of how the film was released in US arthouses but also how it was promoted to the large Spanish-speaking audiences in New York and the Southwest and Western parts of the country before becoming a cross-over mainstream hit. The promotion included the two stars, the director and the Mexican and Hollywood star Salma Hayek – who Miller describes as a 'fantasy object' in the film. Hispanic-Americans comprise 15 per cent of the US film audience and they are the most frequent cinema-goers. Miller's argument is that neither the film industry nor film studies properly appreciates the potential of this audience – which was shown by the success of this 'Mexican/US' film.

Guillermo del Toro commented on the success of *Amores Perros*, stating that 'The foreign market that Mexican cinema has conquered is Mexico' (Miller 2010: 148). In other words, in appealing to an international market but representing Mexico in ways that don't conform to stereotypes, films like this also attract a domestic audience more used to watching Hollywood.

Research and Explore 3.2: *The politics of identity*

Watch *Y tu mamá también* and *Rudo y cursi* or *Casa de mi Padre*. If this isn't possible at least read the comments on these films on the appropriate IMDb Bulletin Board (and/or the User Comments). What kinds of questions are being raised about Mexico and Mexican identity – from both Spanish-speaking and 'Anglo' Americans? What does this suggest about the reception of foreign-language cinema in the US?

We have spent a great deal of time on one film, primarily to demonstrate the potential richness of a transnational film – as long as we are prepared to take the time and effort to discover something about the social and political context and how the formal aspects of the film are used to foreground these issues. On the other hand the treatment of universal generic elements of the narrative has helped us into the story. We want now to turn to a film that adopts a very different approach, and in which genre and the conventions of popular cinema are not likely to help as much.

Case study 3.3: *At 5 in the Afternoon (Panj é asr*, Iran/France, 2003)

In this film we have to start simply from the images and sounds placed before us and then proceed based on an interrogation of our own ideas about some recent history.

The opening of the film seems wilfully obscure. The first shot shows a desolate landscape with two women walking towards the camera, one with a yoke carrying pails of water, the other leading a laden horse. On the soundtrack a woman's voice, barely above a whisper, delivers some lines about '5 in the afternoon'. The image then cuts to a closer shot of a woman entering a yard, again with a yoke carrying pails of water. Is it the same woman? We cannot tell, because this woman is wearing a *burqa* and her whole head and face are covered. She proceeds to put down the yoke and pick up a shoulder bag carrying a large and rather battered book that she takes out and clutches as she climbs into a horse trap. Behind her an old man appears. He turns to face the wall as two young women (wearing long headscarves but with their faces uncovered) walk by. After they have gone he asks God for forgiveness, climbs aboard the trap into the driver's seat and the couple set off down the road.

As they drive into the background a long shot reveals that there are dwellings seemingly carved out of a hillside in the distance. At first, the only sounds are of the street with a distant voice that may be a call to prayer. We see the woman reading from the book and chanting lines of scripture. As the trap enters a busy market area, which we see from a high-angle long shot, we hear singing, seemingly more musical and accompanied. Finally the trap comes to a halt, and the woman alights and walks towards us down a dark alley. The soundtrack now carries a mix of women's voices and some instrumental music (pipes or horns). As the woman sweeps past us, she disappears into the darkness of the alley to reappear a few moments later in the light as she walks away.

At this point four minutes have passed, and we may be bewildered by what we have seen and heard. Whatever our background, we have probably worked out that this is a strict Islamic society and that the woman is reading from the Quran. Given his behaviour, the old man is probably her father, and although the *burqa* could suggest many locations, its colour, the father's clothes and the city sights suggest that it is most likely to be Afghanistan. What is most striking however is how little has been explained. What were those lines read out at the beginning? What does the title mean? Who is this family? This seems wilful because in the next few moments of the film much will be revealed – we see the woman briefly join a religious school group (all dressed like her and reading from the

A *burqa* is a garment that completely conceals a woman's body, leaving only a small mesh window to see through. A *niqab* is a veil that leaves the eyes exposed. A *chador* is a full-length cloak. All three relate to *hijab* – the 'veiling' of women in Islam.

Fig 3.4
Samira Makhmalbaf on set, checking a tracking shot – an image from her sister Hana's film about her 'making of' *At 5 in the Afternoon*.

Quran). But almost immediately she leaves down another alley and, after stopping to lift her veil and slip into a pair of white court shoes, she joins a much larger group of young women all dressed in white headscarves and black uniforms in what is clearly a new school/college for women. When the teacher queries her dress, Nogreh (as we now know she is called) explains that her father would be suspicious if she wore the uniform.

We can probably now work out that the theme of the film is women's status in this Islamic society (and the damaged and part-abandoned buildings seem to confirm that it is Afghanistan). Nogreh is our protagonist and she is striving to do something. Later we will learn that she wants to be elected as the first female president of Afghanistan (initially as part of a school project). This seems to be a more familiar idea for a film – a recognisable hero with a quest. Why the obfuscation in the opening? We will have to dig quite deep to find out what the title means. It comes from a 1934 poem 'Lament for Ignacio Sánchez Mejías' by **Federico García Lorca**, the young and highly acclaimed Spanish writer who was assassinated in 1936. The line is repeated many times in the poem and it forecasts the time of death of a bullfighter.

If you are able to find the DVD of the film (available on a Region 2 disc) you will have the option to view an interview with the director Samira Makhmalbaf either before you see the film or immediately afterwards. Many people prefer to see a film cold without too much prior knowledge and let the film tell its own story. In this case it may help to know something first – and possibly to be fired up by the director's enthusiasm and engaging approach. Her own background is unusual and knowing about it will help to set up the film.

The 'Makhmalbaf Film Family' from Iran is remarkable. Mohsen Makhmalbaf (born 1957) was a tear-away young radical who stabbed a policeman in his attempt to rob a bank to fund his revolutionary plans. At age 17 he was sent to prison where he began to educate himself and to try to learn how to become a filmmaker. He emerged as a free man many years later after the Islamic Revolution of 1979. He then did become a filmmaker – a very good one – who, alongside Abbas Kiarostami and later Jafar Panahi, would become well known on the international arthouse circuit as a leader of the New Iranian Cinema in the 1990s (see Chapter 6). But he was still a rebel and he fell out with the new authorities. Frustrated, he decided to turn his home into a film school; his first students were his second wife Marziyeh Meshkini and his children Samira, Maysam and Hana. Mohsen has continued to make films and he has been joined by the rest of his family, each leading on different projects. You can discover more on the family website at http://www.makhmalbaf.com.

Samira Makhmalbaf became the youngest person to win a prize at the Cannes Film Festival for her second feature *The Blackboard* (*Takhté siah*, Iran/Italy/Japan, 2000). She received the Jury Prize as a 20-year-old (having won several festival prizes for her first feature *The Apple* in 1998). Still only 23 when she released *At 5 in the Afternoon*, she was very confident about her abilities and she knew that she had the support from the family with her father writing the original story and her stepmother as assistant director. She worked on some of the cinematography herself and Mohsen edited the film.

Samira Makhmalbaf may reasonably be said to have made a 'personal' film. In her many interviews she makes reference to various films and filmmakers who have influenced her. Perhaps the most important film she mentions is *Bicycle Thieves* (*Ladri di biciclette*, Italy, 1948), one of the best-known titles associated with Italian **neo-realism**. Samira Makhmalbaf is not the only Iranian filmmaker (or indeed filmmakers from many other countries) to be identified as being influenced by this approach to filmmaking, so it is worth exploring what it means in some detail before we return to the streets of Kabul.

Federico García Lorca (1908–1936) was gay and a radical who wrote many plays as well as poetry: his death at the start of the Spanish Civil War could have been because of either his sexuality or his politics.

The Region 2 DVD of *At 5 in the Afternoon* includes a 'making of' documentary by Samira's young sister Hana (then aged 14) who also directed *Joy of Madness* (Iran, 2003), a 70-minute documentary about the difficulties in casting for Samira's feature.

Neo-realism

The term **neo-realism** is generally associated with Italian cinema in the immediate aftermath of the Second World War when many Italian cities were in ruins, Rome's famous Cinecittà Studio was closed, and materials and infrastructure for filmmaking were generally missing. On a simple practical level, films needed to be made as cheaply as possible, 'on location' in those very streets and ruined buildings.

The ideas behind what became neo-realism had in fact already been developed in France in the 1930s, particularly by Jean Renoir, beginning with his 1934 film *Toni* set among a community of migrant Italian workers in the South of France. One of the young filmmakers who worked with Renoir during the 1930s was Luchino Visconti, whose first feature *Ossessione* (Italy, 1943) used aspects of Renoir's approach in what was actually an unacknowledged adaptation of James M. Cain's Depression-set American novel *The Postman Always Rings Twice* (1934).

Fig 3.5
Father and son in *Bicycle Thieves*. Source: The Kobal Collection/ www.picture-desk.com.

We don't usually associate neo-realism with literary adaptations, but *Bicycle Thieves* was also a (very loose) adaptation of a novel by Luigi Bartolini. The story is very simple. An unemployed man finally gets a job as a bill-poster, but it requires that he has a bicycle. He must retrieve his own bicycle from the pawnshop. When the bicycle is stolen on his first day at work he is distraught, and with his small son he desperately searches for the thief. The adaptation was by Cesare Zavattini, one of the main creators of the neo-realist approach. Drafting his ideas quickly after reading the novel, he took the script to the director Vittorio De Sica who had been searching for:

> action which would be less apparently 'extraordinary', which could happen to anyone (above all to the poor), action which no newspaper wants to talk about.
>
> (De Sica 1948, reprinted in Overby 1978)

What emerges from De Sica's explanation of the genesis of the film is that he has a clear artistic aim, but it concerns the question of how to represent:

> the modern dimension given to small things, that state of mind considered 'common'. Thanks to the camera, the cinema has the means to capture that dimension. That is how I understand realism, which cannot be, in my opinion, mere documentation. If there is absurdity in this theory, it is the absurdity of those social contradictions which society wants to ignore. It is the absurdity of incomprehension through which it is difficult for truth and good to penetrate. Thus, my film is dedicated to the suffering of the humble.
>
> (op. cit.)

De Sica's inherent **humanism** – his interest in the importance of 'small things' to ordinary people – is the essential ingredient of *Bicycle Thieves*. The film does reveal what happens to working people in the face of official indifference, and the audience cares about the man and his son. The film has a social message, but not one tacked on artificially. De Sica, who had been a star actor in the 1930s, got tremendous performances from his non-professional cast and this was one of the attractions for audiences. His neo-realist films were also melodramas that generated an intense emotional response in audiences. The other two figures most closely associated with neo-realism, Visconti and Roberto Rossellini, had a more theoretical/political approach than De Sica (although he arguably had more impact with the public). Rossellini made some of the most important observations:

> The subject of the neo-realism film is the world; not story or narrative. It contains no preconceived thesis, because ideas are born in the film from the subject. It has no affinity with the superfluous and the merely spectacular, which it refuses, but is attracted to the concrete . [...] It refuses recipes and formulas ... neo-realism poses problems for us and for itself in an attempt to make people think.
>
> (Roberto Rossellini in *Retrospettive*, April 1953, reprinted in Overby (1978))

In these few sentences, Rossellini summed up the essence of the neo-realist approach that would go on to influence so many filmmakers around the world. Filmmakers who want to say something about the world should look for material in the events of the daily lives of ordinary people. If that daily life involves struggling just to find something to eat or to keep a roof over one's head you don't need a scriptwriter to invent a story.

Neo-realism 'refuses formulas' according to Rossellini, but it does suggest some common elements in films following the same approach:

- stories taken from the 'real world'
- inclusion of the ordinary details of everyday life
- 'non-professional' actors where possible
- location shooting and authenticity derived from real world décor
- a camera style that is 'free to move' and that uses long shots and long takes
- an avoidance of visible special effects.

This isn't a prescriptive list, and there are neo-realist films using film stars as well as musical scores and elements of theatrical performance, but overall the films avoid the contrivances and artificiality of big-budget studio pictures.

The impact of neo-realism since the 1940s

There were relatively few neo-realist films as a percentage of overall Italian production between 1945 and 1955 but their influence abroad was noticeable. Most often quoted is the impact on the Bengali filmmaker Satyajit Ray who, having already met Jean Renoir (who made *The River* in West Bengal in 1949), saw *Bicycle Thieves* in London in 1950 – and who immediately determined that his first film would be made using De Sica's approach. The international success of the low-budget film *Pather Panchali* (India, 1956) confirmed his belief (Robinson 2004: 73) (Satyajit Ray's approach is discussed in Chapter 10).

It isn't surprising that neo-realism seemed so suited to films depicting peasants in the countryside or making their way on to the streets of a big city. It promised a way of creating stories that would not require a big budget. It is also noticeable that many first-time directors in countries that hadn't developed a film industry previously had trained abroad and possibly seen neo-realist films as part of their film courses. This was true of directors like Sembène Ousmane, who shot the short feature *Borom Sarret* in Senegal in 1963 – often seen as the beginning of Sub-Saharan African cinema made by Africans. The title refers to a cart driver in Dakar – using a trap not dissimilar to that in *At 5 in the Afternoon* (see Chapter 8).

More recently, the Chinese director **Zhang Yimou**, best known perhaps for either his sumptuous early melodramas like *Raise the Red Lantern* (China, 1991) or later epics such as *Hero* (China-Hong Kong, 2002), has also made smaller films like *Not One Less* (China, 1999) – in many ways an exemplary neo-realist film (Stafford 2011: 60–61), in which a young teenage girl is employed to run a village school when the teacher is called away unexpectedly. But she will only be paid if she can keep the children attending the school. A younger Chinese director Wang Xiaoshuai borrowed much of the narrative of *Bicycle Thieves* to create *Beijing Bicycle* (France/Taiwan/China, 2001), in which a boy from the countryside gets a job in Beijing as a bicycle courier, only to have his new bike stolen.

Some critics have seen the impact of neo-realism on another Bengali filmmaker Bimal Roy, who was making Hindi 'social films' such as *Do Bhiga Zamin* (*Two Acres Of Land*, India, 1953) in Bombay (see http://theseventhart. info/2008/08/10/ flashback-28/).

It is important to note that a neo-realist approach will incorporate 'local' ideas about representation. We can compare films from different cultures that share the approach, but they won't necessarily use it in the same way.

Fig 3.6
The temporary village schoolteacher Wei attempts to teach a dance to the children in *Not One Less*.

Neo-realist films are usually seen as 'progressive'/liberal/ socialist but Zhang Yimou has been accused of making films that are 'conservative' in promoting government policies in films like *Not One Less* and *The Story of Qiu Ji* (China, 1992).

Several other Iranian filmmakers, as well as the Makhmalbafs, have been identified as drawing on the neo-realist legacy seen as a key ingredient in New Iranian cinema (see Chapter 6).

There are many modes of realism used by filmmakers in contemporary cinema. Sometimes the emphasis is more on the realism effect that might be created by the introduction of various new camera technologies or the adaptation of certain institutional styles such as the handheld camera, CCTV footage, 'home movies', etc. Some of these may be used in ways which form part of an approach associated with the origins of neo-realism but others may have simply been absorbed into mainstream cinema and become part of what may be termed 'Hollywood realism' (see Chapter 2). One of the other elements of the neo-realist approach that is more difficult to pin down is the **humanism** of certain films.

Humanist film

It isn't straightforward to explain exactly what a humanist film might be. A dictionary definition would suggest a film that does not deal with a religious or supernatural perspective, but this would be true of the majority of films. More useful is the recognition that humanism in conjunction with neo-realism was primarily a product of film criticism in the immediate post-war period in the late 1940s and 1950s. There was a general appreciation at this time of films that had progressed from the nationalist propaganda and ideologically driven narratives of wartime to explore complex moral dilemmas in the lives of individuals. In the 1950s many popular films from Hollywood drew directly on fears about communism during the Cold War so they presented obvious heroes and villains. But humanist filmmakers are prepared to offer us characters who have good and bad sides, who make rational decisions in a crisis, and who are conflicted in their reactions to new developments. These filmmakers are also interested in all the characters in a narrative; there are no 'good' heroes and 'bad' villains, there are just people in all their complexity. The issue here is that a humanist approach coupled with the realist depiction of everyday events is likely to produce a film narrative that is very different to the entertainment film of mainstream popular cinema.

Consider the concept of the 'feel-good film', often quoted as a likely box office winner and the kind of film that everyone wants to see on a Friday night after a hard week – something to sit back and enjoy. Typically, we like to see characters with whom we can identify and we don't mind seeing them struggle through adversity, but we expect them to win in the end and we don't mind if that involves them winning the lottery or taking part in an unlikely chase sequence. Most of all we want a satisfying ending. But a film adopting a neo-realist/humanist stance doesn't want to do this – and neither does its audience. They want to feel that the story is somehow 'real' or 'truthful', and they want to be moved by the way in which different characters respond to events. Of course, the same audience could enjoy both sorts of film at different times. The problems arise when audiences have expectations of one type of film and find themselves watching another.

This humanist ethos of 1950s cinema was challenged by the modernist cinema of the 1960s and again by the postmodernism of the 1980s (see Chapter 2). In this sense we see the New Waves of 1960s cinema at first drawing on a neo-realist tradition but then developing new kinds of anti-hero and beginning to experiment with narrative structures. The hybridity and playfulness of postmodern films also at first sight seems antithetical to neo-realism and humanism. But it would be a mistake to underestimate the ways in which filmmakers can draw on seemingly disparate elements and make them work together – which brings us back to the Makhmalbafs.

In her striking debut film *The Day I Became a Woman* (Iran, 2000), Marziyeh Meshkini deftly brings together episodes representing the different 'ages of woman' in which she mixes realism with elements of what seem in the Western perspective to be almost magic realism. In the final episode of the film, an elderly woman enters a shopping mall on the duty-free island of Kish, commanding a small army of boys to carry her purchases of furniture, kitchen items, etc. These are assembled on the beach and presented in a parody of modern living. Finally they are loaded precariously on to a fleet of rafts and taken to a container ship on the horizon. It seems fantastical but it is rooted in the material world.

The usefulness of the humanist film concept is not recognised by some film scholars. See Andrew Tudor's objections on: http://newhumanist. org.uk/966/ projecting-the-human.

Magic realism is a concept mostly associated with Latin American literary fiction in which certain fantastical elements are included in stories with an otherwise realist base.

Fig 3.7
The surrealist imagery of the last section of *The Day I Became a Woman*.

Research and Explore 3.3: *Humanist characters*

Explore your own response to a 'humanist film' through the following exercise:

■ Make a comparison between a lead character in a film labelled humanist or neo-realist (e.g. Antonio in *Bicycle Thieves*) and a lead character from a contemporary popular action film or other popular genre.

■ Are the characters very different in the way in which they are used in the narrative, or the ways in which the audiences engage with them?

Back to Kabul and the Makhmalbafs

If we return to *At 5 in the Afternoon*, it is soon apparent that Samira Makhmalbaf is interested in the visual possibilities of the dress code. We have already seen Nogreh changing her dress and shoes and in later scenes she often stands out in scenes where she is unveiled when all the other women she is with are veiled. Although the film maintains its neo-realist approach, there is sometimes the suggestion that the director has also chosen scenes because they have both a sense of political symbolism and a sense of the absurd. Thus, for instance, Nogreh, with her father, sister-in-law and baby, is constantly seeking places to sleep and make a temporary home. On one occasion they stay in the shell of the fuselage of a crashed aircraft and in another they are to be found camping out in a ruined palace or municipal building – in which their horse and a shepherd's flock can be seen moving through the rooms. The devastation caused by occupying armies and the destruction wrought by the Taliban on Afghani culture is neatly caught in these images.

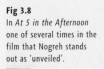

Fig 3.8
In *At 5 in the Afternoon* one of several times in the film that Nogreh stands out as 'unveiled'.

At 5 in the Afternoon is only complex in its ambitious mix of issues and themes. Within each little scene it is relatively straightforward. At the broadest level it is, as the director says, about 'Men and women, about fathers and daughters, about America and Afghanistan'. What plot there is sees Nogreh meeting a refugee poet who will help her in

her school campaign to be president. Mainly this will involve helping Nogreh to literally find her voice in public (which is where the poem comes in) – and also to be seen. In another of those absurd/symbolic moments the poet takes her to a street photographer to have her photo taken for a poster. The photographer insists on taking a photo of her wearing her full *burqa* – so she is effectively invisible.

In the latter part of the film Nogreh also has a conversation with a French soldier who has some form of peacekeeping role. The conversation is conducted in halting English, since neither knows the other's language. This is quite a common feature of contemporary films in which modern English (American English?) has become a *lingua franca*. This in itself is symbolic of contemporary politics and international relations – whatever is happening on the streets of Kabul depends to some extent on decisions taken in Washington and London.

When you get to the end of *At 5 in the Afternoon*, you won't be presented with a 'resolution'. There cannot be a 'satisfactory' ending to Nogreh's experience of her time in Kabul in the same way that an entertainment film might provide. Nogreh is an interesting and engaging character, and we need to respond to whatever experiences she has and how she manages them. But as an audience we should have learned something, or at least started to question our assumptions, having been provoked by the sounds and images representing Samira Makmalbaf's view of life on the streets of Kabul.

Case study 3.4: *Ten Canoes* (Australia, 2007)

Our final example film is also challenging, but in a different way. It raises questions about identity, our approach to the stories of indigenous peoples and how film as a medium attempts to present those stories. We might argue that engaging with this material presents us with a colonial rather than a post-colonial situation, since the original or indigenous peoples of Canada, Australia, Brazil and several other countries are still struggling for full autonomy over their lives. (For instance, you may feel differently about some of the issues in *Y tu mamá también* after watching *Ten Canoes*.)

Background

In one of the most remote parts of Australia, the Arnhem Land Peninsula in the Northern Territories, there are several small indigenous communities that were able to resist the incursion of European culture until relatively recently. In the 1930s when a remarkable social anthropologist, Donald Thomson, visited the Yolngu people he found a way of life seemingly unchanged for several millennia. He shot several thousand feet of nitrate film that was subsequently lost in a fire, but also some 4,000 still images on glass negatives that have survived to provide a unique record of daily life in the region.

David Gulpilil, one of the most high-profile indigenous Australians in the film industry, is himself from the Yolngu community. His career began in the 1970s with films such as Nic Roeg's *Walkabout* (UK/Australia, 1971) and Peter Weir's *The Last Wave* (Australia, 1976). More recently he appeared in *Rabbit-Proof Fence* (Australia, 2002) and *The Tracker* (Australia, 2002). On this last film he met the Australian director Rolf de Heer and invited him to visit Arnhem Land and to make a film there. Gulpilil and de Heer, in discussion

The United Nations statement on 'Indigenous Issues' (www.un.org/ esa/socdev/unpfii/ documents/5session_ factsheet1.pdf) suggests that rather than defining 'indigenous', local groups should be free to identify themselves as they see fit. We will refer to 'Indigenous Australians' but 'Aboriginal' is still in use in Australian documents.

www.12canoes.com.au/ is a web-based audio-visual presentation about the history and culture of the Yolngu people with a downloadable study guide.

Fig 3.9
One of the original Donald Thomson photographs from 1937 showing the hunt for magpie goose nests. Source: The Donald Thomson Ethnohistory Collection, Museum Victoria.

with many of the local people, eventually decided on the unique structure of *Ten Canoes*. The title comes from one of Thomson's photographs, showing a hunting party taking their canoes across the Arfura swamp in search of the eggs of the magpie goose.

Telling stories

Ten Canoes presents three versions of a story, each 'nested' within another. David Gulpilil is the off-screen voice (in English) introducing the landscape from an aerial view and then taking us back to a time when the Yolngu hunted for goose eggs as part of an annual cycle of food gathering. This story is shown in black and white and the look of it derives from Thomson's photographs (see Fig 3.9). The time period is not given, but it could be any time during the 300 years or so leading up to the 1930s, and might be termed 'Thomson time'.

As the men (no women on hunting parties) go about the dangerous and uncomfortable task of finding eggs and fending off crocodiles and mosquitoes, one of the older men begins to tell a story to his younger brother. The older brother, who has three wives, is worried that his sibling is getting too interested in the youngest of the wives. The story he tells is a cautionary tale about what desiring another man's wife in a close-knit community can lead to. The 'story within a story' is set within the same community many years previously, in a 'mythical time'. Of course, it looks exactly like the world in 'Thomson time', but, like the opening shots of the film, it is shown in colour. We get to hear the whole of this story and its consequences.

Fig 3.10
A production still from
Ten Canoes. Source:
The Kobal Collection/
www.picture-desk.com.

Life in the Yolngu community in mythical time is both 'simple', but also sophisticated in terms of ritual, justice, honour, etc. The story involves conflict with another community and two deaths – and, of course, a lesson for the younger brother. It is important to note that the Yolngu were not at the time of these stories struggling hunter-gatherers at the margins of subsistence. The land supported sufficient flora and fauna to allow the Yolngu to eat well, to build shelters, and to have the 'spare time' to create rituals and develop societal structures.

The Yolngu world is presented as patriarchal. The older men live with one or more wives in the central community – adolescent males must live separately in a boys' community. Full initiation into the adult world is controlled and organised.

Filmmaking, culture and the European gaze

How should we engage with a film like this? What kinds of assumptions do we make? The story in mythical time concerns 'characters' in a world that is truly alien to us. It is a 'pre-colonial' culture and therefore we face different problems about how we should respond. In a sense we are being placed in the position of Western social anthropologists meeting a community for the first time. One of our concerns must be a question about how much the film crew misrepresents or distorts/disrupts the lives of the people in the community and misrepresents their story. To a certain extent, this is a consequence of all media production. Yolngu culture can only appear on screen in a mediated form. However, there are several mitigating features in the approach adopted here.

First, it is worth stressing that the fictional world presented on screen is just that – a re-created fiction. The contemporary Yolngu live in a world that uses SUVs, internet banking and satellite television. When the idea of the film was first discussed, the goose egg hunt had lapsed as an annual event and it was the circulation of photographs from the Thomson Archive that stimulated interest. The idea to develop the story around the 'Ten Canoes' photograph came from within the community.

When it came to actually shooting the film, the small crew led by de Heer (the 'Balanda' as white men are termed) lived within the community for the duration of the shoot, much like the 'participant observers' of social anthropology. All of the characters in the story are played by Yolngu people, many of whom are, or have been, artists or live performers, but none were previously film actors. Casting and scripting was not straightforward. Individuals wanted to play the characters who were recognisable in the photographs as their ancestors and tradition forbade people from representing characters from the 'wrong' family group. As a consequence some roles had only one possible player. The script (everything is spoken in one of the Yolngu languages) was difficult to formalise, since some players spoke different local languages and the lines had to be translated and re-translated to create some form of continuity. One of the community, Peter Djigirr acted as co-director as well as actor and translator.

In the completed film it is clear that all these difficulties were overcome and ownership of the narrative appears to rest with the Yolngu themselves – certainly they express themselves as more than satisfied with the outcome. In fact, the process of filmmaking became a vibrant exercise in oral history and rediscovery of a way of life. There was sufficient knowledge among the older Yolngu to make it possible to build the canoes shown in the photographs, and the work on memory and culture has subsequently spawned a whole series of cultural productions, including exhibitions, books and training programmes. The film also exists in three different versions with the narration available in English and the local language and the subtitles removed for local screening.

The unique structure of the film derives from the compromise between the demands of American/European film narratives and the sensibilities of the Yolngu. The local people were attracted to the idea of reconstructing the goose egg hunt, but this was essentially non-dramatic. For the Yolngu it would be wrong to insert dramatic conflict into the reconstruction – but it was allowable in the 'mythical time', and this was how the film developed.

If the film had remained as an interesting cultural project enjoyed by the Yolngu, it would have been a worthwhile project in itself. But a feature film is a potentially universal cultural artefact. How would other audiences, especially non-indigenous Australian audiences, react? In her blog, the Australian academic Liz Conor, a former editor of the Australian media education magazine *Metro*, offers a perceptive observation. She describes an Australian audience anticipating something that will take them into the mythical time (the 'dreaming', as Australian writing has it) – a time when 'original Australia' was not sullied by capitalism and industrialism. They are, as she puts it, 'Western Moderns appraising the difference of the "Native"'. What will happen?

> With utmost respect the non-indigenous patrons take in the opening scene. Naked, perfectly fit men, with all the gravitas of millennia of tradition, stride out in single file to hunt. Very intently we watch as the trailing man calls them to halt. This is surely serious but unfathomable 'business' of some sort. 'I refuse to walk at the back' he declares. Has some law been violated? Is this a challenge to customary command? Has the hunt lost its way, or an ancestor made a sign? 'Somebody is farting' he says, and audible relief staggers down the aisles.

Conor's short entry is well worth reading in full (at <lizconorcomment.blogspot. com/2006/07/ten-canoes-timely-release_15.html>). She argues that *Ten Canoes* allows us to think about a particular kind of society that survived for thousands of years and to do so without suffering the curse of the colonialist's imagination and treating indigenous communities as either noble savages or primitive people. Part of the success of the film is in the leisurely pacing and refusal to over-dramatise the conflicts. This is a different, not inferior, mode of storytelling and we may have to work to appreciate it – working hard to resist the urge to look for conventional narrative pleasures, enjoying what else is on offer and thinking about Yolngu culture in new ways. *Ten Canoes* has been generally well received, but it still represents a mediated view of another culture, a useful starting point, but not a definitive representation.

One of Conor's concerns is that representations of life in indigenous Australian communities are often caught within an **orientalist** perspective:

> For the earliest white writers, brawling Aborigines were shocking mimics of their own excess. Yet they also saw violence as inherent in the 'savage' and not as the manifestation of displaced peoples suffering loss of livelihood and status, and loss of the only place to be who they knew themselves to be.
>
> (Conor, ibid.)

Ten Canoes offers an alternative to this, but it also prompts us to think about films that might be made from directly within the indigenous Australian communities and which would deal with the contemporary issues facing such communities. One such film – controversial in its depiction of family life – is *Toomelah* (Australia, 2011).

Toomelah is the name of an 'Aboriginal reserve', also known originally as a 'mission' (this is the director's description) in New South Wales. The film is directed by Ivan Sen. His mother came from Toomelah and he has maintained contact with the community. Made for virtually no money, with Sen himself acting as the sole 'crew', it is a powerful film which offers no viewing framework as such, throwing an audience straight into a

See Chapter 5 on **Orientalism** and chapter 8 on **postcolonialism**.

Fig 3.11
Young Daniel Connor is the central character in *Toomelah*.

narrative about a young boy and his relationships with his own family and a local drugs gang. It isn't immediately clear whether this is a documentary or fiction. Either way it exposes the kinds of situation that Conor refers to – this community has many social problems. One of the older characters refers to the 'stolen generation' of children taken away from their families by the white authorities (a 'secret history' that was revealed through popular films such as *Rabbit-Proof Fence*).

Like *Ten Canoes*, *Toomelah* is available on DVD, and there is interview material with Ivan Sen on YouTube and an official website at http://www.toomelahthemovie.com/.

Summary

The four main film titles discussed in this chapter have been presented in order of accessibility for film readers relatively new to films from another culture – and film industry and culture outside North America or the UK. Accessibility is partly about familiarity and partly about what else you need to know in order to be able to not only read the film to make sense of it, but also to feel confident about your own perspective on what is being presented. *Die Welle* and *Y tu mamá también* may be understood and enjoyed without any prior knowledge – but they need to be studied in detail and in context for a richer reading. *At 5 in the Afternoon* and the Australian films need some context before you begin. Watching a film like *Toomelah* 'cold' is not advisable unless you are already aware of the issues.

The Iranian and Australian films have appeared at film festivals and been warmly received, but the context of festival viewing is not the same as watching a film on release in a cinema or renting/downloading a film for personal viewing (see Chapter 7). If possible, it is useful to search for an official website and to look for a press pack or director's statement or to read a review from a writer you have come to trust. Official websites tend to disappear after a few years, but for a film like *Ten Canoes* there have been many carefully considered postings (e.g. http://blog.cinemaautopsy.com/2010/06/14/yolngu-storytelling-in-ten-canoes/ and many others).

References and further reading

Arroyo, Jose (2002) 'Review of *Y tu mamá también*', *Sight and Sound*, April.

Basoli, A.G. (2002) 'Sexual Awakenings and Stark Social Realities: Interview with Alfonso Cuarón on *Y tu mamá también*', *Cineaste* 27(3), June.

Brooks, Xan (2002) at http://www.guardian.co.uk/Archive/Article/0,4273,4463899,00.html (accessed 8 August 2004).

De Sica, Vittorio (1948) 'Why *Ladri di Biciclette*?', *La fiera letteraria*, February, reprinted in David Overby (1978).

Heuser, David at http://www.davidheuser.com/YTuMama.htm.

Lawrenson, Edward (2002) Interview with Alfonso Cuarón, *Sight and Sound*, April.

Miller, Toby (2010) 'National Cinema Abroad: The New International Division of Cultural Labour, From Production to Viewing', in Nataša Ďurovičová and Kathleen Newman (eds) *World Cinemas, Transnational Perspectives*, New York and Abingdon: Routledge.

Overby, David (ed.) (1978) *Springtime in Italy: A Reader on Neo-realism*, London: Talisman.

Robinson, Andrew (2004) *Satyajit Ray, The Inner Eye*, London: I. B. Tauris.

Smith, Paul Julian (2002) 'Heaven's Mouth', *Sight and Sound*, April (http://www.bfi. org.uk/sightandsound/feature/49).

Sorlin, Pierre (1991) *European Cinemas, European Societies 1939–1990*, London: Routledge.

Sorlin, Pierre (1996) *Italian National Cinema, 1896–1996*, London: Routledge.

Stafford, Roy (2011) 'Global and Local in Media Education', in Elaine Scarratt and Jon Davison (eds) *The Media Teacher's Handbook*, Abingdon: Routledge.

Williams, Christopher (ed.) (1980) *Realism and the Cinema*, London: Routledge & Kegan Paul/BFI.

Further viewing

These films are all in some sense 'youth pictures', some featuring school/college scenes, others using different genre mixes:

4 Minutes (*Vier Minuten*, Germany, 2006)
The Class (*Entre les murs*, France, 2008)
Drømmen (*We Shall Overcome*, Denmark/UK, 2005)
The Edukators (Germany, 2004)
Knallhart (*Tough Enough*, Germany, 2006)
NEDS (UK/France/Italy, 2010)
Sin nombre (Mexico/US, 2009)
Turn Me On, Dammit! (*Få meg på, for faen*, Norway, 2011)
You Are the Apple of My Eye (*Na xie nian, wo men yi qi zhui de nu hai*, Taiwan, 2011)
La Zona (Mexico, 2007)

The following are interesting in terms of neo-realism and the work of the Makhmalbafs:

Stray Dogs (Iran/France/Afghanistan, 2004) directed by Marziyeh Meshkini
Buddha Who Collapsed Out of Shame (Iran, 2007) directed by Hana Makhmalbaf

Films about indigenous communities in Australia:

Rabbit-Proof Fence (Australia, 2002)
Samson and Delilah (Australia, 2002)
The Sapphires (Australia, 2012)

CHAPTER 4

National cinemas in Europe: contrasting experiences

In the introduction to this book we noted that the analysis of specific national cinemas has been one strategy for exploring cinema outside Hollywood. Often it has seemed that defining what is 'national' has been part of keeping Hollywood at bay. But there are many problems associated with the concept of the national, and in this chapter we explore what a focus on national cinemas means in the context of a supranational 'European cinema'.

Defining national cinema

The concept of **national cinema** sounds straightforward until you begin to investigate it in any detail. In a special issue of *Screen* on 'Questioning National Identities' in 1989, Andrew Higson suggested the following possible ways of conceptualising 'national cinema':

• as an economic entity equated with the 'domestic' film industry of a country with questions about ownership and control;

• through a text-based approach: what kinds of themes do domestic films deal with; how do they conceive nationhood or national character?

- through an approach via all the kinds of films distributed and enjoyed by audiences within the nation state, irrespective of the films' national origins – an approach often fuelled by fear of **cultural imperialism;**
- as a category for film criticism associated with 'quality art cinema' steeped in the high culture and/or **modernist** heritage of a particular nation state – the conscious attempt to say something about the nation/national culture through artistic expression.

(Higson 1989: 36–37)

The year 1989 was a particularly interesting time to be questioning national identities, as the fall of the Berlin Wall a few weeks after Higson's paper was published was the start of a process that would eventually produce several new nation states in Europe. It was also a time when critical theory itself was in flux with the impact of **postmodernism** and the promotion of ideas about local, global and **transnational** as well as questions about identities. We will explore ideas about aspects of national identity later, but the four approaches outlined above have remained relevant ever since and they will be discernible in different ways in how we tackle national cinema in this chapter. It may also be worth adding a fifth approach:

- how is the national cinema of one country understood by audiences in other territories, i.e. in the form of film exports?

In a collection of papers edited by Justin Ashby and **Andrew Higson** (2000), Pierre Sorlin discusses how British films were viewed in 'Continental Europe' in the latter half of the twentieth century and Marcia Landy discusses their appeal in the US during the same period. These observations are useful in suggesting some of the ways in which British films could be both 'national' and 'international' when viewed against other local productions. Both Britain and France have again become strong film-exporting countries over the past ten years and together they will provide one focus. In addition, we will look at one other single European territory and one small regional European grouping in order to explore specific questions. Covering a range of national industries in this way emphasises the diversity of 'national cinemas' in Europe. Europe-wide agencies such as the EU and the Council of Europe consider film and the audio-visual sector more broadly to be of great importance – both as economic and cultural 'drivers' of development across the continent. Some of the European policies on film are considered in Chapter 6.

There are many other discussions of what national cinema might mean, several of them referenced or re-evaluated in *Theorising National Cinema* by Valentina Vitali and Paul Willemen (2006). Higson's 1989 paper has been used simply because it offers what seems to be a useful set of accessible ideas.

Andrew Higson revisited his argument about national cinema in 2006, recognising that although much of his earlier work was still valid it was problematic to suggest that what 'fitted' into a British context could be taken as a model for the diversity of global cinema.

Defining the domestic film industry: national cinema as economic entity

How do we define what constitutes 'national' production? For instance, are all films that are physically made within a country's boundaries part of its national cinema? Does this include films made by overseas companies and crews? What about the opposite scenario in which 'our' filmmakers travel abroad to make films? Perhaps ownership of the production (i.e. who has invested in the film and who owns the rights to the film) is most important? If the issue is also about ownership of cultural property, should we focus on who wrote the script or who is in the cast and crew? In many European countries where public money is being invested in film production these questions become important in terms of accountability – why are we (as taxpayers) funding this film (and not that one)?

	Cultural Test	Points
A	**Cultural Content**	
A1	Film set in the UK	4
A2	Lead characters British citizens or residents	4
A3	Film based on British subject matter or underlying material	4
A4	Original dialogue recorded mainly in English language	4
	Total Section A	**16**
B	**Cultural Contribution**	
	Film represents/reflects a diverse British culture, British heritage or British creativity	4
	Total Section B	**4**
C	**Cultural Hubs**	
C1	Studio and/or location shooting/ Visual Effects/ Special Effects	2
C2	Music Recording/Audio Post Production/Picture Post Production	1
	Total Section C	**3**
D	**Cultural Practitioners**	
D1	Director	1
D2	Scriptwriter	1
D3	Producer	1
D4	Composer	1
D5	Lead Actors	1
D6	Majority of Cast	1
D7	Key Staff (lead cinematographer, lead production designer, lead costume designer, lead editor, lead sound designer, lead visual effects supervisor, lead hair and makeup supervisor)	1
D8	Majority of Crew	1
	Total Section D	**8**
	TOTAL ALL SECTIONS (pass mark 16)	**31**

Fig 4.1 The UK 'cultural test' for film productions. Source: British Film Institute. This summary of the cultural test is a living document and is accurate at the time of going to press.

A good example of a structured response to these questions was formulated by the UK Film Council with its **cultural test** as set out in Fig 4.1. (The responsibilities undertaken by the UK Film Council – the cultural test refers to Schedule 1 of the Films Act 1985 – passed to the British Film Institute on 1 April 2011, and in June 2013 the test was listed at http://www.bfi.org.uk/film-industry/british-certification-tax-relief/cultural-test-film.)

The cultural test is applied to any film production that seeks public funding or tax relief in the UK and does not otherwise qualify as an official **co-production**. Co-productions are legally agreed according to contracts governed by **bilateral**

agreements between countries or via the European Convention on Cinematographic Co-production (see http://conventions.coe.int/Treaty/en/Reports/Html/147.htm).

To pass the test and qualify as sufficiently 'British', a production must score at least 16 points out of 31. This has resulted in several surprising decisions. For instance, in 2009 the animation film *Fantastic Mr Fox* qualified as 'British' under the cultural test, as did *The Dark Knight* (as listed on the UKFC website, downloaded from http://industry.bfi.org.uk/ctproductions on 20 April 2012). *Fantastic Mr Fox* was made by Fox Animation (part of News Corporation) in conjunction with three other US companies, two of which had connections to its American director Wes Anderson. Not surprisingly, IMDb lists the film as simply American. How then does it become 'British'? It is a British cultural property (Roald Dahl's stories). The studio facilities were at Three Mills in London's East End. Music was recorded at Abbey Road and much of the post-production was also completed in London. The (voice) cast and crew also had British members, but even so it must have been a close decision to rack up 16 points and IMDb carries at least one User Comment complaining that the Dahl stories have been 'Americanised'. *The Dark Knight* has a British director and scriptwriter, but its content is resolutely 'American'.

These two productions are good examples of **'Hollywood UK'** – a more suggestive term than the official **inward investment** to describe Hollywood studio films made in the UK. We could also find examples of American films made by UK-based companies or by British creative teams working independently in the US. The Coen Brothers' early international success *Fargo* (US/UK, 1996) was a British film made by two UK-based companies and in a study of 'British cinema' we might not be surprised to see discussion of director Michael Winterbottom's work on two North American films *The Claim* (UK/France/Canada, 2000) and *The Killer Inside Me* (US/Sweden/Canada/UK, 2010). Canadian involvement in British films is partly explained by the co-production treaty between the UK and Canada. The Swedish identity of several films made by Revolution Films, the British company owned by Winterbottom and producer Andrew Eaton, is explained by the presence in the production credits of Film i väst, a public film fund in Western Sweden which aims to bring at least part of a film's production to its region – and which since 1997 has co-produced around 200 international features (see Screenbase on Screendaily.com).

Trishna (UK/India/ Sweden, 2011) is a Revolution Films production shot entirely in India, but sound-mixing was carried out in Sweden.

Fig 4.2
The Claim, shot in the Canadian Rockies with a multinational cast, was described by *Time Out* as 'The most remarkable British film'.

Thus, in the UK, there has been a strong central agency dealing with 'official' policy towards the British film industry and British film culture since the establishment of the UK Film Council in 2000. Before that there were government policies without clear coordination. The UK has had to create a national policy to deal with an industry involved in **transnational** production. To explore what this kind of approach means in more detail, we will compare the British and French situation.

France and the UK: the same but different?

France and the UK have the two biggest film industries in Europe and in terms of **filmed entertainment** (the total revenue generated by films in cinemas, on TV, video and online), the UK is the third most valuable market internationally (after the US and Japan). France has the biggest cinema market in Europe with the best export performance for films not in English. French film exports go first to other territories with francophone markets, including Belgium, Switzerland, Canada (Quebec) and francophone Africa. France and the UK have often been contrasted because of differences in outlook both by commercial filmmakers and by cultural policy-makers, and indeed there are interesting differences between them. But there are also several important similarities.

Public support for film industry and culture

As film industries to study, France and the UK offer one important advantage. They both publish detailed statistics on all aspects of film industry and culture. These data are free to download from the CNC and the British Film Institute.

The CNC (Centre National du Cinéma et de l'Image Animée) was set up in 1946 to oversee all aspects of French cinema – and later television. Data are available (in English) from various parts of its websites but the annual report is available from www.cnc.fr/web/en/publications.

The British Film Institute (BFI) was set up in 1933 and its role, alongside other public bodies, has changed over time. In 2011 the BFI took over most of the functions undertaken by the UK Film Council which operated in a similar way to the CNC between 2000 and 2011. The BFI website covers the whole range of its activities but the former responsibilities of the UKFC are accessible via www.bfi.org.uk/film-industry/ and www.bfi.org.uk/education-research/film-industry-statistics-research.

These two territories were among the first to react to the impact of Hollywood imports in the 1920s when American films took over 70 per cent of box office in both countries. From the 1930s onwards the following public policies have been tried at different times in both the UK and France as a means to support local producers and productions:

- **quota systems**, requiring cinemas (or TV stations) to show a percentage of local films;
- production support for local films funded by taxes on cinema ticket sales or levies on TV broadcasters;
- **tax incentives** for local productions (which may include inward investment from Hollywood);
- **bilateral co-production deals** with non-Hollywood partners;

- **regional support funds** to attract productions to particular regions (often as part of cultural industries regeneration projects);
- **film commissions** to support location work (again, attracting Hollywood);
- direct **public funding** of experimental/'cultural' filmmaking;
- support for **distributors** and exhibitors to encourage screenings of local and 'world' cinema;
- a *film export* support programme.

In extremis, both countries in the late 1940s attempted to restrict/reduce imports from the US (without success).

These same policies have been adopted in many other countries – especially in Europe where the development of Europe-wide audio-visual support organisations via both the European Union and the **Council of Europe** have become increasingly important (see Chapter 6).

A useful diagram showing the French support system is shown in Fig 4.3.

The general point to make here is that government policy in both countries is designed to protect and encourage the local audio-visual sector and to support specific cultural aims related to film. Both aims have been seen as opposed to the free market capitalism of the American film industry. The relationship between Hollywood and these two industries is explored in detail by Toby Miller and colleagues in *Global Hollywood 2* (2005). They suggest that the argument is conventionally presented as an opposition between *laissez-faire* industries such as Hollywood, Bollywood and Hong Kong, and *dirigiste* industries driven by cultural policies – but that the situation is actually much more complex than a simple binarism (Miller *et al.* 2005: 4).

The French agency Unifrance is recognised as one of the most successful international organisations supporting exports of its national film industry (see http://en.unifrance.org/)

The Council of Europe represents 47 countries in a broadly defined 'Europe' and enables legal agreements and support structures covering many aspects of contemporary social relations, including 'Cinema and audio-visual' (see http://hub.coe.int).

Laissez-faire (literally 'leave it to do its own thing') is the concept from classical economics associated with the 'self-regulating market'. Both it and *dirigiste* (or 'state-directed') are heavily loaded terms, often used as insults by opposing sides of the argument.

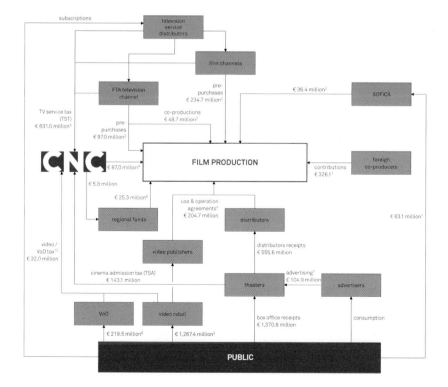

Fig 4.3
Primary sources of funding for cinema production in France in 2011 (€ million). Source: From 'Results 2011' available from: http://www.cnc.fr/web/en/publications/.

The term *dirigiste* implies government direction of the industry and the main infrastructure-building policies in both the UK and France have tended to come from Labour/Socialist Party governments. However, similar policies have also been adopted by Conservative governments in other countries. The really important point is that public funding, sometimes rather sneeringly termed **soft money** in the international film business, is actually a feature of most film-producing territories. Some form of tax incentive exists in most countries, including the US – and of course, Hollywood productions benefit from those incentives if they decide to locate a production in the UK or France. Fig 4.3 shows that the biggest element in French film investment comes from 'foreign co-producers'. In the UK, 'inward investment' by Hollywood studios is key.

If we look at the difference between the UK and France, we do see less direction from government and a less direct connection between the sources of funding and production outcomes in the UK. Whether this has made a big difference in terms of what the policies have achieved is open to debate. In France, the use of levies and quotas has ensured that TV and film companies are forced to contribute to production funding. In the UK, the publicly owned TV channels BBC and Channel 4 have engaged in film production according to their own internal policies, whereas commercial companies like ITV and BSkyB have been open to criticism for their limited support for British films. The British system of taxing cinema seats, the Eady Levy, was instigated by Labour in 1950 and abolished by the Conservatives in 1985. It has generally been seen as benefiting American producers coming into the UK more than local producers (Walker 1986: 460–461; Street 2009: 19).

Support funds for production and distribution in the UK come from two sources, so-called 'Treasury money' from general taxation, via the Department for Culture Media and Sport, and dispensations from the National Lottery, both now distributed by the BFI. Tax relief remains the largest single source of public funding. Like France, UK producers also receive relatively small amounts of EU funding. Both countries also fund National Film Schools.

The French system of film subsidy is part of the French government's policy of '**cultural exception**' – the commitment following the 1993 GATT talks to treat cultural industries as 'different' in terms of regulation and subsidy.

Some of the differences between the two countries' funding policies produce interesting results. France has tended to produce more films each year (200-plus as compared to around 120 in the UK – but see recent changes in definitions below). This may be partly due to the *avance sur recettes* (advance on receipts) first instituted in 1960. This advance (you pay it back only if you make profits) was set up to target 'creative' films of 'quality' in order to try to stimulate an industry facing declining audiences (Hayward 1993: 46). Its introduction coincided with the development of auteur cinema in France (see Chapter 7). Combined with other policies to support regional art cinemas, small-scale auteurist production has survived in France. The criticism has been that since the advance is only awarded after a script has been accepted by a committee at CNC, there is 'safe innovation, eclecticism going mostly by the board' (Hayward 1993: 48).

In the UK, similar processes have developed at different times but never with the simplicity and consistency of the *avance sur recettes*. This has produced a much more mixed bag of 'alternative content', sometimes more experimental or more political. The establishment of Channel 4 as a 'publisher-broadcaster' instigated a new independent film and TV sector in the UK in 1982. Alterations in funding in the 1990s changed practices again but it is interesting that in the 2000s a wave of '**micro-budget**' productions in the UK, several hundred films with budgets too low (under £500,000) to register in UKFC statistics, began to appear – some funded with small amounts of public money, others privately (*Low and Micro-Budget Film Production in the UK*, UK Film Council, 2008). Compared to auteurist French productions, these micro-budget films are more genre-orientated. In its *2012 Statistical Yearbook* the BFI incorporated these films into overall production numbers and revealed that in 2010 there had been 343 films produced in the UK, with over 200 micro-budget productions. Only a handful of these films have been seen by significant audiences in cinemas.

The French system of support has its critics. Vincent Maraval of the production and sales company Wild Bunch created a public debate when he claimed (*Le Monde*, 28 December 2012) that French production costs were being inflated by artificially high fees paid to actors. Maraval's argument is that because TV companies are required to fund French film productions they compete to attract local stars in order to get good ratings from broadcasts of the films. But often these same stars have no international appeal and the films don't sell abroad. The inflated fees also drive up fees for other film productions. While agreeing with much of his argument, other French commentators fear that this debate will be used to attack cultural funding in more general terms – especially at a time of austerity and cuts in public expenditure.

Film culture in France and the UK

> The cultural myth of the French *cinephile* is just that – a myth. The French are not and, with the exception of one period in history, have never been avid filmgoers.
>
> (Hayward 1993: 48)

Susan Hayward's pithy comment points to a number of contradictions about film culture in France. In 2011, French cinemas achieved 215.6 million admissions, the highest for 45 years. However, French pre-eminence in Europe was only established after the massive declines in audiences in the UK, Germany and Italy between the mid-1950s and the late 1970s. French audiences peaked at 424 million in 1947. In 1946 UK audiences peaked at 1,635 million. Those UK audiences moved to TV much more quickly but today they are more likely than their French counterparts to spend money on subscription channels, DVD/Blu-ray, VOD, etc. (see Fig 1.13 in Chapter 1 for figures on 'filmed entertainment').

The other aspect of the myth is that French audiences love art cinema. Despite the structures in place as outlined above, most French audiences still watch American films dubbed into French, or French popular comedies or action films. CNC statistics obscure the American market share by referring to films such *Harry Potter*, *Inception* and *Clash of the Titans* as 'British' (i.e. 'European'). Nevertheless, the same figures do suggest that the French market is more receptive to films from other European countries, or from Asia, Africa and Latin America.

British commentary on French cinema from industry and general media commentators is split between those who want film to have the same cultural status as it does in France and those who dismiss French cinema as pretentious precisely because of its cultural aspirations. Hayward's myth is alive and well in these attitudes – which are based mainly on the 30 or so French films that reach the UK each year. But actually France and the UK have quite similar proportions of funding and audience support for specialised as distinct from mainstream cinema. The differences are that France has more cinemas designated as *d'art et d'essai* (see Chapter 7) which may be found in almost every town across the country. In the UK, such cinemas are only in larger towns and cities, and specialised cinema fans must seek out both the occasional multiplex screen and alternative venues such as film societies and community cinemas.

But what kinds of films receive public funding support in the UK and France? It would not be appropriate here to discuss the wider issues about cultural policies in the two countries, but it is useful to point to the support for 'diversity' – films for diverse audiences and films about diverse cultures. This means a recognition of the changing nature of the demographics of the two states as a result of migration and also the changes in attitudes to a range of social issues. In theoretical terms, as Higson (2006: 16) points out, 'it has become conventional to define the nation as the mapping of an **imagined community** with a secure and shared identity and sense of belonging, on to a carefully demarcated geo-political space'. This is a reference to Benedict Anderson's 1983 book on *Imagined Communities* which has proved highly influential. Anderson suggests that it has become a function of media discourse in any country to sustain a sense of a shared national culture. However, that sense of a shared culture is not bounded by the borders of states and individuals, and groups can imagine themselves as part of more than one 'community' in the case of exiles and migrants. At the same time, the **fragmenting** of national media audiences means that not everyone in the nation shares an interest in the same events and issues. Questions of personal and national identity have become increasingly important in debates about film culture. We will investigate this through the development of diaspora cinemas in the UK and France.

Britain and France received significant groups of exiles from other European countries in the nineteenth and early twentieth centuries, including filmmakers fleeing Germany after 1933. Emeric Pressburger was one such exile who (in partnership with Michael Powell) then focused on stories about British 'national identity' in the 1940s.

Diaspora cinema in Europe

Diaspora filmmakers – and diaspora audiences – have been an important feature of European cinema since the 1970s when the first generation of post-war migrants from Asia, Africa and the Caribbean began to press successfully for opportunities to develop their own ideas about film culture. The diaspora concept was established well before that period and it is an element in several discussions in this book, so we will try to define it here.

Diaspora

The term diaspora comes from Classical Greek for 'disperse' or 'scatter across' and was used to describe the exile of Jews from the area now known as Palestine in the seventh to eighth centuries. It refers to both the process of dispersal and to the dispersed population. In contemporary usage, diaspora is used to refer to many contemporary movements as well as other important historical migrations. In particular, the European slave trade has been recognised as responsible for the creation of an African diaspora in the Americas, and European colonialism and imperialism has been responsible for the forced movements of labour from South and East Asia (see Chapter 10). Contemporary migrations may be encouraged by economic conditions or forced by political persecution.

Recognised diasporic communities share some of these features:

■ a definable community associated with ethnicity, language or religion which sustains specific cultural practices;

■ a retained sense of identity with the country of birth (or the country of parents or grandparents);

■ an expressed wish to return 'home', but often without a real will to do so;

■ an interest or even involvement in political issues 'at home';

■ an ambivalent attitude towards the national identity of the host country – which may range from enthusiastic embrace to some form of negotiated isolation.

In a globalised world of hybrid and transnational cultures, diasporas are widely recognised – and also quite complex in make-up. For example, the expansion of the European Union in 2004 and the possibility of the free movement of labour saw a temporary migration of large numbers of Polish workers to the UK. This large group would not necessarily comprise a diaspora – especially when many would return to Poland after a few years. But the UK has had Polish migrant communities in several parts of the country since the 1930s and therefore the new temporary migrants found existing communities with a distinct social infrastructure in place (but also perhaps different notions of what a Polish identity might mean). The increase in numbers has meant that film distributors and exhibitors have identified a new market for contemporary Polish films which now make appearances in English subtitled prints at various locations in the UK on a regular basis.

Besides the UK and French experience discussed below, the Turkish diaspora in Germany is served in similar ways to the Indian/Pakistani diasporas in the UK, with films from Turkey attracting significant audiences and a number of Turkish-German filmmakers gaining a national and international profile (see Chapter 6).

Diaspora filmmaking in the UK

The UK government encouraged migration from the Caribbean in the late 1940s and early 1950s in order to fill labour shortages. Migration from South Asia started a little later. Economic migration was then restricted by the infamous Commonwealth Immigrants Act of 1968 (which withdrew access to a British passport for most non-white Commonwealth citizens). Despite this legislation, the UK has remained a relatively open society and further diasporic communities have developed.

One of the first diaspora filmmakers in the UK was **Horace Ové**, whose feature film *Pressure* (1975) was funded as a low-budget production by the British Film Institute. The film took several years to make and then to achieve a limited release. It dealt with the experience of a second-generation Caribbean youth, born and educated in the UK, who is at first at odds with his parents and older brother (educated in the Caribbean) but is then politicised by the prejudice he encounters in searching for a job. Further films funded by the BFI followed, including *Burning an Illusion* (1981) by Menelik Shabazz. Black British filmmaking (as it was called at the time) then became associated with the new opportunities offered by Channel 4, the UK's new TV channel established with an aim of both catering for diverse audiences and commissioning work from a similarly diverse range of new filmmakers. The campaigning Greater London Council with its anti-racist cultural strategies became an important focus for the same filmmakers.

The 2011 UK Census revealed that 579,000 UK residents were born in Poland, making them the second largest 'foreign-born' group after Indians. Similarly, Polish as a 'first language' is second only to English in England.

You Are God (*Jesteś Bogiem*, Poland, 2012), a film about a Polish rap group, was released simultaneously in Poland and the UK – where it made the Box Office Top 20 for two weeks.

Izzat (Norway, 2005) is an example of a diaspora genre film – telling the story of young second-generation Norwegian-Pakistanis involved in gang culture and criminality using a narrative structure not dissimilar to that of *Goodfellas* (US, 1990).

Horace Ové (b. 1939 in Trinidad) came to the UK in 1960 to study painting, photography and interior design, eventually moving into filmmaking.

Fig 4.4
The brothers at the breakfast table in *Pressure*. Tony (Herbert Norville) has bacon and eggs but the older Colin (Oscar James) has an avocado.

Retake Film and Video was a North London-based South Asian collective whose short feature *Majdhar* (1984) told the story of a young Pakistani woman brought to the UK for marriage to an older man.

Handsworth Songs is a meditation on the history of African and Caribbean migration to the UK using archive material edited imaginatively with footage of the 'uprisings' of black youth and community resistance to racism in London and Birmingham. John Akomfrah's 2012 film *Nine Muses* makes for an interesting comparison.

The 'Workshop Agreement' between the UK film union, the ACCT, and the Independent Filmmakers' Association (IFA) made it possible for new workshop franchises to be funded to work on films for broadcast on Channel 4. The agreement allowed for new kinds of working practices and four groups were established in London by African-Caribbean and South Asian filmmakers. Black Audio Film Collective, Sankofa, Ceddo and the **Retake Film and Video Collective** all produced work that was seen in a variety of community-based and educational screenings as well as broadcast on Channel 4 and screened in specialised cinemas.

In 1984 to 1985 the Greater London Council's Anti-Racist Film Programme and similar initiatives such as Channel 4's late night film screenings not only screened material by the new groups but also imported material from African-American, African and Indian 'New Cinema' filmmakers. The work in the UK was intensely political and educational, with the result that the British diaspora filmmakers became part of the international networks of Third Cinema activists (see Chapter 8).

The Black and Asian Workshop filmmakers were heavily engaged with issues of identity and with forms of cultural resistance that included explorations of colonialist imagery and an attempt to create different narratives of British history (see Hill (1999: ch. 11) for a detailed study of these developments). The most successful and influential film from the workshops was Black Audio and Film Collective's *Handsworth Songs* (1986, winner of the John Grierson Award for Best Documentary Feature); but there were two linked problems. The avant-garde approach of some of the work and the political nature of most of it meant that it did not have a popular (as distinct from activist or art cinema) audience. Because of this, commercial producers were unlikely to fund further films. The GLC was abolished by the Thatcher government in 1986 and by the early 1990s public funding of the arts was being cut and Channel 4 was beginning to change direction. Some of the major names from the period, most notably John Akomfrah (from Black Audio) and **Isaac Julien** (from Sankofa), have since become known as 'artist filmmakers' with their films appearing as gallery installations as well as on cinema screens.

In contemporary British cinema, the most successful Black British filmmakers are associated with a genre known in the film industry as the 'urban film'. Perhaps drawing on the notion of 'urban music', this categorisation covers films focusing on youth stories involving romance, crime and music set in multicultural UK cities (usually London). The key film in this cycle is *Kidulthood* (UK, 2006) and the key figure is actor/writer/director Noel Clarke. Clarke is a good example of how young Black British talent tended to move into television (where he first gained celebrity status in *Dr Who*), music or theatre rather than specialised film from the late 1990s onwards and who are now engaged in mainstream rather than specialised cinema.

Theatre and television as well as the novel provided the launchpads for filmmakers from the South Asian diaspora. The playwright and novelist Hanif Kureshi provided the scripts for several important British films of the 1980s and 1990s, including key films about British Asian culture in *My Beautiful Laundrette* (1985) and *My Son the Fanatic* (1999). Other established writers such as Meera Syal (*Anita and Me*, 2002) and Ayub Khan-Din (*East is East*, 1999) provided autobiographical scripts. All of these films address life in the UK as a British Asian, but they do so with some confidence about discussions of identity. Although some of the films (e.g. *East is East*) have created controversy in their representations of Asian cultures, most of them mix comedy and drama successfully for UK audiences. Part of that confidence comes from the relative prosperity and security of some British Asian communities (but certainly not all) and by the fact that since the 1970s there has been a significant South Asian film distribution circuit in the UK, in 'Asian cinemas' in the 1970s, on video in the 1980s and in selected multiplexes since the late 1990s.

Isaac Julien was a Cannes prize winner with *Young Soul Rebels* (UK, 1991) and in 2001 he was nominated for the Turner Prize (the major UK art prize).

The first British Asian film is recorded as *A Private Enterprise* (1974) directed by Peter K. Smith and written by Dilip Hiro for the BFI (http://www.screenonline.org.uk/film/id/490687/index.html).

Case study 4.1: Gurinder Chadha as a British diaspora filmmaker

Gurinder Chadha was born into a Punjabi family in Kenya but migrated to the UK as an infant in the early 1960s. She grew up in Southall, West London, a key location for various Indian diaspora communities. Her early career was as a broadcast journalist but in 1989 she directed a short documentary for Channel 4 and the British Film Institute, *I'm British But ...*, which explored the then still relatively new designation of 'British Asian'. Interviewing young people like herself whose parents had left India, Pakistan or Bangladesh and started new lives in the UK, she was able to present articulate witnesses, carefully chosen from Wales, Scotland and Northern Ireland as well as England, who deliver reasoned arguments about how they feel both Asian and something else (which may be Scottish, Welsh or Irish rather than British).

More conventional in structure than the workshop films of only a few years earlier, Chadha's film also focused on the developing ***bhangra*** music scene which was then providing new opportunities for performers and new social opportunities for young South Asian women at special dance events in Central London. Discussing the film more than 20 years later, Anupama Arora and Sandrine Sanos (2011) suggest that the film may not have been fully appreciated at the time. They begin by referencing a quote by Chadha herself reflecting on how she felt watching a presentation of 'Black and British' films around the time she made her own documentary:

Bhangra is an example of a hybrid form of popular music, developed in the UK in the 1980s, with traditional Punjabi folk songs married to Western 'beats'.

Fig 4.5
Kalapreet perform 'Oos Pardesh' on the roof of a shop on Southall Broadway in *I'm British But …*

a lot of the discussion around the films focused on the pain of exile, the pain of separation, and the pain of racism. The problem with my film is that it's actually very celebratory, and at that moment in time, it couldn't easily be accommodated within the framework of the anguish of exile.

(Original quote in Koshy 1996: 148–161)

Arora and Sanos (2011: 90) go on to argue that:

the force of Chadha's short film lies in the melancholia that rubs up against her avowedly celebratory project. It emerges out of her interviewees' complex responses and the weaving together of history and memory.

If we agree with this new reading it means that Chadha's work was much closer to the kinds of ideas (e.g. the importance of the experience of migration and racism in post-colonial Britain) explored in the Workshop films – even if it was formally conventional and less openly political.

Chadha's first fiction feature after three more short films, *Bhaji on the Beach* (1993), was well received by critics and audiences. With its strong script (written with Meera Syal), and one of the founders of Sankofa, Nadine Marsh-Edwards, as producer, the story of a small group of South Asian women of all ages going on a day trip from Birmingham to Blackpool was welcome in many ways. Charlotte Brunsdon and Karen Alexander picked out important innovations in the presentation of the characters:

Chadha and Syal are concerned with questions of feminine destiny and identity, but they show these being lived out in the complex post-colonial hybridity of contemporary Britain.

(Brunsdon 1999: 168)

What engaged critics and audiences alike was the opportunity of seeing and hearing from a section of the community so often constructed as silent.

(Alexander 1999: 112)

After two more shorts and a TV drama, Chadha's next feature took her to the US where, with her American scriptwriter husband Paul Mayeda Berges (of Japanese-Basque descent), she explored the potential hybridity of Los Angeles culture. *What's Cookin'?* (US, 2000) follows the family celebration of Thanksgiving in four different households: African-American, Jewish, Mexican and Vietnamese. The American connection would also be present in Chadha's next two films and she was linked in terms of the subject matter of one part of the *Bhaji on the Beach* narrative with Mira Nair's *Mississippi Masala* (US, 1991), another diaspora film involving a Ugandan Asian family moving to Mississippi and the ensuing 'unacceptable' romance between the daughter of the family and an African-American man (played by Denzil Washington).

Bend It Like Beckham (UK/Germany, 2002) is one of the most successful independent British films of all time. A number of reasons have been suggested as to why this story about a young British Asian woman who wants to play football as a career choice was such a popular film around the world. One reason must be because of the untapped market for women's sports films, particularly football ('soccer') in North America. The celebrity of David Beckham, named in the film's title, may have been a factor (even though Beckham was not at that time a celebrity figure in the US), but the two most important features are likely to have been, first, the way in which Chadha was able to weave aspects of public and domestic Punjabi culture into the narrative, including the set piece of a Punjabi wedding; and, second, the general 'feel-good' tone of the film – associated with the success of its young heroine. The setting is a relatively prosperous household in Hounslow, West London, and the film largely steers clear of the social realism and issue-based or class-based comedy of films like *East is East*. An interesting comparison can be made with the film adapted from the autobiographical novel *Anita and Me* by Meera Syal (UK, 2002). Both films feature a Punjabi girl growing up in the UK and developing friendships in the local white community, and both are social comedies. Syal's story, set in a small rural working-class community in Staffordshire in the 1970s, speaks more directly about the issues associated with developing an identity as a British-Asian young woman. *Anita and Me* was nowhere near as popular as Chadha's film and that may be partly at least because the family featured in *Bend It Like Beckham* and the identity questions in 2002 had become more familiar to audiences. Chadha's film ends with her central character, Jes, heading to America to take up a football scholarship.

Chadha's next film took the two winning ideas further, attempting a calculated hybrid of Anglo-American costume romance and mainstream Bollywood film in *Bride and Prejudice* (UK-US, 2004). Chadha herself has called it a 'British musical'. With a script based on Jane Austen's *Pride and Prejudice* and a cast of Indian, British and American actors, the production used several Indian locations as well as London and Los Angeles. It was photographed by the leading Indian director and cinematographer Santosh Sivan and starred Aishwarya Rai, already a major star in Hindi and other Indian cinema industries. Shot mainly in English, the film opened simultaneously in Mumbai and London.

Bride and Prejudice was deemed a success even though reviews and the general reception of the film were mixed. UK Film Council research later showed that the film was

For more on the 'exchange' of filmmakers between the UK and India see Chapter 10.

A different Jane Austen novel, *Sense and Sensibility*, was adapted for a Tamil film, *Kandukondain, Kandukondain* (India, 2000) – also starring Aishwarya Rai.

Several examples of Gurinder Chadha interviews on Indian TV are accessible on YouTube, revealing something about how her identity as a filmmaker has been constructed in India.

particularly successful in London (UKFC, *Statistical Yearbook 2005*) but in the international market it was unable to attract audiences on the scale of *Bend It Like Beckham*.

With the release of *Bride and Prejudice*, Chadha confirmed her status as a filmmaker who could work with material in the UK, North America or India. In 2012 she was reported to be working on a historical drama based on an American book about the central characters in the lead-up to Indian Independence in 1947.

Research and Explore 4.1

Try to watch as many of Gurinder Chadha's films as you can and explore what she has said about them and how they have been received.

Do you see her as essentially a British filmmaker with a distinctly Punjabi perspective or as a transnational filmmaker whose films are universal in appeal?

Bhaji on the Beach was seen as offering some kind of social statement about Asian women's lives in the UK. Have Gurinder Chadha's films since then been less analytical?

Diaspora filmmaking in France

The history of diaspora filmmaking in France is significantly different – partly because of the different colonial policies adopted by Britain and France and how these policies have influenced film culture in the post-colonial period, and partly because of the other differences in cultural policy outlined earlier in this chapter.

'African-Caribbean French' films similar to the Black British/British Asian films discussed above are difficult to identify from outside France. Paris has become a centre for both francophone African music and francophone African cinema, and many films are officially described as co-productions between France and various African countries. The Burkinabe filmmaker Idrissa Ouedraogo made a film in France, *Le Cri du cœur* (*The Heart's Cry*, Burkina Faso/France, 1994) about the experience of an immigrant African youth. Earlier, Med Hondo created a fierce satire about French colonialism in *Soleil Ô* (Mauritania/France, 1967), and Euzhan Palcy from Martinique directed the period film *La rue cases-nègres* (*Sugar Cane Alley*, France/Martinique, 1983) about growing up in the colony in the 1930s.

Martinique in the Caribbean is constitutionally part of the French Republic as an 'overseas department'.

Black actors in the UK also argue that there are not enough high-profile roles in local film and TV, but that they are able to find work in the US (e.g. Idris Elba, Chiwetel Ejiofor, Thandie Newton).

The Maghreb is usually taken to be the Northwestern region of Africa, including the former French colonies in Tunisia, Algeria and Morocco. Mauritania, also a former part of the French empire, is now also included in the definition.

Many African directors who have become internationally known on the art film circuit from the 1970s onward have either lived or trained in France and then worked on French co-productions (see Chapter 8). But the lack of a significant presence for African-Caribbean French actors on French cinema and TV screens has been raised in France alongside recent controversies about how long it took to recognise the contribution of Omar Sy to the French blockbuster *Intouchables* (France, 2011) and the poor distribution record of African-American films in France such as *Think Like A Man* (US, 2012) (see Flessel 2012; Keaton 2011).

By contrast, Maghrebi-French films have been a significant category of French cinema since 1985 when Mehdi Charef's *Le thé au harem d'Archimède* won the Jean Vigo prize for best first film. For a while this category was known as '*beur* cinema' in France but this is now seen as a derogatory and patronising term owing to its 'ghettoising appropriation by dominant discourses' (Tarr 2007: 32). '*Beur*'

Fig 4.6
Driss (Omar Sy) is the 'carer' for Philippe (François Cluzet) in *Intouchables*. Source: The Kobal Collection/www.picture-desk.com.

is French back-slang (*verlan*) for 'Arabe' and initially the term was used, as both Christian Bosséno (1992: 47) and Peter Bloom (2006: 131) point out, deliberately as a kind of commentary on the ignorance of most of the French population about the Maghreb. Many, probably the majority, of the Algerian and Moroccan migrants to France were of Berber rather than Arab origin. The term '*beur* cinema' is also confusing because it has been seen to cover films made by first-generation as well as second-generation Maghrebi-French directors (for whom issues of identity are clearly different) and films about Maghrebi communities by non-Maghrebi filmmakers. Tarr points out that Anglo-American critics and scholars use the term 'Maghrebi-French', but in France this kind of hyphenated identity is not possible because 'the universalism of French republicanism refuses to acknowledge differences between its citizens' (2007: 32).

The first films by North African migrants in France appeared in the 1960s and 1970s (see Bosséno 1992).

For a long time this issue remained 'local', since relatively few of these films got distribution deals overseas. Outside France the best-known film of the 1990s to offer an insight into Maghrebi-French culture was *La haine* (France, 1995) directed by Mathieu Kassovitz with its trio of young men, '*blanc, beur et noir*' – white Jewish, Maghrebi-French and West African-French (see case study in Chapter 1). This was sometimes described as a '*banlieue*' film – referring to the housing estates built outside Paris to house workers, many of whom are now unemployed. Even though most of these films didn't travel widely outside of France they could attract significant audiences, especially in Paris.

The export possibilities of Maghrebi-French films changed in 2006 with the popular success of *Indigènes* (*Days of Glory*, 2006) directed by Rachid Bouchareb.

Bouchareb was born in France in 1953 'of Algerian descent' and began making films in the 1980s, winning prizes and international recognition for his early short films and features. *Indigènes* was a big-budget film by European standards and it told the story of the French Army of Africa – the colonial troops from North and West Africa who fought with the Free French forces during the liberation of France. The impact of the film, which ended with a contemporary sequence at the cemetery where many of the fallen soldiers were buried, was such that it prompted the French authorities to act. They finally agreed to pay pensions that had been denied to many of the African soldiers. The film was selected as the French entry for the Foreign Language Oscar in 2007 and received a nomination.

Indigènes was a co-production between France, Morocco, Belgium and Algeria. Its budget was possible because the four actors who played the lead characters are well known in France, in particular the TV performer and mainstream film star Jamel Debbouze who co-produced the film.

Bouchareb's success no doubt helped two more French-Maghrebi directors to get international distribution. Abdellatif Kechiche wrote and directed *La graine et le mulet* (*Couscous*, France, 2007) which, unlike his earlier films, received wide distribution after winning the jury prize at the Venice Film Festival. Kechiche was born in Tunisia in 1960 and *Couscous* deals with a fisherman forced into retirement who decides to open a fish couscous restaurant. His is an extended Tunisian-French family in the Mediterranean town of Sète – rather a different setting to *les banlieues* of Paris – and the film is a family melodrama.

Ismaël Ferroukhi, born in Morocco in 1962 but educated in France, had an international festival success with *Le grand voyage* in 2004. This featured a Moroccan father and French son who share a car journey through Europe and the Middle East on the *hajj* to Mecca. Ferroukhi made the film as a story about 'ordinary Muslims' at a time when most narratives featured Muslims as victims or terrorists. However, his next film, released in France in 2011, was *Les hommes libres* (*Free Men*), a fictional story based on real events in which a young Maghrebi man becomes involved in helping North African Jews in Paris escape from the Gestapo in 1943. Ferroukhi's style is slightly softer than Bouchareb's but the film's rewriting of French wartime resistance history is just as powerful and the presence of the rising star Tahar Rahim helped it to a Top 10 entry in France.

Research and Explore 4.2

Tahar Rahim and Riz Ahmed are rising stars of European and international cinema. Investigate their careers and the kinds of films in which they have appeared.

Do their careers so far suggest any differences between opportunities for actors from diaspora communities in the UK compared to France? Or does it suggest that talented actors can move freely across international projects?

London River explores issues of identity through the meeting of a French-West African man and a mother from the Channel Islands who conversing in basic French help each other in searching for their children missing following the London bombings of 2005.

Rachid Bouchareb made *London River*, a co-production with the UK, in 2008, and in 2010 again caused controversy with a film exploring the beginnings of the campaign for Algerian independence on the streets of Paris in the 1950s. *Outside the Law* (*Hors la loi*, Algeria/France/Belgium/Italy, 2010) was again a spectacular film with the same quartet of actors who had proved popular in *Indigènes*. The struggle for Algerian independence, both directly in Algeria and on the streets of Paris,

Fig 4.7
Roschdy Zem (left) and
Jamel Debbouze as two
of the three brothers in
Hors la loi. The boxing
club where an Algerian
fighter is being trained
is an iconic setting for a
polar or a *film noir*.

remains perhaps the most contested period of French modern history. Bouchareb
makes direct links in the film between anti-colonialist struggles in Indo-China (where
the French Armed Forces were defeated in 1954) and in Africa. He also uses aspects
of the **gangster film** tradition in France in presenting the Parisian revolutionary
struggle. This co-option of a popular French genre, the *polar*, and statements in
which Bouchareb acknowledges the influence of **Jean-Pierre Melville**, are key factors
in 'repositioning' the diaspora film in the French mainstream. The *polar* refers to
the crime film generally (there is no English-language equivalent term) and has, at
various times in French cinema history, been the most popular genre after comedy.
Phil Powrie (1997: 75–76) suggests that the *polar* is a good indicator of changes
in French society in the way that it finds new settings and themes. The *polar* also
acts as a conduit for French filmmakers to engage with American crime films – thus
The Godfather (US, 1971) and *Once Upon a Time in America* (US-Italy, 1984) are
also influences on *Hors la loi*. Bouchareb has been criticised for presenting political
struggle in a populist manner, but he has argued that this is the way to attract
audiences to a reconsideration of this area of almost taboo history.

These three Maghrebi-French directors have maintained an international profile
for the local film industries of the Maghreb and at the same time broadened the
presence of diaspora films in the French domestic market. Rachid Bouchareb looks
beyond the local Maghreb-French connection however and in 2012 he completed an
American-based film exploring the Arab experience in Chicago in *Just Like a Woman*
(UK/US/France) – the first film in a planned trilogy:

> 'I'm always interested in what happens between the Arabic world and the
> West,' Bouchareb said this week. 'I come from North Africa, I lived in Paris
> and I made North African and Algerian and French movies, and now movies
> in America. But the stories are universal.'
>
> (Bouchareb, quoted on reuters.com, 12 August 2011)

Jean-Pierre Melville
(1917-1973) was
best known for *polars*
and films about the
résistance during the
Second World War. He
combined the two in his
most celebrated film
L'armée des hombres
(*Army of the Shadows*,
France, 1969).

European regional filmmaking: Nordic cinema

Within Europe there are several categories of 'local' or 'national' industries. National
film cultures are recognised in countries with large populations that can sustain
local production in some form of industrial structure (e.g. France, UK, Russia,
Germany, Italy, Spain and possibly Poland). Smaller countries are sometimes brought

together into regional groupings by both critics and the international film industry. The reasons for this are often purely pragmatic. The number of films produced in a year in a small country isn't sufficient in number to justify international trade press coverage, or the film market in a single country isn't big enough to support a separate distribution system.

The most prominent of these regional groupings at the time of writing is the designation of Nordic cinema. From 2008 onwards a number of Nordic titles have managed some form of breakout into international distribution. Much of the interest has been created by the success of crime novels that have been adapted for television and in some cases cinema release (e.g. the *Millennium* trilogy of Stieg Larsson adaptations led by *The Girl With the Dragon Tattoo* (Sweden, 2009) and TV series such as *Wallander* (based on the novels and characters created by the Swedish writer Henning Mankell) and *The Killing* (original stories produced for Danish TV)). This phenomenon is discussed in relation to 'global television' in Chapter 9. Each of the five film industries in the Nordic region is small by international standards but together they represent a market of over 25 million people and a production base for as many as 120 features each year (including documentary features).

'*Nordic*' is the term used to describe the North European culture of Sweden, Norway, Denmark, Finland and Iceland as well as Greenland and the Faroe Islands. This isn't a homogeneous grouping, but there is a sense of geographical and cultural contiguity. In terms of cinema, it is a group of small European producing countries linked by a similar language base (apart from Finnish – a distinctive language related to Estonian and Magyar in Hungary – and Greenlandic Inuit languages). Historically, Denmark and Sweden have been most successful in exporting films for international distribution. Most larger budget films (still modest by Hollywood standards) have tended to be co-productions between Nordic countries and another major European funding partner – usually in Germany or the UK.

'*Scandinavia*' is the term used to describe Sweden, Norway and Denmark, three countries with strong cultural links, since they have a shared history over several hundred years. Although Swedish, Danish and Norwegian are different languages, most adults across Scandinavia can make sense of the other languages. Many Scandinavians can also speak English and possibly German as well. Iceland and Finland are to some extent marginalised by geography and political history, but they share many cultural concerns. The film industry tends to use the term 'Nordic cinema' to include all five nations (though historically Iceland is a separate 'territory' for distribution rights).

National and regional

The four ways of defining 'national' set out by Andrew Higson at the start of this chapter are readily identifiable in the discussion about *Nordic National Cinemas* by Soila and colleagues (1998). They suggest three approaches to treating the region as a grouping of national cinemas (but cover all four definitions). First, they argue that the film industries in these countries are producing films almost completely for their own domestic markets. Relatively few of the film titles are even exported to their Nordic neighbours. This is one way in which Nordic cinema is different to American cinema, which is both national and international. The only major exception that Soila *et al.* mention is the sex film boom of the late 1960s and 1970s when Swedish films were widely exported.

The second approach is to consider the question of 'the audience and its expectations in relation to national film'. The important point here is that in the

Nordic countries there have been some periods when national cinema has engaged closely with the audience and other times when it has been criticised, but this has always been in relation to the concept of 'home' and 'abroad'. Thus, each Nordic country sees itself as having a unique film culture that potentially represents its individuality, and this is shown in relation to both its neighbours – the other Nordic countries with whom there is an affinity and the possibility of collaboration – and the US (and, possibly to a lesser extent, the UK and Germany).

The third approach to 'the national quality in Nordic cinema is via the search for specific elements in the actual film texts which constitute national markers' (Soila *et al.* 1998: 4). Inevitably this boils down to the ways in which Nordic films carry signifiers of 'not Hollywood'. In the following case study we will consider some films from the past 10 to 15 years. We may find that the situation in the Nordic film industries has changed since 1998; nevertheless, the weighty presence of Hollywood remains. In 2011 after a number of successful film exports 'Sweden's official website' (http://www.sweden.se) reported:

> Most Swedes (64.7 percent) prefer to watch US films, while 19.8 percent favour Swedish, and 9.5 percent like British movies best. The most popular film in Sweden was *Harry Potter and the Deathly Hallows: Part 2*.

This split between 'domestic' and Anglo-American film culture in Sweden (only 6 per cent of the market is left for other Nordic countries and the Rest of the World) is perhaps not so surprising. Like many European countries Sweden has, since the late nineteenth century, developed a relationship with the US on the basis of emigration.

The Nordic country with the highest population (9 million), Sweden has a significant history of film production, especially during the 1950s and 1960s when a group of Swedish directors gained international recognition. The film and theatre director Ingmar Bergman was active as a writer and director between 1944 and 2005. In the 1950s and 1960s Bergman established himself as one of the leading auteurs in European cinema with a name that resonated throughout international art cinema. Although Bergman's long list of credits cover a range of very different films he became associated with a dark and intensely dramatic vision which was not necessarily popular with the domestic Swedish audience. Even so, because of his long career and international status Bergman has exerted an influence, positive or negative, on several generations of Swedish filmmakers. His reputation also means that views of Swedish cinema from outside the region are somewhat skewed. Mainstream Swedish genre films have struggled to get distribution both at home and via export. For several years during the 1960s, Swedish films in the US were either Bergman films or sex films.

Abroad, distributors preferred for a long time to look for new Swedish auteurs – thus the interest in directors such as Lukas Moodysson following the success of his 1998 film *Fucking Åmål*. The title refers to the way teenagers describe what they see as their boring hometown Åmål in Central Sweden, and the film deals with a relationship between two rather different high school girls. Following success at the Cannes Film Festival, the film's US distributor required a new title because advertising the film would be difficult in North America. *Show Me Love* became the title in the English-speaking world – an indication of different sensibilities? Moodysson followed up with his most successful film internationally, *Tillsammans* (*Together*, Sweden, 2000), a satirical comedy about a left-wing commune in

Ib Bondebjerg and Novrup Redvall (2011) report that Nordic countries rarely show each other's films but that each national film industry has a bigger share of its own market than most other European countries.

The American Independent film *Winter's Bone* (US, 2010), set in a forested area of the Ozark Mountains, had its best box office performance in Sweden – perhaps because of some kind of cultural affinity to the landscape and people (boxofficemojo.com).

Stockholm in the 1970s. Since then his films have become both less commercial and less obviously 'Swedish'. His particular auteurist image perhaps no longer fits industry assumptions about the kinds of Nordic films that might get into international distribution. Case study 4.2 discusses two examples of recent Swedish films that typify issues related to Nordic films.

Case study 4.2: Two Nordic films

Everlasting Moments (Maria Larssons eviga ögonblick, Sweden/Denmark/Norway/Finland/Germany, 2008)

Everlasting Moments is a major Swedish film by one of the most celebrated Swedish directors Jan Troell (born 1931). It was the Swedish nomination for Best Foreign Language Film at the 2009 Academy Awards and has been recognised in several other awards ceremonies. The film tells the story of a Finnish woman who marries a big and powerful working man in Malmö (Sweden's third city and Troell's home town) in the early twentieth century. Her husband is a good worker and a good father but he is susceptible to alcohol, and when drunk he beats her. Her only escape from a hard life bringing up her children comes from the discovery that she has a natural talent for photography which is uncovered and encouraged by the man who opens the first photography shop in her neighbourhood.

Everlasting Moments stands as a representative of 'quality' Swedish filmmaking. It is a personal film – i.e. an auteur film (see Chapter 7) – in two ways. First, Troell is both a photographer and a filmmaker, and he clearly relishes the opportunity to meld the two art forms and to explore the creativity in the still image and how it can best be interpreted in a feature film. Second, the central character is an ancestor of Troell's wife and the couple were able to access documentary footage of one of the children in her family and to interview that woman's daughter. Jan Troell is one of the directors who emerged from Bergman's shadow in the 1960s and 1970s. Swedish cultural policy supports his work as an acknowledged Swedish artist. Even so, putting together the relatively modest budget this film needed required funding from all three Scandinavian countries as well as Finland and Germany.

Fig 4.8
Maria (Maria Heiskanen) takes the decision to enter the photographer's shop in *Everlasting Moments*.

Everlasting Moments is not a 'heritage film' as such and it differs from a mainstream costume picture. Troell works hard to represent the historical period as accurately as he can, but also to create an appropriate aesthetic for his film. It is engaging and rewarding in many ways, and justifies its public funding. (The Region 1 DVD for the film features the original print but the Region 2 DVD features a version cut by some 20 minutes.)

Headhunters (*Hodejegerne*, Norway, 2011)

This Norwegian film offers an interesting contrast to *Everlasting Moments*. It's a completely commercial venture that brings together Norway's best-selling crime writer Jo Nesbø, one of its star performers Aksel Hennie and the Swedish TV company Yellow Bird (behind many of the films and TV series known as 'Nordic *noir*' and seen in the US and UK during the past few years). Yellow Bird is discussed in a case study in Chapter 9.

The 'headhunter' of the title is Roger Brown (played by Hennie), a man who makes up for his lack of stature by having big ambitions which have led him to buy a very expensive house for his beautiful (and tall) wife and to help her open an art gallery. His job is to find the right applicants for senior management posts, but in order to fund his lifestyle he also needs to be an art thief. This lifestyle requires some careful juggling and one day it all goes terribly wrong.

Headhunters has become one of the most successful Scandinavian film exports, doing particularly well in the UK and the US. It wasn't particularly popular in Sweden but in Denmark it was a major hit. Jo Nesbø 'broke out' as an international best-selling author around the time of the film's production. *Headhunters* is a one-off – not part of Nesbø's long-running series of crime novels featuring Inspector Harry Hole. It seems inevitable that the Hole books will be adapted as films and/or television series, and Martin Scorsese has already been discussed as the director of one such adaptation to be produced by the UK company Working Title. Although Nesbø's novels feature recognisable Norwegian characters and locations – and tell what might be described as 'Nordic stories' – he has often expressed his interest in American culture. The tone and feel of his novels is less like 'Nordic *noir*' and more like a Nordic form of American *noir*.

*Jackpot (*Arme riddere*, Norway, 2011), a second 'crime comedy' based on a Nesbø story, was released in UK cinemas in 2012 at the same time as *Headhunters* appeared on DVD.*

Fig 4.9
Roger Brown (Aksel Hennie) is the art thief in *Headhunters* who uses his interviews with clients to find information to help him steal paintings.

Nordic cinema: the American and British connection

Headhunters production company Yellow Bird has already entered into television production in Germany and has co-produced the Kenneth Branagh series *Wallander* in the UK. The company is now aiming to produce in the US. In her very useful article on the generic hybridity of *Låt den rätte komma in* (*Let the Right One In*, Sweden, 2008), Rochelle Wright (2010) outlines the ways in which this successful film was received in Sweden, the US and the UK – exploring the fifth approach to national cinema suggested at the start of this chapter. In Sweden the film won some prizes and performed moderately well at the box office but was also compared unfavourably to the original novel (even though the writer John Ajvide Lindqvist adapted his own novel for the film directed by Tomas Alfredson). The film was actually seen by more people in cinemas in the US and also in the UK, and was also more widely praised outside Sweden. At the Academy Awards in 2009, Sweden nominated *Everlasting Moments* (see above) rather than *Let the Right One In* as its official entry.

Let the Right One In featured in Sight and Sound magazine's list of the year's Top 10 films for 2009 as selected by international critics.

Wright suggests various reasons for the different reception inside and outside the country. Her central point is that the originality of the film – it deals with a relationship between a 12 year-old boy and a girl seemingly of the same age who moves into his block of suburban flats one winter – involves a genre hybridity that is much more easily appreciated by Anglo-American critics. The inference is that in Sweden the vampire genre is something associated with imported English-language films.

> English-language reviewers tend to respond differently than Swedish ones to the Swedish suburban setting. In a domestic [i.e. Swedish] context, the vampire motif is strikingly uncommon while the locale is familiar and easily identified, which underscores the elements of social realism in the narrative. Many of the film's character types also seem ordinary and recognisable, whether from cinematic tradition, the source text, personal exposure or some combination of the above. Critics in the English-speaking world, deluged by native vampire narratives, instead construe the Swedish environment as exotic and out of the ordinary, which in turn reinforces the innovative aspects of the story itself.
>
> (Wright 2010: 65)

Here is a central issue about national film culture in a country where cinema screens are dominated by English-language films. Critical/cultural responses to domestic films are caught or constrained in an exchange about local and global films. A genre film produced in the Nordic countries is unlikely to attract the popular audiences that rush to see a Hollywood film – or to be appreciated/validated in the same way as a specialised film that fits assumptions of 'quality national cinema'. But overseas the combination of generic hybridity and 'exotic' setting fits the specialised cinema category perfectly. In the US and the UK, *Let the Right One In* was compared favourably by critics and horror fans with the first film in the *Twilight* series. In Sweden, *Twilight* took 50 per cent more at the box office than *Let the Right One In*.

Aiming for export

In 2010/2011 the Norwegian film industry broke away from the profile suggested by Soila *et al*. In 2011 a total of 40 local titles were released in what was the best year for Norwegian box office admissions since 1976. Some of those local titles had

Fig 4.10
Thomas (Glenn Erland Tosterud), one of the student filmmakers, with the troll hunter's syringe (for taking a blood sample) in *Troll Hunter*. The film is a spoof documentary edited from 'found' footage.

budgets that were ambitious and prompted a more concerted effort to export the finished films. *Troll Hunter* (*Trolljegerne*, 2010), a cultish horror film comedy, had a budget of 27 million NOK or £3 million (twice the average of a British film) and was successfully sold to the UK, US, Australia, etc.

Each of the Nordic countries has a public policy on film culture and a publicly funded agency concerned directly with film and television. *Troll Hunter* received significant support from the Norwegian Film Institute (www.nfi.no) in the shape of 30 per cent of its production budget.

See also:

Swedish Film Institute (www.sfi.se)
Danish Film Institute (www.dfi.dk)
Finnish Film Foundation (www.ses.fi)
Icelandic Film Centre (www.icelandicfilmcentre.is)

This state support is matched by the development of companies with filmed entertainment interests across two or more Nordic countries (and in some cases wider international ownership):

Svensk Filmindustri (SF) (svenskfilmindustri.com)
Nordisk (www.nordiskfilm.com)
Yellow Bird (www.yellowbird.se)
Scanbox (film distribution) (www.scanbox.com)

Both *Troll Hunter* and *Headhunters* have been reported as potential American remake material. Mark Wahlberg, who starred in *Contraband* (US, 2011) – the remake of an Icelandic crime thriller – expressed interest in *Headhunters*.

Spanish national cinema: shaped by history

Perhaps more than any other European cinema, Spanish cinema has been shaped by the national trauma of its twentieth-century history – something that may come as a surprise to younger audiences outside Spain. For most of cinema's history up until the 1980s, Spain was severely restricted in access to the rest of European culture. In the nineteenth century Spain had to deal with the consequences of loss of empire

– defeat in the Spanish-American War resulted in the loss of the Philippines and Cuba at the end of the century. In her introduction to *Spanish National Cinema* in the Routledge series, Núria Triana-Toribio offers three points to note about Spanish ideas of nation and nationalism:

1   it [Spain] was one of the oldest and most established political units in Europe, but
2   ideas of nation came to it slightly later than much of the rest of Europe, and finally
3   whereas the nineteenth century was the era of successful nation-building in Europe, in Spain it was an unqualified failure.

(Triana-Toribio 2003: 4)

The twentieth century was not much better and the Second Republic, finally established in 1931, was faced with Civil War by 1936 with the invasion of an army under General Francisco Franco based in Spain's remaining African colonies. Franco headed forces supported by the Church and the monarchists alongside the Spanish fascist party, the Falange. The rebels won the Civil War which formally ended in 1939, although guerrilla fighters on the Republican side remained in action for several more years. Franco remained in power, latterly as a figurehead, until his death in 1975 – 36 years in which Spain was 'protected' from the dangerous elements of European culture and filmmaking was strictly controlled. By the 1980s a new Spanish cinema was almost literally exploding on to screens as the pent-up desire to express emotions openly was finally let loose.

During the Civil War and the long fascist aftermath, the Spanish population was divided between Republican and Nationalist/Francoist, sometimes within the same family or within the same town or village. Civilians were executed and placed in mass graves on a large scale alongside the military war dead. The experience of the horror of the Civil War and its legacy – the troubled memories of so many individuals, families and communities – has been so great that allusions to the war and its aftermath have become a recurring feature in Spanish cinema. Referring back to Higson's classification at the beginning of this chapter, we may argue that it is one of the stories or themes that in some ways defines Spanish national cinema.

Álex de la Iglesia is 'the present, and possibly the future of Spanish Cinema. At the same time, his films may also be the death-knell of the very idea of a Spanish national cinema' (Triana-Toribio 2003:1). De la Iglesia's vicious satire on the legacy of the Civil War, *Balada triste de trompeta* (Spain/France, 2010), is a good example of what she means.

Fig 4.11
In a much discussed scene, members of the POUM militia and local villagers have a long political debate (mainly in Spanish) about collectivisation of the land in *Land and Freedom* – is this a Spanish film?

Despite the extensive censorship restrictions under Franco that effectively prescribed the acceptable genres for Spanish film production, certain filmmakers found ways round the prescriptions and produced disguised critiques of the regime that worked through metaphor and allegory. The most celebrated examples are Carlos Saura's *La caza* (*The Hunt*, 1966) and *Cría cuervos* (*Raise Ravens*, 1976), and Victor Erice's *The Spirit of the Beehive* (*El spiritu de la colmena*, 1973). By the 1980s such strategies were no longer needed, but the memories of the war and its aftermath remained important for audiences. Countless titles over the next 20 years were either set in the Franco period or referenced the period directly. Few, however, attempted to explain the politics behind the war or to present detailed accounts of how it was fought.

Ken Loach's Spanish Civil War film *Land and Freedom* (UK/Spain/Germany/Italy, 1995) was ostensibly a British film but its 'authenticity' was one of the factors that made it successful at the Spanish box office:

> *Land and Freedom* was an enormous hit among Spaniards, not just because it reclaimed part of their history but because it had authentic images, real faces and true accents.
>
> (Spanish actor and director Icíar Bollaín, interviewed in the *Independent*, 1
> May 1997 (Bollaín appeared in the film))

Many young Spaniards learned about the history of the Civil War from Loach's film. Should we count it as part of Spanish national cinema? It included Spanish actors in the cast, was shot mainly in Spain, and the Spanish TV companies TVE and Canal Plus Espana were among the production's backers – but the film uses English extensively and its central character is a young volunteer from Liverpool.

Following Loach and his collaborators, the next overseas director to recognise the possibilities of exploring the memories of the Civil War was Mexican writer-director-producer Guillermo del Toro. Many Mexicans had supported the Republicans in the

Fig 4.12
Ophelia (Ivana Baquero), the young heroine of *Pan's Labyrinth*, comes across evidence of the 'old kingdom' underground as soon as she enters the forest on her way to meet her stepfather, a captain in the fascist forces.

1930s and del Toro has said that he learned about the history from his grandmother. *The Devil's Backbone* (*El espinazo del diablo*, Spain/Mexico, 2001) is set during the Civil War with its young hero, the child of Republican parents, sent to a school in La Mancha, Central Spain to escape the fighting. The school, run by a socialist couple, has its own problems that contribute to a microcosm of Spanish society in its little community. The hero meets a ghost who has been mistreated by the fascist caretaker, and the narrative drives the hero to discover the truth about what has happened.

Although a modest success as a specialised film outside Spain, the detail of del Toro's metaphor was not fully appreciated at the time. It was his second film in Spain that became an international box office hit. *Pan's Labyrinth* (*El laberinto del fauno*, Spain/Mexico/US, 2006) is set in the early 1940s when the fascists are attempting to capture the surviving Republican fighters now acting as a guerrilla army in the mountains. This time the hero is a young girl whose fascist stepfather is in charge of the 'clearance' operation. Del Toro explores the fantasy world of the fairy kingdom that the girl discovers close to her new home. Her adventures 'underground' are very carefully interwoven, again through metaphor, with the struggle of the guerrillas above ground. The fantasy elements of the film (combined with high-quality CGI and production design) attracted a much larger audience, especially in North America. Some of the new audience will certainly have made the connections in the narrative.

In 2007, del Toro as producer put his weight and new international reputation behind *El orfanato* (*The Orphanage*, Spain, 2007). This ghost story focuses on a woman who was a small child in 1976 living in a remote orphanage (a typical 'Gothic' house – see Chapter 2) before being adopted. Now aged 37, she returns and buys the house, hoping to open a school for children with disabilities. Her plans soon go awry when her own small son disappears in mysterious circumstances. She is convinced he is still in the house and that his disappearance is connected to the 'imaginary friends' he had acquired soon after moving in. The local police – and her husband – begin to worry that she is becoming irrational when she brings in a medium and paranormal investigators. This aspect of the narrative draws on elements of **melodrama**.

El orfanato came top of the Spanish box office for 2007, a much bigger success than the del Toro-directed films. Outside Spain it matched *Pan's Labyrinth* in many territories but in the US it was noticeably less successful at the box office. In a *Sight and Sound* review in the UK, Maria Delgado (2008) suggested that one of the key factors in its success in Spain was its timing – it was released a few weeks before the Law of Historical Memory was passed by the Spanish Parliament. This law marked a key moment in modern Spanish history, with official recognition of the 'illegitimate' trials after the Civil War that resulted in the deaths of thousands of Republicans. The new law stirred up fierce controversy and the film helped to bring the debate further to life with its narrative involving the mysterious deaths of children in an orphanage at the end of the Francoist period in 1976.

Research and Explore 4.3

Watch *El orfanato* and *Cría cuervos* (see above). The casting of Geraldine Chaplin in *El orfanato* is a deliberate reference to the earlier film. Both films offer metaphors for life in Spain under Franco. How do these metaphors work and, in universal terms, how do they work through small children – often central to Gothic ghost stories?

Branston with Stafford (2010: 98–105) and Stone (2002: 85–109) offer extended discussions of *El orfanato* and *Cría cuervos* respectively.

Summary

Europe is a continent of nation states, most of which are members of some form of supranational organisation. In terms of film culture, each national film culture retains a semblance of local distinctiveness, though there are great similarities in the funding of films (often through television and public funding) and in the types of films that are made. At the same time, the different languages of Europe do hold back the free exchange of films and allow distribution to be dominated by Anglo-American and French products.

Local distinctiveness has been exploited in terms of successful local film titles in most European countries in recent years but in the three largest territories (the UK, France and Germany) there has been an openness to co-productions and the development of forms of diaspora cinema.

From outside Europe, and particularly in East Asia and North America, Europe is possibly seen as more homogeneous than it might be in reality.

References and further reading

Alexander, Karen (1999) 'Black British Cinema in the 90s: Going Going Gone', in Robert Murphy (ed.) *British Cinema of the 90s*, London: BFI.

Anderson, Benedict (1983) *Imagined Communities*, London and New York: Verso.

Arora, Anupama and Sanos, Sandrine (2011) 'Bhangra Blues: Melancholy, Memory, and History in Gurinder Chadha's *I'm British But ...*', *Journal of Postcolonial Writing*, 47(1): 89–100.

Ashby, Justine and Higson, Andrew (eds) (2000) *British Cinema, Past and Present*, London: Routledge.

Bloom, Peter (2006) 'Beur Cinema and the Politics of Location: French Immigration Politics and the Naming of a Film Movement', in Elizabeth Ezra and Terry Rowden (eds) *Transnational Cinema, The Film Reader*, Abingdon: Routledge.

Bondebjerg, Ib and Novrup Redvall, Eva (2011) *A Small Region in a Global World: Patterns in Scandinavian Film and TV Culture*, Centre for Modern European Studies – CEMES, University of Copenhagen (available for download at http://filmthinktank.org/fileadmin/thinktank_downloads/Patterns_in_Scandinavian_Film_and_TV_Culture.pdf).

Bosséno, Christian (1992) 'Immigrant Cinema: National Cinema – The Case of *beur* Film', in Richard Dyer and Ginette Vincendeau (eds) *European Popular Cinema*, London: Routledge.

Branston, Gill with Stafford, Roy (2010) *The Media Student's Book*, London: Routledge.

Brunsdon, Charlotte (1999) 'Not Having It All: Women and Film in the 1990s', in Robert Murphy (ed.) *British Cinema of the 90s*, London: BFI.

Delgado, Maria (2008) 'The Young and the Damned', *Sight and Sound*, April: 44–45.

Flessel, Fabienne (2012) 'Martinique: "Think Like A Man", Just Not in France', http://globalvoicesonline.org/2012/05/08/martinique-think-like-a-man-just-not-in-france/.

Hayward, Susan (1993) *French National Cinema*, London: Routledge.

Higson, Andrew (1989) 'The Concept of National Cinema', *Screen* 30(4): 36–47.

Higson, Andrew (2006) 'The Limiting Imagination of National Cinema', in Elizabeth Ezra and Terry Rowden (eds) *Transnational Cinema, The Film Reader*, Abingdon: Routledge.

Hill, John (1999) *British Cinema in the 1980s*, Oxford: Oxford University Press.

Keaton, Rica Danielle (2011) 'The Defiant One: Euzhan Palcy'. Available at http://thefeministwire.com/2011/05/the-defiant-one-euzhan-palcy/.

Koshy, Susan (1996) 'Turning Color: A Conversation with Gurinder Chadha', *Transition* 72: 148–161.

Miller, Toby, Govil, Nitin, McMurria, John, Maxwell, Richard and Wang, Ting (2005) *Global Hollywood 2*, London: BFI/Palgrave Macmillan.

Powrie, Phil (1997) *French Cinema in the 1980s*, Oxford: Oxford University Press.

Soila, Tytti (ed.) (2005) *24 Frames: The Cinema of Scandinavia*, London: Wallflower.

Soila, Tytti, Soderbergh Widding, Astrid and Iversen, Gunnar (1998) *Nordic National Cinemas*, London: Routledge.

Stone, Rob (2002) *Spanish Cinema*, Harlow: Pearson Education.

Street, Sarah (2009) *British National Cinema*, London: Routledge.

Tarr, Carrie (2007) 'Maghrebi-French (Beur) Filmmaking in Context', *Cineaste* 33(1): 32–37 (this issue carries 'a special supplement on French-Maghrebi cinema').

Triana-Toribio, Nuria (2003) *Spanish National Cinema*, London: Routledge.

Vitali, Valentina and Willemen, Paul (eds) (2006) *Theorising National Cinema*, London: BFI.

Walker, Alexander (1986) *Hollywood England*, London: Harrap.

Wright, Rochelle (2010) 'Vampire in the Stockholm Suburbs: *Let the Right One In* and Genre Hybridity', *Journal of Scandinavian Cinema* 1(1): 55–70.

Further viewing

There are many specific film titles mentioned in the chapter. If you would like to extend your viewing or to test the five approaches suggested in the chapter, the following titles are examples of contemporary German cinema:

Lore (Australia/Germany/UK, 2012, dir. Cate Shortland) and *Anonyma – Eine Frau in Berlin* (Germany/Poland, 2008, dir. Max Färberböck) – re-imaginings of 1945 and the end of the Nazi period.

Das Leben der Anderen (*The Lives of Others*, 2006, dir. Florian Henckel von Donnersmark), *Yella* (2007, dir. Christian Petzold) and *Barbara* (2012, dir. Christian Petzold) – films about East Germany before and after the end of the Cold War.

Das letzte Schweigen (*The Silence*, 2010, dir. Baran bo Odar) – a German version of 'Nordic Noir'?

Gegen die Wand (*Head-On*, Germany/Turkey, 2003, dir. Fatih Akin), *Auf der anderen Seite* (Germany/Turkey, 2007, dir. Fatih Akin), *Die Fremde* (*When We Leave*, 2010, dir. Feo Aladag) – examples of Turkish-German diaspora films.

The Edukators (*Die fetten Jahre sind vorbei*, 2004, Germany/Austria, dir. Hans Weingartner) and *Requiem* (2006, dir Hans-Christian Schmid) – contrasting genre explorations of youth in contemporary Germany.

CHAPTER 5

Decentring the Hollywood domination debate: Japan and South Korea

- Problematising the study of Japanese cinema
- Orientalism
- Japanese films in the contemporary UK market
- The contemporary filmed entertainment market in Japan
- Japan and its 'classical' cinema
- *Manga* and *anime*
- ☐ Case study: 5.1: *The Girl Who Leapt Through Time*
- Cinema of South Korea
- The South Korean blockbuster
- The Korean Wave: *Hallyu*
- A mature industry of variety?
- Summary: cinemas in opposition to Hollywood or going their own way?
- References and further reading
- Further viewing

Japanese cinema is going to be a part of any study of global film for several reasons, some of which we touched on in Chapter 1. The cinema of South Korea has perhaps been a more recent entrant into the international film marketplace and is now important as one of the major national markets in which domestic producers have managed to match and recently overtake Hollywood in their home market. For nearly 40 years in the first half of the twentieth century Korea was a colony of Imperial Japan and the after-effects of this experience are evident in both countries. Since the resurgence of film industry and culture in South Korea from the late 1990s onwards the 'exchange' of films and other forms of popular culture between the two East Asian producers has developed significantly. South Korea has become an important agent in boosting the circulation of East Asian films and television in both regional and international terms. This chapter will also move us towards an understanding of both regional and 'Pan-Asian' film exchanges and transnational productions.

Problematising the study of Japanese cinema

Of all of the film cultures outside Hollywood, it is Japanese cinema that seems
to have created the most problems for Anglo-American film scholars. Yoshimoto
Mitsuhiro recognises this anxiety in the introduction to *Kurosawa: Film Studies and
Japanese Cinema* (2000: 2–3):

> Kurosawa, who occupies a central position in the study, consumption, and
> construction of Japanese cinema, arouses the feeling of anxiety in Japanese and
> Western critics because his films problematise Japan's self-image and the West's
> image of Japan.

It is now more than 60 years since Kurosawa's *Rashomon* won a prize at the 1951
Venice Film Festival and 'introduced' Japanese cinema to new audiences in Europe
and North America, but Kurosawa remains perhaps the best-known Japanese
filmmaker around the world. Kurosawa found himself the first beneficiary of the
creation of the concept of 'world cinema' – but also its first victim. In Japan he was
dubbed 'most Westernised' of the leading directors of his period, but in the West
his films were assumed to represent important aspects of 'Japaneseness'. Kurosawa
became influential outside Japan as remakes of his films appeared, and other
directors, especially in Hollywood, studied his techniques. But Kurosawa as the
first global film auteur also presented film critics and scholars with other problems.

Fig 5.1
Mifune Toshiro and
Kyo Machiko in a
promotional image from
Rashomon. Source:
The Kobal Collection/
www.picture-desk.com.

Although his films appeared in film festivals and in art cinema distribution, he was a commercial filmmaker in Japan – often commanding the biggest budgets on his films and, for a period in the early 1960s, being the most successful director at the Japanese box office. At the same time, he was not a conventional figure in the Japanese film industry.

The struggle over Kurosawa's identity and how his films were interpreted reveals some important issues about film scholarship and Japanese cinema. *Rashomon* (an adaptation of a short story set in twelfth-century Japan which introduced the idea of different perspectives on an incident as seen by various participants) was an 'experimental' film in which Kurosawa wanted to try out new ideas, but it wasn't conceived as a film for festival submission. Its genesis is understandable only in the context of filmmaking in Japan in the late 1940s. At that time Kurosawa was working as one of a group of independent directors following a strike at the Toho studios where his previous films had been made. *Rashomon* was funded by one of the new studios, Daiei, which emerged from the reorganisation of the Japanese film industry after 1945. It was the head of Daiei who had the idea of sending the film to Venice in the hope of creating a market for the studio's films overseas. *Rashomon* was also unusual at the time because the Occupation Authorities in Japan (1945–1952) vetted all film scripts. Stories about feudal Japan that might encourage the 'military ethos' of the samurai tradition were not usually allowed. Kurosawa's script got past the censors because it was set in an earlier period than the popular *chanbara* or 'swordfight films' of the 1930s and 1940s that focused on samurai warriors during the long Tokugawa or Edo period (1603–1868). This explains partly why the film wasn't expected to do well in Japan.

Rashomon's success outside Japan was therefore in some ways accidental but it was exploited by Daiei which then sent further historical Japanese films to Venice and Cannes, winning prizes for established directors such as **Mizoguchi Kenji** over the next few years. Mizoguchi and Kurosawa were feted in the West for their historical films. Their contemporary-set dramas were generally not exported, and the other two directors now regarded as major figures during this period, Ozu Yasujiro and Naruse Mikio, who both concentrated on contemporary family dramas or **melodramas** (see Chapter 2), took much longer to be fully appreciated outside Japan. This is an example of the circulation of what was often seen as 'quality cinema' in a Japanese context (i.e. for a popular, albeit more middle-class audience) being received as 'art cinema' elsewhere. The anxiety about how these films were interpreted coalesces around the concept of **orientalism**. Orientalism is an important concept throughout much of global/transnational film studies and it crops up in several chapters in this book. The work of Edward Said and his book *Orientalism* (1978) has been central to studies in this area and in the development of **postcolonial studies** (see Chapter 8).

Edo was the former name for Tokyo. It was the capital for the Tokugawa clan who became *shoguns* of Japan.

Mizoguchi Kenji (1898-1956) was the other leading Japanese director taken up in the West during the 1950s. He seemed to offer an alternative to the younger Kurosawa, and Western critics associated him with female-centred melodramas.

Orientalism

Orientalism may be identified in a range of activities by Westerners concerned with understanding and appreciating the cultures of 'the East' (the 'Orient') from the sixteenth century onwards. European powers colonised, or gained effective control over, significant parts of Asia, and as early as the mid-nineteenth century the United States had become part of this process when Commodore Perry's arrival in Tokyo Bay in 1853 marked the first step towards 'opening up' Japan to Western trade and cultural influences.

Orientalist practices included the administrative procedures of colonial agents, trading agreements, travel writings, missionary work and social anthropology studies – each of which attempted to describe and classify local cultural practices from a Western perspective. Artists also created images of the Orient and in several cases 'acquired' local art objects that found their way back to museums in London, Paris and New York. The combined effect of these different activities was to construct an *imagined* Orient, both 'exotic' and **'other'**. To classify something as exotic (literally 'from outside') now suggests in the West something 'strange' used to titillate the palate of a jaded audience. Not surprisingly, being described in this way feels condescending and dismissive for local artists. The later use of the term 'other' in academic studies refers to the colonial relationship, a relationship between dominant and subordinate entities in which the subordinate is defined only by the ways in which it displays the negatives of the qualities assigned to the dominant. This is the **binarism** of colonialism, the relationship of **coloniser** and **colonised**. Here is a list of some of the binary oppositions associated with the colonial discourse:

educated	vs.	ignorant
religious	vs.	superstitious
honourable	vs.	devious
civilised	vs.	uncivilised
moral	vs.	licentious
wise	vs.	childlike, etc.

These **binarisms** underpin the racism inherent in the colonial relationship and define the colonised. The social typing of colonial subjects developed in slightly different ways in Africa and Asia, but the coloniser–colonised relationship has shown similar features. The coloniser 'names' and defines the subordinate other.

The popularity of the orientalist construction became evident in the fashion in Europe for *chinoiserie* and much later *japonisme* – French terms for the influence of oriental arts and crafts. Orientalism is generally discussed at the level of **discourse** – what is written or said and reproduced textually. But interest in the exotic like this also had real economic import with European industries effectively 'replacing' (i.e. stealing) certain kinds of local Asian technologies and artistic designs such as the cotton textiles industry of India or aspects of Chinese porcelain manufacture – a process that was to some extent reversed in the late twentieth century.

As far as 'narrative production' is concerned, European taste was attracted to oriental stories and characters they recognised from within the *imagined* orient rather than the real world of contemporary Asian societies. We can see this in the emergence of heavily typed East Asian characters in late nineteenth- and early twentieth-century narratives such as Sax Rohmer's *Fu Manchu* (1913 onwards), or the stories associated with the 'Yellow Peril', a term used by populist politicians and journalists in response to the perceived threat of Chinese migrations to the West. By contrast, Japanese contact with the West was limited before the 1930s and the two best-known representations in the West were Gilbert and Sullivan's light opera *The Mikado* (1885) and Puccini's opera *Madame Butterfly* (1904). The former used exoticism as a backdrop for a satire on British politics and the latter was derived from several sources (including an 1898 short story by John Luther Long), and dealt with a 'romance' between an American naval officer and his 15-year-old Japanese bride.

Fig 5.2
Cary Grant and Sylvia
Sidney in Paramount's
1932 film adaptation of
Madame Butterfly. Source:
The Kobal Collection/
www.picture-desk.com.

Research and Explore 5.1

Madame Butterfly remains a very popular opera, but a hundred years after its first appearance it has
also become the focus for discussion of the stereotypical submissive and self-sacrificing Asian woman
in American society. Research the play *M. Butterfly* (1988) by David Henry Hwang. What have critics and
cultural commentators said about this play and how do you link such discussion to the problems of
orientalism?

We might expect that nearly a century after *Madame Butterfly* first appeared and
given the greater awareness in the West (including the migration of many South
Asians and East Asians to Europe and North America) things may have changed. But
Gary Needham argues that orientalist ideas were still deeply embedded in the culture
in the 1990s when the UK film and video distributor Metro Tartan launched its 'Asia
Extreme' brand:

> The language of its promotional material speaks for itself, announcing that 'If
> the weird, the wonderful and the dangerous is your thing, then you really don't
> want to miss this chance to take a walk on the wild side'. The promise of danger
> and the unexpected is linked in the way that these films are marketed according
> to their otherness from Hollywood, and subsequently feeds in to many of the
> typical fantasies of the 'Orient' characterised by exoticism, mystery and danger.
>
> (Needham 2006: 9)

We can follow up Needham's useful introduction by listing some of the types of films
and characters from Japan that have proved popular in Europe and North America
over the past 20 years:

- ghost stories (combining the contemporary and the traditional), e.g. the *Ring* series;
- extreme violence, e.g. the films of Takashi Miike;
- *anime* – all kinds of characters appealing to a wide range of Western audiences (and linking to TV, videogames and *manga*);
- 'crazy' Japanese TV shows, e.g. *Takeshi's Castle* (the 1980s series exported and viewed as 'cult TV').

As Needham points out, films and TV programmes like these are available in the West through DVD, TV and occasionally multiplex cinemas rather than just art cinemas, as was the case in the 1950s. Some of them have also seen Western remakes. Also important is the way in which certain trends in Japanese cinema have been taken up within other East Asian cultures (e.g. the relationship between certain kinds of teen horror branded as 'J-horror' – or 'K-horror' in South Korea). However, these links are rather different to those resulting in Hollywood remakes of East Asian properties, since the cultural differences between Japan and Korea are not couched within that same orientalist perspective. At this point we should stop and consider the odd situation in which Western and Japanese film scholars find themselves in relation to ideas about orientalism and colonialism. Japanese culture has been viewed from the West within an orientalist framework. Yet from the end of the nineteenth century, Japan itself was a colonial power in China and Korea. After 1945, Japan was occupied and forced to relinquish its colonial possessions. Some scholars (e.g. Tezuka 2011) have suggested that during the Occupation period, Japanese culture demonstrated signs of **self-orientalism**. Self-orientalising implies in this case that Japanese producers decided on a strategy of 'positive affirmation' in which they represented their Japanese culture in ways that they thought would fit the Western conception of the imagined Orient (e.g. Daei's presentation of *Rashomon* to Western audiences). At the same time, contemporary Japanese popular culture attempted to copy aspects of the occupiers' culture – a process that had been in play since the nineteenth century but which was now happening in a different context with occupiers in place and a demoralised local population. During the 1950s, as well as working through these developments, Japanese culture would also need to begin to work through the aftermath of its own colonial relationships.

Kurosawa's second film of 1950 gives a different picture of Japan. *Scandal* deals with the sensationalist Japanese tabloid press, unleashed after years of military control. Unlike *Rashomon* this film was not exported.

The tendency to self-orientalise is also discussed in relation to Chinese cinema in Chapter 11.

Japanese films in the contemporary UK market

With the demise of Metro Tartan in 2008, Japanese films in the UK have struggled to achieve a cinema release and therefore a **platform** for strong DVD sales. Here we will discuss four successful Japanese films from 2010 that were released in the UK in 2011 with significantly different results in terms of box office and critical reception. (To some extent, the UK experience is indicative of how the films might fare in other Western markets as well.)

Fig 5.3 shows the box office performance of each film in Japan and then in the UK. All four films were among the Top 40 titles showing in Japanese cinemas in 2010. *Confessions* and *Villain* appeared on only a handful of screens in the UK so they barely register in UK industry figures. They were distributed primarily on DVD in the UK by Third Window Films, a specialist label set up in 2005 with the specific intention to bring 'quality' Japanese cinema to UK audiences. *Confessions* (*Kokuhaku*) and *Villain* (*Akunin*) were the two most celebrated Japanese films of

Title	Japanese B.O. (US$)	Japanese B.O. Chart Position	UK B.O. (US$)
Confessions	42,577,000	(10)	50,000
Villain	22,265,000	(25)	8,000
13 Assassins	17,304,000	(34)	500,000
Norwegian Wood	16,339,000	(38)	550,000

Fig 5.3 The box office performance of four major Japanese films (figures from boxofficemojo.com, screendaily.com and bfi.org.uk) Note: box office revenue is an approximate figure for purposes of comparison. When admissions figures are low, exact figures for box office revenue are difficult to obtain.

the year. *Confessions* was the Japanese entry for the Foreign Language Oscar after winning several awards in East Asian film festivals and it was voted No 2 film of the year by *Kinema Junpo* magazine in Japan. *Villain* was voted No 1 by *Kinema Junpo* in every category.

By contrast, the other two titles were less successful at the Japanese box office but performed well in the UK by the standards of foreign-language cinema. How do we explain this difference between the Japanese and UK reception of each film? What can we learn about both the distribution process and the assumptions of industry professionals and film critics – as well as the audiences themselves?

Confessions is an example of a high-profile genre film by an established director, Nakashima Tetsuya. As in his earlier two films that received some form of international distribution – *Kamikaze Girls* (2004) and *Memories of Matsuko* (2006) – *Confessions* has a striking colour palette, careful use of popular music and an overall approach that is distinctive. (Nakashima previously worked in advertising films.) The film is a revenge tale that focuses on a schoolteacher who announces to her class that she is resigning and that a terrible crime has been committed. She knows who is responsible but instead of naming the two 13-year-old culprits in her class, she describes them in a way which makes their identity clear. Then she

Fig 5.4
One of many expressionist images in *Confessions*, this composition isolates one of the students in the school gym.

Fig 5.5
Yuichi (Tsumabuki Satoshi)
and Mitsuyo (Fukatsu Eri)
go 'on the run' in *Villain*.

announces that she has tricked them and that they will soon learn their fate. All hell breaks out. The title refers to the way in which four characters 'confess' by narrating their own stories. This complex narrative structure is derived from the best-selling novel by Kanae Minato.

Confessions combines many of the elements that are familiar from Japanese horror films distributed in the West through Tartan's Asia Extreme. The high school setting is in some ways reminiscent of the South Korean cycle of *Whispering Corridors* films (1998–2009). The idea of a teacher taking revenge on school students is the basic premise of *Battle Royale* (Japan, 2000), one of the best-known Japanese titles of recent years on the international circuit. There are also references back to the central films of the J-horror cycle such as *Dark Water* (Japan, 2002) focusing on a young divorced woman and her small child. The stigma of divorce and single parenting is a recurring element in films that seem to be critiquing the failures of Japanese society, especially in relation to young people.

Given the possible familiarity with these genre elements in various Western territories, why was *Confessions* not picked up by a major distributor in the UK or the US – especially after its awards successes? Could it be that distributors felt that 'J-horror' had reached the end of its cycle and was no longer marketable? The audience that relied on Tartan's branding may have drifted away with the demise of the label. As a relatively new label, Third Window consciously tried to move away from the Tartan legacy, but in doing so perhaps emphasised the artistic qualities of *Confessions* instead of its genre appeal. As we frequently note in other parts of this book, genre films in foreign languages are often treated as specialised films when they enter markets such as the US or the UK.

We can contrast the fate of *Confessions* with that of *Norwegian Wood*, the least successful of the four films in Japan but the best performer at the UK box office. The film also achieved a release in most major film territories around the world, though unusually the UK was one of the strongest overseas markets. This film too was distributed by one of the smaller UK independents, Soda Pictures, but they are more established than Third Window and have more resources to support a cinema release. Like *Confessions* (and many other Japanese films), *Norwegian Wood* is a literary adaptation, but this time of a novel by the best-known Japanese writer in

Fig 5.6
Mizuhara Kiko and
Matsuyama Ken'ichi in
Norwegian Wood.

the West, Murakami Haruki. The novel was first published in 1987 but was not translated into English until 2000. Murakami's interest in Western culture has not prevented him from becoming popular in Japan and *Norwegian Wood* was one of his most popular novels with Japanese youth. It is set mostly in the 1960s when the central character is at university against a backdrop of student unrest. However, he is recovering from the shock of his friend's suicide and more concerned with his own personal relationships.

The film adaptation was written and adapted by the Vietnamese filmmaker Tran Anh Hung, who has won prizes at Cannes and Venice, and was photographed by Mark Lee, the celebrated Taiwanese cinematographer who has worked with the international auteurs Wong Kar-wai and Hou Hsiao-hsien (see Chapter 11). Music for the film was specially written by Jonny Greenwood of Radiohead and included tracks by the German band Can, active mainly in the late 1960s and early 1970s. The film's title refers to the Beatles song from 1965.

Norwegian Wood is a 'difficult film' compared to *Confessions*. It is relatively slow and long at 133 minutes (even though the adaptation leaves out part of the novel's narrative) and it doesn't use generic conventions as such. How do we explain its relative success in the UK? First, its distributor had the confidence to

Fig 5.7
The *13 Assassins* preparing
to take on the huge force
assembled by the Shogun's
younger brother in late
Tokugawa period Japan.

put out 33 prints and to promote the film. That confidence was founded on two main factors – the high international profile of the filmmakers involved, attracting broadsheet reviewers and feature articles, and the literary following of Murakami, attracting audiences who wanted to check out the adaptation. Soda was also able to successfully bid for a UK Film Council Award from the 'Specialised Cinema P&A Fund'. The distributor received £103,900 of National Lottery money to make extra prints available and to promote the film through advertising. Soda's initiative saw the film in the Top 20 for its opening weekend with a screen average of US$4,500 – one of the best returns of any film title that weekend.

In Japan, both *Confessions* and *Norwegian Wood* were distributed by the major studio Toho and the genre picture had a bigger box office. In the UK, the film that was seen as more akin to an international arthouse film was the box office winner. Adam Torel (2012) of Third Window explains that small distributors have great difficulty getting films into cinemas, especially when so many UK specialised screens are controlled by just two companies – Artificial Eye (see below and in Chapter 12) and City Screen/Picturehouse. *Confessions* received some very good reviews, including a rave on the prime television show covering new releases, *Film 2011*. However, the strong interest in the film that this review helped to generate could not be exploited, since the film was shown in only four cinemas and extra bookings were not possible at such short notice. If we now consider the other two titles we discover similarities and differences but overall a confirmation of how Japanese films are handled in a UK context.

Villain is again a literary adaptation but this time of a crime fiction novel by Yoshida Shuichi. The novel was translated into English and published in the UK in 2010 but without the coverage given to a Murakami novel. In Japan, however, Yoshida is a major figure. Although *Villain* is a crime film, it does not follow the conventions of most Western crime thrillers. In some ways it is a 'whydunnit?' rather than a 'whodunnit?' (a young female office worker is murdered and there are two possible male suspects). Generically it is perhaps a 'crime melodrama', involving the families of two of the main characters and focusing on one of the young male characters and his relationships. The film is also long (139 minutes), slow-paced and rooted in local culture (of the island of Kyushu, the most southerly of Japan's four main islands). The mix of crime and social commentary is similar to that in the Korean film *Memories of Murder* (2003) (see below) and perhaps some of the Swedish and Danish TV crime series and serials (see Chapter 9). The nearest type of Hollywood film might be the 1940s/1950s *film noir*. In this sense, Western audiences may see the film as 'old-fashioned'. At one point in the narrative there is a 'matter-of-fact' appearance of a ghost – something not unusual in Japanese cinema.

13 Assassins is a film by the prolific director Takashi Miike (more than 80 titles in 20 years). Takashi is renowned for making a wide range of genre films, episodes of TV series and low-budget **V-cinema** films. Few of these films have been seen on cinema screens in the UK. Notable exceptions were *Audition* (Japan, 2000) and *Ichi the Killer* (2001), both notorious for their attitudes to violence – Miike was in many ways the leading director associated with Tartan's Asia Extreme brand. He has also made mainstream comedies and surreal films like *The Happiness of the Katakuris* (2001). The three titles listed here are all contemporary-set films. *13 Assassins* is a *jidaigeki*, a period film, and a remake of a 1963 film with the same title. In the history of Japanese cinema there are two great 'meta genres' described as *jidaigeki* or **gendaigeki** – 'period' or 'contemporary'. The Japanese films that first entranced

The director of *Villain* is Lee Sang-il who is a *zainichi* from an established Korean-Japanese family. Although his first film did include Korean characters, his films mostly deal with 'rebel' or 'marginal' characters such as the central character of *Villain*.

V-cinema is the Japanese industry practice of producing low-budget films for video distribution. Unlike in the West, the V-cinema label does not imply that the films are lower in artistic quality. The format may in fact allow more artistic freedom (see also Chapter 9)

Western art cinemas tended to be *jidaigeki*, either melodramas or *chanbara* – swordfight films. In the West the latter came to be known as 'samurai films'.

Although it was the *jidaigeki* of Kurosawa Akira that first attracted Western audiences, films like his *Seven Samurai* (Japan 1954) tended to be more 'realist' and historically accurate about the civil wars at the end of the sixteenth century than the *chanbara* that were so popular in Japan in the 1960s. Takashi's film represents a 'genre remake', but one in this case approached with something of the dedication of a Kurosawa, even if the subject matter itself is a samurai story set during the latter years of the Tokugawa shogunate. This combination of cult genre film and art film selected for competition in Venice is in some ways typical of contemporary cinema. It does however raise questions about how to distribute the film, since the genre fans may not go to the specialised art cinema to see the film and the art cinema audience may be put off by genre and Takashi's reputation. As a UK co-production via the Recorded Picture Company and legendary international producer Jeremy Thomas, *13 Assassins* was in a good position to be picked by the biggest specialised cinema distributor in the UK, Artificial Eye.

Samurai characters in Japanese film narratives

Samurai warriors in Japanese society were traditionally servants of their feudal lords and so the historical films set in the sixteenth century during the Civil War are often concerned with military battles (e.g. Kurosawa's later films such as *Kagemusha* (Japan, 1980)). In the Tokugawa period the focus of the film narratives switches to the so-called 'masterless samurai' or *ronin* who roam the country looking for work as 'swords for hire'. Stories about samurai were sometimes adapted for the new form of popular theatre, *kabuki* – which in turn would eventually feed into cinematic narratives. Finally, during the Meiji Restoration in the late nineteenth century, when Japan is moving towards a modern state, the samurai struggle to find new roles in society and to confront their demise as warriors (e.g. in films like *Twilight Samurai* (Japan, 2002)).

There is an interesting parallel between these different sets of stories and the different types of American western, with soldiers in the US cavalry and 'gunslingers' in the most common genre narratives and finally the 'death of the West' cycle in Hollywood during the 1960s and 1970s.

Artificial Eye is part of the Curzon group in the UK that owns four of the leading arthouse cinemas in London's West End, and is thus best placed to promote its titles. *13 Assassins* received significant coverage in the UK media that helped to confirm its status for arthouse audiences – who were then able to find the film in the leading specialised cinemas.

Our case study of four films has provided an insight into some of the questions about the film exchanges between Japan and the West. We will draw some useful conclusions:

- successful distribution of Japanese films (and all foreign language films) is heavily dependent on access to cinemas and sufficient funds for prints and advertising;

- a high profile as an 'international art film' is more useful in specialised cinemas than a popular genre profile;
- the exoticism of a *jidaigeki* is sometimes an easier sell than the realism of contemporary Japanese society;
- stories that are 'too Japanese' in their contemporary 'otherness' suffer in comparison with films in which Japanese authors embrace aspects of Western culture.

The DVD sales of the same films may tell a slightly different story, since discs may be purchased online from any territory, and UK DVDs are bought by customers in North America and Japan (UK discs are much cheaper).

The contemporary filmed entertainment market in Japan

Because of high ticket prices in Japan, the Japanese cinema market remains in the top three most valuable in global terms even as it declines in terms of admissions. Japanese audiences are concentrated into older audiences that will still watch a more diverse range of films and younger audiences who currently favour domestic blockbusters associated with TV productions. What's missing is the solid mainstream audience in the middle. As a consequence, average annual attendance in Japan is much lower (around 1.2 visits per head) than in the major English-speaking markets and considerably lower than in South Korea – which matches the Japanese total admissions figure with less than half its population.

Japanese films have always had lower budgets than equivalent Hollywood/ European productions, and even though the industry has always been dominated by three or four 'majors', the low production costs have helped to maintain very high levels of production. In 2010 around 400 new Japanese productions were released but only 29 were deemed hits (http://film.culture360.org/magazine/observations-on-japanese-cinema-after-311/). Having recovered from a very difficult period in the 1990s, the Japanese market now favours domestic production again. Hollywood blockbusters, especially franchises, still sell but 'medium-budget' Hollywood has been squeezed and foreign specialised films are also struggling in 'mini-theatres'. Some East Asian blockbusters have been successful, including *Red Cliff* (HK/China in two parts, 2008/2009).

The main Japanese film exports to the West fall into three main categories:

1 art films recognised via film festival exposure;
2 *anime*, mostly for DVD distribution apart from Studio Ghibli (see below);
3 cult cinema, again mostly via DVD with occasional theatrical releases.

The same kinds of films are also exported to other East Asian markets, where they may stand more chance of a cinema release. Exports to East Asian (and Southeast Asian) markets are also likely to include popular Japanese 'blockbuster cinema' films such as the *Umizaru* franchise. *Umizaru 3* took US$94 million in Japan in 2010 and had a limited release in Taiwan, Hong Kong and Singapore. Japanese blockbusters in 3D offer a potential alternative to Hollywood and Chinese production for distributors in these three territories as well as Malaysia and Thailand. The exchange of films between Japan and South Korea is something we will discuss later in the chapter.

The *Umizaru* franchise refers to a *manga* series about the Japanese Coast Guard service and its exploits. Following TV adaptations, the films are live action blockbusters.

The relatively 'slimline' theatrical market in Japan is partly explained by the impact of television from the mid-1960s and later the popularity of video rental and then pay TV and online – although these also now seem to have reached saturation, so that any growth in the revenue for Japanese films is matched by a fall in revenues for imported films. But in a regional and global ecology of film-producing nations, the history of Japanese films remains important. Twice, during the 1930s and again in the 1950s and early 1960s, Japan produced the most films of any film industry in the world. These two periods have been referred to as 'golden ages' for Japanese cinema. We need to understand something about Japanese cinema during these periods in order to fully appreciate the challenges facing film scholars interested in global film.

Japan and its 'classical' cinema

We began this chapter with a concern about the ways in which Japanese cinema was received in the West in the early 1950s as an 'other cinema' – a film culture defined simply by being 'alternative' to Hollywood. The set of assumptions which accompanied that reception has since been challenged as Western scholars have become more familiar with the history of Japanese cinema and Japanese writing on film has become more accessible in the West. For many years, film scholars took the Hollywood studio system (approximately 1930–1960) to be the 'classical' model for cinema – as we explored in Chapter 1 in relation to the work of Bordwell, Staiger and Thompson. A recent sustained critique of this position has been offered by Catherine Russell who has argued that 1930 to 1960 could also be considered as the period of 'Classical Japanese Cinema', i.e. not as an alternative to Hollywood but as:

> another structure of cultural imperialism, and another discourse of modernity, that became a dominant form of mass culture in the twentieth century. The influence of Japanese film on neighbouring Asian nations remains largely undocumented (or more accurately, underresearched).
>
> (Russell 2010: 16)

Russell's argument, which draws on her research into the long career of **Naruse Mikio** (over 37 years) and which calls for further research from other scholars, ties in with our overall polycentric approach to the development of global film. Here is a studio system eventually producing films on a large scale to put alongside others in Asia such as India and Hong Kong. Japanese film history offers us some interesting examples of how a large-scale industry operated in an Asian context.

Naruse Mikio (1905–1969) was a major director of contemporary melodramas and another director, like Ozu and Mizoguchi, prolific from the 1930s through to the 1950s.

The beginnings of cinema in Japan

Japan experienced rapid industrial growth at the end of the nineteenth century alongside tumultuous social changes. Compared to Western Europe and North America which began the process earlier, the modernising of Japan was compressed. To illustrate this, Donald Richie (2001: 9) imagines a 50-year-old in Japan seeing an imported film for the first time at the end of the nineteenth century. This would be someone who in their own lifetime had experienced the move from a traditional, feudal society into the modern world and with it new modes of dress, new foods and public services alongside railways, postal services and new work practices. As Richie also notes, the Japanese population learned to accept these imports and

In 1868 the Japanese Emperor was restored to the throne after the fall of the Tokugawa shogunate. 'Meiji' is the 'era name' and 1868 is one of the most important dates in Japanese history.

Chikamatsu monogatari (Japan, 1954), literally 'a story from Chikamatsu', is a film by Mizoguchi Kenji.

Fig 5.8
Veteran actor Hasegawa Kazuo plays an *onnagata* in nineteenth-century Japan in Kon Ichikawa's *An Actor's Revenge* (1963), reprising a role he first performed for Nikkatsu in 1935. The widescreen is used imaginatively to represent the *kabuki* stage.

swiftly assimilate and incorporate them into contemporary life so that they became 'Japanese' in some way. It is something of a cliché perhaps, but modern (i.e. post the 1868 Meiji Restoration) Japanese culture has often seemed to develop with a tension between the 'new' and the 'traditional'. As Richie points out, the idea of foreign imports in 1896, when the Lumière Brothers' films first appeared in Japan, was only a few decades old but Japanese culture was nearly 2,000 years old.

In most film cultures we can recognise that cinema in its early development drew on other forms of popular entertainment, especially popular theatre and popular literature – as well as classical literature and fine art forms. In Japan there were three forms of traditional theatre, each of which in some way influenced cinema. The most traditional form is *noh* in which performers sing or chant in a musical drama – at one time four or five such dramas were interspersed with lighter performances. Characters wore masks and men traditionally played both male and female roles. Originating around the fourteenth century, *noh* is Japan's 'classical theatre'. The popular theatre that developed in the Tokugawa era (1601–1868) was *kabuki* – a much more audience-friendly form that developed in the *ukiyo* or 'pleasure gardens' of Tokyo and later in Osaka and Kyoto. Still stylised and with traditional stories, it was performed in bigger theatres, often with spectacular stage designs. Like *noh*, *kabuki* then required men to play female roles – actors doing this were known as *onnagata*. In some ways *kabuki* resembled the spectacular melodramas of Europe during the same period. The third traditional form, *bunraku*, was a puppet theatre that developed from the end of the seventeenth century and told stories similar to those in *kabuki*. Chikamatsu Monzaemon was the best-known Japanese playwright of both early *bunraku* and *kabuki*.

Given this background we shouldn't be surprised to find that early Japanese cinema included versions of *kabuki* plays, performed by *kabuki* players – and including *onnagata*. One of the major companies in Japanese film history is Shochiku which was founded in 1895 to manage *kabuki* theatres and which went on to add *noh* and *bunraku* theatres to its portfolio. It finally became a film-producing studio in 1921 and immediately had a modernising influence on the Japanese film industry. A second Japanese major was Nikkatsu, formed in 1912 and bringing together four smaller film companies. The third major, Toho, was formed in the mid-1930s and again was first a *kabuki* theatre company in Tokyo, part of a duopoly with Shochiku.

The social turmoil at the end of the nineteenth century in Japan also saw the development of new forms of theatre. *Shinpa* or 'new school' theatre developed from the 1880s, still traditional in the form of melodrama but now focusing on contemporary social issues. *Shinpa* was influential on early Japanese film narratives, but was superseded by *shingeki* or 'new drama' which was based on Western realist theatre of the period and which in turn again changed Japanese cinema.

Another early influence on Japanese cinema was visual culture – forms of woodblock printing, ink drawings and other traditional forms. East Asian visual culture has a different history to that of the West – Japan had been isolated from Western influences for hundreds of years. What was described as 'Western painting' was yet another element in the opening up of Japan in the early twentieth century and Kurosawa Akira studied Western painting as well as watching American movies and European plays. But this does not mean that traditional Japanese forms had been lost. A surprising number of well-known Japanese film directors had backgrounds in different forms of the graphic arts and this means that across Japanese cinema we may expect to see a range of approaches to representing landscapes, architecture and human interaction, some referencing Western and some Eastern aesthetics (see the various contributions in Ehrlich and Desser (1994)).

A studio system in Japan

By the late 1930s the Japanese studio system was well established with newly formed Toho vying for leadership with Shochiku and Nikkatsu as well as a number of smaller companies that were still able to make up to two films per week. Freda Freiberg (1987) quotes Japanese government figures showing 1,362 talkies and 701 silent films produced in 1938 – a figure down from the previous year! The transition from silent to sound cinema took much longer in Japan and other East Asian territories. Freiberg does not tell us whether the figures refer to feature-length films and whether all the films actually reached cinemas. But even if only half the total films are feature length, it seems likely that this was the biggest film industry globally during this period. (Most other estimates suggest 300–500 films per year, but that Japan had the biggest output is not disputed.)

The number of cinemas in Japan increased steadily, from 1,057 in 1926 to 2,363 in 1940, and attendances rose from 154 million to 440 million over the same period.

From the mid-1920s onwards, Japanese cinema gradually modernised its production methods. *Chanbara* remained popular but Shochiku also produced contemporary-set dramas about life in the modern big cities of Tokyo and Osaka. In 1938, again from figures quoted by Freiberg, around 25 per cent of Japanese cinemas showed American or European films at some point, but only a fraction of these cinemas showed foreign films exclusively. Foreign films would usually only show in Tokyo or other large cities. Toho and Shochiku were vertically integrated and could guarantee outlets for the films they produced. Double bills in Japan were often 'balanced' in offering a *gendaigeki* produced in a Tokyo studio and a *jidaigeki* produced in a Kyoto studio.

Cinema in Imperial Japan

Following rapid industrial and military development in the late nineteenth century, Japan went to war with both China (1894–1895) and Russia (1904–1905) primarily over control of Manchuria and Korea. Japanese victories led to colonisation of part of the Russian island of Sakhalin (1905) and Taiwan (from 1895). Japan formally annexed Korea in 1910 and set up a colony in South Manchuria in North East China in 1905 from which Japanese forces would eventually move out to control the whole of Manchuria and set up the puppet state of Manchukuo in 1932. The result was that Imperial Japan expanded its population by 90 per cent so that in 1940 it controlled over 140 million people, as well as the Chinese in territories occupied since the start of the second Chinese War in 1937. When the Pacific War was extended in 1941, the 'Greater East Asia Co-Prosperity Sphere' represented the Japanese attempt to claim the whole of East Asia from Burma to the Philippines and Singapore to Inner Mongolia – comprising Japanese colonies, occupied lands and 'puppet regimes'.

Catherine Russell suggests that the role of cinema in cultural policies designed to bind these new territories to Japan is one of the areas where more research is needed. This has already begun (see in particular Baskett 2008), and the history of the Manchukuo film industry from 1937 to 1945 is now emerging in detail. With international scholars working in this area, film history will be transformed if it represents the activities of Imperial Japanese cinema in its 'classical' phase alongside the colonial cinemas of Britain and France and the global reach of classical Hollywood. The Japanese Empire ended *de facto* with defeat in 1945, but the legacy of Japanese administration and cultural policies, especially in Taiwan and Korea, has proved to be lasting (see Chapter 11 as well as the latter part of this chapter). Several Japanese films of the 1950s refer to the experience of colonialism much as British and French films refer to their own imperial narratives.

Manga and anime

The importance of *manga* and *anime* both as part of Japanese popular culture and as exportable media products is another aspect of the distinctiveness of Japanese popular culture. The Japanese word '*manga*' has been translated as 'whimsical pictures' and the origins of the *manga* style have been traced back to the eighteenth century and later to the various woodblock series of artists such as **Hokusai** and **Hiroshige**. The contemporary commercial *manga* publishing industry developed after 1945 and *manga* now represent a large proportion of reading material for all ages in Japan.

Katsushika Hokusai (1760-1849) and **Utagawa Hiroshige** (1797-1858) were two of the best-known woodblock artists of the early nineteenth century.

Wikipedia suggests that there are 3,000-plus *mangaka* in Japan who both create and draw stories. Occasionally a story will be written by an author and passed on to a *manga* artist to draw. Stories that begin as *manga* are then often adapted for *anime*, many of which appear as TV series. Some have become successful feature films and have circulated widely (including in export markets) on DVD.

Anime are animated films that employ slightly different conventions to Hollywood-style animations. The clearest difference is in the lower frame rate which means that *anime* are less smooth in terms of motion. Although many famous *anime*, such as those from Studio Ghibli and its founder Miyazaki Hayao, are original stories and not adaptations of existing *manga*, they still use the drawing style developed within the (post-war) *manga* tradition. This includes the large eyes used for many characters, sometimes argued to allow drawn characters to express more emotion. The work of Tezuka Osamu (beginning with the *manga* of *Astro Boy* in 1952 and the subsequent TV series in 1963) is often quoted as influential in developing this convention.

The look of *manga* and *anime* is distinctive and there are three important factors in their popularity throughout East Asia and in markets in the West, especially in North America, France and Italy.

- Different sectors of the market cater for specific audience groups – unlike Western forms of animation or comic books, there is less of an assumption of an audience composed mainly of children. Everybody in Japan reads *manga* and *anime* are enjoyed by adults as well as children and teens.
- New genres or combinations of genres in *anime* have extended the range of international cinema's genres, especially in the interrelated genres of horror, science fiction, and mystery and romance/youth cultures. Gender difference and sexual identity is explored in different ways.
- *Manga* and *anime* have prompted the development of new forms of fandom and a new subculture of the *otaku*.

Taken together, these three developments have contributed something new and uniquely Japanese to global film. *Manga* and *anime* have developed out of a Japanese context and not 'in opposition' to Hollywood as such – although part of the sensibility evident in the culture associated with them certainly comes from the experience of war, the end of Japanese Imperialism and the impact of Occupation. They have now found audiences across the world to be receptive to Japanese cultural products. In academic terms, *manga* has been recognised as 'a key part of the cultural accompaniment to economic globalisation. No mere side-effect of Japan's economic power, *manga* is ideally suited to the cultural obsessions of the early twenty-first century' (Jean-Marie Bouissou, http://www.eurozine.com/articles/2008-10-27-bouissou-en.html). Bouissou's article is worth reading through, and if you aren't already interested in Japanese popular culture it is certainly worth exploring what *otaku* culture means in more detail.

Otaku refers to a particular kind of obsessive defined by his or her consumption of several types of media: *manga, anime, tokusatsu* (special effects films – 'creature features'), videogames, *aidoru* (female pop performers), *figyua* (scale character models) and so on.

Case study 5.1: *The Girl Who Leapt Through Time* (2006)

The most prestigious *anime* and those that score (very) heavily at the box office are either science fiction-related (e.g. *Akira* (Japan, 1988) and *Ghost in the Shell* (Japan, 1995)) or they are products of Miyazaki Hayao's Studio Ghibli and often ostensibly targeted at younger audiences (but also popular with adults). Both these groups of *anime* are successful on the basis of strong stories and well-designed and drawn characters and backgrounds. Most of Studio Ghibli's work has remained hand-drawn, with computer-generated imagery enhancing rather than replacing drawn artistry.

Although not officially a Studio Ghibli product, *The Girl Who Leapt Through Time* was directed by Hosoda Mamoru (who spent a brief and not very happy period at Ghibli) with a team of other animators, several with Ghibli experience. Based on a best-selling science fiction novel from the 1960s, it mixes the concept of 'limited' time travel with a modern high school teen story. It thus draws on both the trends for successful *anime*. The drawing style of the central characters is slightly different to the Ghibli style but the attention to detail in the backgrounds is just as high. (Critics have commented on the overall representation of that 'last summer' for high school students and the beauty of old Tokyo streetscapes.) The central character, 17-year-old Makoto, discovers (in quite dramatic circumstances) that she has the power to leap backwards in time, but only for short periods. The narrative sees her attempting to use her unique 'superpower' responsibly (and failing badly) as part of her daily life as a normal adolescent and she turns to her (young) aunt for guidance. She doesn't yet know where the power has come from and

Fig 5.9
A street scene from
*The Girl Who Leapt
Through Time* showing
the representation
of 'old Tokyo' and the
elongated human figures.

what she will have to do with it. In the meantime, she is close to two male students and not sure about her affections for them.

This story was first written by Tsutsui Yasutaka (born 1934) as a serial in magazines for secondary schoolchildren in 1965 before being published as a novel in 1967. Since then it has been adapted for several live action films and television series (the latest in 2010 is also available on DVD in the UK as *The Time Traveller – The Girl Who Leapt Through Time*) as well as a *manga*. Some of these adaptations are sequels/prequels or re-workings of the original material.

Reviews tend to suggest that this is 'soft' science fiction – presumably because it is associated with 'romance' rather than technology. In UK literary terms it is closer to ideas of 'hard SF' – where the focus is more on ideas than on 'action/adventure'. This confusion also relates to its *manga* categorisation. Although it might be expected to be categorised as *shojo manga* (the market segment for girls) it was in fact published in a *shonen* (boys') magazine by the major publisher Kadokawa (also an important producer/distributor in Japanese cinema).

The most useful insight into how the *anime* was received by fans may be found on the following websites:

http://www.animenewsnetwork.com/review/the-girl-who-leapt-through-time
http://www.animevice.com/the-girl-who-leapt-through-time/13-1227/

The fans' reviews sometimes indicate the very close relationship they have with *anime* characters – possibly because there are no stars or celebrities to get in the way? *Manga* and *anime* have become successful both within Japan and in export markets where they seem to have overcome some of the hurdles of 'accessibility' that face live action Japanese drama outside East Asia. Alongside Japanese videogame culture (see Chapter 12) they represent the possibility of a different kind of engagement with Japanese culture, especially with younger audiences who first encountered them as children.

Research and Explore 5.2

If you aren't already familiar with *otaku* culture, visit a bookstore or videogames store or seek out fans of *manga* and *anime*. What is the attraction of these media forms? To what extent do you think that these fans have learned about Japanese culture? Do they prefer genuine Japanese media or local variations? Does their consumption of *manga* and *anime* allow them to explore identities in different ways than is possible with Western media?

Cinema of South Korea

The story of South Korean cinema's remarkable growth from the late 1990s onwards deserves a whole chapter to itself. We don't have that much space, so here are some of the important points that may be explored through the films.

As noted above, Korean production began under Japanese colonial rule. In the aftermath of the Korean War (1950–1953), film production was split between North and South. North Korean films have been seen only rarely in the West and then only in sponsored touring seasons or very occasionally at festivals. Reliable statistical information is almost impossible to obtain but it seems likely that film production was highest in the 1980s when the country was still able to exchange films with other communist countries.

By contrast, the film industry in South Korea experienced periods of extensive production followed by retrenchment at various times between the 1950s and 1990s. Then, in the space of a few years, what had been a largely local industry with little impact on the international scene was transformed into a modern film industry that began to sell films across East Asia and to create a strong impression internationally. This transformation has been intriguing because it appears to have been prompted by some of the factors associated by scholars with globalisation and other factors that are unique to South Korea.

Darcy Paquet explains the transformation from the sorry state of the Korean film industry in 1993, when Hollywood had forced its way into what was a declining cinema market, to the astounding success of 2001. He suggests that a key factor was the resolve of a new group of producers to build a 'commercial' cinema, but he doesn't mean 'commercial' as distinct from 'artistic' – rather that the determination was to make the industry self-sufficient and able to make films of all kinds that would at least cover their costs from domestic theatrical and ancillary markets like video or export. It sounds an obvious point to make, but many film industries have fallen into the trap of simply accepting that films need to be subsidised or that only certain kinds of films can be made, etc. In South Korea the new producers were able to look for cooperation from both government and the major South Korean conglomerates (*chaebol* – Daewoo, Samsung, etc.) equally concerned to build a strong industry. This would mean forming larger and more powerful film companies, providing better training, better facilities and infrastructure, and more efficient ways of raising money – such as using venture capital companies (Paquet 2005: 33).

Paquet and Choi Jinhee (2010) point to a number of changes in the 1990s which swept away outdated local practices in distribution, changed accounting practices, increased budgets (and reduced the number of productions), built new cinemas, focused more clearly on certain genres and created more recognised local stars. The

The Flower Girl from 1972 is a 'revolutionary opera' film featuring a young peasant girl in Korea during the 1930s struggle against the Japanese. It was extremely popular in China during the Cultural Revolution and a scene depicting a showing of the film in China is included in *Balzac and the Little Chinese Seamstress* (China/France, 2002).

chaebol didn't last long as direct players in the industry, but when they withdrew they had restructured the industry so that three **vertically integrated** companies – CJ Entertainments, Cinema Services and Showbox – now play a significant role in the South Korean film industry.

Choi argues that the economic crisis in Asia in the late 1990s was a factor in the *chaebol* withdrawing but that other investors saw films as a relatively quick way of earning a return, and that the government both invested directly in production on the European model via the Korean Film Council and Small Business Corporation as well as granting tax benefits through a re-definition of film as a 'semi-manufacturing business'.

Although Hollywood distributors were operating in Seoul, a quota was in place that required cinemas to play Korean films for 146 days in the year. As new screens became available, the saturation distribution of Hollywood films became possible – but because of the Korean films quota, so did saturation distribution of local films. The whole array of changes in the Korean film industry led to the emergence of the 'Korean **blockbuster**'.

The South Korean blockbuster

As Choi explains, the Korean blockbuster is not the same as the American variant. Yes, it does have a bigger budget than other Korean films, but still in the few millions of US$, not the US$50–100 million of Hollywood. Nor is it necessarily a special effects-laden 'super-genre' film. The term refers mainly to its distribution policy and to its primary appeal to Korean audiences through a shared sense of Korean history. This point is important: although films have been sold abroad, the original production targets the Korean audience first, whereas the Hollywood blockbuster assumes universality.

The first blockbuster is generally recognised as *Shiri* (South Korea, 1999) which sold 6 million tickets and was then sold to Japan where it earned US$17.6 million. *Shiri* is an action film involving North Korean agents operating in South Korea. A number of other films at this time also featured stories that focused on divided Korea and the possibility of reunification. *JSA* (2000) or 'Joint Security Area' is a mystery/thriller about a shooting in the demilitarised zone between North and South. *Brotherhood* (*Taegukgi*, 2004), like *Shiri*, directed by Kang Je-gyu, is set during the Korean War when two brothers are separated in circumstances that eventually find them fighting on different sides.

Brotherhood continued the trend for the budgets of Korean films to rise. Estimated to be in the region of US$12.8 million, this was a considerable advance on average budgets of below US$1 million ten years earlier. The film grossed US$64 million in its domestic market. *Brotherhood* is a long film (148 minutes) and it includes a narrative 'bracketing device' whereby in 2003 an elderly man is contacted when some human remains and a military medal are found during excavations. This links *Brotherhood* to a global trend in the 2000s involving personal stories told within a wartime setting – and mechanisms that address an audience thinking about family members. In Europe and North America this has involved the two World Wars, but in Korea the war in the early 1950s is the major national story in which all Koreans have an investment. We may want to also relate the success of the film to the concept of the **national-popular** or to compare it with the **main melody** films of China (see Chapter 11).

JSA introduced director Park Chan-wook and star Kang So-Hoo, who would become known to international audiences through specialised cinema releases in the West.

My Way (2011) was a less successful (but more ambitious) blockbuster from Kang Je-gyu focusing on the rivalry between two athletes, Japanese and Korean, and mainly on their time as soldiers in Asia and Europe between 1939 and 1944 (see the entry on globalfilmstudies. com).

Fig 5.10
The two brothers at the beginning of *Brotherhood*, when the older brother is trying to prevent the younger from being conscripted.

However, films like *Brotherhood* are not 'state-sanctioned' as such. They are commercially driven on the basis of assumptions about audience appeal. This is not to deny the possibility that the films are part of the ideological terrain in South Korea in which arguments about reunification are played out.

The annual blockbuster successes at this time may be recognised through the extensive data publications of the Korean Film Council, KOFIC (http://www.koreanfilm.or.kr). Founded as early as 1973, KOFIC changed its identity in the early 1990s and became a crucial part of the industry's re-emergence as an efficiently organised operation with an international profile. Publications in English promoted individual directors, released market data and analysis, and generally presented the policies supporting Korean film and its strength in its domestic market.

Blockbusters came in various genres, including comedy (see the discussion of *My Sassy Girl* (2001) in Chapter 3 as a romantic comedy) and crime films – and at times comedy-crime films. *King and Clown* (2005) is a period drama, while *Tidal Wave* (2009) is a disaster movie. The one 'failed' genre seems to be science fiction, although South Korean audiences do respond to Hollywood science fiction and superhero films, and *The Host* (2006), one of the biggest hits, combines family melodrama, political satire and a 'monster' movie.

The Korean Wave: *Hallyu*

When *Shiri* was sold to Japan and *My Sassy Girl* was a hit in several East/Southeast Asian countries, Korean film came to be seen as part of a wider concept of the *hallyu* or 'Korean Wave' in which popular culture from South Korea became very attractive in different territories in Asia.

The principal drivers of the Korean Wave in China, Hong Kong, Taiwan, Japan, Vietnam and other territories have been Korean TV drama and Korean pop music, 'K-pop'. Film has links to these other media and a feature of the *hallyu* is the rising profile of Korean stars and media celebrities, partly through the spread of internet culture. South Korea has invested heavily in digital technologies and electronics manufacturing. Videogaming is also a strength, contributing new jobs to the expanding Korean entertainment and cultural industries sector.

In 2012 K-pop's reach
was confirmed when
the whole world went
mad for the 'Gangnam
style' dance performed
by K-pop singer Psy. The
song went to No.1 in the
UK and by January 2013
had attracted 1.2 *billion*
hits on YouTube.

The wave is primarily an Asian phenomenon but YouTube has been seen as partly responsible for the arrival of K-pop in Europe. In a *Guardian* article (16 December 2012), Edwina Mukasa reported on the K-pop phenomenon and noted that at the MTV European Music Awards in 2011 the only real surprise was the winner of the 'best worldwide act' was not Britney Spears but K-pop group Bigband, who attracted 58 million votes from fans. Later in 2011 the first K-pop show in the UK opened the London Korean Film Festival. Similar developments have occurred around the world and fans often travel to other countries to see performances. Mukasa makes the point that this pop phenomenon is related not to reality television talent shows as in the West, but instead to TV drama – serials/soaps. This relates to the discussion in Chapter 9 about the contra-flows of *telenovelas* and other forms of serial TV drama.

The beginning of the wave is often quoted as the transmission in China of a TV drama *What Is Love All About* in 1997. In the early phase, it was mainly within the Three Chinas and diaspora Chinese communities that Korean drama became popular. Then in 2003 *Winter Sonata* was shown in Japan by public broadcaster NHK. The melodrama proved so popular that after initially starting on a satellite service it was rerun four times, eventually on primetime. It was also eventually subtitled rather than dubbed – to give fans the real 'Korean feel'. Korean actor Bae Yong-jun became a celebrity in Japan on the basis of this show.

The success of Korean TV paved the way for greater acceptance of Korean films, and explanations for its success usually include these related factors:

- the exported shows were, at the end of the 1990s (during the financial crisis), much less expensive for Chinese TV to purchase compared to TV material from Japan or Hong Kong (and certainly cheaper than Hollywood), but;
- the technical quality of material was as high as the competitors despite the lower cost;
- Korean culture was both sufficiently 'different' and 'familiar' at the same time to please audiences (an observation that applies to many of the cultural exchanges within East Asia where the similarities give such exchanges preference over Hollywood imports).

The Korean Wave has been recognised as helping to build South Korea's **soft power** in the region and worldwide – cultural exports of music and television have reached markets in every continent, including sometime pariah states such as Zimbabwe and Burma. This hasn't been without some controversies along the way – including reactions in Japan where the earlier colonial relationship and the later question of Korean immigration are still live issues for certain groups. Nevertheless, the buildup of soft power is another reason for the South Korean government to keep on investing in cultural industries.

Film as part of the Korean Wave

Korean films began to appear in the West in larger numbers through limited cinema releases as promotion for more sustained DVD releases in the early 2000s. In the UK, although some films received multiplex screenings as part of the Tartan DVD promotion, most titles followed the conventional route into specialised cinemas, with the result that a Korean blockbuster was often placed in front of an 'arthouse' audience. Here is one example.

Memories of Murder (*Salinui chueok*; South Korea, 2003) was the second film by writer-director Bong Joon-ho who has proved to be one of the major figures of contemporary South Korean cinema, his status confirmed by the massive box office success of *The Host* in 2006. *Memories of Murder* was an earlier success as one of the top box office attractions for its year, selling 5 million tickets. The title is apt for a film that represents the (unsuccessful) investigation of murders in a small community outside Seoul in 1986. These were real events but Bong weaves them into a generic narrative in which he draws out a black humour from the sometimes inept attempts of the local police to find the killer. In fact, the representation is constructed in such a way as to make a social commentary on Korean politics. Generic devices like the arrival of a Seoul detective to help out his 'hopeless' country cousins and the long process of sending forensic evidence off to the US for testing also work as social commentary – as do the night-time curfews, since this was a period of extreme government repression in the country. The film was based on a successful play and therefore the local audience was prepared for the complexities of the presentation – but for a Western audience the richness of the *mise en scène* and the range of performances was a revelation in what appeared at first to be a familiar police procedural/crime thriller.

Choi (2010) picks out two other films released in 2003 as joining *Memories of Murder* under the heading of 'well-made films'. *Untold Scandal* and *A Tale of Two Sisters* were both successful genre or 'commercial' films that also attracted high praise from critics. *Untold Scandal* is a version of the French novel *Les liaisons dangereuses* (previously adapted as *Dangerous Liaisons* (US/UK, 1988) and *Valmont* (France/US, 1989) transposed to eighteenth-century Korea and starring Bae Yong-jun in his first film role. His presence helped the film to a Japanese box office total equalling the local take. *A Tale of Two Sisters* is a Gothic horror film based on a traditional Korean folktale about a stepmother and her two stepdaughters. Director Kim Ji-woon is one of the 386 generation with a number of successful films, including *The Good, the Bad, the Weird* (2008).

The social commentary running through the film refers to the '386 generation' (after the Intel computer chip) – in their thirties during the 1990s, born in the 1960s and attending college in the 1980s. Bong (b. 1969) just fits into this categorisation.

Fig 5.11
The local police attempt to reconstruct a crime – in front of the media and other spectators – in *Memories of Murder*.

Fig 5.12
The two sisters at their lakeside home in *A Tale of Two Sisters*.

The 'well-made film' has echoes of the 'quality film' (see Chapter 2) in the US, UK and France. Choi argues that the adoption of the term was prompted by a fear that output was becoming too commercialised and that it was an attempt to 'bridge the gap between the economics and aesthetics of a commercially-driven industry' (Choi 2010: 144). She devotes a chapter to what she terms 'High-Quality Films', suggesting that their directors are not just '*metteurs en scène*'. This reference to the 'second-rank' of auteurs, directors who simply 'film the script', goes back to the early 1960s attempts to discuss Hollywood directors as 'film artists'. It is a clever way of distinguishing a group of directors and their films who somehow manage to appeal to both critics and popular audiences – and who then become the 'poster boys' of South Korean Cinema's presentation in the international market. Choi's discussion goes on to explore how once again the Korean industry looked towards Hollywood for ideas about how to structure a film industry in terms of production and distribution strategies – but then to create something specific to the local situation. She suggests that these Korean films share something with the kinds of American independent films distributed by Miramax or Focus Features in the 2000s, focusing on 'themes, character relationships and social relevance: themes that have long been associated with European art cinema' (Choi 2010: 146).

The 'well-made films' were box office successes at home and critical successes in Europe and North America where the directors became established names among fans and industry practitioners. In 2013 both Kim Ji-Woon and Park Chan-wook (included in Choi's broader grouping of 'high-quality' filmmakers) released Hollywood films. *The Last Stand* by Kim is an action film featuring the return of Arnold Schwarzenegger, and *Stoker* by Park is a 'Hitchcockian' thriller with Nicole Kidman. Earlier, *A Tale of Two Sisters* had been remade and released by DreamWorks under the title *The Uninvited* (Canada/US/Germany, 2009). The 'Remake Man' Roy Lee of Vertigo Films was involved, as he was with the Spike Lee remake of Park's *Oldboy* (US, 2013) (see Chapter 2 for more on Roy Lee and

Vertigo). When Kim Ji-Woon's gangster revenge thriller film *A Bittersweet Life* (South Korea, 2005) was released in its home market it was described in publicity as 'Melville meets *Kill Bill*' (Choi 2010: 147). This is a reference to the French director Jean-Pierre Melville and it echoes the links between Melville and the **gangster films** of John Woo and Johnnie To in Hong Kong as well as with Quentin Tarantino. Here is evidence of the sophistication of the Korean audience and the local-global stance of its film culture.

The director of *Memories of Murder*, Bong Joon-ho, directed *Snowpiercer* for release in 2013. Based on a French graphic novel series, the South Korea/France/US production, mainly in English, was part-produced by Park's film company Moho Films.

Research and Explore 5.3

Analyse any one of the three films selected by Choi Jinhee as a 'well-made film' (*Memories of Murder, A Tale of Two Sisters* or *Untold Scandal*).

- Does the film transcend its genre and become something more? If so, how?
- How would you assess its technical merits (cinematography, sound, design, performances)?
- Research how it was produced and what kinds of responses it received. How does it refer to aspects of Korean culture, history or politics?

A mature industry of variety?

The South Korean industry is not simply an industry of blockbusters or 'well-made films'. There are relatively low-budget horror and teen films linked to ideas about K-horror and J-horror. There are specialised films as 'art' or auteur films as they would be recognised in the West. Kim Ki-duk (b. 1960) is a sometimes controversial art film director whose films like *Spring, Summer, Fall, Winter …, and Spring* (2003) and *3-iron* (2004) became popular in international art film distribution. *Pietà* (2012) won the Golden Lion at Venice.

The Busan Film Festival has become an important event in the international film calendar and part of the funding process for independent films. South Korean film companies and public funding agencies have invested in various co-productions and many film festivals now expect a number of entries from Korean filmmakers.

The industry has experienced several ups and downs during the 2000s but it appears to have survived a reduction of the local film quota from 146 days to 73 in 2006. In 2012 it was listed as the sixth most important film market globally in terms of admissions, and local films took 58 per cent of the local theatrical market.

Summary: cinemas in opposition to Hollywood or going their own way?

The title of this chapter points to the debate that is central to the whole question of global film and the binarism of Hollywood vs. the Rest. We have tried to demonstrate the ways in which both Japanese and Korean film cultures have developed modes of cinema production and distribution that work in a domestic national, regional and global context. They have both been influenced by – and have borrowed from – Hollywood, but they are not defined solely by their difference from Hollywood.

Japan with its larger population and classical cinema studio system in the 1930s and 1950s has maintained its position as a major producer, albeit now on a smaller scale, within the region. South Korea in the 1990s moved to replace Hong Kong as a major regional innovator and exporter, and in 2013 it is evident that there is a developing system of cultural exchanges of film, TV, music and videogames across East Asia. South Korea may provide some kind of model for ways in which to increase these exchanges. This is really a question best left to Chapter 12, and before that we need a sense of where the two giant Asian film industries/cultures in China and India are heading.

Thanks to Tom Vincent for observations on otaku *culture.*

References and further reading

Baskett, Michael (2008) *The Attractive Empire: Transnational Film Culture in Imperial Japan*, Honolulu: University of Hawaii Press.

Choi, Jinhee (2010) *The South Korean Film Renaissance*, Middletown, CT: Wesleyan University Press.

Ehrlich, Linda C. and Desser, David (eds) (1994) *Cinematic Landscapes: Observations on the Visual Arts and Cinema of China and Japan*, Austin: University of Texas.

Eleftheriotis, Dimitris and Needham, Gary (eds) (2006) *Asian Cinemas: A Reader and Guide*, Honolulu: University of Hawaii Press.

Freiberg, Freda (1987) 'The Transition to Sound in Japan', in T. O'Regan and B. Shoesmith (eds) *History on/and/in Film*, Perth: History & Film Association of Australia.

Hwang, David Henry (1988) *M. Butterfly*, London: Josef Weinberger Plays.

Kim Youna (2007) 'The Rising East Asian "Wave": Korean Media Go Global', in Thussu, Daya Kishan (ed.) (2007) *Media on the Move: Global Flow and Contra-flow*, Abingdon and New York: Routledge.

Napier, Susan J. (2006) *Anime from Akira to Howl's Moving Castle: Experiencing Contemporary Japanese Animation*, London: Palgrave Macmillan.

Needham, Gary (2006) 'Japanese Cinema and Orientalism', in Eleftheriotis and Needham (eds) (op. cit.).

Paquet, Darcy (2005) 'The Korean Film Industry: 1992 to the Present', in Shi Chi-Yun and Julian Stringer (eds) (op. cit.).

Richie, Donald (2001) *A Hundred Years of Japanese Film*, Tokyo: Kodansha.

Rimer, Thomas (1994) 'Film and the Visual Arts in Japan', in Ehrlich and Desser (eds) (op. cit.).

Russell, Catherine (2010) 'Japanese Cinema in the Global System: An Asian Classical Cinema' in *The China Review* 10(2): 15–36.

Said, Edward (1978) *Orientalism*, New York: Vintage.

Shi Chi-Yun and Stringer, Julian (eds) (2005) *New Korean Cinema*, New York: NYU Press.

Shin, Jeeyoung (2005) 'Globalisation and New Korean Cinema', in Shi Chi-Yun and Julian Stringer (eds) (op. cit.).

Tezuka Yoshiharu (2011) *Japanese Cinema Goes Global: Filmworkers' Journeys*, Hong Kong: Hong Kong University Press.

Willemen, Paul (2006) 'The National Revisited', in Valentina Vitali and Paul Willemen (eds) *Theorising National Cinema*, London: BFI.

Xu, Gary G. (2008) 'Remaking East Asia, Outsourcing Hollywood', in Leon Hunt and Leung Wing-Fai (eds) *East Asian Cinemas: Exploring Transnational Connections on Film*, London: I.B. Tauris.

Yoshimoto Mitsuhiro (2000) *Kurosawa: Film Studies and Japanese Cinema*,
    Durham, NC: Duke University Press.
Young, Louise (1999) *Japan's Total Empire: Manchuria and the Culture of Wartime
    Imperialism*, Berkeley: University of California Press. northkoreanfilms.com
    http://www.koreanfilm.or.kr/jsp/publications/books.jsp.

Further viewing

Other aspects of Japanese cinema not considered in this chapter, but that are relevant
to debates in other parts of the book, include the 'New Wave' films of the 1960s
when younger directors were challenging traditional ideas. A wide range of different
films include the following:

Kisses (Japan, 1957, dir. Masumura Yasuzo)
Naked Youth (Japan, 1960, dir. Oshima Nagisa)
Insect Woman (Japan, 1963, dir. Imamura Shohei)
Woman of the Dunes (Japan, 1964, dir. Teshigahara Hiroshi)
Branded to Kill (Japan, 1967, dir. Suzuki Seijun)

Two of the most celebrated 'contemporary masters' of Japanese cinema have films in
international distribution, including the following:

Afterlife (Japan, 1998, dir. Kore-eda Hirokazu)
Tokyo Sonata (Japan, 2008, dir. Kurosawa Kiyoshi)
Still Walking (Japan, 2010, dir. Kore-eda Hirokazu)

South Korean cinema

The films discussed in this chapter are all directed by men. Two examples of films
made by women are as follows:

Take Care of My Cat (South Korea, 2001, dir. Jeong Jae-eun)
Treeless Mountain (South Korea/US, 2008, dir. Kim So Yong). Kim was born in
Korea but educated in the US and her other work has been mainly in the US.

Two films that demonstrate the range of Korean films getting a release in the West,
the first an action/historical film, the second a form of melodrama are as follows:

Poetry (South Korea, 2010, dir. Lee Chang-dong)
War of the Arrows (South Korea, 2011, dir. Kim Han-min)

CHAPTER 6

Middle East without borders

- ■ Where is the 'Middle East'?
- ■ 'Without borders'
- ■ The film industries and film cultures of the Middle East
- ■ Local film industries
- ■ Turkish film culture and industry
- □ Case study 6.1: *Uzak*
- ■ Iranian cinema
- □ Case study 6.2: *Nader and Simin: A Separation*
- ■ Egyptian cinema
- □ Case study 6.3: *Microphone*
- ■ Lebanese cinema
- □ Case study 6.4: *Caramel*
- ■ European funding and support
- ■ Dreams of a nation: Palestine
- □ Case study 6.5: Two films from Hany Abu-Assad
- ■ Israeli cinema and the 'periphery'
- □ Case study 6.6: Young Israelis at war
- ■ Summary
- ■ References and further reading
- ■ Further viewing

This chapter attempts to give an overview of a whole region. Its title is borrowed from the 'Films From the South' Festival held each year in Norway (see Chapter 7). The 'without borders' designation seems appropriate in several different ways. There is no agreed definition of what constitutes the 'Middle East' – middle of what, east of where? Filmmakers are often forced by economics or politics (or both) to work from 'outside' the region as exiles or to find partners inside or outside the region 'across borders', even if those borders are fiercely contested. This amorphous sense of film industries and film culture in the region generates several useful case studies for us.

Alongside Africa, this is the least profitable part of the international market for the major Hollywood studios. None of the top-earning film territories are found here. There are relatively few admissions on a per capita basis, partly because most countries in the region are 'underscreened' by international standards. Nevertheless, there have been some very important and critically celebrated films from the region and there are also significant popular local film cultures as well as controversial films that both provoke and represent political conflicts – the diversity of production and audiences offers a microcosm of global film activity.

Where is the 'Middle East'?

The idea of 'the East' must be a cultural construct, since the Earth is a sphere. The East was initially defined by those who lived in 'the West' (i.e. in Europe). But when the centre of world power shifted to the US, what happened to the concept of 'the East'? If you stand on the dockside in San Diego and look west there is nothing to see until you get to Japan. For Americans, Japan should be 'the West'. But it doesn't work like that.

The British and the French in particular defined 'the East' as part of first mercantile and then colonialist practice. From the start of the eighteenth century up until the aftermath of the First World War, British and French foreign policy referred to the 'Near East' – what was in practice the Ottoman (Turkish) Empire stretching from the Balkans to Iraq and encompassing Egypt and North Africa. Both countries also had interests in the 'Far East' – in Indo-China, Hong Kong and Malaya. India remained a separate issue but there was a gap in this perspective, and that is how Persia/Iran, Afghanistan and parts of Central Asia came to be seen as the 'Middle East' – in the context of the 'Great Game' involving keeping the Russians out of India. Gradually, however, the 'Near East' passed out of usage and the Middle East grew to cover the whole region from the Eastern Mediterranean to Afghanistan.

The detail of these historical changes of terminology is not as important as the recognition that this region has consistently been defined by those outside the region itself. The consequences of this are neatly summarised in the concept of 'Orientalism' associated with Edward Said and his book with the same title first published in 1978 (see Chapter 5). Said was a Palestinian Christian scholar whose arguments will inform our understanding of the film culture of the region.

Mercantilism refers to the period between feudalism and capitalism when controlling trade was the basis of economic power.

'Without borders'

The geographical area that lies between Asia and Europe and which also acts as a bridge into Africa is inevitably going to be characterised by the movement of peoples from one continent to another – fleeing persecution, seeking new trade routes, looking for new worlds to conquer, etc. This is the region associated with 'the cradle of [Western] civilisation' and with learning and conquest flowing from West to East and East to West with the armies of Alexander and Darius and later the Arab caliphs, whose influence extended from Moorish Spain to Persia. Far from being the monolithic entity that seems to have become the common enemy in American popular culture, this is a region of ethnic, religious and cultural diversity. There *are* borders of course and some of them, such as the 'Green Line' that divides Palestine, have become the focus for conflict. Most borders have been set not by physical geography but by external agencies, both colonial and supranational (i.e. League of Nations, United Nations). But people don't necessarily recognise borders and this region has become associated with the modern phenomenon of **diaspora** communities (see Chapter 4) and refugee camps. There is a wide range of diasporic communities, including North Africans, Palestinians, Lebanese and Iranians. They range from the poor in refugee camps still in the region to the more affluent in Paris

The Green Line is the demarcation line drawn after the 1948 Arab-Israeli War. Today it marks the 'boundary' between Israel and the Occupied Palestinian Territories – often represented in Palestinian and Israeli films.

and other European cities as well as in North America, Australia, etc. Some of these communities have been recently formed, but others, such as the trading families from Syria and Lebanon, go back much further into the history of European colonialism. From these movements we get **diasporic** and **exilic** film cultures.

Diversity means that there are several, possibly mutually exclusive categories or self-definitions that have been applied. For instance, the peoples of the region are largely Muslim but there are significant populations of Jews and Christians (and agnostics). All three monotheistic religions in the region are in fact collections of several groups, each of which identifies with different practices or teachings – identity politics in the region is a heady mix of religion, ethnicity and politics as well as gender and sexuality. The region is home to the majority of Arab filmmakers, although Europe and Africa also produce Arab filmmakers and there are people in the region who see themselves as European or African. Again, just as Arabic is the dominant language across much of the region, it isn't the same Arabic in popular speech in each country and the region encompasses other large language groups such as Turkish, Farsi, Kurdish, etc. But when we see scenes from diverse communities in the films, there is a sense in which history and geography have contributed to the development of cultures with some common features, and exploring these will be one of the aims of this chapter.

The film industries and film cultures of the Middle East

Film industry personnel and film scholars have also had difficulty dealing with this region. In the Wallflower Series of *24 Frames* offering essays focusing on key films from specific film territories, the editor of the *North Africa and the Middle East* volume, Gönül Dönmez-Colin, discusses debates about 'West Asia' as the region may more accurately be described by Asian scholars. The region is problematic for film industries because, although there are large centres of population and a history of interest in popular entertainment, there have also been restrictions on cinema exhibition as a result of war and political unrest as well as religious views. Consequently the penetration of Hollywood and international product has been limited at various times and local production has sometimes been stifled. Individual filmmakers in the region have increasingly turned to overseas funding.

However, the region does have three major film-producing centres in Egypt, Turkey and Iran, and there is a new focus for film as both art and entertainment in the oil-rich Gulf States, for example, through the Doha Film Institute in Qatar and the Dubai International Film Festival in the UAE, both of which aim to promote Arab film production. These oil money initiatives have added to the other principal source of funding in smaller countries via the cultural policies of the EU and in particular France as a production partner. Israeli and Palestinian film cultures share similar issues about funding in a social and cultural context dominated by current political struggles and reliance on overseas involvement, including American as well as European exiles and funders. It would be wrong, however, to see the region as linked only to film industries and cultures in Europe and North America. Local audiences in the Middle East have long been interested in Indian cinema, especially in the Gulf which now receives first-run films from India.

MENA (Middle East and North Africa) is an acronym used in business and politics. See also the London MENA Film Festival (menafilmfest.com).

Local film industries

As with other parts of Asia and Africa (and Latin America), building a profile of the region in terms of film industries and film cultures based on statistics is difficult. The international film industry only publishes information on territories with an organised market for international product. (Research reports by industry consultants are commissioned for internal consumption by specific companies.) Countries where the number of cinemas is too small to produce a significant admissions figure or where international films are not distributed according to (American/European) industry practices are generally ignored. The figures for Iran need to be considered in the light of government policies, discussed in more detail later in this chapter.

Turkey is potentially the dominant player in the region with a large population, the highest production levels and the most cinema screens on which it manages to deliver a majority share of admissions for domestic productions. If Turkey were to follow up its foreign policy moves with a concerted attempt to sell its films across the region, it could consolidate its position through 'soft power' (see Chapter 9 on Turkish TV exports).

There is a clear disparity between two groups of countries in terms of GDP per capita and hence spending power. The Gulf States and Israel have up to ten times the income of the poorer countries. Israel has substantial box office revenue and a domestic production programme to match. The indications are now that some of the Gulf States are also moving in this direction. By contrast, Egypt, a long-time major

Country	Population (millions)	GDP per capita (US$)	Gross Box Office (US $ millions)	Average ticket price (US$)	Admissions (millions)	Domestic productions	Market share for domestic productions	Number of cinema screens
Bahrain	0.8	22,809	16.9	7.95	2.2	–	–	52
Egypt	79.4	2,922	74.7	2.4	31.3	25	80	341
Iran	75.9	6,260	27.9	2.9	9.7	76	99.7	438
Israel	7.6	32,297	99.0	9.9	10.0	16	12	395
Kuwait	3.7	46,460	19.8	9.5	2.2	–	–	61
Lebanon	4.0	10,473	18.4	6.6	2.7	8	4	98
Morocco	32.2	3,162	8.4	3.7	2.2	19	19	68
Qatar	1.8	97,967	13.0	8.8	1,5	–	–	43
Turkey	72.2	10,756	238.7	5.6	42.3	70	50.2	2093
UAE	5.4	66,625	100.4	8.1	10.1	–	–	255

Fig 6.1 Industry data on those countries in 'the Middle East and North Africa' covered by the *Focus 2012 Report: World Film Market Trends* published by the European Audio-Visual Observatory. The report takes data from a variety of sources including Nielsen, *Variety*, *Screen International*, Film Festivals and national film bodies (data for Bahrain comes from *Focus 2010*).

producer, is suffering from low average ticket prices in the poorest country in the region on a per capita basis. Egyptian films still circulate across the region and, after Hollywood, claim the most admissions in Arab countries. (The domestic share of the market is preserved by a strict quota policy on American imports.) The figures for Morocco suggest that it too may be able to build its domestic industry (having for many years benefited from acting as a location for Hollywood and French productions).

Hidden behind these figures is the vigour of Palestinian film culture. Despite having only four full-time cinemas and struggling with all kinds of obstacles created by Israeli occupation, Palestinian filmmakers continue to produce significant numbers of fiction feature films (always as co-productions) and locally produced documentaries.

The difficulties of international film distribution mean that our focus will inevitably fall on what may be deemed the specialised or art cinema productions from the region. Let us briefly consider the three main producers and discover why getting to see popular films outside their home territories is difficult. Turkey, Egypt and Iran are of roughly similar size and population. They all have long histories of film production and they share an Islamic culture – although it manifests itself in different ways in each country. Turkey has a secular government, Iran is an 'Islamic state' and Egypt is at the time of writing still to determine its future after the 'Arab Spring' of 2011.

Turkish film culture and industry

The history of film in Turkey falls somewhere between the experience of India and that of many European territories. Relatively late to develop a local production base, the industry reached its full potency between 1950 and 1970 with the production of 250 films or more per year. Yesilçam ('Green pine') is a metonym for the Turkish film industry, similar to 'Hollywood' and named after Yesilçam Street in the Beyoglu district of Istanbul, where many actors, directors, crew members and studios were based.

Television too came relatively late to Turkey (the first national broadcasts were in 1968) but as elsewhere it quickly drew audiences away from the local popular cinema films and Yesilçam declined. The revival began in the late 1990s and by 2010 the number of cinemas and screens had doubled over 20 years. A closer look at 2010 figures from 'Film in the New Europe' (www.filmneweurope.com/Turkey) suggests that local production was 60 releases but that 'risk-averse' distribution strategies meant that a small number of films were big hits that out-performed Hollywood imports but a large number of local films were hardly seen at all. Even so, in 2010 local productions took 53 per cent of the Turkish box office. The local hits ranged from comedies and romances through to action films and large-scale epic films. In March 2012 a **national-popular** epic *Fetih 1453* (*Conquest 1453*), telling the story of Sultan Mehmet II's conquest of Constantinople in 1453, became the biggest success of recent times, selling 4.6 million tickets in just 18 days. It was also the biggest budget Turkish film at US$17 million (www.todayszaman.com/columnist-273706-fetih-1453-turkish-cinema-on-the-brink-of-a-new-era.html). The columnist on *Today's Zaman* suggests that the film will attract many admissions at box offices across the Muslim world and points out that director Faruk Aksoy has now made four of the Top 10 Turkish films at the box office. *Fetih 1453* was released

Three cinemas opened/reopened on the West Bank between 2009 and 2012 in Nablus, Jenin and East Jerusalem. There are no functioning cinemas in Gaza at the time of writing – although Gaza does have filmmakers and a local film culture.

Fig 6.2
Cinema-goers in Ankara for a screening of *Fetih 1453*. Source: Adem Altan/AFP/Getty Images.

in international markets at the same time as its Turkish release and it entered the International Chart at No. 8 based on returns from just four recognised territories. After a month on release it had taken US$37 million.

While productions like *Fetih 1453* help to grow the Turkish film industry and to push it towards major production status, Turkish cinema admissions are well below European levels with only around 0.5 visits per head per annum. However, two other developments are also beginning to raise the profile of Turkish films.

The **diaspora market** for Turkish films in Germany is significant. With three to four million people of Turkish descent living in Germany, as well as smaller communities in Austria, the Netherlands and the UK, major Turkish hits may expect to do good business. For instance, the franchise of three comedy films, starting with *Recep Ivedik* in 2008, saw European box office running at about 10 per cent of the Turkish total – four million admissions in Turkey and 400,000 in the EU (Lumière Database). Some of these films will have screenings in London and, together with DVD sales in Europe and North America, the Turkish diaspora audience performs a similar function to that of the Indian diaspora.

Research and Explore 6.1: *Popular Turkish film*

Find out what happened to the release of the Turkish film *Kurtlar Vadisi: Filistin* (*Valley of the Wolves: Palestine*, Turkey, 2011) in Germany and explore the responses to the film on IMDb and elsewhere. Compare this with the responses to *Fethi 1453*. What does this tell you about the potential for Turkish film exports?

As well as providing an audience for Turkish-language films, the Turkish diaspora has also produced important filmmakers. The two most prominent are Fatih Akin in Germany and Ferzan Özpetek in Italy. Although these filmmakers get the biggest response in their home countries as well as France and Spain, when they have co-produced with Turkey and featured stories set partly in Turkey they have achieved significant admissions in the Turkish market of between 100 and 200,000. The films of Akin and Özpetek circulate more visibly at international festivals and via specialised film distribution in Europe and North America but there are similarly celebrated Turkish filmmakers producing specialised films as well. Nuri Bilge Ceylan, Reha Erdem and Semih Kaplanoglu have all won major festival prizes with films that are set in Turkey and which deal with aspects of Turkish culture.

Case study 6.1: *Uzak* (*Distant*, Turkey, 2002)

Nuri Bilge Ceylan hosts an impressive website at http://www.nuribilgeceylan.com which includes both photographic galleries and film-related material.

The third fiction feature by the feted Turkish writer-director **Nuri Bilge Ceylan** consolidated his reputation after early festival successes. The narrative is seemingly straightforward. Yusuf is made redundant in his village in Central Turkey and decides to visit Istanbul, planning to stay for a few days with his cousin Mahmut while he looks for work aboard a ship. Mahmut is a photographer. He is divorced from a woman who he persuaded to have an abortion because he couldn't cope with a child. He is now settled in his ways and doesn't really want Yusuf hanging around – he isn't as hospitable as he might be.

This is an **auteur** film – 'authored' like a novel by a filmmaker with a 'personal view' (see Chapter 7 for discussion). It is useful in this case to have some background knowledge about the writer-director. Ceylan (b. 1959) began his studies as an engineer and then became a photographer before developing an interest in cinema. He developed his skills as a filmmaker relatively late and, in his early career, culminating in the production of *Uzak*, he undertook most of the creative roles himself (producing, writing, directing, cinematography and editing) or in conjunction with friends and family. He also cast two non-actors, men he knew, as recurring characters. Emin Toprak and Muzaffer Özdemir, respectively Ceylan's cousin and an architect friend, play Yusuf and Mahmut. In

Fig 6.3
Mehmet Emin Toprak as the 'country cousin' in Istanbul in *Uzak*. Source: The Kobal Collection/ www.picture-desk.com.

Uzak the two characters are similar to those in Ceylan's previous film, *Clouds of May* (*Mayis sikintisi*, Turkey, 1999), in which Muzaffer Özdemir played a filmmaker. Since Ceylan's parents also appeared in that film, we understand that there are autobiographical elements in his films.

There is not a great deal of plot in *Uzak* and some audiences may find the pace of the narrative slower than a mainstream film. However, *Uzak* features excellent cinematography with – for audiences outside Turkey – some surprisingly beautiful shots of Istanbul under several inches of snow. It is also in parts very funny and at other times quite moving. *Uzak* works as a narrative on several levels. At the level of metaphor, the story refers to traditional tales about town and country living, such as the fable of the town mouse and the country mouse. Yusuf comes to Istanbul still with a sense of the country about him. He is quite gregarious and in close contact with his family. Mahmut by contrast has cut himself off in the city and has become disenchanted with his profession. There is also a 'real' mouse story in which Mahmut has set a trap of glued paper to catch a mouse in his kitchen. He explains this to Yusuf as part of his almost obsessive instructions about keeping the flat clean and tidy. It is Mahmut, in a highly comic scene, who gets himself stuck to the paper, but it is Yusuf who must eventually dispose of the mouse when it is caught. We can relate the metaphor to Yusuf's first appearance in the opening shot of the film, walking towards the camera across a valley to the road taking him to Istanbul, and to the film's closing shot of Mahmut staring out across the Bosphorus towards Europe. Is Turkey part of Europe or part of Asia? Should it look west or east? In *Uzak* Yusuf is a much more sympathetic character than Mahmut, which seems to indicate that Ceylan is being very self-critical. There is even a joke against **cinephiles**. Mahmut watches a film on TV, not just any film but *Stalker* (USSR, 1979), the science fiction film by Andrei Tarkovsky and highly regarded by critics. A bored Mahmut switches to a porn channel only to quickly switch back to Tarkovsky when Yusuf appears.

Mahmut behaves very badly – towards everyone. But it is difficult not to be moved when he rushes to the airport to watch his ex-wife board the aircraft that will take her and her new partner to a new life in Canada. When the film ends, Mahmut is staring out across the water and smoking a cigarette – one of the cheap brand that he berated Yusuf for smoking. Like many specialised films, *Uzak* ends on what Hollywood audiences would perhaps call a 'downer'. The film doesn't celebrate Turkish culture like the national popular films, but it makes us think about the lives of two Turkish characters.

In 2011, Ceylan's 157-minute-long police procedural *Once Upon a Time in Anatolia*, in which again very little 'action' occurs by popular genre standards, won the Cannes Grand Jury prize and was at the top of many cinephiles' lists of the films of the year. More important perhaps in the long run, the film has won prizes at Asian film festivals and looks set to be distributed in East Asia where it will help promote Turkish cinema and confirm Ceylan's international profile.

Iranian cinema

Iranian cinema currently occupies a unique place in global film culture. Iran's film industry had begun domestic production tentatively in the late 1920s, battling against foreign films in distribution and some resistance from religious groups in the country. The industry really began to develop from 1948, first with popular genre pictures and later with the beginnings of an avant-garde in the late 1960s.

The Islamic Revolution in 1979 was a major disruptive force in all forms of cultural work but a new (conservative) commercial industry and a revived arthouse sector began to emerge in the mid-1980s and it was the new filmmakers of this group who started to dazzle international arthouse audiences from the 1990s onwards (see Mehrabi (2006: 38) on this history). This success has been despite the actions of the Iranian government in banning films and imprisoning filmmakers, and in the process almost closing down a potentially vibrant domestic popular cinema. As a result of the government's stance, it is almost impossible to present a considered view of that popular cinema. The films are not exported and there is little reliable industry data for admissions or box office of individual films.

In a BBC Report from Tehran on 8 January 2012 (www.bbc.co.uk/news/ entertainment-arts-16458859) Mohsen Asgari visits a cinema in the city and tells us that it is one of the few still operating that attracts a Friday night crowd to a comedy film, the most popular genre in Iran. The auditorium is modern but quite small (perhaps 100 seats). Asgari tells us that Iran still produces 150 films a year but that only 10 per cent of Iran's 80 million people go to the cinema. He goes on to say that there is little private investment in film productions so that most films must be financed by the state. But since the state requires all scripts to be vetted before funding is awarded, many directors are prepared to risk potential imprisonment by making films outside the system, sometimes with overseas monies. Asgari's report tallies with an earlier *Financial Times* report: 'Iranian film industry's star dims' by Monavar Khalaj (22 September 2010). Rather different reports may be found on the website of Press TV, the Iranian government's English-language channel (presstv.ir).

The infrastructure for an Iranian industry is all in place with film and drama schools producing the personnel and agencies like the Farabi Cinema Foundation (http://www.fcf.ir/en/index.php) overseeing production and organising distribution and exhibition, but government policy is in danger of driving the industry underground. In January 2012 it forced the closure of the Iranian House of Cinema, the main agency for independent films in the country, and replaced it with a more compliant new organisation. The House of Cinema has represented 5,000 members, including many leading Iranian filmmakers. The most celebrated of Iran's filmmakers such as Abbas Kiarostami and Mohsen Makhmalbaf (see Chapter 3) have already exiled themselves abroad, and Jafar Panahi was arrested in 2011 and sentenced to imprisonment. Banned from making films, his 2011 documentary *This is Not a Film* was smuggled out of the country on a USB stick hidden in a cake and subsequently released worldwide.

Closed Curtain, a second Panahi film set in a single room, was shown at the Berlin Film Festival in February 2013. His co-director Kambuzia Partovi presented the film with Panahi banned from travelling.

Iranian Cinema has reached a point where it resembles the film industries that operated in Spain under Franco between 1940 and 1976, in the USSR and Eastern European countries between 1948 and 1989 and in China for much of the time since 1949. The authorities can censor films, ban filmmakers and restrict screenings but they cannot always stop the films being made and screened at international festivals or distributed in overseas territories. Filmmakers can move abroad or they can stay at home and make films that operate via allegories and delicate codes. In the report from Asgari above there is an interview with Khosrow Sinaei, an Iranian director who argues that the restrictions may actually help filmmakers to become more 'artistic' in their approach (i.e. the artistic strength of Iranian cinema has developed partly *because of* the restrictions, not in spite of them). This echoes some of the arguments by the Polish auteur Andrezj Wajda:

Interviewer: *Why were such fantastic films made during the communist years in Poland, and now that everything is free, Polish films are so weak?*

Wajda: In a totalitarian state, in one where fictional elections mean that people have no political representation, artists become their voice. For years and as far as our capabilities, talent, and political situations permitted, we tried to be the voice of Poles. Political cinema requires a large audience. The artist cannot lean out the window and call out to society. How many people will hear?

(www.wajda.pl/en/wywiad80.html)

Wajda's comments make a lot of sense but he refers to events some 30 to 40 years ago. In contemporary Iran that 'large audience' mostly watches films, Hollywood and Iranian, on pirate DVDs and online. YouTube carries many clips from Iranian films – and many complete films. *The Lizard* (*Marmoulak*, Iran, 2004), directed by Kamal Tabrizi, is a good example of a popular comedy available online with English subtitles. It tells the story of a man who escapes from prison in the guise of a priest and who finds himself feted by his congregation in a village near the border where he has gone, hoping to escape abroad. See a detailed synopsis at http://en.wikipedia.org/wiki/Marmoulak_(film).

Research and Explore 6.2

Compare the situation in contemporary Iran with that in China as discussed in Chapter 11.

What are the similarities and differences between the actions of the Iranian state towards cinema and the authorities in the PRC and Taiwan between 1949 and 1987?

Is there any similarity between 'dissident directors' in China and in Iran?

Chapter 3 includes a discussion of a film by Samira Makhmalbaf which is in some ways typical of successful Iranian specialised films, bringing together forms of realism and surrealism and dealing with issues and characters which may be seen as marginal or peripheral by a popular audience in Iran. Here we will focus on the highest profile Iranian film to get an international release in recent years – and one which is rather different from the Makhmalbaf family films in its mix of ingredients.

Case study 6.2: *Nader and Simin: A Separation (Jodaeiye Nader az Simin, Iran, 2011)*

Beginning with its appearance at Cannes in May 2011, *A Separation* by writer-director Asghar Farhadi steadily conquered the international film market. It followed two earlier films with similar ingredients from the same director: *Fireworks Wednesday* (*Chaharshanbe-soori*, Iran, 2006) and *About Elly* (*Darbareye Elly*, Iran, 2009). All three films are ensemble pieces featuring couples from Tehran's middle classes whose bourgeois marital relationships are to some extent disrupted by young women who have come into the group from 'outside'. In *Fireworks Wednesday*, a young woman from the suburbs works as an agency cleaner and finds herself in an apartment where, through no fault of her own, she gets caught up in the lies of adultery. In *About Elly*, a young nursery schoolteacher is invited to a 'weekend away' with three married couples and their

Fig 6.4
Taraneh Alidoosti as Roohi tries on her wedding dress at the agency where she registers for temporary work as a cleaner in *Fireworks Wednesday*.

divorced university friend who has just returned from Germany. But when she is left in charge of the group's children on the beach, Elly disappears and the group is again caught up in lies told to the police and Elly's family. These two films are both universal in terms of families and relationships, but also distinctively Iranian in their concerns over gender roles and social etiquette. As such they have attracted audiences both at home and at international festivals.

A Separation begins with Nader and Simin in front of a judge (who is unseen but whose 'point of view' we are forced to adopt). Simin wants to leave Iran and take their 11-year-old daughter Termeh with her. Nader refuses to leave because he must stay and look after his father who has Alzheimer's disease. The judge tells them that they must both agree to the divorce and that they should go away and sort it out between them. Simin then decides to leave the family apartment and go to her mother's. Termeh decides to stay put. This is the inciting incident in the narrative. Without his wife in the household, Nader begins to realise that getting carers for his father during the daytime (when he is at work and Termeh is at school) is going to be an issue. When he does hire Razieh, a woman from the suburbs, to come to his apartment the problems become real. He is not aware that Razieh has taken the job without telling her husband (which local custom says she must do) and there are other complications, so that when a dispute arises Nader's actions have a very unfortunate outcome. It is important that the audience remain alert throughout all the early stages of the narrative because what happens later depends, as a legal dispute, on tiny pieces of information revealed in these early scenes.

The intricate plotting across just over two hours never lets up in intensity. It is presented via a simple and clear aesthetic with handheld camerawork that operates fairly close to the characters in the confined spaces of rooms, offices, stairways, etc. and a couple of roadside locations. There is no musical score – only dialogue, sound effects and direct sound. The great strength of the screenplay and characterisation is that in the true humanist sense we are able to recognise that everyone has their good and less good sides – with the possible exception of Termeh who is forced by circumstances into

Fig 6.5
Simin (Leila Hatami) and
Nader (Peyman Moaadi)
face the judge at the start
of *A Separation*.

impossible situations that she tries desperately to resolve. (Termeh is played by the
director's own daughter.)

The film has a terrible fascination, partly because of its universality. Tehran (for the
middle classes) is in many ways no different to London, Paris or New York. Alzheimer's is
an issue with older relatives everywhere in the developed world (again a different kind of
problem in poorer societies). The social class divide is just as important in Iran. Nader is
a bank executive with some kind of responsibility. Simin's profession isn't clear, but this is
a middle-class household with working professionals. The would-be working-class carers
face a long commute across the city and they desperately need the money.

All the women in the film cover their hair, but Razieh wears a full *chador*. She is also
concerned about what is 'allowed' in a strangers' (i.e. non-family) household but the
moral questions – about truthfulness and fidelity – are presented in such a way that they
are relevant whether or not the characters are devout Muslims. The film does in many
ways invite us, the audience, to ask what we would do in the same circumstances.

The Iranian judicial process involves a single investigating judge. The system is
presented as thorough but somewhat inflexible in its process. It appears to treat
plaintiffs and defendants on an equal basis but still seems biased towards the middle
class who can more easily get 'respectable' people to vouch for them. Unlike some of the
other Iranian art films that focus on much more obvious 'issues' and political discourses,
A Separation seems 'ordinary' in its story elements but extraordinary in its presentation.
Even so, there is a subtle critique of society and it is likely that the film will be seen by
bigger audiences than some of the more overtly 'political' films.

Asghar Farhadi (b. 1972) began making films as a teenager and studied scriptwriting
and theatre. After graduation he worked in television and theatre before directing his
first feature in 2003. He is both younger and has a different background compared to
Kiarostami, Mohsen Makhmalbaf and Panahi. He has worked within the Iranian system.
Major prizes for his last two films, including the Foreign Language Oscar for *A Separation*

(plus a nomination for Best Original Screenplay), have brought prestige to Iran. Even so, Farhadi has suffered from pressure from the authorities, including an order preventing him from working in Iran for a month until he apologised for supporting exiled and banned directors. It is no surprise that in May 2012 he was presented with the EU Media award, promising funding for his next feature to be made, in French, in France in autumn 2012. (*A Separation* was a French co-production and made US$8 million at the French box office.) Another Iranian director has become at least a temporary exile.

Farhadi's approach shares certain neo-realist elements with the Makhmalbafs and Jafar Panahi in its subject matter and its humanist approach towards characters. On the other hand, the films are very carefully scripted, casting is crucially important with a great deal of preparation time (including rehearsal time) and the choreography of characters in confined spaces is similarly planned. The scenes are mainly shot on location but the court scenes had to be shot in disused school buildings. The discipline of theatre and television shooting is evident in several scenes. Added to this is a sense of a balance between the seeming realism of some scenes and a suspicion that the dramatic situation has been artfully constructed. The ending of the film is 'open' and Farhadi has said that he wants audiences to leave his films asking themselves questions:

> I believe that the world today needs more questions than answers. Answers prevent you from questioning, from thinking. From the opening scene, I aimed to set this up. The film's first question is whether an Iranian child has a better future in his or her own country or abroad. There is no set answer. My wish is that this film will make you ask yourselves questions, such as these ones.
>
> (From the UK press pack for the film)

All forms of realism in cinema are 'constructed' by definition but there is a difference between a scene that appears to develop out of a 'real world situation' and one which exists because it has been written in order to create drama.

Iranian cinema has attracted more critical attention than most national cinemas. The reasons for this are partly associated with the high quality of the films in international distribution. Some of the attention is specifically focused on gender issues, particularly the question of the veil and the relationship between the cinematic gaze and the portrayal of women. See, for instance, Hamid Naficy's (1999) complex essay which explores the apparent contradiction between a society which demands that women 'cover' themselves and a film culture that has seen the emergence of several high-profile female directors and strong female characters represented on screen – such as in the work of Samira Makhmalbaf discussed in Chapter 3.

The other main focus for much of the critical work has been on its **exilic** nature. Iranian filmmakers working abroad are like filmmakers from other parts of the 'post-colonial' world or the 'Global South' who move to New York or Paris. These exilic and diasporic filmmakers are discussed by Naficy as part of what he calls '*accented cinema*'. They are

> 'situated but universal' figures who work in the interstices of social formations and cinematic practices [...] they exist in a state of tension and dissension with both their original and their current homes.
>
> (Naficy 2001: 10)

Expressed in less rigorous terminology, these filmmakers exist between two worlds. They find supporters and develop ways of working outside the studio systems of the West as well as avoiding the structures of the local industry they have left behind.

It is clear from the brief discussion above that several Iranian filmmakers fall into this category. They are 'local' and 'global' in outlook. Many of the film scholars who focus on this issue (e.g. Naficy and Hamid Dabashi) are themselves part of an Iranian or other Middle Eastern diaspora in the US and in Europe, especially in France. This diasporic community retains a keen interest in Iranian cinema and its exiled filmmakers.

The politics of this exilic filmmaking are complex. **Mohsen Makhmalbaf** has been described as a 'borderless' filmmaker since he stopped making films in Iran after 1999. From a base in Paris he has returned to make films in other Central Asian countries such as Afghanistan or Tajikistan, maintaining an international profile and being celebrated by Dabashi (2007) as a 'rebel filmmaker'. But Makhmalbaf has also been fiercely attacked for his representation of the local cultures of the territories in which his 'filmmaking without frontiers' is located. *Scream of the Ants* (France, 2006) deals with a visit to India by an Iranian couple and Shahab Esfandiary (2012: 106) finds that:

> Makhmalbaf's attitude towards India and its inhabitants in this film resembles the view of an eighteenth century European anthropologist who is baffled by the (apparent) ignorance, barbarism, and superstitious beliefs of the people of the Orient [...] reminiscent of the project of colonialism.

Makhmalbaf in these terms is acting like a Western orientalist. This is an unfortunate echo of something that Hamid Dabashi himself discusses in an essay on Makhmalbaf's 1996 film *A Moment of Innocence* (Dabashi 1999: 119–121). Dabashi argues that intellectuals in Iran are 'inorganic' – not connected to any working-class movement or even to a 'rooted' middle class. This is because Iran's 'modernising project' since the early nineteenth century has created what he calls a 'comprador bourgeoisie' – a term referring to the agents of Western powers who managed the plantations and mineral extraction of Asia. Iran has been completely

Makhmalbaf's 2001 film *Kandahar*, set in Afghanistan, was a surprise hit in the West after 9/11 in New York. Later it emerged that the Bush administration used ideas from the film in formulating a presentation of US war aims (Esfandiary 2012: 108).

Fig 6.6
Avaz Latif as Agrin, one of the refugees at the centre of *Turtles Can Fly*. Source: The Kobal Collection/ www.picture-desk.com.

dependent on oil that has paid for consumer imports without the development of domestic industry – a situation akin to control by an external colonial power. Iranian intellectual filmmakers have to work through ideas about how they address this colonial situation before they can comment on contemporary Iran. Dabashi argues that Makhmalbaf has begun this process but that praise from film festival critics is irrelevant – the films need to be discussed by Iranian audiences in Iran and in the diaspora.

These questions about exiles and colonialism also remind us that Iran is itself a multicultural state. Bahman Ghobadi is a Kurdish-Iranian filmmaker who has made films about Kurds in both Iran and Iraq (e.g. *Turtles Can Fly* (Iraq/Iran, 2004)). The Kurds form a 'borderless state' of more than 30 million people living in Iraq, Iran, Turkey and Syria, and in a widespread Kurdish diaspora.

The 2011 London Kurdish Film Festival screened 120 films (see lkff.co.uk).

Egyptian cinema

As with Iran, Egyptian cinema is difficult to study because the important commercial films produced in the country are not usually traded outside the Arab world. However, that is slowly starting to change as an independent sector begins to develop with potentially a more open outlook.

The Egyptian film industry has a long tradition with a strong production record steadily developing from the foundation of the first studio in 1934 and reaching a commercial peak between 1948 and 1952 with an average of 48 productions per year. Since then the industry has experienced nationalisation and part-privatisation but the number of productions has remained roughly the same (although not with the same audiences or profitability). As Viola Shafik (2007: 11) points out, this development took place in the colonial period. The British mandate over Egypt was relatively loosely held after 1922 but British forces didn't leave until 1952. After the First World War, most of the Arab world was divided up between the French and the British (the Sykes–Picot Agreement of 1916) comprising settler colonies and mandated territories. Shafik argues that what happened in Egypt couldn't have happened anywhere else in the Arab world. Partly that was because nowhere else had the accumulation of local capital to begin a studio, but it was also because of the different policies adopted by the British and the French. French policy (mirrored elsewhere in West Africa) was to 'acculturate the natives' and insist that they learn French and about France and French culture – films by local filmmakers were definitely not encouraged (as they would be after independence in an attempt to maintain the Francophone cultural activity). In Egypt, however, there was no cultural control as such and the industry developed sometimes in quite similar ways to the industries nominally under the British Raj in India during the same period. See Chapter 8 for more on British and French colonial policy.

Early Egyptian films developed from existing local traditions, including popular theatre and literature – and, very importantly, music. Not surprisingly perhaps the most popular genres have tended to be melodramas, broad comedies and action films. Shafik suggests that the Second World War created an increased interest in Hollywood and that aspects of American film culture were incorporated in a uniquely Egyptian way into Arab popular cinema. In 1952 the overthrow of King Farouk brought to power Gamal Abdel Nasser, a charismatic leader who attempted to introduce socialism into Egypt and to support independence struggles in Africa and other Arab countries. Egyptian cinema became involved with ideas of the 'national' as well as political stories. Towards the end of the Nasser period some more artistic films appeared, but at various points the commercial industry has suffered from low budgets and the impact of television on cinema productions.

We may characterise some of the issues about Egyptian popular films as follows:

- a strong audience desire for entertainment (i.e. audiences have expectations because of a history of popular films);
- a potentially contradictory pull between Hollywood stories and 'national' Egyptian stories (in the same film);
- the popularity of romance, but also controversial stories about social issues concerned with love and sex;
- a star system, often involving star music performers;
- a Hollywood-like appetite to draw in talent from other Arab countries.

Even though Egyptian cinema is distinctive, it is still protected to a certain extent by restrictions on Hollywood imports. The threat from television from the 1980s onwards has been partially offset by the circulation of films on video, especially in the Gulf, and the great popularity of television drama series involving film stars and filmmaking facilities (see Chapter 9). Although relatively few Egyptian popular films make it into distribution outside the Arab world, some of the films of one of the most celebrated Egyptian directors, **Youssef Chahine** (1926–2008), are available subtitled on Region 1 discs. Otherwise, as in Iran, clips from popular Egyptian films are available on YouTube.

Much of the funding for Egyptian cinema comes from the more affluent Arab countries in the Gulf. Some of the cultural foundations in Qatar and Dubai, etc. are increasingly interested in new forms of Egyptian cinema, more in the line perhaps of the **festival films** discussed in Chapter 7. Case study 6.3 is an example of a recent Egyptian festival success.

Chahine's 1982 feature *An Egyptian Story* illustrates much of the history of cinema in Egypt outlined above.

Case study 6.3: *Microphone* (Egypt, 2010)

This example of the new independent cinema in Egypt is a docudrama. It creates a fictional story around the real issues of putting on independent music and art events in contemporary Alexandria, Egypt's second city and the former cosmopolitan 'Utopia of the Eastern Mediterranean' during the 1930s. The director Ahmad Abdalla initially imagined a documentary about a single graffiti artist, but gradually the film 'just grew'. Making it a fiction feature helped it get distribution in Egypt, since documentaries have never figured in theatrical distribution.

Microphone didn't have a formal script and most of the musicians and artists play versions of themselves. The fictional story concerns Khaled (played by a major star of Egyptian cinema, Khaled Abol Naga) who has returned to Alexandria after working for seven years in New York as an engineer. His old friend finds him a job in an organisation that manages projects for art and community work. Khaled finds that the city has changed. On the one hand, there is a vibrant underground art scene that he slowly discovers and comes to appreciate. On the other, the authorities and other social pressures mean that it is very difficult to organise/promote the scene. The central narrative involves Khaled's attempt to put on a concert featuring independent music acts,

Fig 6.7
Yousra El Lozy in the independent Egyptian film *Microphone*. Source: Film Clinic.

including hip-hop, metal and traditional music. At the same time he tries to communicate with his father, and in a scene with his ex-girlfriend (which is chopped up and played intermittently out of sequence) he learns that she is now leaving to do a Ph.D. in London. Khaled says that he will always carry a little bit of sadness with him after he realises that he has lost her.

The film includes many performance scenes as well as skateboarding, graffiti art and an enjoyable narrative strand about a film school (in the Jesuit college) in which a film professor tries to explain the difference between documentary and reportage and fiction. The discussion here (based on a film festival screening with a Q&A) points to a very different kind of film compared to Egyptian commercial releases. Some of the elements are similar to those in the 'New Bollywood' films being produced in Mumbai (especially with the engineer returning from the US), but the intriguing mix of elements is original. The film won the main prize at the Carthage Film Festival in 2010, giving it status in the Maghreb, and independent films such as this are now being introduced to festival audiences in Cairo and Dubai.

Lebanese cinema

One of the smaller countries in the region, Lebanon has suffered greatly from civil war and its location between Syria and Israel. The diversity of its own population and the presence of so many Palestinian refugees does however make for a rich cultural mix. Added to this, up until the 1970s Beirut had developed into perhaps the most cosmopolitan and sophisticated of Arab cities through which exchanges in commerce and art could be arranged. Lebanon was, and can be again, an alternative base for Arab culture compared to Egypt.

Lebanon was part of the French mandate in the 'Levant' after the First World War and, as in other former French colonies, the cultural links have remained since full independence in the 1940s. Lebanese filmmakers may have attended French medium schools and trained in Paris – and funding may be possible via French production partners and public funding from European sources.

Case study 6.4: *Caramel* (Lebanon/France, 2007)

Nadine Labaki (b. 1974) trained as a filmmaker and made her name in advertising and the Arabic music video industry. She began acting in short films in 2003 and gradually moved into features. *Caramel*, her own first feature film, was the result of long preparation during which she participated in a screenwriting workshop organised by the Cannes Film Festival. Her second feature, *Where Do We Go Now?* (2011), won the Audience Prize at the Toronto Film Festival. As in *Caramel*, she co-wrote the script, directed the film and took the leading acting role.

Caramel was seen by 1.4 million people in Europe. In the UK the film made the box office Top 10 for three weeks.

 Caramel explores women's lives through a traditional genre. The film is a form of melodrama that uses some of the elements of soap opera in the UK, the *telenovela* in Latin America or its Middle Eastern equivalent as made in Egypt and Turkey. The central character, played by Labaki, is the owner of a beauty salon in Beirut in which 'caramel' is the sugar solution used as a form of depilation agent. It may be that the idea of using the salon as a meeting place for an array of female characters came partly from the very successful French film *Vénus beauté (institut)* (1999) written and directed by Tonie Marshall, although there are other films which use similar settings such as the African-American 'barbershop' films.

 The DVD for the film includes a long interview with the director in which she suggests that her intentions and practice were closer to neo-realism (see Chapter 3) than the genre classification of *Caramel* might imply. Most of the characters are played by non-professionals and although the film was carefully scripted there was also an element of improvisation on set with Labaki herself and two other writers responding to suggestions. The popular audience in Lebanon and audiences around the world have had no difficulty in following the film's narrative and identifying with the five female characters at its centre. Thus, for instance, the narrative thread that deals with the upcoming marriage of one of the characters and the subsequent wedding provides familiar audience pleasures.

Fig 6.8
Three of the women from the beauty salon take a taxi ride in *Caramel*. Nadine Labaki is on the right.

Music is also an important element in the film and was composed by Labaki's future husband. It too relates to the Middle Eastern melodrama. Negative connotations of melodrama mean that in Europe and North America the film has been described as a 'romantic comedy'. The film has comedic moments and it also features various romance sub-plots but the rom-com label is not really helpful, as it promises familiar genre pleasures about a central on/off romance that the film probably doesn't deliver.

The representation issues in the film are particularly interesting. Here is a Lebanese community in which Christians and Muslims mix easily, but in which women who appear completely 'Westernised' are still part of a traditional community with the pluses and minuses which that brings. The film was completed just before the 2006 war in Lebanon which forms a kind of 'structured absence' in the film. The Civil War has been the single most important subject for Lebanese filmmakers since the 1980s, and *Stray Bullet* (Lebanon/France, 2010) in which Labaki starred, and her own recent feature, both refer to the consequences of the Civil War.

As an example of Arab cinema, *Caramel* also raises the issue of language and post-colonialism. Although all five women are Arabs, four are Christians. The fifth, Nisrine, is Muslim. She is required to speak French at one point and it is clear that she is less fluent than the others. This is another possible factor of 'difference' that in conjunction with ethnicity, religion and gender, as well as social class, makes negotiating Lebanese society problematic for the women. The script is clever in the way it exploits these differences in developing a dramatic narrative. For instance, Layale, the central character played by Labaki, is in many ways a privileged woman – she owns her own beauty salon, she is physically attractive with a good personality, and she is a good communicator. But because she is unmarried she must live with her parents and her younger brother, and she is humiliated in her attempts to book a hotel room as a single woman – Lebanese law requires ID to prove that a woman booking a double room is married.

This element of language difference – the importance of French and French culture as a divisor in a post-colonial world – is something Lebanese film culture shares with that of the Maghreb (i.e. the former French colonial territories of Tunisia, Algeria and Morocco as well as Mauritania) and also of Francophone West and Central Africa. Lebanon's film industry is now to a significant extent dependent on European and particularly French production partnerships and funding support.

Je veux voir (I Want to See, Lebanon/France, 2008) by Joana Hadjithomas and Khalil Joreige features the French star Catherine Deneuve playing herself in a form of documentary drama in which she surveys the effects of civil war in Lebanon.

European funding and support

Like Lebanon, other parts of the MENA region are currently struggling to develop a local industrial base. Co-productions with European and/or perhaps Gulf-based agencies are the most likely means by which films from the region are going to be able to reach both domestic and international markets. This is the case for the Maghreb countries, and the role of Maghrebi-French filmmakers in making films about North African culture is explored in Chapter 4.

European audiovisual policies have an impact in several different ways in the MENA region. The Euro-Mediterranean Partnership (Euromed) was relaunched in 2008 so that the 27 states of the enlarged EU were joined by 16 further countries, most of which have coastal access to the Mediterranean. 'Culture' is one of the project areas for the new partnership (www.eeas.europa.eu/euromed/index_en.htm). Earlier, a support programme for the distribution of films from Mediterranean countries was organised through the original Euromed initiative (www.euromed-cinemas.org/supported-films.php). *Caramel* was one of the supported films in 2007. A further programme was launched in 2009 through the MEDIA programme (www.europa-cinemas.org/en/Supports/MEDIA-MUNDUS). These support programmes for distribution and exhibition are 'two way', helping films from outside Europe get more exposure in European cinemas, but also better distribution in other countries outside Europe in the case of 'Mediterranean films'. *Caramel* was released in several other countries in the region – though not all, possibly because of the issues dealt with in the film.

Eurimages is a funding body organised through the Council of Europe. It has 36 European members (including Turkey, but not the UK, which opted not to join). The fund's aims are economic and cultural with most of the fund supporting the production of films that are co-productions between members. Turkish films regularly receive support as do productions from exilic filmmakers from the Middle East (e.g. Elia Suleiman, whose Palestinian film *The Time That Remains* was co-produced by the Netherlands, France, Belgium and Italy in 2007, received €550,000).

In addition to these funds, co-productions between France or other European nations and filmmakers in the Middle East could benefit from the other forms of public funding discussed in Chapters 4 and 7.

Dreams of a nation: Palestine

This chapter concludes with a brief discussion about film culture and film production in Palestine and Israel. It would take a whole chapter to explore even sketchily what has happened over the history of film activity in the sub-region since the Lumière's *operateur* showed the first local footage of Jerusalem in 1896. Instead, we will pick out some of the ways in which filmmakers here face similar conditions to those elsewhere in the Middle East and some ways in which local filmmakers find themselves in a unique position.

In 2002 an exiled Palestinian filmmaker, Annemarie Jacir, began to curate a film festival in New York with the title 'Dreams of a Nation' (see Jacir in Dabashi 2006). The theoretical question of defining a national cinema (as discussed in Chapter 4) is rather more pragmatic in relation to Palestine. Much of Palestine is occupied by Israeli settlers and in all of Palestine economic and cultural activity is constrained by Israeli regulations which affect travel and the movement of goods. Palestine has limited technical facilities for film production and, as noted above, only a handful of cinema screens. Yet Palestinian filmmakers, working in co-productions with European funding, have produced some of the most celebrated Arab films over the past 20 years. We will consider two films by a typically exilic Palestinian director.

Case study 6.5: Two films from Hany Abu-Assad

Hany Abu-Assad is based in the Netherlands and he has returned twice so far to make features in Palestine. Born in Nazareth (i.e. in territory claimed as Israeli), he left aged 18 to train as an engineer in Delft before forming a film production company in 1990 and initially working as a producer. He made a full-length feature documentary in Palestine before embarking on *Rana's Wedding* (*Al qods fee yom akhar*, Palestine/Netherlands/UAE,

2002). As the credits indicate, this film was produced with money from outside Palestine. 'Rana' is played by Clara Khoury, daughter of the Jerusalem-born actor Makram Khoury. Like her father and many other Arab actors she appears mostly in Israeli or American films and television programmes.

Plot outline

Rana lives with her father in (Arab) East Jerusalem. The family are middle class and she has her aunt, cousins and grandmother nearby. The film covers ten hours on the fateful day when her father has decreed that he is 'finally' leaving for Egypt at 4 p.m. Rana, who is not yet 21, should go with him. If she wants to stay in Jerusalem, she must marry one of the 'respectable men' on a list drawn up by her father. She is determined to marry her boyfriend Khalil, an actor whose theatre group is currently based in Ramallah – which the Israelis have made a separate jurisdiction, so travel between the two Palestinian communities is controlled. Islamic law decrees that if Khalil and Rana can present themselves, along with a Registrar, before Rana's father, he cannot refuse permission for them to marry. But this is not so easy to arrange in just ten hours – not when it means getting papers and making the other preparations as well as travelling to and fro between East Jerusalem and Ramallah. (Although Rana is legally a resident of the occupied territories of Palestine she must pass through Israeli roadblocks and a strip of land designated as 'Israel' to reach Ramallah.)

Commentary

The film is a comedy-drama that some audiences have seen as an allegory in which the trials and tribulations of the central character are representative of the way Palestine itself is treated. It seems clear on several occasions that Abu-Assad is influenced in how he responds to the script (by Liana Badr and Ihab Lamey) by the kinds of modernist devices developed in European cinema.

In one of his statements about the film he said:

> In this film I felt that reality was dictating me. It became a bloody fight between reality and fiction, in a country where the normal appears to be absurd and the absurd appears to be normal. I realised this fight had to be a fair one and that in order to win I had to stay honest.
>
> (archives.dawn.com/weekly/images/archive/020922/images5.htm)

And from a blog comment on the film from an American student:

> Khalil jokes around in front of a security camera, which the audience has assumed the point of view of, and he mimes out a fight where he is repeatedly punched, yet he walks away defiantly in the end. Khalil is mocking the absurdity of the security camera and his pantomime is meant to insult the camera, and thus insult Israel's watchful eye.
>
> Finally, as Rana is preparing for her hastily organised wedding, she and her friend, Mary, gaze outside a window as an Israeli demolition crew tears down a house. Rana remarks that they are destroying a home on the day she wants to build one. Facing the camera, Mary tells her not to worry, because the house will be rebuilt the next day.
>
> (thearabicfilmblog.blogspot.com/2009/01/ranas-wedding-rana-as-allegory-for.html)

Fig 6.9
The view from the security camera in *Rana's Wedding* as Khalil (Khalifa Natour) mocks the surveillance suffered by Palestinians.

This absurdity represents a powerful way of maintaining identity and resilience in the face of endless provocation. The film ends with the opening lines from 'State of Siege' by the Palestinian poet Mahmoud Darwish:

> Here on the slopes before sunset and at the gun-mouth of time,
> Near orchards deprived of their shadows,
> We do what prisoners do,
> What the unemployed do:
> We nurture hope.

If *Rana's Wedding* appears optimistic in its comic response to absurdity, Abu-Assad's 2005 second feature, again with external funding, is slightly different. *Paradise Now* is the story of Saïd and Khaled, two young men from the Palestinian city of Nablus, recruited as suicide bombers and sent on a mission to the Israeli city of Tel Aviv. The film is not a conventional suspense thriller but a clever meditation on what motivates young men to consider such an action (again the characters are given only a few hours to come to terms with their decision). There are some darkly comic moments (e.g. during an inept recording of a 'martyr video') but these add to the analysis of what life for young people in Palestine under occupation can mean. The introduction of an exilic character – the return to Nablus of Suha, a young woman who has been educated abroad – provides an outsider's perspective on the young men's state of mind.

Paradise Now received a wider international release than *Rana's Wedding*, winning many awards and an Oscar nomination as best foreign-language film (after the Academy reversed a previous decision that Palestine was not a 'country').

Abu-Assad's public profile following the success of *Paradise Now* tells us something about the difficulties of being an exilic director. Shooting in Nablus had been dangerous with the second *intifada* (2000–2005) heightening tension. Given the lack of local resources, a feature might be possible only every couple of years. Perhaps it isn't surprising then that Abu-Assad took a job that presumably paid well, making a US-set action thriller *The Courier* (US, 2012), and taking his Palestinian storytelling into *Do Not*

One of the revealing comic scenes in the film involves a discussion about films between Saïd and Suha. He has never visited a cinema – except to destroy one during the first *intifada*, the 'uprising' of Palestinians against occupation between 1987 and 1993.

Amreeka (US/Canada/
Kuwait, 2009) is a
family melodrama about
Palestinians moving
to America during the
period of the Iraq War
– in some ways also
an 'absurdist' comedy
about migration and
identity (see more
on the website: www.
globalfilmstudies.com).

Forget Me Istanbul (Turkey/Greece, 2011), a **portmanteau film** celebrating Istanbul's year as European Capital of Culture (see Chapter 7 on the concept of the portmanteau film). Abu-Assad's contribution is a story about two elderly Palestinian sisters who have been separated for 62 years since the Nakba (the flight of thousands of Palestinians into refugee camps when Israel was established in 1948). One of the sisters has been living in Syria and now they meet in Istanbul.

Israeli cinema and the 'periphery'

'Dreams of a Nation' may also be a possible title for a film festival focusing on Israeli society and the film culture it has developed. Israel is still a young country, even if the majority of the population is now Israeli-born. One-fifth of the population in the territory claimed by Israel is Palestinian and there is a significant population of recent migrants from Russia. As we saw from Fig 6.1, Israel is an affluent country with a relatively high number of cinemas, most of which show Hollywood films. The number of Israeli local productions is roughly commensurate with the resources of a country with a population of around 8 million. More noteworthy are the types of films that are now produced and the ways in which the industry works.

Israel regularly produces around 15 films per year. Most of these receive public funding of some kind, from Israeli and sometimes from European cultural agencies. The Israeli cultural model follows that of much of Europe with film schools and specialised cinemas such as the *cinemathèque* in West Jerusalem which would not be out of place in Madrid, Paris or Berlin. In a paper clearly referring in its title to François Truffaut's polemical 1954 attack on French 'quality cinema' (see Chapter 7), Joshua Simon (2007) suggests that these institutional factors have created a specific 'tendency' in Israeli filmmaking.

Like Truffaut, Simon wants to attack the script-led movement in cinema. He argues that the bulk of Israeli films each year are publicly funded on the basis of their well-written scripts which are heavily dialogue-driven and often deal in the kinds of stories which place Israel in the news (he claims that Israel is the third largest generator of international stories after the US and Russia). These scripts work in such a way as to make the actual direction of the films fairly irrelevant – all the director has to do is 'film the script' rather than create something cinematic in a 'personal' sense. In other words, the films tend to be formulaic in presenting the same kinds of stories in similar ways. Simon's argument is complex and provocative. It throws up several interesting ideas about Israeli cinema.

- Funding schemes push cinema towards state-sanctioned modes of expression as the result of funding priorities – both national and supranational (European funding produces a kind of standard 'Euro-funded film').
- The bureaucracy of funding and its involvement with education and training produces a situation in which Israel has 13 film schools for 8 million people (which Simon compares with the six film schools in Germany for 80 million

people); this has a deadening effect on the commercial sensibility of young filmmakers.

- Funding produces the emphasis on the **periphery** with two specific themes: the 'exotic' landscapes and communities of Israel and the 'broken' Israeli family.

To illustrate his thesis, Simon quotes Goel Pinto, a journalist from *Haaretz* newspaper reporting on the Israeli Film Awards of 2005: 'Whores, Arabs, religious Jews, settlers, homosexuals and two Israelis who go out to sell an American car in Germany are at the centre of the five films nominated for the award.'

At one level, Simon is arguing against the aesthetic strait-jacket that funding regimes foster, but he is also noting that this produces a specific cultural outlook. In a relatively affluent and modern society typified by the bars and nightlife of Tel Aviv, we might expect Israeli films to be similarly concerned with the kinds of mainstream genres produced by Hollywood; and indeed at one point in film history this was exactly what 'popular Israeli cinema' produced in the notorious teen comedy series of *Lemon Popsicle* films in the 1980s (www.lemonpopsicleforever.co.uk/themovies. html). Now, however, the subject matter, as the quote from *Haaretz* suggests, is more likely to feature the schisms in Israeli society with films about the problems faced by young conscripts in the Israeli Defence Force, by immigrants and migrants, Arabs and religious Jews, etc. The periphery is a concept associated with marginalisation – the relationship between specific groups on the edge of society with the mainstream. These are issues of identity that are as troubling to some Israeli characters as those of Palestinians denied a right of residence in what they consider as 'home'. The Israeli sense of identity in this context is confused and almost paranoid. Thus the focus on 'broken families' suggested by Simon.

The ideologies explored in these Israeli films are difficult to understand from outside the society, and from a European perspective they seem contradictory, caught up in confused liberal attitudes undercut by what is effectively a coloniser/colonised relationship between the Israeli 'centre' and its Arab periphery. We will explore this in relation to a specific **cycle** of high-profile films made immediately after Simon wrote his piece. Aspects of what he argues are apparent in these three films – but they are certainly not 'formulaic' in an aesthetic sense.

Popular Israeli films are categorised with brief descriptions on the Israeli Film Database (www. israelfilmcenter.org/ israeli-film-database).

A '**cycle**' here refers to films with similar genre elements produced over a limited period. The films may be seen by audiences as being influenced in some way by the previous title in the cycle.

Case study 6.6: Young Israelis at war

The films *Beaufort* (Israel, 2007), *Waltz With Bashir* (Israel/France/Germany/US/Japan/ Finland/Switzerland/Belgium/Australia, 2008) and *Lebanon* (Israel/France/Germany, 2009) are all concerned with the experiences of young men during the Israeli invasion of South Lebanon in 1982 and the subsequent occupation that eventually ended in 2000. The Israeli Defence Force (IDF), as it is somewhat ironically called, is one of the best-equipped and largest military forces in the region. All young Israelis are expected to serve for three years (men) or two years (women). Arabs living in Israel are not included. After service the conscripts remain on a reserve register. The events in South Lebanon pitched these conscripts into action. *Waltz With Bashir* and *Lebanon* are both based on the memories of conscripts during the initial invasion (directors Ari Folman and Samuel Maoz respectively). *Beaufort* is about a young man at the end of his service who has become the commander of an observation outpost in an old Crusader castle in the border region just before the

2000 withdrawal. The director of this film, Joseph Cedar, also served in Lebanon, but the film is adapted from a novel by Ron Leshem. All three films were critical successes on the festival circuit, two being short-listed for the Foreign Language Oscar and one winning the top prize at Venice.

These films show young men under pressure, terrified young men, young men in some ways out of control – raising the possibility that these are in some way anti-war or humanist films. They are not films celebrating valour in battle or presenting Israeli soldiers as heroic figures. But they are films in which the effects of war are felt mainly by young Israelis. There are moments in *Lebanon*, a film in which the world is seen exclusively from the perspective of an Israeli tank's crew, when we see the impact on local villagers, but otherwise the enemy remains faceless. The aesthetics reinforce this view. The observation bunker in *Beaufort* is designed in such a way that it creates a claustrophobic effect – much like that felt by the crew of a spaceship such as the Nostromo in *Alien*. The second 'tank-based' film, *Waltz With Bashir*, is presented as an animation, using a style that seems partly related to Japanese *manga* and the representation of post-apocalyptic landscapes. The film has sometimes been classified as a documentary and it does include some 'found footage' in its closing section. The structure of the film is built around a series of interviews with his ex-comrades that the director uses in order to try to remember what happened and why he still has nightmares about his experience. All three films, though they represent some of the realities of war, to some extent also create a distance from it. None of them make any real attempt to explain the war or why it is being fought.

In an essay focusing on an earlier war film *Kippur* (Israel, 2000), directed by Amos Gitai and dealing with the 1973 war against Egypt and Syria, Nitzan Ben-Shaul (2007: 214) suggests that the idea of being besieged (like the crews inside their tanks or in the bunker) is located firmly in the Israeli psyche.

Waltz With Bashir features the attack on the Shatila and Sabra Palestinian refugee camps in Beirut by Lebanese Christian Phalangists. The invading Israeli forces were found by the UN to have failed to prevent the killing of large numbers of refugees.

Fig 6.10
The Israeli soldiers in their 'pod-like' bunker in *Beaufort*.

War is posited as the sole origin of a society that is morally, emotionally, aesthetically and mentally corrupt. Society is represented as anxious and suspicious, its members being malicious and violent, or naive and therefore lost, confused and in despair. This confusion, anxiety and despair are supported by disjointed story and plot lines, articulated within a closed narrative space.

The siege mentality in Israel has now been represented in a concrete fashion with the building of the Wall across the Occupied Territories and the worry that Israel is turning in upon itself is perhaps being confirmed. A similar reading of Israeli war films since the 1980s is also evident in a review article on *Beaufort* by Shai Ginsburg (2007):

> Israeli feature films seem to turn inside to examine Israeli Jewish society and, with only few exceptions, leave the conflict with the Palestinians to documentary filmmakers.

Ginsburg points out that the real enemy for the soldiers is the military and political leadership of a country that seems to have little interest in their welfare (this quote also refers to the earlier films by Joseph Cedar):

> Those who bear the brunt of Israeli colonialism, whether it be in the Occupied Territories or in southern Lebanon, are not the local Palestinians, Syrians, or Lebanese but, rather Jewish Israelis themselves. Cedar's discussion of Israeli violence turns into a discussion of the effect of that violence on Israeli Jews and, more precisely, on common, simple people, and it is up to them to save themselves from a political, military, and religious system that abuses them.
>
> (Ginsburg 2007)

Just to prove that Israeli cinema is more complicated than may at first be apparent, consider *The Band's Visit* (discussed in the Introduction) and the films of Eran Riklis. Trained at the National Film and Television School in the UK, Riklis has often made films which look outward from Israel or at least deal with social relationships between different groups inside the country. *Cup Final* (Israel, 1991) is a drama again set at the time of the invasion of Lebanon and involving an Israeli reservist captured by Palestinians. Despite the violence, an understanding develops between the prisoner and his captor over a shared enthusiasm for the Italian team in the 1982 World Cup. *The Syrian Bride* (France/Germany/Israel, 2004) is a comedy-drama about the difficulties of a wedding in the Israeli-occupied territory of the Golan Heights that involves several questions of official nationality/identity disputed by Syria and Israel. *Lemon Tree* (Israel/France/Germany, 2008) is about a legal land dispute between a Palestinian woman and an Israeli minister who, as a security measure, wants to clear the woman's land on the 'Green Line' in order to protect his new house. Several profiles quote Riklis as preferring to see himself as a 'world director' rather than as an 'Israeli director' (see e.g. IMDb.com).

Several Israeli films are discussed in detail on www.globalfilmstudies.com.

Research and Explore 6.3

On the basis of this chapter, think about how you would sum up the idea of 'Middle Eastern Film'.

If you were asked to put on a festival of Middle Eastern Film, what would be your approach? If you had 12 film screenings in your programme, what kinds of films, and from which countries, would you select? How would you structure your programme and how would you introduce your brochure?

Summary

The Middle East and North Africa is a region in which social and political change is currently having more impact on the possible development of film industry and culture than in any other region. In the four major producing countries of Turkey, Iran, Israel and Egypt, investment in the film industry and film culture is likely to be affected by changes in government policy. During the writing of this book Iraq has slowly begun to emerge from ten years of war and its aftermath. The country has a relatively large population (30 million) of educated and creative people and the potential for economic growth. Cinemas are beginning to be built and in 2011 Mohamed Al Daradji, an Iraqi filmmaker trained in the Netherlands and the UK, with European and Arab funding made *Son of Babylon* which became a successful film on the international festival circuit. Libya has never had a film industry but perhaps it will in future. At the Venice Film Festival in 2012, *Wadjda*, a film by Haifaa Al Mansoura, a woman from Saudi Arabia (a country without cinemas), was the first film from that country to get an international screening.

On the other hand, Syria, once a significant producer, has seen the outbreak of civil war, and Egypt, though it is experiencing the growth of an independent sector, is still coming to terms with what the Arab Spring of 2011 may mean for the future of the country. In Turkey and Iran there is a large-scale domestic industry – one growing, the other in crisis – but the filmmakers celebrated in the international arena are often exiles or auteurs with co-production funding from the West. Politics and social/cultural conflict are likely to remain as important in film culture in the region as the commercial imperative of entertainment films.

References and further reading

Andrew, Geoff (2004) 'Beyond the Clouds: An Interview with Nuri Bilge Ceylan'. Available at http://www.sensesofcinema.com/2004/feature-articles/nuri_bilge_ceylan/.

Armes, Roy (1987) *Third World Filmmaking and the West*, Berkeley: University of California Press.

Ba, Saer Maty and Higbee, Will (eds) (2012) *De-Westernising Film Studies*, Abingdon: Routledge.

Ben-Shaul, Nitzan (2007) '*Kippur*', in Gönül Dönmez-Colin (ed.) (op.cit).

Dabashi, Hamid (1999) 'Mohsen Makhmalbaf's *A Moment of Innocence*', in Rose Issa and Sheila Whitaker (eds) *Life and Art: The New Iranian Cinema*, London: BFI.

Dabashi, Hamid (ed.) (2006) *Dreams of a Nation: On Palestinian Cinema*, London: Verso.

Dabashi, Hamid (2007) *Makhmalbaf at Large: The Making of a Rebel Filmmaker*, London: I.B. Tauris.

Dönmez-Colin, Gönül (ed.) (2007) *The Cinema of North Africa and the Middle East*, London: Wallflower.

Esfandiary, Shahab (2012) 'Banal Transnationalism: On Mohsen Makhmalbaf's "Borderless" Filmmaking', in Ba and Higbee (eds) *De-Westernising Film Studies*, Abingdon: Routledge.

Ginsburg, Shai (2007) 'Enemies Out of the Frame: Joseph Cedar's *Beaufort*'. Available at http://www.zeek.net/enemies_out_of_the_frame_joseph/.

Hamid, Rahul (2011) 'Freedom and Its Discontents: An Interview with Asghar Farhadi', *Cineaste* 37(1): 40–42.

Jacir, Annemarie (2006) '"For Cultural Purposes Only": Curating a Palestinian Film Festival', in Hamid Dabashi (ed.) *Dreams of a Nation: On Palestinian Cinema*, London: Verso.

Mehrabi, Massoud (2006) 'A Bed and Several Dreams: A Short History of Iranian Cinema', *Cineaste* 31(3): 38–39, 47.

Naficy, Hamid (1999) 'Veiled Visions/Powerful Presences: Women in Post-revolutionary Iranian Cinema', in Rose Issa and Sheila Whitaker (eds) *Life and Art: The New Iranian Cinema*, London: BFI.

Naficy, Hamid (2001) *An Accented Cinema: Exilic and Diasporic Filmmaking*, Princeton, NJ: Princeton University Press (an extract from this book is included in Elizabeth Ezra and Terry Rowden (eds) *Transnational Cinema: The Film Reader*, Abingdon: Routledge under the title 'Situating Accented Cinema').

Nicholas, Joe (1994) *Egyptian Cinema*, London: BFI.

Öztürk, Ruken S. (2007) '*Uzak/Distant*', in Gönül Dönmez-Colin (ed.) *The Cinema of North Africa and the Middle East*, London: Wallflower.

Said, Edward (1978) *Orientalism*, London: Routledge & Kegan Paul.

Shafik, Viola (2007) *Arab Cinema: History and Cultural Identity*, Cairo and New York: American University in Cairo Press.

Simon, Joshua (2007) 'A Certain Tendency in Israeli Cinema', */seconds 5*. Available at http://www.slashseconds.org/issues/002/001/articles/jsimon/index.php.

Simpson, Catherine (2006) 'Turkish Cinema's Resurgence: The "Deep Nation" Unravels'. Available at http://www.sensesofcinema.com/2006/featurearticles/turkish_cinema/.

Further viewing

Turkey

Yol (Turkey, 1982, dir. Yilmaz Güney)
Honey (*Bal*, Turkey/Germany, 2010, dir. Semih Kaplanoglu)

Egypt

Cairo Station (Egypt, 1958, dir. Youssef Chahine)
An Egyptian Story (*Hadutha Misriyya*, Egypt, 1982, dir. Youssef Chahine)
Scheherazade, Tell Me a Story (*Ehky ya Scheherazade*, Egypt, 2009, dir. Yousry Nasrallah)

Iran

The Wind Will Carry Us (Iran, 1999, dir. Abbas Kiarostami)
Offside (Iran, 2006, dir. Jafar Panahi)

Lebanon

West Beyreuth (*À l'abri les enfants*, France/Lebanon/Norway/Belgium, 1998, dir. Ziad Doueri)

I Want to See (*Je veux voir*, Lebanon/France, 2008, dir. Joana Hadjithomas and Khalil Joreige)

Where Do We Go Now? (*Et maintenant, on va où?*, Lebanon/France/Egypt/Italy, 2011, dir. Nadine Labiki)

Palestine

Divine Intervention (Palestine/France/Morocco/Germany, 2002, dir. Elia Suleiman)

The Time That Remains (Palestine/UK/France/Belgium/Italy, 2009, dir. Elia Suleiman)

5 Broken Cameras (Palestine/Israel/France, 2011, dir. Emad Burnat and Guy Davidi)

Israel

Broken Wings (*Knafayim Shvurot*, Israel, 2002, dir. Nir Bergman)

Lemon Tree (Israel/Germany/France, 2008, dir. Eran Riklis)

Ajami (Israel/Germany, 2009, dir. Yaron Shani and Scandar Copti)

CHAPTER 7

International art cinema and the festival circuit

The origins of 'art cinema'

The history of 'art' or 'alternative cinema' involves several changes of terminology. Although the term **art film** can be traced back to the early period of cinema at the start of the twentieth century, it attained its most familiar profile in the 1950s. Initially an art film was literally a film presenting an already validated work of art such as an opera, play or novel. The term *film d'art* was used in France in 1908 to describe *L'assassinat du Duc de Guise,* a film directed by a celebrated theatre director and performed by leading stage actors of the day. The company that produced the film called itself 'Film d'art' and francophone art cinema is still categorised today as *film d'art et d'essai* – covering auteur films, experimental films, essay films, short films, re-released classics and foreign-language films. In the 1920s and 1930s film was the medium for avant-garde artists such as the **Dadaists** and **Surrealists**, and film clubs appeared in various European cities where the new kinds of films were screened.

In retrospect, several distinctive **film movements** within European cinema have been recognised and appropriated as art cinema, even though they sometimes reached large audiences and influenced popular entertainment. The idea of a film movement is derived from fine art and refers to the recognition that a group of artists appear to be working on similar subjects and developing a common aesthetic.

The **Dadaists** came from many different art forms and developed a critique of conventional ideas about art as a response to the horror of the First World War. Man Ray (Emmanuel Radnitzky, 1890–1976) was an American who was part of both the Dadaist and the later Surrealist movement in Paris. His own specialism was photography but he appeared in *Entr'acte* (France, 1924), a film by René Clair.

Surrealist films appeared in the 1920s as part of an attempt to use the still relatively new art form to challenge conventional ideas with shocking images and provocative juxtaposition of ideas, often related to dream imagery. *Un chien andalou* (France, 1929) by Luis Buñuel and artist Salvador Dalí is a good example.

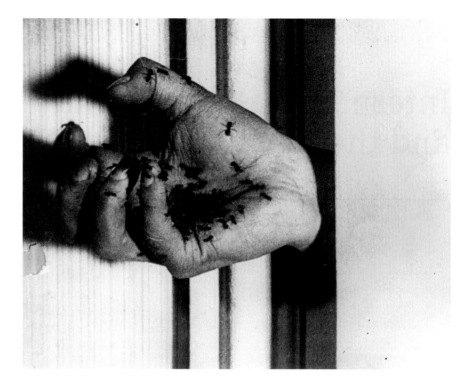

Fig 7.1
One of the startling images from *Un chien andalou.* Source: British Film Institute Stills Collection.

Sometimes the group may be located in the same place or know each other through membership of a social group, a shared education or some other institutional process. This produces particular 'schools' of art practice. However such groups come together, their work is promoted through institutional means. They have patrons – funders who want to buy their artworks, galleries that want to show the work, critics who want to write about them, etc.

Film movements also became associated with concepts of **national cinema** such as German Expressionism in the 1920s, French Poetic Realism in the 1930s, Italian Neo-realism in the 1940s, etc. (See Chapter 4).

The development of the term 'art film' came partly through how some films were shown in film clubs or societies in Europe and then how European and other foreign language films were distributed, exhibited and received by critics and audiences in the US – and how 'different' they were seen to be from mainstream Hollywood films. Susan Hayward summarises several of these 'differences', including the 'disturbance of narrative codes and conventions', the 'fragmented narrative line' and the focus on characters rather than heroes. Overall, she suggests:

> [This cinema's] rupture with classic narrative cinema intentionally distances spectators to create a reflective space for them to assume their own critical space or subjectivity in relation to the screen or film.
>
> (Hayward 2006: 28)

The emergence of *la nouvelle vague* (**New Wave**) in France in the late 1950s came at a time when the cinema audience was beginning to decline in the US and UK but was near its peak in France, Italy and Germany. Improvements in education and living standards in Western Europe and North America meant that the possibilities for the wider circulation of new kinds of cinema were clear to film exhibitors and distributors, and they were able to build on the established interest in a relatively limited range of art cinema directors that had developed in the 1950s, often through the promotion of films via screenings at the Venice and Cannes film festivals and coverage in specialist journals.

The French New Wave marked a moment in film history – and a change in the film industry to accommodate and exploit a wider interest in alternative films. It is now generally agreed that the term 'New Wave' was a journalistic invention to describe the very large number of films by first-time directors produced in France around this time. Most of these films have been long forgotten but the association with youth and the 'new' was important, and the high profile of the group of critics from the journal *Cahiers du cinéma* who themselves became directors at this time (François Truffaut, Jean-Luc Godard, Claude Chabrol, Jacques Rivette, Eric Rohmer, etc.) created a focus for other critics, festival directors, film marketers, distributors and exhibitors.

The success of key films like Truffaut's *Les quatre cent coups* (1959) and Godard's *À bout de souffle* (1960) helped create a new kind of 'hip' and 'cool' art cinema with young stars to match the new young directors. This new cinema market could be exploited in France and overseas by linking it to the already existing group of French art filmmakers sometimes known as the 'Left Bank Group' of Alain Resnais, Chris Marker and Agnès Varda as well as more commercially minded young directors such as Louis Malle, Claude Lelouch and the unique talent of Jacques Demy.

The Danish **Dogme** movement of the late 1990s deliberately targeted the 'failure' of the New Wave cinemas of the 1960s, suggesting that though their aims were good, their execution wasn't. Dogme 'succeeded' in the sense that a handful of directors became well-known names, other young filmmakers around the world were

Cahiers du cinéma is one of two **specialised film** journals in France, alongside *Positif*. Both journals have a long history of serious coverage of film, including the politics of film. *Cahiers* became more well known outside France because of the writings of one of its founders, André Bazin, as well as the famous directors of *la nouvelle vague*.

Fig 7.2
Anna Karina and Michel Subor in Jean-Luc Godard's second film *Le petit soldat* (*The Little Soldier*, France, 1960). Karina later married Godard and became one of the stars of *la nouvelle vague*, but the film's release was delayed because of its controversial representation of Algerian independence struggles.

Fig 7.3
Anette Støvelbæk as
Olympia and Ann Eleonora
Jørgensen as Karen, two of
the evening class students
in Lone Scherfig's *Italian
for Beginners* (Denmark,
2000), Dogme film #12.

inspired by new ideas and Danish Cinema as a whole received a huge boost through the marketing opportunities that media attention to the Dogme films aroused.

Research and Explore 7.1: *Dogme '95*

The original manifesto and 'vow of chastity' of the Dogme '95 group may be found at http://pov.imv. au.dk/Issue_10/section_1/artc1A.html. (There are several different websites carrying this material, including lists of 'official' Dogme films.) Study these documents carefully and then watch one or two of the early Danish Dogme films such as *Festen, Idioterne, Mifune* or *Italian for Beginners*. Why do you think that the movement attracted so much attention and inspired young filmmakers?

This view of art cinema is a European concept of filmmaking and film exhibition that took on a similar but slightly different form in Anglophone countries and other major film-producing countries. When Kurosawa Akira's *Rashomon* won a major prize at Venice in 1951 and began to introduce European and North American audiences to Japanese cinema, it was received as an art film (see Chapter 5 for more on Kurosawa's profile at home and in Asia).

The definition of art cinema is constantly shifting and now seems to be more associated with how films are distributed rather than the ways in which certain films produce meanings. Take the term **'quality'** that might be used to describe Kurosawa's films in Japan. The same term could be applied to many films made in France, the UK and Hollywood in the 1930s to 1950s when there was still a mass audience for cinema. These 'well-made films', sometimes with quite serious adult themes (i.e. for thoughtful older audiences) and big name stars, could command a sizeable audience in upmarket circuit cinemas. Unlike the European art films of the 1950s from directors like Fellini, Antonioni, Bergman, etc., these quality films often had straightforward linear narratives and offered a range of genre pleasures – they weren't necessarily radical or 'alternative'. Celebrated British films of the 1940s such as *Brief Encounter* (dir. David Lean, 1945), *The Third Man* (dir. Carol Reed, 1949) or *The Red Shoes* (dir. Michael Powell and Emeric Pressburger, 1948) were in effect specialised films for a middle-class audience (and often treated as such in North America).

In the current cinema environment, similar films (what are now often deemed **awards films** because they are promoted during the period of the Oscars, BAFTAS, Caesars, etc.) may well be categorised as specialised and only screened in certain venues. This phenomenon is now apparent in all the major film nations with a sense of **mainstream** and **specialised** implied in the treatment of certain films and directors, and in the building/conversion of cinemas divided between mainstream multiplexes and smaller 'artplexes'. Art/specialised films appear in similar cinemas and in similar modes of presentation in Tokyo and Taipei, Mexico City and Manchester, Barcelona and Beijing. This chapter sets out to discover what kinds of films these are, how they get to be made, and how they are distributed and received by audiences globally.

> 'Specialised films' were originally defined by the UK Film Council in order to monitor the diversity of films in UK distribution. Cinemas that received support in acquiring digital projectors and joining the Digital Screen Network (DSN) in 2008 were required to demonstrate that they had screened a set target of specialised films. Other agencies such as the Europa Cinemas Network which supports cinemas showing European films require something similar. The current British Film Institute definition (http://industry.bfi.org. uk/specialisedfilms) includes all foreign-language films, documentaries or archive films and certain genre films where generic categories are unclear or hybridised. Specialised films will usually be independently produced outside the major Hollywood studios.

Arthouse – a description of certain kinds of films in terms of the cinema in which they are likely to be shown. 'Arthouse' is now largely a historical term, referring to the development of cinemas showing primarily foreign-language art films in the 1950s and 1960s. Such cinemas would sell film books and magazines and have bars and restaurants rather than popcorn and coke.

Europa Cinemas has a network of over 400 cinemas in the EU and nearly 200 in Asia, Latin America and the Mediterranean (http://www.europa-cinemas.org/en/Supports/EUROPA-CINEMAS-MUNDUS).

'Alternative content' in UK cinemas refers to 'non-cinema' material streamed via satellite link – live opera, ballet, theatre, sports or music events. This does not qualify as 'specialised film' according to the BFI definition.

Auteur filmmaking

The concept of an auteur filmmaker – literally a filmmaker who is an 'author', akin to the writer of a novel – is one of the most used terms in certain parts of the public discourse about film, but also one of the most misunderstood and contested. It is important to emphasise that the emergence of the concept began in France in the late 1940s and early 1950s and was taken up by film critics and publicists in the US and around the world during the 1960s. This coincided with the growth of new film movements associated with the concept of a New Wave in different countries and the introduction of new film festivals and distribution systems for arthouse cinema, as outlined above. As the festival circuit expanded, festival programmers needed criteria for selecting new films. Naming key directors became one of the ways of distinguishing films that would appeal to festival audiences.

The unofficial manifesto for an 'authored' cinema was set out in a 1954 polemical essay by the then young firebrand critic François Truffaut. In 'Une certaine tendance du cinéma français', Truffaut referred to 'la politique des auteurs'. It is unfortunate perhaps that 'la politique' became seen as a theory about cinema when it began

In global cinema the best-known 'New Wave' was *la nouvelle vague* in France. The British New Wave occurred at around the same time (1958–1963), while in West Germany, Czechoslovakia and Japan 'New Wave' films appeared slightly later – as they did in many other countries.

to circulate as an idea among Anglo-American film critics. Truffaut meant it as a polemic and a call to arms for critics and filmmakers (as he himself became later). His argument was against the 'quality cinema' of the time that relied on carefully written scripts and high production values. Truffaut wanted to promote those directors who wrote their own scripts and impressed themselves upon their material, using a 'personal vision'. (See Chapter 6 for a similar polemical essay about contemporary Israeli cinema.)

Obviously, despite the 1950s championing of certain Hollywood directors as auteurs, the idea of a single authorial vision in an industrial production system doesn't make much sense as a theory about how films work, and 'auteurism' was soon being dismissed in academic film studies. However, in relation to **artisanal cinema** (i.e. the work of artisans or craft workers), the identification of key individuals (rather than studio marketing departments) certainly makes sense for distributors and film festival organisers. To make the obvious point, festivals can invite an auteur director (or a scriptwriter or cinematographer) as a guest to discuss their films – but they cannot invite a studio or a production company. In addition, certain funding schemes in both national and international contexts find it useful to support 'named' directors responsible for culturally important films (see Chapter 4 on auteur filmmakers in France).

The casual adoption of auteurism is hard to shake off – the work of specific directors is frequently used as the basis for case studies in this book. But it is important to distinguish the role of key personnel within an industrial system – films are made by teams of creative people working in a particular industrial and institutional context.

Before we leave concepts of 'arthouse' and specialised cinema, we should flag up the use of **independent** as an associated label. 'Independent' is another slippery term when used to describe a category of cinema – independent of what? The Hollywood studios have a simple definition: an independent film is any film not distributed by one of the six members of the MPAA. This notion of studio vs. independent also has some currency in other territories where there is a commercial industry akin to the studios and then an 'independent sector' (e.g. in the UK, Japan, India, China, etc.). Independent in this sense includes commercial films distributed by companies such as Lionsgate or eONE. StudioCanal is the largest European film company but it is still seen as an 'independent' when compared to the Hollywood studios in the UK and North America.

A different definition of 'independent', developed by critics and film scholars in the 1980s, focused on low-budget films made outside the studio system. These sometimes 'political' and sometimes genre-bending films constituted 'American Independent' cinema. Key directors included John Sayles, Spike Lee, Jim Jarmusch and Lizzie Borden. To some extent, these films took the screening slots once occupied by European art films in cinemas in North America and Europe. By the mid-1990s this form of cinema began to be replaced by more commercially orientated independent films, encouraged by the enormous success of Quentin Tarantino's *Pulp Fiction* (US, 1994). Because 'indy films' are largely an American phenomenon they are not explored in detail here. Issues related to American Independent cinema are covered in Pierson (1996), King (2005) and Tzioumakis (2006).

The role of film festivals

Film festivals developed mainly after the Second World War and they have proved to be an essential component of the international film industry as well as important cultural events in their own right. Today there are major film festivals in most countries that have a developed film culture and in many countries there are numerous festivals with some cities housing several different festivals across a year.

A film festival may be defined as a specific programme of films offered across one or more cinemas with only a limited number of screenings of each title. Festival screenings comprise either new films that haven't been seen yet in the local area or archive titles that have been collected together under a particular theme – or perhaps a combination of the two. The films on offer will be mostly specialised films and they may not yet have a local distribution deal. Festivals also expect to feature guests and to offer the chance for audiences to meet directors, writers, stars, critics and others associated with film culture. A festival is a celebration of film and therefore it is most easily defined by how 'different' the experience of watching a film might be when a director is present or a film is 'unknown' – and perhaps unlikely to be seen anywhere else again in the locality. A large film festival will usually present itself as 'international' and include films and guests from overseas. Smaller festivals may promote themselves mainly to a local audience.

Why might a festival be set up?

- A film festival is a cultural event that may be used to build the profile of a town or city in the same way as music or literature festivals. A successful festival can boost the local economy by bringing in visitors and attracting businesses whose staff want to live in a town with cultural attractions.
- For specialised cinemas, a festival may be simply a way of 'rewarding' local audiences with something extra – and thus helping to grow the local audience over time. Offering a festival may also be part of the cultural remit of the cinema. Many specialised cinemas are either charities or are publicly funded in some way. Few commercially operated cinemas run their own film festivals as such – although many will be used as temporary venues by different film festivals.
- As a showcase for the film industry, festivals have a dual function of upholding the prestige of the industry and also providing practical services; thus festivals might include:
  – competitions for best film, acting performance, direction, etc.;
  – a showcase for local films;
  – a market for buying and selling the rights to films;
  – a chance for film professionals to meet each other;
  – an opportunity for film bookers to see new films and for journalists to preview films and develop stories around them.

All three of these factors point to the need to find extra funding, often through some form of sponsorship. A successful festival is often a hybrid venture of specialist film exhibition staff, volunteers, industry personnel and passionate fans. Festival screenings become part of the process of promoting many films, either for eventual local release or possibly the re-release of a cult or classic film.

Thomas Elsaesser has theorised about the importance of film festivals at some length, and his chapter on festivals in *European Cinema: Face to Face With*

Many smaller festivals include one or two previews of big films that will open only a few weeks later. These may attract more mainstream audiences who may then watch 'unknown' titles as well. The BFI's London Film Festival is a big festival that is often used to 'showcase' major films that will eventually open in the UK.

Fig 7.4
Claire Denis and Isabelle
Huppert pose for
photographers at the
Venice Film Festival in
2009 when *White Material*
was nominated for the
Golden Lion. Source:
photo by Venturelli/
WireImage/Getty Images.

Hollywood (2005: 82–107) expands many of the points made here. Elsaesser
identifies the importance of festivals as part of a 'network', especially important in
conceptualising categories of cinema. In a sense the festival circuit acts like another
'platform', fulfilling some of the same functions as Hollywood: through competitions
and awards, submission rules and support for filmmakers, the festival network
influences the production, distribution and exhibition of 'art' and 'independent'
cinema.

Because of these different possible reasons for their existence there are several
different kinds of film festival. The most important festivals, classified as 'A'
festivals by the international critics' association FIPRESCI, play a crucial role in the
international distribution of films. Let us pick out just four festivals. The annual film
year starts with Berlin in February where prizes of Silver and Golden Bears are given
to films that are often seen as some of the edgier or more socially conscious examples
of 'World Cinema'. In May, the Cannes Film Festival awards the Palme d'Or to what
it considers the best film in competition (alongside several other major awards) and
in September Venice awards Golden/Silver Lions on a similar basis. These three sets
of festival prizes are proudly announced in the subsequent promotion of winning
film titles. The status of Cannes means that all the films selected to be shown 'in
competition' carry a marker of quality that will probably help the title gain wide
international distribution (though it can also backfire if the film turns out to be
terrible). It is their track record of return visits to Cannes that enables filmmakers
like Ken Loach, the Dardennes Brothers or Nuri Bilge Ceylan to maintain a status as
a major director in the international market.

Films gain distribution deals on the back of competition screenings but Cannes
also operates a huge film market where hundreds of films are sold outside of
competition. In dozens of small hotel rooms, producers show whole films and teasers
to potential buyers from TV stations, DVD labels and cinema distribution companies
across the world.

The Toronto International Film Festival also takes place in September immediately after Venice. In some ways, Toronto is the most important festival, even if it isn't the most glamorous. It doesn't have a major competition (though its 'Audience Award' is often taken to be a useful marketing asset for a new film) but it does show a very large number of films, often for the first time in North America. It is therefore the event which attracts most industry personnel and which often works as the first step in promoting a film in the world's most valuable film market. In the past few years, Toronto has also been the starting point for Oscar campaigns for small independent films, for example *Juno* (Canada/US, 2007), *Slumdog Millionaire* (UK, 2008), etc.

So far we have only mentioned festivals in Europe and North America. Festivals are equally important in Asia where currently major festivals in Busan (South Korea's second city), Hong Kong, Shanghai and Tokyo vie for attention as the best place to launch a film into the East Asian market. India also has several international festivals (Delhi, Goa, Mumbai, Kolkata (see Chapter 10) and Trivandrum) that range from cultural to industry events. In Africa, where film distribution and exhibition is difficult to organise, the festivals in Ouagadougou and Carthage are biennial in alternating years and have become essential events for critics, filmmakers and cultural commentators dealing with African films and films from the Arab world. There are also major festivals in Latin America, Australia and the Middle East, as well as many more in Europe.

Some festivals aim to stand out by focusing on one aspect of film culture or one category of films. Sundance, the festival set up by Robert Redford in Colorado, has become the festival for 'independent films', both American and overseas titles. Dinard in France holds an annual festival of British films and Frightfest is an annual horror film festival held over a weekend in London's West End – one of many similar festivals across the world.

Case study 7.1: Films from the South, Oslo

There are festivals for every interest, from 'Mountain Films' to 'Cycling Films', Science Fiction Films to Literary Adaptations, Animation, Documentary and First Films. The Films From the South Festival (Film Fra Sør) specialises in showing films from Latin America, Africa and Asia. Its aim is to bring films from these regions to the general public in Oslo. There is a strand for children's films (a key element of Nordic film culture) and an educational programme. The festival runs in October each year and there is a linked event in the spring which deals specifically with Arab films.

Norway is one of the richest countries in the world with a major aid programme in many parts of the South. It also has a connection to the attempts to find a solution to the Israel–Palestine conflict (i.e. with the 'Oslo Accords' in 1993). Oslo is a small city in which cinemas were municipally owned until 2013. Catering for a local audience and its array of different migrant groups is part of the festival's mission plan. The following is an extract from the 'About Us' section of the festival's website (http://www.filmfrasor.no):

Since 1991 the festival has presented the best films and filmmakers from Asia, Africa and Latin America to a diverse audience. Each year approximately 100 feature films and documentaries are screened, in the course of ten festival days and across 230 screenings.

Identity

The festival considers itself an important part of the cultural life of Oslo and the Norwegian film industry. Through great film experiences, seminars, international guest appearances and events all through the year, Films From the South is an important arena for cultural exchange.

Films From the South will give you fine film experiences, dialogue and atmosphere in various areas like politics, film poetry, topical documentaries and entertainment.

The festival is a film-political corrective to a Western-oriented film scene.

Fundamental values

The festival screens films of quality from the non-Western part of the world – films that will give you cultural experiences, insight and understanding. Films From the South combines idealism with a professional organisation and promotes values like tolerance, receptiveness and respect.

In 2011 the festival invited directors Nadine Labaki (Lebanon), Eric Khoo (Singapore), Fernando Pérez (Cuba) and Matías Bize (Chile). Each was honoured with screenings of their latest films plus two or three earlier films. Although he wasn't able to attend, there was also a selection of films from Asghar Farhadi (Iran). Nadine Labaki and Asghar Farhadi are profiled in Chapter 6 and Eric Khoo in Chapter 12.

Norway has other major festivals in Oslo, Bergen and Tromso.

Fig 7.5
Eric Khoo introduces an exhibition of the original drawings for his film *Tatsumi* at the Films From the South Festival in 2010. Source: Films From the South Festival.

Research and Explore 7.2

Find your nearest international film festival or choose one from the database on www.festivalfocus.org. Visit the website of your chosen festival:

- What is its mission statement/aims?
- Does it specialise in films of a specific genre or from a specific region?
- Check out last year's programme (or the next programme if it's coming soon) – are the films listed different from the films you usually get to see?
- What kinds of events or visitors in the programme look attractive for audiences?
- Would you like to visit the festival? Which are the elements that attract you?

The 'festival film'

Festivals show all kinds of films and it isn't unusual for American Independent films featuring well-known stars to win prizes at Cannes or Venice. However, many titles are classified simply as **festival films** which tour festivals in different countries even though they may never get an official film release in that territory. Without the festival circuit these films might not exist at all – and global film culture would be the poorer. How do they get made?

Some festivals (e.g. Rotterdam, Busan) run schemes that enable new filmmakers to gain advice and support from the festival before they make their films. These films then stand a much greater chance of being screened at that particular festival. Other festivals offer a competition or strand for new filmmakers (e.g. 'Un certain regard' at Cannes). Festivals also work with funding agents so that a young filmmaker may have another source of funding – and support to get a festival screening. Specialised films will usually have some form of public funding (see Chapter 4), and this may be dependent on whether or not the funders think that the film will receive festival screenings (and thus generate cultural prestige, developing **soft power**). This is particularly important for public funders in small territories where commercial interest in local films may be limited.

Larger festivals like Cannes will seek competition entries from 'name' filmmakers, but the majority of festival organisers may simply invite filmmakers to submit their films for consideration or go to festivals themselves to find new filmmakers and sales agents. Festival programmers then have to sift through piles of DVD 'screeners' and attempt to select titles that match the aims and objectives of their particular festival.

A typical 'festival film' will be made by a filmmaker who aims to 'say something' – either about an aspect of his or her own culture or about some form of universal social issue. Alternatively their main emphasis may be in developing a personal style of filmmaking. Festival films must appeal to international festival audiences, so they won't usually be entertainment films targeting a local audience. The festival audience is expected to be relatively well educated and ciné-literate, and 'liberal' in terms of politics. As we have seen, there are specialist festivals that will screen horror films, science fiction or martial arts films from around the world, but these are less likely to appear at mainstream festivals. In some film industry circles, the term 'festival film' may be mildly pejorative, since a festival film is sometimes seen as a film which couldn't be commercially released – it will only be expected to find an audience at a festival.

The most high-profile festival films will also be seen as auteur films, since the identity of the director is often more important than the genre or star. The most important auteurs will usually get a release for their films in major film territories, but this isn't true for all auteurs. There are many filmmakers discussed as auteurs in film journals whose films rarely escape the festival circuit. Even in their own home territory they may not receive a wide release. The 'auteur film' is a category in the international film business, so even if film scholars may find the concept questionable as a theoretical concept involved in reading a film, it must be recognised as a meaningful term in film industry practice. We will explore auteur filmmaking through a detailed study of one director in particular.

Claire Denis, auteur filmmaker

A **portmanteau film** is feature length, comprising several short films by various directors (with different 'personal visions') all working with a similar theme or setting (e.g. *Tickets* (UK/Italy, 2005) features three stories directed by Ken Loach (UK), Ermanno Olmi (Italy) and Abbas Kiarostami (Iran), all set on the same train travelling through Italy).

A **cinephile** has a passionate interest in cinema as an art form, i.e. ahead of an interest in stories or entertainment. *Cinephiles* seek out particular films and filmmakers who are often unknown by the mainstream audience. *Cinephilia* refers to a whole culture of blogs, specialist magazines and DVD labels such as Criterion or Masters of Cinema.

Claire Denis (b. 1948) became a director relatively late, having served a form of traditional apprenticeship (after leaving film school) working as an assistant for such distinguished auteur filmmakers as Wim Wenders and Jim Jarmusch, among others. Since then she has made ten features and an equivalent number of other films such as shorts, documentaries and contributions to **portmanteau films**.

Denis has been selected as the focus for a case study, since she has been celebrated by *cinephiles* as one of the best contemporary filmmakers currently on the festival circuit and also because several of her films deliberately explore ideas related to migration, postcolonialism, identity, etc. – issues addressed in several chapters of this book. However, rather than addressing social or political issues directly, Denis constructs very beautiful films that place the artistic possibilities of cinema above the desire to entertain through narrative. We will define Claire Denis as an auteur and an 'art director' using the following criteria:

- unconventional narratives;
- preference for music, camerawork, editing to create stories rather than explicatory dialogue;
- similar themes, often concerned with migration/post-colonial situations;
- sometimes films that are transgressive of French cultural norms;
- little relationship with ideas of French national cinema or typical French genres;
- films that are 'personal' in some way, expressing a personal approach to cinema or connecting personally to the story elements and themes;
- well-developed working relationships with a small group of actors (and occasionally French stars with art cinema credentials);
- similarly close relationships with scriptwriter Jean-Pol Fargeau, cinematographer Agnès Godard and musician Stuart Staples (of Tindersticks), etc.

Whenever films are described as unconventional, there is an assumption that they will be difficult for audiences. Certainly, many of the films made by Claire Denis may be thought elliptical in their presentation of stories – things are not 'said' (Denis

Fig 7.6
The legionnaires performing choreographed exercises in *Beau Travail*.

plays down dialogue) and audiences are required to infer connections between events. However, any frustration at having to 'work' in this way is compensated for by the real pleasures offered by sound and image. This was famously the case in *Beau travail* (France, 1999) in which Denis transposed Herman Melville's story *Billy Budd*, about British sailors in the Napoleonic Wars, into a contemporary story about the French Foreign Legion set in Djibouti (previously the French colony in Somaliland in Northeast Africa). Denis employed a choreographer for scenes of bare-chested soldiers exercising in locations featuring unusual landscapes. These sequences, featuring music from Neil Young and Afrobeat performers among others, drew critical praise from all quarters. Denis seemed to create emotional narratives from music and imagery alone.

Here we will focus on a single Denis film as a case study and relate it to four others that share some elements. These five films are also the most accessible in terms of available DVDs. The five are:

1 *Chocolat* (France/West Germany/Cameroon, 1988). A young woman, France, returns to the West African country where she had been a child living in a colonial outpost during the 1950s.
2 *Beau travail* (1999) (see above).
3 *L'intrus* (France, 2004). The central character is an older man who lives in an isolated mountain region in France but who then travels to South Korea for a heart transplant and then to a former French colony in the South Pacific.
4 *35 rhums* (France/Germany, 2008). Set among a community of French African-Caribbeans who work on the Paris suburban rail system, the main focus of this narrative is a father and daughter relationship.
5 *White Material* (France/Cameroon, 2009). A Frenchwoman runs a coffee plantation in an unnamed African country during a difficult period when civil war appears to be breaking out.

Earlier films by Denis, including *S'en fout la mort* (*No Fear, No Die*, 1990), have also been read as post-colonial (see Hayward 2002).

All of these films take French characters out of France at some point, often to parts of Africa that were once French colonies, and all explore the post-colonial identity in some way. Claire Denis was the child of a French civil servant who moved between postings in French colonies up until the 1960s when they achieved independence. He then carried on working with newly established African companies. Denis spent most of her early childhood in Africa, attending schools with both French and African students. She returned to Senegal from France when she was 17 (see Reid 1996). Her first three films all featured lead male roles for African or Caribbean actors. We should note here that the practice of reading auteur films 'through' the autobiography of the director is controversial, but in the case of Claire Denis it seems perverse not to recognise that she draws on her own life experiences that she 'recovers' in highly creative and original ways.

Case study 7.2: *35 rhums* (*35 Shots of Rum*, France/Germany, 2008)

The idea for this film came from the Denis family story. Claire Denis had a Brazilian grandfather who found himself bringing up his daughter alone in Paris. Father and daughter developed a very close, loving relationship that was apparent to granddaughter

Claire even when she was a small child. Years later in the 1990s Claire took her mother to a season of films by the Japanese director Ozu Yasujiro running over several nights at a Paris cinema. Her mother recognised something in these films and their depictions of family relationships (most of Ozu's later films are family dramas), but one film stood out. *Late Spring* (Japan, 1949) is a film in which a widowed father, a professor in Tokyo, decides that he must help his daughter find a husband. In turn, the daughter is concerned about what will happen to her father if she marries and so she plans to encourage him to marry again. *35 rhums* is a contemporary story about a close father–daughter relationship. The title refers to a drinking ritual involving tots of rum – a ritual that is saved for very specific occasions.

Production context

The budget for a Claire Denis film is usually quite small. The films are not financed as a commercial proposition, since the theatrical audience is small and investors are only likely to receive revenue from DVD and TV sales. Typically this kind of film will receive funding from several different sources. The Internet Movie Database lists 16 organisations that have contributed something to the production budget of *35 rhums* – the majority are public institutions (regional/national funding organisations in both France and Germany: see Chapter 4 on French public funding).

Opening sequence

The film opens with a montage of shots of the track photographed from the cab of an RER (rapid transit, suburban) train heading out of Central Paris towards the suburbs. This cuts to a middle-aged man smoking by the side of the railway tracks and then back to the train shots. A shot cut into the sequence shows the train driver and another frames a young woman in medium close-up strap-hanging on a crowded train. Finally, the man by the track puts on a helmet and clambers on to his motorbike. We see the young woman looking at electric rice cookers in a shop. We then see her inside an apartment having bought a cooker (which she puts away). She loads a washing machine and begins preparing a meal. We are more than seven minutes into the film and so far there is no dialogue – but there has been a music track throughout, complementing the rhythm of the editing. Then the man enters the apartment (carrying another, larger, rice cooker) and the young woman greets him with a kiss and fetches his slippers. She comments on his smoky breath and he goes to shower and change his clothes. Not until they start their meal and she has graciously thanked him for remembering to get the rice cooker does she say 'thanks Dad', so ending any lingering doubts about how these two people are related. We are now 10 minutes into the film.

If we analyse this opening, a number of issues arise which may be puzzling for a mainstream audience. First, the lack of dialogue and any specific indication of where we might be, or who the characters are, goes against the mainstream convention of getting the audience on board early by feeding them clues. We don't have any expectations of what the story might be about – except that both characters have bought rice cookers and there are several shots of trains. The refusal to confirm the relationship between the two characters is slightly disturbing. Could they be lovers? How intimate are they? There is no dialogue but the music from the British band Tindersticks certainly helps to set a mood. The train sequences are still confusing however, suggesting a montage of shots taken at different times of the day. Instead of a simple narrative of 'taking the train home', this suggests a representation of something else, and later on we will discover

Fig 7.7
Hara Setsuko as the
daughter and Ryu Chisu
as her father on a train
trip in *Late Spring*.

that the man Lionel, played by Alex Descas, is himself a train driver who knows the driver of the train in the sequence. Depending on what we know of French urban society we may be surprised by something else – all the characters we see in this sequence (and indeed most of the characters we see in the film) appear to be African-Caribbean. Is this a realist depiction of a specific community or is there some significance for the story in focusing on only these black characters? We should also note that very little in terms of narrative or character development happens in the sequence, at least on the surface. The film feels slow but if the audience is engaged a narrative of emotions rather than actions is well underway.

For a *cinephile* audience who have seen other Claire Denis films, this opening is less potentially alienating. They will possibly recognise Alex Descas, an actor from the Francophone Caribbean who has appeared in several of the director's films. If they know Ozu's films or they have read any of the promotional material around the film, they will recognise the trains and the rice cooker as referencing Ozu family dramas. *35 rhums* actually follows Ozu's 1949 film *Late Spring* (*Banshun*) quite closely in parts of the narrative structure. Most importantly, they won't be put off or confused by any of the above, but instead will be prepared to go along with the narrative as it unfolds.

We haven't the space to analyse the whole narrative so we'll just mention two of the sub-plots and then look more closely at a key scene later in the film. In the opening sequence we briefly see the train driver René who will retire in the near future. Denis tells René's story in a very emotional manner. We see him at his leaving party being given presents – two African art objects and an MP3 player. We hear him tell Lionel in a very

Railway journeys – or even just shots of trains or station platforms in the extensive Japanese rail network – appear in most of Ozu's later films (i.e. in the 1950s).

Café Lumière (Japan/Taiwan, 2003) (discussed in Chapter 11) was commissioned as a film celebrating the centenary of Ozu Yasijuro's birth and makes an interesting comparison with *35 rhums*.

morose tone that he wanted to die young but that he could live to be 100. This seems to be a reference to the possible fate of the immigrant rail workers but there is no direct comment on why he should feel like this. In the same part of the narrative we see the young woman, Joséphine, in a classroom where she is presenting a formal argument to her classmates about the unequal economic exchange between the South (Africa) and the North (Europe and North America) in a detached, objective way. Her teacher is both praising her and being quite critical in his attempts to improve her performance but her classmates are passionate about the injustices surrounding the 'debts' that the South supposedly owes to the North and they accuse Joséphine of being too cold and detached. Denis takes no prisoners here. One student quotes Frantz Fanon (see Chapter 8) and Joséphine refers to Joseph Stiglitz, the Nobel prize-winning American economist. There is no 'outcome' to this scene, so an audience must decide for themselves whether to relate it to the employment of people from the South on the railways. Or is it there to hint at Joséphine's dilemma about choosing rationality over emotional attachment?

One of the crucial scenes in the film takes place at night in a small African bar-café where Lionel and Joséphine are marooned during a rainstorm because their car has broken down. They are with the other two principal characters in the story. Gabrielle is their neighbour in the apartment block (and the car owner – she runs it as a taxi). She has clearly known Lionel and Joséphine for a long time and there is an uneasy familiarity about her relationship with them. Noé (played by Grégoire Coline, another very familiar actor in Denis films) is a young man upstairs in the apartment block who has a tentative relationship with Joséphine and who has also been around the older couple for a long time. This is clearly a kind of family group with a huge emotional investment among its four members.

Again, the whole sequence is largely bereft of dialogue but a seemingly diegetic music track (i.e. played through the bar's sound system) runs throughout, carefully segueing from one song to another. The first track is African and quite light, the next is a classic Cuban song 'Siboney' and the third the Commodores' 1985 international soul hit 'Night Shift'. The characters begin to dance between the tables in the tight space and the camera picks out the looks they give each other. Lionel dances first with Gabrielle and then with Joséphine who he then 'gives' to Noé. The young couple embrace and kiss but

Denis, like many auteurs, works with a stock company of actors. She also sometimes casts actors whose presence refers to other films. Joséphine is played by Mati Diop, the niece of Djibril Diop Mambéty, the Senegalese director of an important African film, *Touki Bouki* (Senegal, 1973).

Fig 7.8
Mati Diop and Grégoire Colin in the bar dance sequence in *35 rhums*.

they are tentative and uncertain – and therefore their contact is possibly more erotic and affecting. Lionel, as if to assert himself after giving away his daughter, then persuades the beautiful woman who owns/runs the bar to dance with him. Gabrielle is forced to watch. But as the scene reaches this level of intensity, Denis suddenly cuts to the quartet travelling home in an empty night bus.

The bar dance sequence has prompted a great deal of discussion because of its use of music and its emotional intensity. Check YouTube and look for a commentary on the scene taken from an interview with Claire Denis (who also discusses Ozu's films on another YouTube clip).

Denis completes the film narrative but doesn't allow the audience the simple pleasure of resolution. Nothing is explained and we cannot be sure exactly what will happen to the characters. In the latter part of the film, Lionel and Joséphine make a trip to Lübeck in Eastern Germany. In terms of the narrative the trip makes perfect sense, but we still cannot be sure what else to read into the German location. Since the film is a co-production with Germany, perhaps it is simply a contractual obligation that a section of the film is shot there? Would it make a difference if Lionel and his daughter had travelled elsewhere in France or perhaps gone to Senegal or Guadeloupe? We could ask the same question about the film overall. In one interview (of the many available on the internet) Denis discusses the autobiographical elements of the story and her casting decisions: 'I think the real thing is that there is a community that is French and also has black skin, that is integrated but also rejected' (Hughes 2009).

> Claire Denis tells Kevin Lee (2009) that 'There was something that led me to Germany, not the Germany of the war, but a Germany that is so different from France, northern Germany'.

Reception

It is useful to read some of the many reviews of *35 rhums* on a variety of websites and social media outlets. For many critics this was their film of the year and they are passionate in their discussions about why Claire Denis is to be celebrated. Equally, you will find viewers angry about what they see as a slow, boring film that they feel is pretentious and offers no narrative pleasure.

The 'body of work'

The arthouse audience is likely to follow the work of auteurs – perhaps not remembering everything that they have seen by a particular director but ready to be prompted by promotional material. Knowledge across several of the same auteur director's films is likely to enhance understanding and enjoyment. In some cases the personal stamp will be about style or theme. In the case of Denis we can relate *35 rhums* to the other four titles mentioned here (and others if they were available) through both theme and the personal connections to places/locations and working colleagues in cast and crew.

If we study *35 rhums* and then watch the other films, we note that Grégoire Colin also appears in *Beau travail* and *L'intrus*. Each time we see him we build up a slightly stronger sense of the kinds of character he plays. His performance begins to resonate. We wonder about how Claire Denis sees him. Also in *Beau travail* and *L'intrus* is Michel Subor, an actor who first gained an international profile in the early Jean-Luc Godard film *Le petit soldat* (France, 1960) (see Fig 7.2). His is a powerful presence but as he ages the nature of that presence changes and he becomes representative of decline in some way – in these films perhaps the decline of the power of the coloniser? This is certainly a possible reading of his role in *White Material*.

Gender and individuality

Focusing on the director of a film as the creative force at its centre (while recognising the important creative contributions of the other members of the team) inevitably leads into discussions about gender and individuality. Claire Denis is a very visible female director with a distinguished body of work – at a time when in most film industries it is still difficult for women to enjoy the same access to directing that is available to men, and particularly to do so consistently over a 20-year period. Denis attempts to distance herself from being a role model as such or to see herself as defined by a label such as 'woman filmmaker'. She repeats the same response to many interviewers on questions like this:

> Although she is a product of feminism and is loyal to its ideas, her subject matter is not the battle of the sexes: 'This does not interest me.' She is a feminist icon by default rather than by design.
> (Interview by Hermoine Eyre, *Prospect* Magazine, 21 June 2010)

Denis has done what she needs to do to make the films she wants to make. Of the five films discussed here, *35 rhums* is perhaps the most 'gender-balanced' across four central characters. *Beau travail* and *L'intrus* are films about men whereas *Chocolat*

Fig 7.9a
Isabelle Huppert's character seems vulnerable in her pink dress as she emerges from the bush in *White Material* ...

Fig 7.9b
... but she seems much stronger hanging from the back of the bus that picks her up.

and *White Material* have female central characters. Denis is certainly interested in masculinity and male stories, and her recurring use of the same actors perhaps suggests that certain types of men are to be found across her films. Auteurism in effect seduces us into speculating what the connections between the films may be. We might expect that in the films in which there are strong central female characters there is something of Denis herself, especially given the strong autobiographical influences on *Chocolat*, *35 rhums* and *White Material*. But *Beau travail* is set in Djibouti, also with connections to Denis's childhood. Does the (erotic) gaze that captures the physical displays of the young soldiers come from the young Denis herself?

These questions (which don't necessarily have answers) are prompted because we are looking across the five films. *White Material* poses another problem for us, since it features Isabelle Huppert in the central role – the same role that might be connected to Denis herself through France, the young woman in *Chocolat*. Huppert is a strong woman and in some ways not unlike Denis as a 'film personality' who has made frequent appearances at film festivals, including as a member of judging panels for awards. In one scene in *White Material* she is shown, seemingly vulnerable and abandoned on a dirt-track, her vulnerability emphasised by the flimsy cotton dress she is wearing. But when a bus arrives and she literally hangs on to the back, her arm muscles bulging and hair flying, we know how strong she is. For many of Denis's admirers this is likely to be an image of the director herself as a strong character. But Huppert also represents something else: star power. She brings to the film a formidable star image, with meanings accreted over many years in films made by other auteurs and aspects of her own strong personality. How do we deal with this complex Denis/Huppert image embodied in a single character? Perhaps Isabelle Huppert is also an auteur?

Even if we cannot answer these questions without much more research, we can recognise that Claire Denis has a distinctly personal view on the world. She puts herself into situations, into debates and takes her own stance. The five films discussed here all tell their stories in what some critics have described as the space opened up by debates on the coloniser/colonised relationship (see Chapter 8 and also the extended discussion by Kaplan (1997: 160–172)), a fictional world open to the gaze of postcolonial film studies. Denis enters this space with her own views but no fixed agenda and proceeds to expose aspects of it to us in her own way. In this sense she is an auteur.

The auteur in programming and cinema exhibition

We've noted that film festivals are important institutionally in enabling the distribution of films. Similar activities to those in festivals also feature in the regular screening programmes of specialised cinemas. Auteur cinema provides one of the organising principles of such programmes. A cinema screening a new film by an established auteur can also programme earlier films by the same director alongside talks and discussions about the director's work as well as, if possible, an appearance by the director and/or collaborators such as writers, actors, etc.

A good example of this is the programme 'Intense Intimacy: The Cinema of Claire Denis' put together by Mark Cosgrove at Watershed Cinema in Bristol, UK in 2010 around the time of the UK release of *White Material*. Aspects of the programme then toured selected cinemas in the UK. You can explore the programme and access some of the video materials on: http://www.watershed.co.uk/dshed/intense-intimacy-cinema-claire-denis.

Such programmes are very time-consuming and expensive to put together (and film prints may need to be imported). They will usually have some form of sponsorship or a funding partner such as a national cultural agency like Instituto Cervantes.

A comprehensive listing of useful scholarly material on Claire Denis as auteur is available at http://filmstudiesforfree.blogspot.co.uk/2009/04/35-shots-of-claire-denis-and-more.html.

Case study 7.3: A 'festival film'?

It is quite difficult to select a 'festival film' as a case study (as distinct from an auteur film), since by definition it is the kind of film that tends to appear only at festivals – distributors being unwilling to risk a proper release in cinemas. This in turn means that it is less likely to be picked up for wide DVD distribution.

The Colors of the Mountain (*Los colores de la montaña*, Colombia, 2010) had only been released in Colombia, Spain, Poland and the US by 2012 (according to IMDb). A Region 1 DVD is available from The Film Movement (http://www.filmmovement.com/aboutus/), an organisation set up specifically to release festival films that other distributors haven't picked up. This Colombian film has won prizes and acclaim, so why wasn't it picked up in other major territories?

FARC guerrillas have been fighting as a 'people's revolutionary army' against Colombian government forces since the mid-1960s. The guerrillas finance themselves through various forms of criminal activity aimed at the Colombian bourgeoisie – but inevitably encouraging condemnation from international agencies.

The film tells the story of a small community in a mountain village in Colombia situated on the edge of the area controlled by the FARC guerrillas. The village experiences periodic visits from both the guerrillas and the Colombian security forces. The focus of the story is the series of adventures of 9-year-old Manuel and his friends. The title refers to Manuel's passion for painting. His other passion is football, but when his father buys him a new ball it is soon kicked into what the locals fear is a minefield. The boys of course are determined to get the ball back. As the director's statement tells us:

> The soccer ball on the minefield – a leitmotif throughout the film – is a symbol of our harsh and absurd reality [i.e. in Colombia] and, at the same time, carries universal resonance.

> (Press pack)

Manuel is oblivious to the stress in his parents' relationship caused by the threat of violence and of the problems faced by a new, enthusiastic teacher who arrives at the local school that is losing children withdrawn by parents fleeing to the city.

There are definitely 'cycles' and trends in international cinema. In 2012 in the UK it became much easier to sell Nordic films because of the success of Nordic crime fiction (novels and TV serials; see Chapter 9).

It isn't difficult to understand why the film succeeded at festivals. Colombia is rarely seen on film, so that in itself is appealing. The director, Carlos César Arbeláez, is a documentarist making his first fiction feature and he shoots on location with a cast of mainly non-professionals. Audiences feel that they are getting access to some kind of authentic representation – they may even recognise the approach as similar to that of

Fig 7.10
The boys on their hill-top
football pitch in *The
Colors of the Mountain*.

some Iranian films (see Chapter 6). Added to this, the story about childhood in what is effectively a war zone is likely to appeal to politically liberal festival audiences. But it isn't an art film in the way that *35 rhums* certainly is. Arbeláez is yet to be recognised as an auteur – though perhaps he will be in future if he is able to produce several films of a high standard and to develop some kind of personal 'signature'. If he were to become an auteur, his first film may then get a retrospective release.

The same features that make *The Colors of the Mountain* a festival film can also mean that it will not be considered for a general cinema release. Colombia is 'different' but it doesn't have a high profile in terms of film culture – unlike, say, Iran or Mexico. The director is unknown internationally and a distributor would find the film difficult to promote. Even as a film 'for children' there is the problem that such films are usually expected to be uplifting. *The Colors of the Mountain* is actually quite difficult to classify because of the violence or threat of violence. It may mean a distributor being faced with an exhibition certificate that prevented it from being shown to younger audiences, even though its story is accessible. Note that the decision not to distribute is often based on pragmatic issues like this. A film like *The Colors of the Mountain* needs critics behind it and ideally an experienced sales agent in order to be sold to overseas territories.

If we compare this film to a Claire Denis title – and put aside the subject matter and Denis's status as an auteur – we can identify some other factors that would help the film to be seen more widely. One possibility is to seek some form of co-production deal. As we note in Chapters 4 and 6, some countries have a policy of supporting production overseas. In this case, a co-production with Spain – a common practice in much of Hispanic Latin America – guarantees a Spanish release and may help in further sales in Europe (this film did get Spanish distribution but not much more widely in Europe). Co-production deals also sometimes involve European TV channels, especially public service broadcasters. Such deals are mutually beneficial. For a modest contribution a broadcaster might purchase broadcast rights – and meet some of its own cultural programming targets. This is also likely to lead to DVD distribution deals in that country. Unfortunately in the current funding climate TV channels are cutting back on investment in foreign-language programming.

The Colors of the Mountain in Manchester

Cornerhouse, the specialised cinema in Manchester, Northwest England, runs ¡Viva!, a festival of Spanish and Latin American Cinema, in March each year. *The Colors of the Mountain* was shown as part of ¡Viva! in 2011, alongside two other films from Colombia. In addition, because Cornerhouse also features art galleries, there was a display of the work by the Colombian artist Oscar Muñoz programmed as part of the festival – this included a video installation project (http://www.cornerhouse.org/art/art-exhibitions/oscar-munoz-biografias).

The Colors of the Mountain was screened three times during the festival, including once for school students studying Spanish. (A local '12A' certificate for the film was negotiated.) The screenings were well attended and it is likely that the audience for the festival screenings was roughly what might have been expected if the film had played a typical engagement in the normal film programme of the cinema (i.e. several screenings, probably in a smaller auditorium, over a week). This suggests that the festival met the local audience demand for the film – a distributor would have to work hard to find a larger audience for a conventional release.

Contemporary art cinema prospects

We have noted that specialised cinema covers a range of different kinds of films. In recent years the sector has benefited from two developments. First, there has been a revival of interest in documentary films in **theatrical** distribution. Documentaries had a long history in cinema programming up until the 1970s by which time the format had almost completely migrated to television. The huge success of 'authored' documentary films such as *Bowling for Columbine* (US, 2002) and *Fahrenheit 9/11* (US, 2004) directed by and featuring Michael Moore has prompted distributors to release more documentaries in cinemas. Documentary festivals such as Sheffield Doc/Fest in the UK or *Rencontres internationales du documentaire de Montréal* (RIDM) are thriving. The most recent example of a successful cinema documentary was *Senna* (UK, 2010) which with total box office of over £3 million in the UK and Ireland became the most successful documentary to date in the UK and the biggest specialised film of the year. *Senna* (a documentary biopic about the Brazilian Grand Prix driver Ayrton Senna) is an interesting title for two reasons. It attracted audiences of motor-racing fans to cinemas that they might not have visited before – a major promotional bonus for the sector as a whole. It also demonstrated that the relatively new system of digital distribution could indeed bring new benefits to specialised cinemas.

Digital distribution – films released not on 35mm film but as a **DCP** or **Digital Cinema Package** – could have a profound impact on the specialised film sector. The concept of digital cinema is explored in detail in Chapter 12. Here we will refer to just one aspect of the changes.

A physical 35mm print comprising several reels can only be in one cinema at a time. It costs around US$1,000 to make each print and transport costs are significant. If the film proves popular, it isn't feasible to instantly create more prints so that it can be shown in other cinemas at the same time. A DCP is much less expensive to produce and then the same portable hard drive can be sent to

Fig 7.11
The rivalry between
Ayrton Senna and Alain
Prost is central to *Senna*.

several cinemas before the release date and the DCP copied to a computer server
in each cinema. The distributor then provides the cinema with a key code enabling
projection for an agreed number of screenings. *Senna* was one of the first films to
demonstrate how effective this process could be in allowing cinemas to both obtain
the film and then *retain* it for future showings. Much of *Senna*'s success came from
word-of-mouth promotion and the new flexibility that cinemas found in meeting
growing audience demand over several weeks. The scale of the film's box office
success would not have been possible without this new flexibility.

We need to be a little careful here. As in all new systems, digital distribution and
exhibition will take some time to 'bed in' and there are still unresolved issues such
as the cost of installing projectors, etc. and who should pay for this. There are also
other issues about the distribution of specialised films which digital conversion won't
necessarily cover. But the new digital environment does change the outlook. So-called
'alternative content' such as streamed live video of opera, ballet, etc. is also part of
digital exhibition practice.

Film festivals are also part of the new digital ecology. Imported films and
submissions from filmmakers now arrive at festivals in a bewildering array of digital
formats from DCPs down to DVDs. This perhaps means more access to the 'diversity
of films' for audiences, but also headaches for the projectionists at festivals, since
many of the 'prosumer' and domestic entertainment digital technologies are not
designed for cinema projection. So, if you go to a festival and see a low-grade print,
don't automatically blame the projectionist!

One aspect of digital
cinema that is not so
welcome is that in most
cases equipment failures
have to be repaired
by an external agency.
Projectionists have less
chance of solving the
problem.

Artists' films

At the beginning of this chapter we recognised that the term 'art cinema' or
'arthouse' has evolved over many years. One of the original meanings refers to a
classification sometimes now termed **artists' films** when a fine artist uses film or video
as a medium for a single artwork or as part of a larger art project. Avant-garde film
might involve an exploration of film or cinema as an artistic medium or as a social
or political statement such as those of the underground or experimental film art
movements of the 1950s to 1970s and their contemporary equivalents.

For various reasons – institutional and technological – the distinction between artists' films and other forms of arthouse cinema have begun to blur. Certain fine artists have now become successful filmmakers. Steve McQueen (*Hunger*, UK/Ireland, 2008, and *Shame*, UK, 2011) and Sam Taylor-Wood (*Nowhere Boy*, UK/Canada, 2009) are two British artists who have become successful filmmakers. Two other earlier filmmakers Isaac Julien and John Akomfrah (see the section on UK diaspora film in Chapter 4) have made films that have shown in galleries as 'installations' and also in cinemas as 'films'. The blurring of these distinctions has created at least the potential for some audiences to 'cross over' to another medium and another type of venue – or to sample both forms in multi-arts venues. Cornerhouse in Manchester has now moved into distributing films from artists/film artists beginning with Gillian Wearing (*Self Made*, UK, 2010) and Andrew Kötting (*Swandown*, UK, 2012). (See http://www.cornerhouse.org/art/art-events/artist-film).

Summary

The definition of art film and specialised film is changing. Some audiences may regret that the arthouse concept of showing films from acknowledged auteur directors is under challenge – especially from Hollywood studio-backed 'awards films'. But we have noted that initiatives like digital projection make a wider variety of material available in more venues and encourage new initiatives, including artists' films.

Film festivals are a major part of the whole process of film production, distribution and exhibition, and the wide variety of festivals is now being supported by social media and the growth of online discussion and open access archive material. In the past few years, film festivals have been recognised in academia with the establishment of a Film Festival Research Network (www.filmfestivalresearch.org/) and a regular publication *The Film Festival Yearbook* published by 'Film Studies at St Andrews University'.

Many thanks to Rachel Hayward, Programme Manager (Films) Cornerhouse, Manchester for help with this chapter.

References and further reading

Beugnet, Martine (2004) *Claire Denis*, Manchester and New York: Manchester University Press.

Elsaesser, Thomas (2005) *European Cinema: Face to Face With Hollywood*, Amsterdam: Amsterdam University Press.

Hayward, Susan (2002) 'Claire Denis's "Post-colonial" Films and Desiring Bodies', *L'Esprit Créateur* 42(3): 39–49.

Hayward, Susan (2006) *Cinema Studies: The Key Concepts* (3rd edn), Abingdon: Routledge.

Hughes, Darren (2009) 'Dancing Reveals So Much'. Available at http://sensesofcinema.com/2009/50/claire-denis-interview/.

Kaplan, E. Ann (1997) *Looking for the Other: Feminism, Film and the Imperial Gaze*, London: Routledge.

King, Geoff (2005) *American Independent Cinema*, London: I.B. Tauris.

Lee, Kevin (2009) 'Spectacularly Intimate: An Interview with Claire Denis'. Available at http://mubi.com/notebook/posts/spectacularly-intimate-an-interview-with-claire-denis.

Murphy, Ian (2012) 'Feeling and Form in the Films of Claire Denis', *Jump Cut* 54 (autumn) (www.ejumpcut.org).

Pierson, John (1996) *Spike, Mike, Slackers and Dykes*, London: Faber and Faber.

Reid, Mark A. (1996) 'Claire Denis Interview: Colonial Observations', *Jump Cut* 40 (March): 67–72. Also available at http://www.ejumpcut.org/archive/onlinessays/JC40folder/ClaireDenisInt.html.

Tzioumakis, Yannis (2006) *American Independent Cinema: An Introduction*, Edinburgh: Edinburgh University Press.

Web material

http://www.guardian.co.uk/film/2010/jul/04/claire-denis-white-material-interview.
http://www.filmmovement.com/downloads/press/THE%20COLORS%20OF%20THE%20MOUNTAIN%20FM%20PRESS%20KIT.pdf.

Further viewing

If you really want to understand art films, specialised cinema and film festivals, the best option is to visit your nearest specialised cinema on a regular basis and sample the range of films that it shows. If that isn't practical, the next best option is to use the festival websites at:

www.berlinale.de/en/HomePage.html
www.festival-cannes.fr/en.html
www.labiennale.org/en/cinema/

Use the 'archives' section of each site to find out which films won prizes in previous years. See if you can find the films of any one year on DVD. They may have taken some time to get distribution in your country. You can make up your own mind what you think about the films but it is also useful to compare the lists of prize-winners with the nominations for 'Best Foreign Language Film' at the Academy Awards each year:

http://awardsdatabase.oscars.org/ampas_awards/BasicSearchInput.jsp

The Academy tends to be more conservative in its selections than festival juries. Is there any difference in the lists? If so, what do you think it means?

CHAPTER 8

Cinema that needs to be different?

- Defining 'Third Cinema'
- 'Imperfect cinema' in Cuba
- From Third Cinema to postcolonialism
- Basic concepts associated with postcolonialism
- 'African cinemas'
- The legacy of British colonialist policies for film culture
- Film in Francophone Africa
- Sembène Ousmane and sub-Saharan African filmmaking
- ☐ Case study 8.1: Third Cinema and Sembène's *Xala*
- FESPACO, the diaspora and the academy
- Nollywood
- ☐ Case study 8.2: *Araromire*
- Summary
- References and further reading
- Further viewing

This book deals with filmed entertainment being produced and 'received' everywhere in the world. Most of the organisations in the international film business focus on the three biggest continental markets: North America, Europe and Asia. Australia and New Zealand are also significant markets and sometimes the term 'Asia Pacific' is used to include them. Central and South America are also covered, but mainly in terms of the three major industries in Mexico, Brazil and Argentina. Last and almost an afterthought comes 'Africa and the Middle East' – an enormous geographical area with a potential audience of over a billion and some new, and wealthy, regional producers. As we saw in Chapter 6, the commercial cinema in this region is included alongside Europe, almost as an afterthought.

The main concern of the film business is the revenue that can be generated from film production, distribution and exhibition. Alternatively, film in many affluent countries not large enough to sustain a fully commercial domestic film industry can become instead a cultural activity that brings social benefits. Both these versions of film industry and culture demand not only relatively high levels of per capita income and sources of investment funding but also an infrastructure of theatrical venues and distribution systems as well as production facilities and training for crews and creative talents.

In Europe, production is often subsidised through forms of tax relief, loans and grants (see Chapter 4). In poorer countries, **cultural production** may be the only possibility for local filmmaking – raising a series of different questions about state control over cinema – as well as the political decisions necessary to divert scarce resources towards such production. In this chapter we will look at Cuba and parts of sub-Saharan Africa in order to explore what film industry and culture might mean in countries where domestic production is difficult and there are likely to be reasons, political or cultural, why Hollywood, Bollywood and other forms of international film production are not necessarily welcome or appropriate.

Since we are dealing here with film provision that often lies outside the commercial mainstream, there is also an issue about access to films. New digital technologies offer one possibility of overcoming this. Access is also about the **gatekeepers** of film culture – the distributors of films. Film territories in Africa have been among those most heavily affected by colonialism. They may now face a form of **neo-colonialism** in which the infrastructure of the international film business restricts their capacity to develop an indigenous film culture. All film production is political in the sense that films construct a discourse in which ideas and values are presented and explored. As we noted in Chapter 2, Hollywood and the national mainstream film culture of the major producing countries present the problem of **transparency** – the mode of presentation that attempts to appear 'natural', that disguises its own 'constructedness'. Commercial filmmaking is predicated on the idea that audiences shouldn't be encouraged to think about who is making the film or how it is creating its meaning.

Defining 'Third Cinema'

Dissatisfaction with the film experience available locally was a feature of the cultural environment in the 1960s alongside different forms of anti-colonial struggle in Africa and Southeast Asia and political upheaval across Latin America and the Middle East. These developments were oppositional to the ideological thrust of Hollywood and European films, and they saw the emergence of a set of political ideas enshrined in a call for a **Third Cinema**, initially from Fernando Solanas and Octavio Getino, Argentinian filmmakers who produced and directed a powerful political documentary *La hora de los hornos* (*The Hour of Furnaces*, 1968). 'Towards a Third Cinema' was the title of an article published in the journal *Tricontinental* in October 1969 in Havana. It attempted to bring together oppositional filmmakers from Asia, Latin America and Africa. Solanas and Getino had first heard the term 'Third Cinema' in Cuba earlier that year and they emphasised that their ideas, although collected together during a production in Argentina, were meant to be applied much more widely.

For these Argentinians, 'First Cinema' is mainstream Hollywood – and by extension any other mainstream commercial industry operating on a Hollywood model. 'Second Cinema' is the art cinema model (see Chapter 7). Whereas Hollywood is defined as an entertainment cinema, art cinema is defined by the concept of the bourgeois artist or auteur expressing an individualistic viewpoint. Again, other forms of specialised cinema made by 'film artists' could be included in this category (e.g. films by auteurs in Hong Kong or Iran, no matter what the politics of the filmmaker may be). By contrast, Third Cinema would be made *collectively* with the intention of providing information and analysis that would engage audiences in *local* issues of economics, politics and culture. Third Cinema would be *international* in ideas, sharing with other producers and audiences, but also *local* in terms of specific issues for investigation.

It is important not to confuse the concept of Third Cinema with 'Third World Cinema'. The latter term was in common usage during the 1970s and 1980s before falling out of use, since the notion of a 'Third' World was thought by many to be demeaning. It implied a ranking of different regions. It was replaced by concepts of 'North' (i.e. North America and Europe) and 'South'. Alternatively, some commentators preferred the term 'underdeveloped' which implied that Africa, Asia, etc. had yet to reach their full potential (and that they had been deliberately kept back by colonialism).

Third World Cinema referred to all cinemas/film cultures in the Third World – which included both the highly commercial popular cinemas of India and the state-controlled cinemas of both Communist China and Taiwan and the commercial cinema of Hong Kong. Although there were connections between Third Cinema practitioners and certain Chinese and Indian filmmakers, they need to be distinguished from the overall practice in those countries.

During the 1960s, Latin America was the site for various forms of revolutionary struggle against governments that were seen as dictatorial and agents for American capitalism. Mexico, Brazil and Argentina had film industries that had developed sustained local production, peaking in the 1940s. But the commercial film market in each country was always vulnerable to domination by Hollywood. Opposition to Hollywood by local filmmakers was initially based on the combination of desire for local stories and recognition of local traditions and links to European film cultures.

How Europe Underdeveloped Africa was the title of an important book by Guyanese historian, writer and political activist Walter Rodney, published in 1972.

'Imperfect cinema' in Cuba

After the Cuban Revolution of 1959, the revolutionary leaders, recognising the paramount importance of cinema, established ICAIC (Instituto Cubano de Arte e Industria Cinematográficos) as the cultural agency that would ensure that cinema in the new Cuba would serve the revolution. The aim was to use what resources were available to make a new kind of cinema.

The pre-revolutionary cinema legacy in Cuba was thin in spite of a vibrant local film market. A weak entertainment cinema had been subservient to Hollywood and it was necessary to make a fresh start. Julio García Espinosa was one of the founders of ICAIC and one of the only directors in Cuba, alongside Tomás Gutiérrez Alea (see below) to have any experience of a formal film school. Espinosa's essay 'For an Imperfect Cinema' was published in Cuba in 1969. A 1979 translation by Julianne Burton is available online from *Jump Cut* magazine at: http://www. ejumpcut.org/archive/onlinessays/JC20folder/ImperfectCinema.html. The essay begins with what may be seen as a prescient observation about the possibilities that video technology might open up for all kinds of filmmakers. Espinosa is excited by this because he seeks a genuinely popular cinema which instead of being a mass entertainment by a few for the many would become a cinema made by everyone for everyone.

The concept of the imperfect as something to strive for is a response to the problem of 'seeking the perfect' that Espinosa identifies as caused by the status of

Cuba in the 1950s was a country dominated by American culture and American business interests. The American mafia were involved in the local tourist trade, including forms of sex tourism.

Cuba has a history of film production, beginning in 1897, that covers fiction and non-fiction features and co-productions with the US and Latin American and European partners (see Douglas 2008).

'high art' made by artists trained to serve élite audiences. Imperfect for Espinosa does not mean flawed or amateurish. Instead he wants to create art for everyone, but art that asks its audience to 'work' in order to get pleasure and also to learn from the process of 'reading' the film.

This perception of what a Third Cinema could become involved the production of documentaries and short films as well as features (in fact documentaries were a priority). The challenge in Cuba was to educate audiences and to raise political consciousness – but also to replace the pleasures of a Hollywood cinema that had dominated Cuban screens. The relatively small group of Cuban filmmakers was charged with delivering new forms of cinema. The best known of these filmmakers was Tomás Gutiérrez Alea (1928–1996) and his work is often singled out, partly because it was the most widely seen outside Cuba, especially *Memorias del Subdesarrollo* (*Memories of Underdevelopment*, Cuba, 1968). This film, Alea's fifth based on a novel by Edmundo Desnoes, deals with a writer from a bourgeois family who decides to stay in Cuba after the revolution even though his wife and friends flee to the US. Alea, trained at the Centro Sperimentale di Cinematagrafia in Rome, represents Sergio's struggle almost as a stream of consciousness, including documentary footage, stills, extracts from newsreels and Hollywood films. The film resembles the modernist cinema of the European New Waves of the 1960s with its anti-hero, who is almost a redundant figure in the new Cuba, unable to come to terms with the revolution and what it means – and is therefore of no use to society.

Alea's films form a formidable body of work that is worth exploring for its own sake as marvellous cinema as well as an indication of what the 'New Latin American Cinema' could be. Cuba became the centre for aspiring filmmakers across the region, symbolised later by the establishment of the Havana Film Festival in 1979. However, Alea's work also presents problems. It is difficult to know what popular audiences in Cuba made of such a complex work as *Memories* – although some other Alea films have had much more direct audience appeal. His films took time to be released in the US because of the blockade of Cuba and, when they were seen, *Memories* in particular, they were often misunderstood. In an interview, Alea picks out *Sight and Sound* in the UK as deliberately misunderstanding *Memories* and equating Alea with Russian dissidents who sought to criticise the regime (Alea 1990: 187).

For our purposes, a film that is available and which perhaps illuminates Espinosa's ideas about the imperfect cinema approach more directly is his own film *The Adventures of Juan Quin Quin* (Cuba, 1967). The central character, Juan, is familiar from many traditional Hispanic stories – the poor young man whose adventures in the world with his faithful sidekick will mean finding a beautiful young woman and rescuing her after defeating the evil king, landowner, brigand, etc. Think Don Quixote, but also *The Cisco Kid* (a western series on US television in the 1950s). This character is immediately attractive to the Cuban audience and Espinosa uses him to represent the ordinary person's capacity to defeat the enemies of the revolution. He does this by placing his hero in situations that parody the Hollywood films and TV series Cubans would recognise from the 1940s and 1950s as well as more up-to-date references. The settings are the familiar Cuban landscape and village events such as cockfights, bullfights and a travelling circus, and Juan battles with oppression by a priest, the local mayor and a landowner – as well as trying to become a revolutionary leader.

Centro Sperimentale di Cinematagrafia is the Italian film school established in 1935 (with the support of Benito Mussolini). Alea was a student there in the early 1950s along with Julio García Espinosa.

Fig 8.1
Juan (Júlio Martínez) adopts an iconic pose as he tries to fight for justice in the sugar cane factory in *The Adventures of Juan Quin Quin*.

Alienation was one element of Brecht's approach to political theatre in the 1920s and 1930s. It was pursued in film studies in relation to devices that 'make strange' the experience of watching a film, exposing its conventions and constructedness. In the 1970s it was discussed as 'distanciation' in relation to work by Louis Althusser.

Scratch video was the basis for a politicised video art form in the UK in the 1980s, using found footage and exploiting the new possibilities of relatively inexpensive video editing. It developed during the Thatcher period when many artists and filmmakers were 'politicised' by their experience of contemporary culture.

The film is presented in black and white CinemaScope with rousing Hollywood music and title credits borrowed from spaghetti westerns. Later there are spoofs of James Bond, silent film comedies, musicals, 1950s war films, etc. A detailed critique of the film from the archives of *Jump Cut* magazine is available online (Taylor 1979). This analyses the film in some detail and considers Espinosa's approach in the light of the **alienation** effect promoted by Bertholt Brecht. The conclusion is that, two years ahead of Espinosa's essay, the film doesn't really encourage the audience to 'participate', and risks confusion through its 'play' on familiar genres and typical characters. Anna Taylor suggests that Espinosa's later documentaries such as *Third World, Third World War* (Cuba, 1971) might be better examples – but unfortunately these are difficult to find.

The other important Cuban directors of this period include Sara Gómez (1943–1974) and Santiago Álvarez (1919–1998), both specialising in documentary. Clips of their work are available on YouTube, including *Now* (1965) by Alvarez, which perhaps justifies Espinosa's observations about the possibilities of new technologies and techniques by presenting a precursor of later mash-ups or **scratch videos**, cutting a montage of newsreel clips and news photos on the theme of Civil Rights in the US to a soundtrack including Lena Horne's 'Now'. Another notable Cuban film from the 1960s is *Lucía* (1968) directed by Humberto Solás (1941–2008), a historical film in three parts focusing on the lives of women, all called 'Lucía', from the Spanish colonial period through the 1930s and up until the 1960s. Like the documentaries, *Lucía* would go on to provide a potential model for filmmakers elsewhere concerned to explore colonial legacies and questions of identity.

ICAIC controlled the Cuban music industry and a group of artists who produced the posters for films. It also provided mobile cinema vans and projectionists to tour the countryside. Mobile cinemas can be traced back to the travelling cinemas at fairgrounds in early cinema, but the Soviet 'agit-trains' and the mobile units used by the British Colonial Film Unit in Africa and Asia (see later in this chapter) and the United States Information Agency (USIA) in Cuba itself before 1959 were designed specifically to promote the ideologies of the central government or colonising power. The American activity is summarised by Tamara Falicov (2010: 104–105). She then describes the comprehensive policy of ICAIC in taking cinema to the Cuban people in a structured cultural programme that ran parallel to a major literacy project. Falicov also refers to the writings of Michael Chanan (1985/2004) who describes the scene in a documentary about a projectionist's visit to a small and remote village

Fig 8.2
A poster for ICAIC Cine Movil project featuring a Chaplin image. Source: International Institute of Social History, The Netherlands.

where many people, even in the 1960s, had not seen a film before (Chanan 2004: 25). The villagers are entranced by Charles Chaplin's *Modern Times* (1936) – a film largely without dialogue featuring Chaplin's 'little tramp'. (Although a Hollywood filmmaker, Chaplin was exiled from the US in 1952 following accusations of communist sympathies during the McCarthy period.) The mobile film project Cine Movil was attracting up to three million viewers in 1976 (Falicov 2010: 104).

Whatever the faults of *Juan Quin Quin*, Espinosa's film was a comedy that did reach large audiences in Cuba and this was an important lesson for films with political intent. Cuban cinema's attempts to create a Third Cinema were joined by other filmmakers working elsewhere within the New Latin American Cinema, especially after the Havana Film Festival was established in 1979 and the International Film School outside the city in 1986. Cuba became the centre of this new cinema. It had a healthy domestic cinema market and up until 1990 was able to compensate for the damage caused by the American economic and cultural blockade with the support of trade with the Soviet Union and Eastern Europe. After 1990 the loss of that support led to the 'Special Period' of austerity which, coupled with the decline in cinema admissions, made life for ICAIC extremely difficult.

With funding limited, ICAIC had to reduce its activities and turn increasingly to co-productions, especially with Spain and other European and Latin American countries. The films produced in Cuba in the past 25 years have become more conventional but there are still elements of the 'New' Cuban cinema of the 1960s and ICAIC is still involved in most Cuban films. In February 2013 the web 'portal' of ICAIC (in Spanish) at http://www.cubacine.cult.cu/ gave an overview of Cuban film culture in which cinemas were screening a new Cuban-Spanish film *La película*

The International Film and Television School of San Antonio de los Baños (EICTV) was founded by Colombian journalist and writer Gabriel García Márquez, Argentinean poet and filmmaker Fernando Birri, and Julio García Espinosa as a centre for training filmmakers from Asia, Africa and Latin America. See http://www.eictv.org/en/.

Fig 8.3
The streets of Havana in *Juan of the Dead*. Source: The Kobal Collection/ www.picture-desk.com.

The Lumière database of the European Audio-visual Observatory (http://lumiere.obs.coe. int/web/search) records over 70 Cuban films, mostly as co-productions that have received a release in European territories since 1960.

de Ana (*Ana's film*, Cuba/Austria, 2012) alongside selected French and American commercial releases. At the same time work by young Cuban filmmakers was touring the country and other Cuban filmmakers were preparing for appearances at overseas festivals such as Guadalajara in Mexico and Berlin, where *La piscina* (Cuba, 2012) from Carlos M. Quintela was to be shown in the Panorama section. *La película de Ana* is a comedy drama about a struggling actress forced into prostitution, whereas *La piscina* is more like an experimental film about a group of young people at a swimming pool. ICAIC was involved in both films' production and had an interest in a further seven films in production.

Research and Explore 8.1

Seek out *Juan of the Dead* (Cuba/Spain, 2012), the 'zombie comedy', which should be easily accessible. What do you think it is saying about contemporary Cuban society? Try to compare it to earlier satirical Cuban films such as *The Death of a Bureaucrat* (Tomás Gutiérrez Alea, Cuba, 1966) or *The Waiting List* (Juan Carlos Tabío, Cuba/Spain/France/Mexico, 2000).

Since its 1959 revolution Cuba has had a complex relationship with several African states, partly because of its own history of slavery and concerns about African-Cuban culture in the new society but also because of direct Cuban intervention to support African liberation struggles.

Our aim is to see what kinds of similarities and links there may be between the Cuban experience and what happened in Africa from the mid-1960s onwards. But first we will take a short diversion to consider changes in the priorities of film studies as a discipline.

From Third Cinema to postcolonialism

The 1980s proved a period of transition in film studies and film theory – linked to political changes in other areas and the developments in cultural studies and other academic disciplines. A quick glance at some of the covers of *Screen* magazine in the period reveals 'Racism, Colonialism and the Cinema' (1983), 'Other Cinemas,

Other Criticisms' (1985), 'The Last "Special Issue" on Race?' (1988), and 'Over
the Borderlines: Questioning National Identities' (1989). In crude terms what we
see here is a gradual move away from directly political, if not revolutionary, Third
Cinema ideas to consideration of more 'personal' political ideas – from investigating
anti-colonialism and **neo-colonialism** to exploring **post-colonialism**.

Susan Hayward (2006: 293) attempts to avoid confusion when she points out
that the hyphenated term '**post-colonial**' refers to the historical concept of the state
following the end of colonial rule. '**Postcolonial**' without a hyphen then refers to
theory, literature, culture, etc. concerned with the transition to experience of the
post-colonial state. We will try to stick to that distinction.

It is possible to trace back ideas about the postcolonial to theorists emerging from
different disciplines during the colonial period. Thus, for instance, **Frantz Fanon**
(1925–1961) is now seen as an influential figure in postcolonial studies, even though
his books were written before most of the French colonial possessions gained a
degree of autonomy. Fanon was born in Martinique and worked as a psychiatrist
in Algeria where he supported the FLN struggle for independence in the 1950s.
His work inspired writers such as Ngũgĩ wa Thiong'o in Kenya. Other politicians,
writers and academics who grew up under British colonialism included Kwame
Nkrumah and Julius Nyrere, C.L.R. James, Walter Rodney and Stuart Hall – all of
whom contributed to understanding about the struggle against colonialism up until
the late 1960s and then the questions of neo-colonialism that followed as newly
independent countries discovered that in economic and cultural terms little had
changed. Basil Davidson was also important in attempting to change understanding
about the process of colonisation and, like Walter Rodney, the 'underdevelopment'
of Africa in particular.

But the historical trajectory of colonialism/post-colonialism/neo-colonialism is
seen as an unhelpful distraction by some postcolonial theorists. Instead, the focus
is on discourse and power relationships. Who speaks – and from what perspective?
The most quoted theorists, alongside Fanon, have been Gayatri Chakravorty Spivak,
Homi K. Bhabha and Edward Said, and postcolonial studies is found situated mainly
in cultural studies as a discipline – though what actually constitutes cultural studies
differs in terms of 'British/Australian', 'American' and other European conceptions.
This means that we have to tread carefully in discussing postcolonialism in terms of
global film.

Basic concepts associated with postcolonialism

Many of the writers listed above are/were themselves colonial subjects and much
of their work has been concerned with questions of identity and the formation of
personal ideologies in the context of specific colonial and post-colonial academic
experiences. Edward Said (1935–2003) was born in Jerusalem as a Palestinian
living under what was termed the British Mandate for Palestine. Said's father had
an American passport and the family moved freely between Cairo and Jerusalem
before the 1948 war, after which the Christian Said family moved to America. In
his later life as an American academic Said had a different 'colonial' experience as a
member of the Palestinian National Authority engaged in struggles with Israel and its
American backers.

Said's exploration of **orientalism** underpinned every way in which the coloniser/
colonised relationship became manifest. This meant that it influenced not just

social, governmental, military, etc. attitudes by the West towards the East, but it ran through all forms of representation including fine art, literature, reportage, administrative documents – and, of course, cinema. Crucially, it also informed academia so that the study of the Eastern world is potentially 'orientalist' if undertaken by any student in a university and on a course/research project that derives its study materials or approaches from Western academic institutions. We discuss orientalism in chapters 5 and 11.

One of the issues in postcolonialism is the invidious positioning of scholars from an Eastern/Southern background. These scholars, like Said himself, are part of the élites of the East, often educated in English medium schools. However, the links are not straightforward. Those same scholars/writers/politicians who may have 'internalised' colonialist ideas are also individuals who may be 'different' or '**other**' owing to their religion, gender orientation, class, etc. Said himself was a Christian investigating Western attitudes primarily concerned with Muslim cultures in the 'Middle East' (see Chapter 6 on the construction of the 'Middle East').

The concept of the 'other' is key to the **coloniser/colonised** relationship. The colonised is often defined simply through the opposite (and negative) set of characteristics which describe the coloniser (e.g. such as civilised/uncivilised, strong/weak, honest/devious, etc.: see Chapter 5). But relationships characterised by crossing definitions of 'difference' allow spaces and margins to develop and, more importantly perhaps, '**hybridity**' and '**creolisation**' – the process of mixing West and East to produce something new and potentially subversive.

These concepts are interrogated by Gayatri Spivak (b. 1942 in Calcutta) in an important text for postcolonial studies, 'Can the Subaltern Speak?' (1988). The term 'subaltern' in general discourse means a person of lesser standing but in postcolonial studies it is derived from Antonio Gramsci's writings. We cannot hope to do other than present a very broad statement here about Spivak's complex paper and her challenge to the idea of a homogeneous mass who are collectively the subaltern. We take the impact of her critique to be that in the inequalities of the postcolonial world there are many subaltern groups defined by gender, ethnicity, class, religion, etc., each of whom is in a different position in wanting to speak about different issues. Spivak's own situation is important to her as a South Asian woman in a Western university.

Filmmakers conscious of the debates about postcolonialism are found in different parts of this book. For instance, the discussion of diaspora filmmakers in the UK and France in Chapter 4 is concerned with voices speaking from within a specific position in relation to both the history of colonialism and the current post-colonial structures of society. In this chapter we can discern voices in the debates about which direction film industry and film culture in Africa should take. It is to these voices and these discussions we turn now.

Pan-Africanism began as a strong political movement in the 1960s following decolonisation with a desire to overcome the 'divide-and-rule' approach of the imperial powers. These ideas underpinned the establishment of institutions such as the film festival known as FESPACO (see later in this chapter).

John Akomfrah also makes the important point that other forms of cultural output such as *Drum* magazine from South Africa and popular music forms such as highlife music from West Africa have a long history of popularity across the continent.

'African cinemas'

Although you will find frequent references to 'African cinema' in books and magazines, the concept of a single cinema culture stretching across the continent is not viable and we need to think about 'African cinemas' alongside political ideas about the attempt to create **pan-African** responses in the post-colonial environment of the 1960s. **John Akomfrah** (2006: 274–292) argues carefully for a consideration of the different factors – cultural, political and economic – that have seen some filmmakers manage to address both local/national and pan-African/international audiences while others have opted (or been forced into choosing) one over the other. One of our objectives here will be to investigate some of the background to the development of local film culture and film production in different parts of Africa.

There are three African countries with large populations and economic activity at a level that has sustained a film culture in the way that it is understood in territories elsewhere in the world. *Egypt* has long been the leader of Arabic-language film production exporting its mainstream and now occasional independent films to other countries in North Africa and the Middle East (see Chapter 6).

South Africa has an established film industry that services international Hollywood productions as well as 'local' productions in English and Afrikaans. The industry is well organised and has developed a profitable line in attracting international advertising shoots to attractive locations. In the past 20 years there has also been the emergence of some locally produced films that are associated with the different ethnic groups inside the Republic of South Africa. South Africa also has the most developed television ecology in Africa and, through satellite broadcasting and exports of recorded programming, South Africa has come to dominate much of the television culture of Anglophone Africa. We will discuss South Africa briefly at the end of this chapter, but because of its strong links to Hollywood it won't be our main focus here.

Nigeria has Africa's largest population and there are now claims that the unique form of Nigerian video film production, often termed **Nollywood**, is the world's biggest producer of films with more than 1,000 titles produced each year. We will discuss Nollywood a little later. At this point we will simply note that the history of film in Nigeria (and Ghana) is rooted in the legacy of British government policies on film culture in the colonial period. We want to study what has happened in terms of film industry and film culture in sub-Saharan West Africa through a comparison of the Francophone and Anglophone post-colonial regions.

Languages in post-colonial Africa

Most Africans have a first language that is 'local' or perhaps regional (e.g. Swahili in East Africa). But in terms of education, international trade and cultural exchange, it is essential to be able to speak one of the languages associated with the ex-colonial power: English, French or Portuguese. Arabic fits into a slightly different category but still carries vestiges of colonial domination. These languages are also 'localised' or creolised to produce interesting hybrids. Selecting which language to use for an African film production raises interesting questions in a post-colonial world.

The legacy of British colonialist policies for film culture

British colonial policy had effects on all parts of Anglophone Africa. Rosaleen Smyth (1983: 129) quotes British concerns in the 1920s about the impact of Hollywood films in Africa – both because 'trade follows the film' and because American films threatened the prestige of the coloniser and therefore the proper administration of the colonies. In the period between 1930 and the late 1950s, when the process of de-colonisation began in earnest, colonial film policy had the following aims:

- to use film as a tool of education and propaganda;
- to train local African technicians (to support British producer-directors);
- to establish filmmaking facilities in key cities (e.g. Accra in the Gold Coast – now Ghana).

This was the approach often described as 'indirect rule' or 'association'. It meant that the British District Officer in, for example, Nigeria was seen as an 'adviser' to a local ruler. The British would not usually intervene locally. The contradictions of this approach were apparent in British attitudes towards African education. They didn't want to promote an African colonial élite and they operated a colour bar to prevent any potential élite mixing with colonial administrators. On the other hand, they allowed African schools to use local languages, and British District Officers were encouraged to learn local languages and culture in order to be more effective in their role. The colonial administration built only one university in West Africa and one in East Africa, but these did help to produce an intellectual class (which also studied at UK universities). One side effect of all of this was that nationalist movements were stimulated by the spur of visible racial prejudice – and were able to retain a sense of their own culture. Both of these features were less noticeable in French colonial practice, as we will see below.

The outcomes of British colonial policies for film – and representation of some of the issues described above – are now viewable via the work of a major research project into 'Colonial Film: Moving Images of the British Empire' undertaken

Fig 8.4
Amenu's Child (1950) is a production from the Gold Coast Film Unit. A 'social development' film shot by a British crew in the 'idiom of the African folktale' – but presenting a British perception of African culture (see the film's entry on colonial.film.org.uk). Source: British Film Institute Stills Collection.

between 2007 and 2010. Some 6,000 films produced by a variety of film units are on the project's database and around 150 are viewable online, including some from the Gold Coast Film Unit.

> In September 1948, the Colonial Film Unit set up its first 'school of instruction', at Accra in the Gold Coast. The school was intended to train six local film workers in the hope that 'these trainees will form the nucleus of production units' in West Africa (*Colonial Cinema*, December 1948, 80). The school was part of a drive, outlined at 'The Film in Colonial Development' conference of January 1948, to develop and encourage local film production within the colonies.
>
> Filmed at Accra, at Kedze and in Keta over a period of a year from October 1950 until September 1951, *The Boy Kumasenu* was the first feature film made by the Gold Coast Film Unit and brought together a non-professional all-African cast.
>
> (From http://www.colonialfilm.org.uk/production-company/
> gold-coast-film-unit)

The Boy Kumasenu is viewable online accompanied by a critical commentary. It was shot on 35mm film with an 'Associate Producer' credit for Basil Wright, one of the leading figures of the British Documentary Movement of the 1930s. The critical commentary points to the way in which the film is constructed around a British perspective on Africa (the story is about a boy who comes to the city from the countryside) and couched in Hollywood narrative terms. Even so, the location shooting and African cast (who don't speak much in the film which has a British voiceover) were an attraction for a local audience. The film had prestige showings

Fig 8.5
The local men recruited as potential game wardens look bemused as the English couple act out an 'official opening' of their game park in *Where Vultures Fly*.

in West Africa but was then sold for a lump sum to a local Syrian exhibitor who reputedly made a 'five-figure sum' (in UK pounds) from large local audiences – 40,000 saw the film in three weeks.

At the same time, British commercial producers became interested in exploiting African locations (especially in East Africa and Southern Africa) for spectacular adventure films, sometimes in conjunction with Hollywood studios. *Where No Vultures Fly* (UK, 1952) was an early 'eco-themed' thriller produced by Ealing Studios. It dealt with the struggle to set up a game park in Kenya. Filmed in Technicolor, it was a commercial success in the UK. Whereas that film dealt with a white settler family in Kenya, *Men of Two Worlds* (1946), shot in what is now Tanzania, attempts to explore the dilemma faced by an 'educated African' returning home to his village from London.

These various production initiatives were all consistent with British policy that saw African colonies as resources to be exploited. The result of these policies in the 1960s was that the newly independent African states with a British colonial history were presented with a rather different set of problems to those faced by the new Francophone states in West Africa.

Film in Francophone Africa

French colonial policy in Africa differed considerably from the British variety (see also Chapter 6 on Egypt). African colonies were treated as parts of metropolitan France and the focus was on 'French medium' education and an introduction to French cultural ideas. As far as cinema was concerned, French policy meant that an educated African élite was encouraged to appreciate French cinema. Manthia Diawara (1992: 22) refers to the 'Laval Decree' of 1934 setting up French censorship procedures for any films produced in the African colonies. He argues that, though rarely applied, this decree 'postponed the birth of francophone African film'. Little was done in respect of African production until close to the time of independence when training in Paris was available, as well as funding for production in Africa via cultural initiatives involving French agencies. The result in West Africa was that newly independent states such as Senegal, Ivory Coast and Gabon in the 1960s had budding filmmakers eager to make films, but no local facilities. They were expected to remain in the French cultural ambit rather than to create their own way. At the same time in Anglophone Ghana, local filmmakers had facilities for film production but no specific training in how to make feature films. The obvious solution was some form of co-production – which did develop in certain ways but not in the joint production of films.

A second cultural difference between Francophone and Anglophone African countries was the importance of the concept of *négritude* developed in Paris in the 1930s by Aimé Césaire from Martinique and Léopold Senghor from Senegal, among others. Although this was an anti-racist and anti-colonialist movement that promoted pride in the cultural achievements of African and Caribbean people, it did so within Francophone culture, and after independence it was opposed by some African writers and filmmakers. The Nigerian scholar Femi Okiremuete Shaka (2004: 333) describes the 'astonishment' felt by Anglophone Africans about the extent to which the new leaders of Francophone Africa had lost touch with their African culture and traditions. Senegal, with Senghor as president, was the new African country most clearly associated with French culture – much to the distaste of Sembène Ousmane, the Sengalese director sometimes called the 'father of African Cinema'.

The whole British involvement in filmmaking in Africa may be explored (with online clips for education users) on Screenonline starting at: http://www.screenonline.org.uk/film/id/1082830/.

Belgian colonial policy set up colonial film units in francophone Congo following the British model (Diawara 1992: 12).

Samba Gadjigo provides useful background on Sembène on: www.newsreel.org/articles/OusmaneSembene.htm.

Sembène Ousmane and sub-Saharan African filmmaking

Most writing about African film culture will at some point reference the work of Sembène Ousmane (1923–2007). Sembène was a fisherman's son from Southern Senegal who took manual jobs until he was recruited by the French Army of West Africa during the Second World War. On his discharge in 1946 he became a railway worker and experienced a major strike. In 1947 he moved to France and, up until 1960, worked in the Marseilles docks. He became a trade unionist and joined the French Communist Party. An accident forced him into lighter work and in his free time he educated himself through public libraries, becoming a committed political activist. He also began to write – poetry, essays, and in 1956 his first novel *Le docker noir*. On his return to Senegal (after a tour of other African states) following independence in 1961, he decided that he wanted to make films and took the opportunity of a scholarship to train at the Gorky Studios in Moscow. He returned at the end of 1962 with an old Russian camera and a desire to put 'ordinary Africans' on the screen. Over the next 40 years his output of both literature and films comprised five novels, five collections of short stories, four short films, ten features, and four documentaries. The practical difficulties associated with film production in Africa are immense and Sembène spent a great deal of time attending festivals, giving interviews and working on the distribution and exhibition of his films to African audiences. In this context Sembène's legacy represents a considerable achievement. It still has an importance for us now in terms of that desire to put ordinary Africans and their lives on screen – using a language with which they could identify.

Influences and themes

Sembène's early films show the clear influence of Italian neo-realism, and in particular of *Bicycle Thieves* (Italy, 1948). There is no surprise in this and we have already discussed the neo-realist legacy in Chapter 3, and in relation to Iranian cinema in Chapter 6.

The training in Russia marked out Sembène from some of the other West African filmmakers of the 1960s and 1970s who were trained in France. The Russian experience was something Sembène shared with some Cuban filmmakers as well as other Africans. He would eventually work with French cultural agencies (though not without conflicts). From the outset, Sembène's aims were pursued as part of a cultural politics, examining Africa's history and attempting to influence its future. The American academic Manthia Diawara (1992: 141–166) has suggested three types of films that provide basic categories for many African filmmakers:

1   *Social realist narratives* – 'thematising current sociocultural issues'. These are often concerned with conflicts between tradition and modernity, agrarian and urban industrial societies, oral and written culture, and subsistence economies and cash economies. The heroes of such films are often marginalised characters who suffer during this transition period. The films are presented in 'realist' style (e.g. via neo-realist principles) but also use satire, melodrama and comedy. Such films have a real potential to please popular African audiences who have otherwise been exposed to mainly cheap imports of American, French, Indian and Hong Kong 'exploitation' films, largely action and melodrama. Middle-class audiences in Francophone Africa would have had more access to quality French films (the audience would be French speaking, unlike the popular audience).

Fig 8.6a

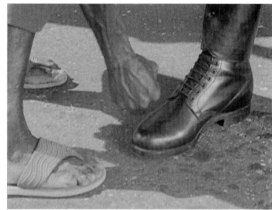

Fig 8.6b

Borom Sarret (*Cart-Driver*, Senegal, 1962) is a 20-minute film shot on the streets of Dakar in a neo-realist style. A cart-driver is stopped by a police officer when a customer takes him into the restricted area where the rich live. Director Sembène offers a reference to Soviet cinema with an Eisenstein moment when the police boot stamps on the man's wartime service medal which has fallen out of his papers. The police offer impounds the man's cart, making it impossible for him to earn any money.

2   *Colonial confrontation* – films dealing with the colonial era. These may be historical reconstructions of the early conflicts between Africans and Europeans or more recent conflicts, particularly around twentieth-century wars in which Africans fought for the French, experiencing racism and rejection (see discussion of *Indigènes* in Chapter 4).

3   '*Return to source*' films – narratives in which Europeans are not present and which attempt to explore African culture in African terms. The key film here is Souleymane Cissé's *Yeelen* (Mali, 1987) in which a son seeks his uncle's help to fight his sorcerer father in a mythical past. Diawara suggests that filmmakers have turned to this kind of film for various reasons, including a desire to avoid censorship, to look for ideas in pre-colonial culture that might help with contemporary problems and also to seek a new 'African' aesthetic for filmmaking.

Diawara makes the point that although Africans are proud of their filmmakers, the films themselves have to go abroad and win prizes at festivals to gain a profile. Of the three categories, the first is usually the most popular (and the most likely to be exhibited to African audiences).

   We could argue that Sembène has made films in all three categories, although only *Moolaadé* (Senegal/France/Burkina Faso/Cameroon/Morocco/Tunisia, 2004) might relate to the last category. Sembène's early films are nearly all in the social realist mode, with the exception of *Emitai* (Senegal, 1971) (which features resistance against French military demands during the Second World War) and the related *Camp de Thiaroye* (Senegal/Algeria/Tunisia, 1988). *Ceddo* (Senegal, 1976) is virtually in a category of its own, but fits best as a historical reconstruction under (2). Sembène always wanted to draw a popular audience, so social realism was the obvious choice; but he also saw the value in appearing at European festivals and American universities. Throughout his career he sought to make films in Africa with African producers for African audiences. In the beginning, however, he needed European support.

Fig 8.7
Aoua Sangare in the
'return to source' film
Yeelen. Source: British Film
Institute Stills Collection.

Spoken language

A major feature of Sembène's work was his attempt to work in the vernacular languages of the people of West Africa. This was a highly charged issue. French was the language of the coloniser, and it became the language of the educated African and the 'official language' of the newly independent nations in the 1960s – barring the majority of the population from full participation in society. Because of their strong oral traditions, African languages were not formalised in written form and had low cultural status. Sembène's insistence on making his films, from *Mandabi* (France/Senegal, 1968) onwards, in local languages such as Wolof, Doula or Bambara was a powerful political statement. At first he thought that the French dubbed over Wolof would be seen as politically provocative, helping to stimulate the local audience, but instead they found it alienating.

One problem was the difficulty Sembène discovered in using non-actors who could speak 'naturally' in their own language. Local forms of conversation were difficult to incorporate into film dialogue (the local convention includes the repetition of formal greetings during conversation). Sembène had to develop strategies to modify the conventions without losing the naturalness of speech delivery.

Case study 8.1: Third Cinema and Sembène's *Xala* (Senegal, 1974)

Although some of them were made over 40 years ago, Sembène's films are still studied and discussed, and fortunately some are easily accessible in DVD format. *Xala* is one of the most interesting because it provides case study materials for many of the arguments in this chapter.

Xala was made some 14 years after Senegal gained independence and 11 years since Sembène's first short film *Borom Sarret*. The film was made on 35mm filmstock and in colour. In 1974 a low-budget film would still have been cheaper if shot on 16mm in black and white, but Sembene wanted to balance two considerations. First, he wanted to be free of French control through funding and post-production, so his Senegalese company Films Domirev had to find the funding alongside a state funding agency. Second, he wanted a popular audience to see the film, so he had to offer colour (to compete with imported films) – he also managed to offer music from one of Dakar's top bands. Diawara argues that Sembène's insistence on 35mm film and colour restricted the number of films he could make because of the expense.

Characters in *Xala*
speak Wolof or French
depending on their
status.

'Xala' is a Wolof word that refers to a curse of impotence and the film suggests that the central character is suffering from a *xala* which is not only preventing the consummation of his marriage to a new (third) wife but is also taking away his sense of self and his status in the community. El Hadji is a businessman and a politician, part of the new élite in the country.

The country is never named, but the audience knows we are in Dakar. Sembène focuses on a 'chamber of commerce' as a metaphor for the Senegalese government within the wider allegory about corruption and loss of authentic identity. At the beginning of the film the new members of the chamber throw off their African clothes, don morning coats and pledge allegiance to their president – for which they each receive a briefcase full of money and a chauffeur-driven car. These are the new 'neo-colonialist'

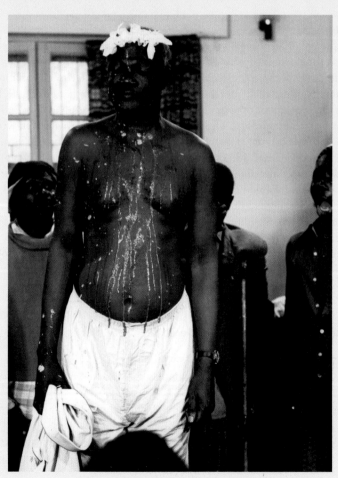

Fig 8.8
El-Hadj submits to
humiliation in a desperate
attempt to free himself
from the *Xala*. Source:
British Film Institute Stills
Collection.

bourgeoisie in Senegal – the French-speaking, Westernised Africans who, as the new bride's mother puts it, are 'neither fish nor fowl, neither a black man nor a white man'.

El Hadji already has two wives: his first is 'traditional' and his second 'modern', but both are disdainful of the third marriage undertaken simply to confirm his status. The *xala* appears to be a form of revenge by a person or persons he has trodden on to get to the top. In the course of the film El Hadji will resort to various strategies (including appeals to *marabouts* – one a real priest, one a charlatan) to lift the *xala*. But he cannot prevent an inexorable decline as his corrupt business practices are revealed and his colleagues from the chamber of commerce abandon him (replacing him immediately with an equally corrupt character introduced earlier in the narrative). *Xala* is a broad satire. It isn't intended to be a modernist art film but something that an African popular audience would identify with and enjoy. On the other hand, the film displays a sophisticated visual style that pleases Western cinephiles. There are plenty of jokes and observations, some more meaningful to the local audience, but one, in which El Hadji's chauffeur uses imported French bottled water to clean his limousine, is understood by all audiences.

Not surprisingly, the Senegalese president Senghor did not take kindly to the depiction of corrupt neo-colonialists. Sembène was known to be opposed to the implications of the *négritude* movement, so it is surprising perhaps that *Xala* received any form of state support. The film was banned for a time and censored. Diawara (1992: 61) reports that it was one of three state-supported films in 1974 that were commercial successes. Sembène himself says in an interview that there were ten cuts in what appeared as a full print in the West (Ghali 1976: 42).

Kenneth W. Harrow's critique of *Xala* attacks Sembène from a postcolonial theory position. He argues that Sembène does not allow the audience to make up its own mind and that he commits the cardinal sin of speaking 'for' the dispossessed in the allegory. He makes the point strongly in terms of the representation of women in this (and indeed in all Sembène's films):

> Sembène has always assumed the power of ideological, and especially Marxist, class-based truth to sway his audience [...] assumed with the narrative position of the camera the very role of spokesman [...] a role eschewed by [...] feminist film critics and filmmakers for whom speaking for has always been understood as the conventional role of the phallocentrist.
>
> (Harrow 2004: 125)

This quote about feminist filmmakers is a reference to the work of Trinh Ti Min-ha and her film *Reassemblages* (US/Senegal, 1982), a film showing women in a Senegal village. Harrow also maintains that Sembène's approach is counter to Espinosa's ideas about 'imperfect cinema'. These are important objections to raise, since in Sembène's films there are many forceful women in central roles, and in *Xala* it is El Hadji's educated daughter who shows most resistance to him within his family. For an alternative and carefully nuanced view of *Xala* alongside *Yeelen* and Djibril Diop Mambey's *Touki-Bouki* (Senegal, 1973) – an experimental youth-orientated film displaying the influence of New Wave films from around the world – see David Murphy (2006). Murphy raises important questions about the three films and echoes something that we come across in other parts of this book: the mixing of 'local' and 'global' ideas in many of the most interesting films. As Murphy suggests, Sembène in *Xala* is not 'anti' all Western ideas, but is specifically against Western capitalism.

Research and Explore 8.2

Watch *Xala* or either of Sembène's last two films with central female characters, *Faat Kine* (2002) or *Moolaadé* (2004). What do you make of the women's roles and actions? How would you respond to Harrow's critique? Sheila Petty (1996: 67–86) also discusses women's roles in Sembène's films, and Beti Ellerson (2004: 185–202) discusses the work of Sembène's compatriot Safi Faye. Do their ideas differ from Harrow's?

FESPACO, the diaspora and the academy

In the late 1980s and into the 1990s, 'African Cinema' became one of the new trends in 'world cinema'/international art cinema. The films of Sembène and his contemporaries from the 1960s and 1970s and a new generation of filmmakers, mainly from Francophone Africa, began to get more regular distribution in France and occasional screenings in the UK and North America. These films began to be recognised at major film festivals such as Cannes where Souleymane Cissé won the Jury Prize with *Yeelen* in 1987. By this time, 'sub-Saharan Africa' had also got its own film festival in Ouagadougou (capital of Burkina Faso), FESPACO (Festival Pan-Africain du Cinéma et de la Télévision de Ouagadougou, http://www.fespaco-bf. net). First established in 1969, the festival gradually expanded to show films from across Africa. It has become a biannual event, alternating with the Carthage Film Festival that focuses more on North African films (see Chapter 6). FESPACO has developed a cultural and political role, fostering film as a pan-African cultural project. It has five main aims as a festival organisation (collected together here from different documents on the festival website):

See Chapter 7 for a more general discussion about film festivals.

1   To screen African films, to provide a forum for filmmakers and other industry professionals to meet, and to participate in a film and television market.
2   To publish newsletters and catalogues, and act as a focus for research.
3   To build an archive of African film prints and publications.
4   To organise not-for-profit screenings to promote film in rural areas.
5   To promote African films through the international film festival circuit.

Each year the festival has a theme. In 2013 it was 'African Cinema and Public Policy in Africa'.

In the late 1980s FESPACO began to attract a new group of filmmakers and activists, including what it saw as diaspora African filmmakers, as well as political activists and film studies academics interested in Third Cinema. This led to meetings between leading African directors and Black British filmmakers such as the Ghanaian-born **John Akomfrah** (see Chapter 4). African and African-American academics also made the trip (see **Manthia Diawara**'s report on FESPACO 1989 in *Framework 37*), and a new outlet for African films in North American universities began to emerge. The discussions at FESPACO were part of a wider discussion about Third Cinema that was pursued in journals like *Screen* (e.g. in the 'Racism, Colonialism and the Cinema' issue in 1983).

Although the concept of Third Cinema has rather faded away, FESPACO and the kind of African cinema it has promoted has survived. Indeed, in 2010 another African film won the Jury Prize at Cannes – *A Screaming Man* (*Un homme qui crie*,

John Akomfrah made *Testament*, a partly autobiographical film, in Ghana in 1988.

Manthia Diawara, born in Mali, is a Professor at New York University, Director of NYU's Institute of Afro-American Affairs and Director of the Africana Studies Programme.

Fig 8.9
Senegalese director Alain
Gomis receives the award
of the Golden Stallion
for Best Picture for *Tey*
(*Today*, Senegal/France,
2012) at FESPACO in
March 2013.

Chad/France) directed by Mahamat-Saleh Haroun. Born in Chad, Haroun trained in
France and has lived there since 1982. Abderrahmane Sissako, born in Mauritania,
trained in the Soviet Union and also now living in France, is the only other African
filmmaker of recent years to have achieved festival success and a wide international
release for his films.

Festival success but cinema closures in Francophone Africa

Sissako's 2006 film *Bamako* is one of the few directly political films in modern
cinema, linking itself to some of the ideas first explored in Third Cinema films.
Bamako is the capital of Mali. In the film, a family house in Bamako (the house
Sissako grew up in during part of his childhood) and its large courtyard becomes
the setting for a trial hearing in which 'the West', in the form of the World Bank
and the IMF, is accused of deliberately underdeveloping Africa by stealing its
resources. With statements read in beautiful French by real advocates and cross-
examination by African writers and ordinary Africans using African languages, the
hearing reveals a great deal about the inequalities of international business. In the
background of the trial life goes on, and a family melodrama develops. There is also
a third element in the film. When the family sit down in the evening, they watch a
spoof 'spaghetti western' on local television. 'Death in Timbuktu' features a group
of bandits (including the director under a pseudonym and the Palestinian director
Elia Suleiman) and a 'man with no name' character played by Danny Glover, the
Hollywood actor known for his activism in African-American politics. Sissako,
like many African youths in the 1970s, watched cheap action pictures from France
and Italy (and probably Hollywood and Hong Kong). In creating this spoof he is
referring to the Africans who have conspired to kill and starve their own people (as
in *Xala*'s narrative). This choice of a spaghetti western as the vehicle for a satire
takes us back to *The Adventures of Juan Quin Quin* (see above).

Fig 8.10
Danny Glover as a cowboy
in the spaghetti western
spoof featured in *Bamako*.

Bamako, along with Sissako's earlier films and the four films by Haroun, has been
seen in France and the UK/US and at film festivals. None of the films are likely to
have been seen by ordinary Africans in local cinemas. There is one simple practical
reason for this. The only cinema in Chad is in a French cultural institute and in
Bamako, where there were once many cinemas, most have now closed. Only one
remains, refurbished and showing Hollywood films. In 2010 Abderrahmane Sissako
took a BBC World Service reporter around the abandoned cinemas of Bamako.
He has formed an association to reopen at least one old cinema in order to show
African, European and 'world' films (see http://www.cinemasforafrica.com). Sissako
is on the ground doing something for film culture in Mali, but the truth is that
throughout Francophone West Africa, cinemas have largely disappeared. When they
were open they rarely showed African films, except as festival screenings. There have
never been African distributors motivated to develop audiences for local films. The
story is different in Anglophone Africa.

The prize winners at FESPACO have not all been from Francophone Africa.
Kwaw Ansah (Ghana), Newton Aduaka (Nigeria) and Zola Maseko (South Africa)
have all been winners. But film directors in these countries (especially Ghana and
Nigeria) have a different attitude towards getting their films seen.

Entrepreneurs in Anglophone Africa

Filmmakers in Anglophone West Africa were fortunate perhaps in having access to
facilities in Accra not available to the Francophone directors and they also benefited
from having strong theatre traditions of travelling players (especially the Yoruba theatre
companies in Nigeria) – but they didn't have any money or a production system of any
kind. Kwaw Ansah raised his own money (with his father-in-law's house as collateral)
in order to finance *Love Brewed in an African Pot* (Ghana, 1981), which went on to
become one of the most popular films by an African director with African audiences.

Nigeria and Ghana have bigger populations than any of the countries of
Francophone West Africa. As in many Francophone countries, the state controlled

chains of cinemas in Ghana after independence and the colonial legacy included mobile cinema vans used to travel to remote villages. The combination of filmmaking facilities (apart from processing labs), a distribution/exhibition system of sorts and the touring theatre groups meant that when cinema audiences declined and production became more expensive (partly due to financial issues generally in the Nigerian economy), Ghana and Nigeria were prepared to shift to video production. The two countries both had TV broadcasting systems. Nigeria had the first TV broadcasting system in Africa. By the early 1980s many Nigerian TV employees had been trained abroad and local TV production had reduced imports to only 20 per cent of Nigerian programming (Umeh 1989: 59).

'The single most interesting fact about Nollywood is the entrepreneurial spirit of its workers' (Okome 2007: 5). These filmmakers were prepared to take on Hollywood and Bollywood and win the local audience. Whatever the precise mix of factors which contributed to its launch, 'video film' started in Ghana or Nigeria (there are many claims for both) some time in the 1980s.

Nigeria's population tripled from 55 million in 1971 to over 170 million in 2012. Ghana's population over the same period rose from 8 to 24 million. Senegal's population has been half the size of Ghana's over the same period.

Nollywood

Nollywood is another of those terms first used by a journalist and then adopted by practitioners despite criticism by more serious cultural commentators. Some reports refer to 'Nigerian video films' (nvf) and various claims about '1,000 films per year' have been made. Certainly productions seem to be in the high hundreds. However, the circulation of films on VHS, **VCD** and DVD is often of quite short films (70–80 minutes). Many titles have sequels listed simply as 'Part 2'.

Ghanaian video films are usually released in English, whereas films from Nigeria are produced in several languages – Yoruba (55%) from the South and West, English (24%) and Igbo (1%) from the Igbo region in the Southeast, Bini (4%) from Edo state in the South and Hausa 16% from the Muslim North (UNESCO Institute for Statistics, 2012). Yoruba-language films are exported, but the English-language films have the most appeal across Anglophone Africa. There is an attempt to use 'Ghallywood' to distinguish films from Ghana but in writings about Nollywood the distinction is not always clear.

Up until around 2002 Nollywood remained relatively unknown to film audiences outside Africa and the African diaspora. *Film International* published a special issue in 2007 which featured several different discussions useful for this chapter. The collection suggests an industry that had reached a form of maturity during the previous five years with films being sent to overseas festivals and an established star system that not only satisfied local fans with a need to find their own heroes, but was also beginning to be acknowledged by those overseas festivals.

As noted, production is in several languages and, as with Bollywood, it is important not to allow a single term to mask diversity. Production is also characterised by religious differences between Christian, Muslim and secular genres. But also, as in India, genres overlap and actors and crew straddle different genre cinemas. Okome suggests the emergence of specific genres:

VCD is a cheap digital video format in which a feature film is released on a double CD. The overall quality is about VHS standard, and in Asia and Africa VCDs at half the price of DVD (and playable on DVD players sold in many countries) have powered the local market.

In the Muslim North of Nigeria there is a strong local link to Indian cinema which became a passion for many fans who saw imported Hindi films as offering an alternative cultural space in which to explore a local identity. When local Hausa video films appeared they often copied storylines and/ or songs from Bollywood hits. Some scholars argue that Hausa videos should not be included in 'Nollywood'.

[T]he city video film, which also has as a subgenre, the occult video; the epic video with its narrative locus on historical subjects rather than on the dimensions of the history engaged in; the hallelujah video and the comic video.

(Okome 2007: 6)

But Okome also warns that although the industry seems to be established (and
he sees it as topping Hollywood and Bollywood in West Africa), there is not yet a
critical or academic consensus about how it should be approached as film culture.
Many critics still dismiss the films as crude/amateurish/trashy. Yet auteur directors
are emerging. There are concerns about sex and sexuality in the films (though little
overt sexual activity is shown) and about how the video films relate to literature and
theatre. Okome also poses the question of what Nollywood means in terms of Third
Cinema:

> [T]here is no one discernible cultural or even political project in Nollywood, as
> is the case with the project of 'third cinema' practice in Latin America of the
> 1960s. But Nollywood is extremely aware of its local audience.
>
> (Okome 2007: 6)

Nollywood producers have built up an industrial infrastructure and they have
achieved a form of 'globalisation from the bottom' – introducing local audiences
to global experiences having 'eluded the watchful eyes of the state and corporate
capital' (Okome quoting Arjun Appadurai 2000: 1–9).

What is undoubtedly true is that Nollywood reaches audiences in all of Africa,
including Francophone Africa. Language does not seem to be a problem, and in
Anglophone East Africa co-productions have taken place between Nigeria and
Tanzania with the snappily titled *Dar 2 Lagos* (Tanzania/Nigeria, 2007) ('Dar' refers
to Tanzania's biggest city, Dar es Salaam) and *She's My Sister* (Tanzania/Nigeria,
2007). The latter film (in English rather than Swahili) features local Tanzanian stars
Stephen Kanumba and Yvonne Cherry with two Nigerian stars and a Nigerian
director. An urban melodrama with a moral message, the film charts the rise and
fall of a woman from rural Tanzania who goes to university and starts a business in

Fig 8.11
Steven Kanumba and
Yvonne Cherry are the
stars of *She's My Sister*.

Dar es Salaam. She returns to her village and brings her childhood sweetheart to the city, marries him and settles down but things go wrong when she introduces him to her girlfriends. The title refers to the flashback device that introduces the film when the woman's sister arrives in Dar, only to discover that she no longer lives in her big house with its security guard.

The world depicted in *She's My Sister* is not representative of most parts of Tanzania. Mhando and Kipeja (2010) explore the circuit of local *Kideo* (video) halls in Tanzania and Uganda where cinemas have virtually disappeared but a distribution system still operates. Nollywood has joined Hollywood and Bollywood in competing with local Tanzanian producers – undercutting them owing to economies of scale based on the large Nigerian market.

Nollywood is also popular in South Africa – challenging the still largely Anglo-American local film industry – and in the Caribbean. However, around 2007, Nigeria started to return to cinema building with Silverbird multiplexes appearing in Port Harcourt, Lagos and Abuja (as well as Accra in Ghana). Should Nollywood ignore these cinemas designed specifically to show Hollywood or should it attempt to compete?

At the same time, Nigerian film entrepreneurs are starting to make more effort to release films in cinemas in the UK and North America where there are significant diaspora communities and the possibility of co-productions in the US with African-American producers. This will require a shift in approach compared to the video films of the 1990s and early 2000s. What might these new films look like?

Swahili is the language understood in many parts of East Africa and acts as a regional language.

Multiplex chains also operate in South Africa and Kenya as well as in the French quarter of cities such as Marrakech in Morocco.

Case study 8.2: *Araromire (The Figurine*, Nigeria, 2009)

Araromire was widely promoted on its release as the film that would move Nollywood to a new level and transform the industry. It is discussed here primarily because it is one of the few Nigerian films to be accessible via DVD through mainstream retailers such as Amazon.

The film is interesting on several levels. First, the production budget was considerably higher than the norm for video film releases. This is mainly because of the length of the production – several weeks rather than days. Shot on high-definition video the final projection print is presented in CinemaScope (2.35:1) and therefore matches the presentation of Hollywood or Bollywood films shown in African cinemas. The 'yellow carpet' premiere was held in a Lagos multiplex and the film showed in multiplexes in Nigeria's main cities. It then appeared in several international film festivals as well as in public screenings in London and other cities of the Nigerian diaspora. With a running time of around two hours, a music soundtrack and contributions from a leading Nigerian artist and a fashion designer, this is an international feature film. But is it still 'Nollywood'?

The outline story is universal in its blend of generic elements, but distinctively Nigerian in the way that certain themes and discourses are developed. In a prologue set in early twentieth-century Nigeria, a priest under instruction from a deity creates a wooden idol in a district called Araromire – the idol grants the local community seven years of good luck but warns that seven years of bad luck will follow. Around a century later three young Nigerian graduates are preparing for their year of National Youth Service. Sola, a confident and brash young man, is in a relationship with Mona. His friend

Femi loves Mona but he is too shy to do much about it. All three end up in the same camp in Araromire and on an exercise Sola and Femi find the idol in an abandoned shrine in the forest. Sola decides to take it home. From this point on their lives are changed and everything goes well. Femi is cured of his asthma and he is selected to train abroad. Sola marries Mona and remains in Lagos, living comfortably as a successful businessman in a house near the beach. Six years or so later Femi returns but when he has settled into a comfortable job things start to go wrong.

In the latter part of the film the narrative is constructed in such a way that the downfall of Femi and Sola is explored through a form of family melodrama. The work of the idol in creating 'bad luck' is then manifested as distrust, jealousy and revenge. Femi's young sister lives with Sola and Mona who have a small son and are expecting another. Mona has 'matched' Femi with her best friend Linda. Sola is punished seemingly because of his general behaviour (doubts about whether he is an adulterer or that his business is not totally legitimate). Femi seems less 'guilty' but he still loves his best friend's wife. The idol perhaps performs a similar function to the ghosts in Japanese horror films. There is no requirement to use special effects, since the various disasters that befall the characters are all explainable without recourse to the supernatural. The only inexplicable events concern the idol's reappearance in Sola's house on several occasions after strenuous attempts to destroy it or throw it away.

Religion only becomes important when Linda invites priests to attempt to exorcise the evil spirits which seem to be possessing Mona. Sola throws them out and condemns religion as being for the illiterate masses.

Araromire follows Bollywood conventions with dialogue in a local language (Yoruba) and English. The main characters are middle class and switch between the two languages in mid-conversation. At one point Mona teaches her son to speak Urhobo, denoting that she comes from a smaller linguistic community.

Araromire has a star cast (i.e. stars from Nigerian film and television) comprising Ramsey Nouah as Femi and Omoni Oboli as Mona. Sola is played by the writer-director Kunle Afolayan, the son of Yoruba filmmaker Adeyemi Afolayan (aka Ade-love). Since *Araromire* there have been similar films by Nigerian filmmakers such as Andrew Dosunmu (*Restless City*, US, 2011) and Andrew Okorafor (*Relentless*, Nigeria/France/Spain/Germany, 2011).

Fig 8.12
A panoramic shot from *Araromire* showing the new intake for National Youth Service arriving at the camp.

Research and Explore 8.3

Look up the film listings of cinema chains in Nigeria (Silverbird, Genesis, etc.) and Kenya (Fox, Starflix, IMAX, etc.). Are they mainly showing Hollywood or Bollywood? Are there specifically African-American films? Are there any examples of local films? How are they being promoted?

Anglophone Africa has also evolved its own awards ceremony:

> The Africa Movie Academy Awards (AMAA), the continent's most prestigious awards for filmmakers, has received 328 entries from across Africa, up from 220 in 2011. This includes 134 feature films, 88 short films, 57 documentaries and six animations. 43 entries came from Africans in the Diaspora, with the other entries coming from 23 countries across the continent, including Ghana. (March 2012)
> (http://www.ghanacelebrities.com/tag/a-film-scholar-and-critic-and-directors-berni-goldblat-and-john-akomfrah#ixzz1vrscApRL)

This suggests that African filmmaking isn't quite as sparse as the Western commentary focused on Francophone African films in festivals might suggest. To return to Okome's point about Third Cinema, is Africa now ready to create its own versions of cinema? Jeffrey Geiger (2012: 59–63) makes an argument for the importance of Nollywood video films as 'social, narrative, and aesthetic objects of inquiry'. He suggests that the films at least deserve to be investigated using the array of critical tools available to film studies scholars instead of only in terms of their lack of 'quality' in industrial terms (i.e. in terms of use of technology and deployment of techniques). He recognises that there needs to be some form of rapprochement between the video filmmakers and auteurs like Mahamet Saleh-Haroun. He also recognises that despite their success the video filmmakers are faced with huge disparities in income and living standards in Nigeria, which not only threatens the financial security of their industry but also raises questions about the stories and characters they choose to represent.

Summary

This chapter began with a recognition that some film territories in Africa, Latin America and Asia are not considered important in terms of international film business development. At the same time, many of these 'excluded' territories don't necessarily have the resources to sustain publicly funded 'cultural film' production. You may wish to explore this predicament in relation to the one sub-Saharan African territory that *is* part of the international film business. The South African film industry profits from acting as an enormous **facilities house** for Hollywood and European producers. British and American actors play the roles of African characters in international film and television productions. Advertising films also provide important 'inward investment' and South African locations 'stand in' for the US and other parts of Africa. Yet there are relatively few productions in Zulu, Xhosa or Afrikaans – the first languages of the majority of South Africans.

The BBC TV Christmas
schedules for 2012
included two television
films, *The Girl* (UK/
South Africa/US, 2012)
and *Restless* (UK/South
Africa, 2012), both of
which used South African
locations to represent
California and the
American Southwest.

Research and Explore 8.4: *Film in South Africa*

South Africa has the most cinema screens in Africa but they mainly show Hollywood films. In 2010 South Africa produced 23 local feature films – double the number five years previously and gradually increasing. Is this what we should expect from a country with a population of 50 million and the biggest economy on the continent? What kinds of films are being made in South Africa?

Surprisingly perhaps, South Africa does not have a single, central agency presenting industry information. What do you learn about 'film in South Africa' from these different sources?

- National Film and Video Foundation, http://nfvf.co.za/ (see 'Documents')
- www.gautengfilm.co.za/
- www.screenafrica.com (see the Digital Magazine)
- http://www.guardian.co.uk/film/filmblog/2012/jun/13/greater-inclusivity-south-africa-film-industry

The disparity between the multiplex in a South African mall and the *Kideo* hall in a Dar es Salaam suburb is matched by similar disparities in India (see Chapter 10). The documentaries of Anand Patwardhan, for instance, are not likely to be welcome in Indian multiplexes. *Jai Bhim Comrade* (India, 2011) is a film about the deaths of ten Dalits ('untouchables') at the hands of the police in 1997. Patwardhan told the *Guardian* writer Sukhdev Sandhu that the most important audiences for the film were the people it represented:

> All across Maharashtra [where it's set] the film is in constant demand: we bought a powerful video projector, made a foldable 20ft x 30ft screen and for the past five months have done regular open-air screenings in working-class and Dalit neighbourhoods, organised and sponsored locally. As people cannot afford to hire many chairs, the audience squats on the floor or, incredibly, stands through the entire three hours of the film. We wait for darkness before we begin and the film often goes past the 10pm cut-off point when loudspeakers are officially silenced. But at many venues the local police, who often came from the same caste and class background as the audience, look the other way.
>
> … 'Across the country, two Dalits are killed and three raped every day.' The eloquent social critiques delivered by its subjects, as well as the fire and lyrical fervour in their ballads, oratory and street-theatre performances, bear out the claim, delivered by one interviewee: 'In every lane there's a poet, and in every hovel there's a singer.'

> (http://www.guardian.co.uk/film/2012/jun/08/
> india-film-documentary-maker-patwardhan)

'Cinemas that need to be different' could be located anywhere. The development of digital cinema (see Chapter 12) makes this more possible in terms of technologies – but new ideas and creative skills are still required. New forms of cinema also need passion, commitment, some form of political activity and community organisation.

References and further reading

Akomfrah, John (2006) 'On the National in African Cinema/s: A Conversation', in Valentina Vitali and Paul Willemen (eds) *Theorising National Cinema*, London: BFI.

Alea, Tomás Gutiérrez and Desmoes Edmundo (1990) *Memories of Underdevelopment* and *Inconsolable Memories* with an introduction by Michael Chanan, New Brunswick, NJ: Rutgers University Press.

Burton, Julianne (trans.) (1979) 'For an Imperfect Cinema' by Julio García Espinosa, *Jump Cut* 20 (May). Available at www.ejumpcut.org/archive/onlinessays/JC20folder/ImperfectCinema.html.

Chanan, Michael (1985) *The Cuban Image: Cinema and Cultural Politics in Cuba*, London: BFI.

Chanan, Michael (2004) *Cuban Cinema*, Minneapolis, MN: University of Minnesota Press.

Diawara, Manthia (1992) *African Cinema: Politics and Culture*, Bloomington: Indiana University Press.

Douglas, María Eulalia (2008) *Catálogo del cine cubano 1897–1960*, Havana: Editions ICAIC.

Ellerson, Beti (2004) 'Africa Through a Woman's Eyes: Safi Faye's Cinema', in Pfaff (ed.) (op. cit.).

Falicov, Tamara L. (2010) 'Mobile Cinemas in Cuba: The Forms and Ideology of Traveling Exhibitions', in Susan Lord, Dorit Naaman and Jennifer VanderBurgh (eds) *Public: #40 Screens*, Toronto. (Part of the special dossier on mobile screens edited by Tamara Falicov.)

Geiger, Jeffrey (2012) 'Nollywood Style: Nigerian Movies and "Shifting Perceptions of Worth"', *Film International* 10(6): 58–72.

Ghali, Noureddine (1976) 'Interview with Sembène Ousmane', collected in John D. H. Dowling (ed.) (1987) *Film and Politics in the Third World*, New York: Autonomedia.

Harrow, Kenneth W. (2004) 'The Failed Trickster', in Pfaff (ed.) (op. cit.).

McCall, John C. (2007) 'The Pan-Africanism We Have: Nollywood's Invention of Africa', *Film International* 28(5), no. 4: 92–97.

Mhando, M.R. and Kipeja, L. (2010) 'Creative/Cultural Industries Financing in Africa: A Tanzanian Film Value Chain Study', *Journal of African Cinemas* 2(1): 3–25.

Murphy, David (2006) 'Africans Filming Africa: Questioning Theories of an Authentic African Cinema', in Elisabeth Ezra and Terry Rowden (eds) *Transnational Cinema, The Film Reader*, Abingdon and New York: Routledge.

Okome, Onookome (2007) 'Nollywood: Africa at the Movies', *Film International* 28(5), no. 4: 4–9.

Petty, Sheila (1996) *A Call to Action: The Films of Ousmane Sembene*, Trowbridge: Flicks Books.

Pfaff, Françoise (ed.) (2004) *Focus on African Films*, Bloomington: Indiana University Press.

Rodney, Walter (1972) *How Europe Underdeveloped Africa*, London: Bogle-L'Ouverture.

Saul, Mahir and Austen, Ralph A. (eds) (2010) *Viewing African Cinema in the*

Twenty-First Century: Art Films and the Nollywood Video Revolution, Athens: Ohio University Press.

Shaka, Femi Okiremuete (2004) *Modernity and the African Cinema*, Trenton, NJ and Asmara, Eritrea: Africa World Press Inc.

Smyth, Rosaleen (1983) 'Movies and Mandarins: The Official Film and British Colonial Africa', in James Curran and Vincent Porter (eds) *British Cinema History*, London: Weidenfeld & Nicolson.

Spivak, Gayatri (1988) 'Can the Subaltern Speak?', in Cary Nelson and Lawrence Grossberg (eds) *Marxism and the Interpretation of Culture*, Champaign: University of Illinois Press; reprint edition (1 October 1987), available at www.mcgill.ca/files/crclaw-discourse/Can_the_subaltern_speak.pdf.

Taylor, Anna Marie (1979) 'Imperfect Cinema, Brecht, and *The Adventures of Juan Quin Quin*', *Jump Cut* 20 (May). Available at http://www.ejumpcut.org/archive/onlinessays/JC20folder/JuanQuinQuin.html.

Umeh, Charles C. (1989) 'The Advent and Growth of Television Broadcasting in Nigeria: Its Political and Educational Overtones', *Africa Media Review* 3(2): 54–56.

UNESCO Institute for Statistics (2012) *Linguistic Diversity of Feature Films*, UIS Fact Sheet No 17, February. Available at http://www.uis.unesco.org/FactSheets/Documents/fs17-2012-linguistic-diversity-film-en5.pdf.

Vieyra, Paulin Soumanou (1987) 'Five Major Films by Sembène Ousmane', in John D.H. Dowling (ed.) *Film and Politics in the Third World*, New York: Autonomedia. www.newsreel.org/articles/OusmaneSembene.htm http://documentaryisneverneutral.com.

Further viewing

Cuba and Latin America

Strawberry & Chocolate (Cuba, 1993, dir. Tomás Gutiérrez Alea and Juan Carlos Tabío)
Life is to Whistle (Cuba, 1998, dir. Fernando Pérez)

West Africa

Abouna (Chad/France/Netherlands, 2002, dir. Mahamat-Saleh Haroun)
Daratt (Chad/France/Belgium/Austria, 2006, dir. Mahamat-Saleh Haroun)
Waiting for Happiness (Mauritania/France, 2002, dir. Abderrahmane Sissako)
La pirogue (Senegal/France/Germany, 2012, dir. Moussa Touré)

Central Africa

Viva Riva! (DR Congo/France/Belgium, 2010, dir. Djo Munga)
War Witch (*Rebelle*, Canada, 2012, dir. Kim Nguyen). The film was made entirely in DR Congo with local actors and non-professionals.

South Africa

Tsotsi (South Africa/UK, 2005, dir. Gavin Hood)
Life Above All (South Africa/Germany, 2010, dir. Oliver Schmitz)

Global television

At some point, probably in the early 1980s (reliable data being hard to come by), the global number of viewers watching films on television screens each day exceeded the number of cinema admissions. Many of the readers of this book will have grown up watching filmic narratives on a small video screen as a 'normal' activity with trips to the cinema more like 'special occasions'. An audience survey published in the UK in 2012 focusing on 'frequent cinema-goers' found that the sample group watched around 120 films per year – but only 17 of these were watched in cinemas (Mitchell 2012). Perhaps then we should no longer worry about how a film is screened or watched? In the media ecology of 2013 the range of transmitters/carriers has expanded further to include smartphones and tablet computers. At the same time some cinema screens are getting smaller and some domestic video screens are getting larger. The significance

Frequent cinema-goers are identified by market research data usually on the basis of attendance at least once a month or perhaps ten times a year.

of these changes is explored further in Chapter 12, but here we want to note simply that the changes in screen and projection technologies do not negate the importance of the different institutional factors that govern the film and television industries – and to some extent the different academic disciplines of film studies and television studies, even though in some cases these have been subsumed under 'screen studies'.

In this chapter we will look at the following questions:

- How has television developed on a global basis and how has television material been traded in the international marketplace?
- What has been the historical relationship between the film and television industries and is that relationship the same in all countries?
- What might the differences be between film narratives designed specifically for cinema release and those designed with television transmission as their main distribution method?

This discussion will enable an analysis of recent developments with some case studies. One key finding is likely to be that the global 'exchange' of television films and other programme formats is not weighted in favour of Hollywood in quite the same way as it is for cinema films.

Television and non-standard technologies

Television *broadcasting* (as distinct from experimental transmissions) began in the 1930s on a small scale in the UK, Germany, the Soviet Union and the US, but development was constrained in the first three territories by the Second World War. During the 1940s the US leapt ahead with a purely commercial system, overtaking the **public service broadcasting** system (PSB) operated by the BBC in the UK that resumed in 1946 after nearly seven years 'off air'. Most of the other advanced economies took longer to develop the systems that first appeared in the 1950s and it was the 1960s before television spread to most parts of the world.

Unlike the film technologies that became standardised for cinema projection on a global basis fairly quickly (i.e. by the 1910s), television suffered from the development of different electronic broadcasting systems in different territories. At first these were differences in the frequency of the broadcast signal and lines of resolution of the black and white video image but later there were differences in colour systems as well. North America and Japan adopted the NTSC system, the UK and Germany went for PAL, and France, USSR and Eastern Europe used the SECAM system. These three systems were not immediately compatible, so that material recorded on one system had to be converted if it was shown on another. Recording was initially only available for the broadcasters themselves but when videocassettes became widely available to the public, the possibilities of exchanges between countries was at first limited owing to competing video formats as well as different broadcasting systems.

Conversion between two formats
In the 1950s, when most television was broadcast live, recordings were sometimes made by filming the broadcast image ('kinescoping'). The standard practice of videotaping TV programmes didn't develop until the late 1950s/early 1960s. A similar system for broadcasting cinema films on television involved using a form of television camera to scan the film image – a process known as **telecine**.

One of the consequences of this lack of a global television standard and the delay before taped material became available was that in the 1950s and 1960s the US television production companies were able to follow Hollywood film studios in successfully entering the nascent international TV market through the use of film to produce TV material that could be easily exported.

The 'filmed' TV series

Early American television output included a number of genre-based series shot on film. This development took place in a quite specific industrial context. Because the major Hollywood studios feared the impact of TV watching on the cinema-going habit that had been ingrained in the mass audience for the previous 40 years, they initially refused to openly sell rights to any of their films to the new TV stations. (The smaller independent producers quickly sold most of their titles to television.) The major studios changed the nature of mainstream film production to reassert the uniqueness of 'big screen' film entertainment. Increased use of colour with new widescreen formats and experiments with stereo sound and 3D were accompanied by a focus on a smaller number of 'bigger' films shown as so-called 'roadshow' attractions (see Hall and Neale (2010: 150–153) for an insight into producer Mike Todd's ideas). The roadshow concept was designed to make films 'special' with an

Up until the early 1950s, most Hollywood feature films were still monochrome. New colour systems followed the introduction of widescreen formats like CinemaScope in 1953, offering competition to Technicolor.

Outside the US and UK, expensive colour films generally took longer to become commonplace in local production.

Fig 9.1
A scene from the TV show *Wagon Train* being filmed in 1957. Source: photo by Allan Grant/Time Life Pictures/Getty Images.

initial release in key cities, a printed film brochure like a theatre programme and possibly an overture played before the film began with its spectacular scenes. Seat prices were higher, which only added to the sense of occasion for some audiences. But what this 'blockbuster presentation' did mean was that the remainder of the traditional film programme – the newsreel, cartoons and 'B' feature – were omitted. As these aspects of the film programme began to disappear, several Hollywood studio facilities (as well as actors and creative teams) became available for other uses. 'B' movie cowboys easily migrated to new western series made on 35mm film but intended for television and by 1959, when this form of production reached its peak, there were 48 western shows on US television (see Weddle 1996: 133).

Alongside westerns such as *Wagon Train* (see Fig 9.1), early film-based TV series included cop shows such as *Dragnet* and the family sitcom *I Love Lucy*, both of which began in 1951. These were the top-rated TV shows of the period. *Dragnet* had developed from a radio series but Lucille Ball, star of *I Love Lucy*, was already well known as a Hollywood performer, having worked on a wide range of films since the early 1930s before establishing herself as a comedienne. As a sitcom, *I Love Lucy* could have been recorded 'live' for TV broadcast. Instead it used standard 35mm film camera technologies, but in a three-camera set-up before a live audience in a studio complex (Mellencamp 2003: 134). The show was edited and prints were then sent to the TV stations in advance of broadcasts. Later to become the conventional mode for US sitcoms, this method had several advantages. It produced a higher quality programme via post-production and also the better definition and texture of the filmic image. It also produced a product, on film, that could be easily exported when TV broadcasting began to develop worldwide and was seeking new material.

The British telefilm

The 'Hollywood blacklist' – the action against film industry personnel 'named' in the anti-communist witch hunts of the late 1940s and early 1950s – was one of the elements drawing Americans into British film and TV (see Mann 2012).

The Four Just Men (1959) was a UK filmed TV series featuring four well-known film stars from Hollywood, the UK and Italy and prominent UK film industry writers and directors. It was distributed by Lew Grade's ITC, the major exporter of UK filmed series.

In the early 1950s, the second biggest commercial film industry worldwide was in the UK – which also had the other main TV broadcasting system. Hollywood's refusal to release films to US TV opened up the market for British film producers to create films which could play in British cinemas and sell to American television stations. At one point, at least six British film studios were engaged in this practice (Noble 1954: 101–105). British productions were cheaper than those in Hollywood and they attracted American writers and directors to London along with some high-profile talent from elsewhere in Europe. At this point, the UK only had one TV channel but when ITV arrived in 1955 to 1956 as a 'commercial' channel promising more popular entertainment than what was perceived as the 'stuffy' BBC, a new market for filmed TV series opened up.

The development of US television production

The declining Hollywood major studio RKO Radio Pictures was forced to sell its library of film titles to television in 1956 and Warner Brothers sold part of its library to an independent in the same year. The other studios quickly recognised that their libraries could be profitable in a new way. They also began to realise that television could be used to promote new film releases through appearances of stars on TV and the airing of promotional clips. Production of new material for television as well as distribution of library film material had actually begun much earlier. Screen

Gems became the Columbia Pictures television brand in 1948 (though it wasn't until 1955 that Columbia linked the brand to its iconic Hollywood film brand). Walt Disney Productions produced its first television series *Disneyland* in 1954 and Warner Brothers became a television producer in 1955. Revue Productions was set up by MCA in 1950 and became a major television producer – in 1957 it bought Paramount's pre-1950 film library and in 1958 it bought Universal's film studio lots. In 1962 MCA acquired all of Universal. By the 1960s, filmed TV series production in Hollywood matched current affairs and drama produced in New York.

The size of the US market and its development (based on existing radio broadcasting structures) by means of competing commercial networks with local affiliates led to the development of a form of distribution of television material based on **syndication**. There is a long and complex history of distribution in the US television industry but here we will just focus on the idea that certain kinds of programme material (e.g. filmed series) could be rented out in much the same way as traditional film releases. The broadcast rights for a set period might be sold first to one of the three major networks in the 1950s, or perhaps directly to independent operators, for a 'first run'. After completing its run the series might be sold to smaller local networks and then into syndication for further reruns. In this way, a successful series could be earning 'rentals' somewhere in the US for many years. The same concept applies today when there are far more channels. Syndication (which also has a long history in radio and print media in North America) became the economic lynchpin for American television. As with Hollywood, the large American market gave the TV producers confidence that their costs could be covered by domestic rentals. Live television was made by the networks themselves but filmed series were made by Hollywood studios and independents who targeted syndication. The latter included Desilu, the company set up by Desi Arnaz and Lucille Ball to make *I Love Lucy* and other popular series. *Whirlybirds*, a 'helicopter adventure' series, was produced by Desilu for direct syndication with 111 25-minute episodes produced on 16mm film between 1957 and 1960.

Once television markets developed overseas in the 1960s, the rights holders of US filmed TV series discovered an eager band of new buyers for their material. Since their library of titles had already paid for itself through syndication in the US, sales overseas produced almost pure profit (although some actors might receive 'residual' payments). The US sellers decided to maximise this profit through a process of **differential pricing**. In the more affluent countries of Western Europe, TV stations were charged a high price but in Africa and other territories the same shows were sold at very low prices – so low in fact that the local industries could not possibly make their own programming that could compete on price.

From the 1960s onwards, television and then video would prove to be crucially important to the Hollywood majors, both at home and overseas. The major Hollywood studios looked to be in decline as the theatrical film market gradually shrank in North America. Although some of the majors moved discreetly into television production themselves, they also faced competition from not just the television networks but also the music companies. The arrival of cable and satellite television provided further competition for the American public's entertainment dollar – with MTV in the 1980s combining music and television. At one point the famous Hollywood studio logos seemed to be brands that had lost value as they became simply part of the portfolio for one of a group of industrial conglomerates (Branston and Stafford 2006: 244–249).

Ironically, home video was one of the saviours of the studios – and not just in the domestic market. Tino Balio in his discussion of the 'globalisation of Hollywood in the 1990s' (Balio 2002: 206–207) tells us that in 1989 video retail and rentals of films had reached US$10 billion in the US – twice the theatrical total. But they had also reached US$4.5 billion in Western Europe with Hollywood taking the largest share. In North America the video boom also fuelled a boom in film production with new independents entering the market. The new business model assumed that the profits from low-budget film production would come from the video release. The theatrical release would serve to build the film's profile and help promote the subsequent video release. The mid-1980s saw the growth of the so-called American Independent film.

The Hollywood cinema recovery in the 1990s was partly based on the 'reviving' home market, but also on the revival in European theatrical markets following the refurbishment of cinemas and the 'new-build' multiplexes. Cinema box office hits generally meant better video sales. At the same time, de-regulation of the television market in Western Europe as well as the growth of satellite and cable opened up revenues from library film titles as well as new releases. By the 1990s the home video market was also seeing growth rates as high as 20 per cent in the Asia-Pacific region.

The trend in the 1990s was for the Hollywood studios to gradually move out of the general industrial conglomerates that had bought them a decade or so earlier and into new media conglomerates where they found themselves alongside television interests. In 2012 Disney/ABC, Comcast/Universal/NBC, News Corp/Fox, **Paramount/CBS** and Warner Bros/HBO represented combined film and television operations. Sony has its own television operations, including extensive holdings in networks outside North America.

Paramount and **CBS** are separate companies but National Amusements has a controlling share in each.

This brief history emphasises the way in which Hollywood was positioned to retain its hegemony over global filmed entertainment as the industry developed from solely theatrical exhibition towards the primacy of home viewing in a marketplace featuring different exhibition **platforms**. The figures speak for themselves. In 2004 US exports of film and television programmes to the rest of the world totalled US$10.4 billion as against imports of just US$341 million (Thussu 2007: 17). This suggests the scale of the US trade surplus in filmed entertainment. It doesn't show what other trade flows in film and television add up to and this has led in turn to research and theoretical work on what have been described as **contra-flows**, especially of television material. Contra-flows refer to exchanges of film and TV material 'against' the flow of Hollywood product from the US to the rest of the world (e.g. between Latin America and East Asia). Television, because of its different modes of watching in different social situations and its different sense of 'liveness' and 'localism', is not the same as theatrical film, both as industrial product and traded commodity. As a result, television has created possibilities of different connections between cultures.

We will deal with some classic examples of contra-flows later in the chapter. Here, we will just note that following the experience of those British films bought by American television stations in the 1950s, the UK has sustained a successful television export business up until the present. In 2010 UK exports of 'television and related content' rose 13 per cent to well over US$2 billion, including over US$800 million of exports to the US, the best export market for the UK TV industry (figures from PACT, the UK's independent producers association). These figures appear to contradict those from the US government quoted by Thussu above, but there seems little doubt that the UK is a very successful exporter of both film and TV material.

UK government figures suggest a combined film and television trade surplus of over US$3 billion in 2010 (Office for National Statistics). The *film* trade surplus is primarily with Europe.

What is the significance of this? First, it suggests that although Hollywood hegemony extends over films shown in UK cinemas and DVDs rented or downloaded, there is a two-way flow of films and television programmes and services. In reality this means that Hollywood makes films in the UK and that production spend is effectively a UK 'export'. Hollywood also pays royalties/rights fees to writers like J.K. Rowling. This is also a UK export of film services. More importantly, the success of the UK as an exporter of TV programme material (which is what the figures refer to; Hollywood doesn't make much TV in the UK, except as a co-producer on major series) points to a number of institutional differences between the UK and the US.

UK TV programmes are made either by companies with public service broadcasting remits (whether they are public or private sector organisations) or smaller independents from a sector that has developed since the 1980s. In recent years there have been complaints that the combination of competitive markets and the constraints on 'popular programming' that PSB might require have led to unimaginative and 'safe' programming. These complaints have come from audiences who have admired the 'premium cable offerings' from US producers such as HBO (which has the budgets and the freedom from advertising and broadcast television censorship restrictions to make challenging drama). However, HBO-type material is still a minority attraction in the UK compared to locally produced drama that appears in primetime.

The UK television industry is also part of a wider European audio-visual sector – something which is perhaps not always appreciated in public discussion about television in the UK. As we will see in several examples in this chapter, UK producers have worked closely with European partners.

Public service broadcasting (PSB) refers to the regulation of UK television that lays down certain requirements re programme quality and diversity, etc. that must be followed by UK broadcasters.

The principal UK public sector companies (i.e. publicly owned) are the BBC and Channel 4. They have both invested significantly in film production and TV drama. The main commercial broadcasters are ITV, BSkyB and 5. ITV has a longer history of production and export success but BSkyB (part-owned by News Corp) has recently increased local production.

One of the best-known UK format exports is 'Who Wants to be a Millionaire?' – *Slumdog Millionaire* was based around the Indian version of the show.

Case study 9.1: Fremantle Media

One of the major independents working out of the UK is Fremantle Media, perhaps a model for global television companies. The current company is built around three main elements. The earliest operating part of the company was the major German film studio Ufa (see Chapter 1), which following its re-emergence from the Nazi period in 1946 was eventually bought by Bertelsmann, the only major multinational media corporation without a US film or TV base. Bertelsmann placed its acquisition in a group with RTL, the major European radio and TV company (and one-time owner of the UK's fifth terrestrial TV channel).

The UK constituent parts of Fremantle are Thames TV, once a major franchise holder as part of the ITV network in the UK, and Talkback Productions, one of the successful UK independents founded in the 1980s.

Grundy Television was founded in Australia in 1959 and became well known for game shows and soaps – including *Neighbours*, which proved a big success in the UK in the 1980s and was the launchpad for the careers of Jason Donovan and Kylie Minogue (see Moran (1998) for background on Grundy and the development of global TV formats). With this structure and the library of titles owned by the constituent parts, Fremantle

Fig 9.2
A 'wallpaper' image from
Neighbours featuring the
wedding of Scott (Jason
Donovan) and Charlene
(Kylie Minogue) in 1987.
Neighbours has been
seen in 50 countries, and
Donovan and Minogue
went on to become
international music stars.
Source: Fremantle Media.

is in a strong position to exploit its rights and create new formats internationally. Its
game shows and reality formats are now broadcast worldwide, including in the US (e.g.
American Idol).

Research and Explore 9.1: *Fremantle Media*

Look up the range of programmes produced by Fremantle's different production units.

How wide is the spread of Fremantle's programming to different territories?

In what ways do you think having three bases in Australia, the UK and Germany helps Fremantle to
operate globally?

In the next section we will consider some of the forms of television most closely
related to film.

Television films

The concept of a television film is in one sense quite simple – it is a film made primarily to be shown on television. As such, a television film may be a production comparable in length and budget to a feature film and indeed this is currently the case in many countries. Such films may also receive cinema screenings – perhaps when they are exported. However, the concept becomes more problematic when we consider institutional issues concerned with television broadcasting and critical/ aesthetic issues which may mean that certain assumptions about style and content are prompted by the term 'television film'.

As already noted, the early US TV industry was unusual in producing material on 35mm film. Elsewhere, television was first broadcast live with elements of filmed material usually on cheaper 16mm filmstock. Later, videotaping became possible and film formats for television drama standardised on Super 16mm. Although directors favoured 35mm, it was, at least in the UK, considered too expensive for television.

Television films: aspect ratios, filmstock and digital

The TV screen was originally designed as having an aspect ratio of 4:3 (1.33.1) – approximately the same as the standard cinema aspect ratio up to the introduction of widescreen technologies in the mid-1950s. As noted above, the film industry changed ratios as part of the attempt to appear 'bigger' and more visually exciting than TV. Consequently, when films made after the mid-1950s began to be sold to TV stations for broadcast, one of two strategies was open to the broadcaster. Either the film was broadcast in the correct ratio with black bars above and below the film image (known as **letterboxing**) or else the broadcaster attempted to fill the TV screen by cropping part of the film image. This was either a fixed crop from either side of the wide film screen image or the action on screen was followed by a **pan and scan** telecine camera which literally panned across the image. These were unsatisfactory solutions and a film made in the original 2.55:1 CinemaScope ratio could be unwatchable on TV when nearly half the image was missing.

When it appeared that the largest audience for Hollywood films was likely to be on TV, Hollywood film producers began to instruct cinematographers to shoot action within the centre of the frame to limit the negative effects of cropping on TV. Although modern TV sets use a 16:9 ratio (1.78:1), this is still not compatible with the standard cinema ratio of 1.85:1 and certainly not with the wider ratio of 2.35:1 – which for some audiences is what connotes 'cinema'. Films in post-production may now produce several different versions of the same film for theatrical, DVD, TV, etc. in different parts of the world. At least then they have some control over how their product is shown to audiences. Unfortunately, TV audiences may still have their sets wrongly configured so that they produce distorted images which are stretched or squeezed. (Something similar happens with some of the public screenings of digital material projected on screens in public venues.)

The Super 16 and Super 35 film formats used by producers of film for television use the same size stock as standard 16 or 35 but capture a wider film negative (not requiring space for a soundtrack which is recorded separately), and therefore a higher resolution projected image is possible in different widescreen formats. Super 16 became standard in the UK, and in Hollywood Super 35 became standard for 16:9 TV material. Contemporary high-definition TV productions are mainly shot and post-produced using digital formats that can produce a range of aspect ratios as required (see Chapter 12).

Fig 9.3a

Fig 9.3b

Fig 9.3c

Fig 9.3d

Aspect ratios. These images demonstrate the problems faced by producers and broadcasters. **Fig 9.3a** shows the full 2.35:1 frame used for the Zhang Yimou film *Hero* (China/Hong Kong, 2002). **Fig 9.3b** shows how the same image would have to be cropped to fit the traditional TV shape of 4:3 or 1.33:1. **Fig 9.3c** shows that the current 'widescreen' TV shape of 16:9 or 1.78:1 is also unable to show all the action. Any attempt to force the image to 'fill the screen' will produce one of several possible forms of distortion such as the 'squeeze' in **Fig 9.3d**.

How is a TV film different?

Any film intended to be viewed on a video screen may be expected to be planned in relation to expectations about visual style. Most television material will have a higher proportion of medium shots and medium close-ups compared to film where both a greater variety of shot sizes (e.g. long shots and big close-ups) and possibly more complex camerawork may appear more frequently. Films made for television may also be expected to be lit more evenly and not to display the rich textures of the cinema image. However, if producers consider this as a baseline, there may be some discussion about how using a more cinematic style could give a television film more prestige, distinguishing it from routine television drama. There are currently as many comments about TV drama that appears 'cinematic' as about cinema films that are 'televisual'.

Production budgets may be a distinguishing factor. Certainly, a mainstream theatrical film from the Hollywood majors is likely to cost considerably more than a TV film of the same length. However, other production contexts may create the opposite situation. In the UK the average hourly cost of 'quality' primetime TV drama is significantly more than the average for domestic feature film production, with many low-budget films costing under £500,000 for a 90-minute feature. By contrast, the BBC television films adapted from Henning Mankell's Swedish crime novels cost £2.5 million per film.

The institutional context of different TV channels is likely to be the single biggest factor affecting production. Producers hoping for export sales or syndication may have to consider how the same film narrative can be presented in different ways for different institutional contexts. For instance, if a film is likely to appear on broadcast commercial channels with advertising breaks, should potential breaks be accommodated in the editing? On the other hand, subscription cable stations like HBO don't carry in-programme advertising – and the regulatory requirements on swearing, depictions of sexual activity, etc. are less stringent.

American TV films have suffered to some extent because of perceptions about their themes and treatment of content. In attempts to attract a large television audience on a weekly basis the US 'movie of the week' or TV special made by a TV network in the 1980s and 1990s turned to popular news stories. One example was the *Amy Fisher Story* made by ABC in 1993. Amy Fisher was a young woman who shot her lover's wife and the role was played by 18-year-old Drew Barrymore. A rival CBS production aired on the same evening. Other TV films were described as presenting 'disease of the week' or 'social problem of the week'. In the UK, a familiar put-down of any theatrical film is to accuse it of being like a 'made for TV movie'. When US TV movies are imported into the UK they are often screened in the afternoon or late at night because of their low status.

Why do TV companies show imported TV movies that they don't rate highly? Cost is the important issue. Some films may also be included in bulk packages, structured so that a popular lead title enables the sale of less popular ones as filler material.

Research and Explore 9.2

Look through your TV guide for the coming week.

Can you distinguish which films were made for the cinema and which were created directly for TV?

Select one of the high-profile TV drama series/serials made on film – can you explain why the subject matter and its treatment (how it is presented) have led to its production for TV rather than for the cinema?

How do you watch?

The concept of the 'high-quality TV series/serial' has become extremely important for certain audience segments over the past few years. High-budget series shot on film (now mainly using digital film cameras) often with leading Hollywood stars (and directors), have become a feature of American and global television. *The Wire*, *Mad Men*, *True Blood*, *The Tudors*, *Rome*, etc. have been mostly made as co-productions by US cable channels such as Showtime, AMC or HBO, sometimes with European **PSB**s such as BBC, RAI, etc. Part of their success comes from the greater freedom of cable in the US (see above) and the high production values. The restrictions on sales to free-to-air TV mean that some audiences have to wait to see them (fuelling piracy) but this has perhaps been compensated for by the sale of box sets. Sales figures for these are hard to come by but on the evidence of press coverage, 'waiting for the box set' seems to be fashionable. The image of the box set purchaser suggests someone who buys box sets either to supplement or replace purchase/rental of films on DVD. On a large-screen TV how much difference will the viewer see between 'TV' and 'cinema'?

Parade's End (UK/US, 2012) is a high-budget five-part serial listed as a UK/ Canada/Belgium co-production by independent companies for HBO and BBC Worldwide. The cinematography by Mike Eley and direction by Susannah White is notable for long shots and lighting much more akin to cinematic features. The two have worked together mainly on television but also on a cinematic feature. *Parade's End* is a literary adaptation by Tom Stoppard of four books by Ford Maddox Ford, featuring a star-laden cast in a story that runs from before the First World War through to its aftermath. It was broadcast in the UK at the same time as a second Stoppard adaptation, of Tolstoy's *Anna Karenina*, was released as a major UK/French film in cinemas.

Fig 9.4
A production shot featuring Keira Knightley in *Anna Karenina* and showing the studio set. Source: The Kobal Collection/ www.picture-desk.com.

Fig 9.5
A production shot featuring Benedict Cumberbatch from a location shoot on *Parade's End*. Source: Mammoth Screen.

The spread of multi-channel television via satellite and cable in most parts of the world means that a serial like *Parade's End* may become available in as many territories as a cinema release. *Anna Karenina* is the third literary adaptation or 'costume drama' directed by Joe Wright and starring Keira Knightley. The previous two adaptations – *Pride and Prejudice* (UK/US/France, 2005) and *Atonement* (UK/US/France, 2007) – earned US$121 million and US$129 million respectively worldwide with releases in every major territory.

Screendaily featured *Parade's End* during its post-production (27 March 2012) as a case study of 'high-end' TV production. Damien Timmer from Mammoth Screen, the UK production company behind the project, is quoted as saying, 'it is a bit of a golden age. TV is getting more ambitious and the talent you can attract to work in television is better than ever.' The budget for the five-hour programme is reported to be US$19.7 million. The two earlier Joe Wright films had estimated budgets of US$28–30 million (IMDb) but the scale of the TV production matched them with 100 locations in the UK and Belgium and 101 speaking parts (several filled by well-known film actors). Producer David Parfitt (who worked with Tom Stoppard on *Shakespeare in Love* (US, 1998)) commented: 'Apart from trying to shoot a little bit more each day, there is remarkably little difference [from a film shoot] at this scale.' He also suggests that though shooting in Belgium worked very well and the Eurostar rail network brought actors and crew from around Europe together with ease, 'When you go somewhere only used to day-to-day TV and you throw an almost Hollywood-sized production at them, there was some fast learning to be done'. The Belgian shoot and post-production also enabled access to the Belgian tax shelter scheme negotiated through the French bank BNP Paribus.

Parade's End was sold to the Australian Network Nine TV channel early in the production process. Australian actress Adelaide Clemens is one of the three leads. Australia has been a strong market for the Joe Wright/Keira Knightley films as well. Network Nine also takes *Sherlock* (UK, 2010–2012), the TV series starring Benedict Cumberbatch, the lead in *Parade's End*. *Sherlock* is screened in at least 12 territories (IMDb listing), including Germany, France, the US, Japan and Russia. Since HBO is a co-producer, *Parade's End* will also have the *potential* to reach HBO subscribers in territories across Asia, Latin America and Europe as well as North America. If *Parade's End* does eventually reach the same worldwide audience as *Anna Karenina*, it may also serve to highlight the way in which certain forms of TV drama will begin to circulate in a television equivalent of specialised cinema. HBO, as a cable channel, already defines its audiences differently than free-to-air broadcasters, and in the UK the serial was first broadcast on BBC2 on a Friday evening – a calculated indication that this was not intended as a mainstream, Sunday evening costume drama?

See Chapter 12 for discussion of the entry VOD platforms such as Netflix into the production of big-budget drama serials.

The other factor that has supported this new interest in TV drama is the development of internet forums for discussion of specific series/serials. This encourages the longevity of TV material alongside the number of 'rerun' channels and box sets. Where once a TV film had only limited screenings, most TV series/serials are accessible via at least one format at any time – like cinema films. TV production companies now find themselves in the same position as Hollywood in terms of release/transmission dates. Audiences are now prepared to illegally download programmes or import DVDs if they know a specific programme has been shown in one territory but so far not in another.

Classical Hollywood, TV movies and reality TV

The disdain with which some TV critics have treated the 'movie of the week' on TV is worth considering alongside the Hollywood studio strategy of creating films 'torn from the headlines' – as was the policy of Warner Bros. in the early 1930s. Rick Altman in his book *Film/Genre* (1999: 44) quotes Darryl Zanuck writing in *The Hollywood Reporter* of December 1932:

Fragmenting refers to an audience splitting into several smaller audiences. **Segmenting** implies that some of those smaller audiences are mainly composed of viewers of the same gender, age group or social class.

> Somewhere in its [the 'headline film'] make-up it must have the punch and smash that would entitle it to be a headline on the front page of any metropolitan daily [newspaper].

Demographics refers to the same issue as 'segmenting'. Hollywood refers to the largest possible audience as comprising four quadrants: old and young, male and female.

In 1932 Hollywood was making movies for a mass audience and the 'headline film' sought to grab the biggest possible audience for the most contemporary story – whatever it was. By 1982, the mass audience was watching television, so a similar strategy attempted to grab the biggest audience on a Saturday evening for television. However, the development of multi-channel TV (and especially cable television) has since **fragmented** and **segmented** that TV audience. There is no single mass audience any more but TV still looks for the biggest audience associated with specific **'demographics'**.

In contemporary television we can see two attempts to deal with these changes in audiences – both of which are interesting to explore in terms of global trends. Before we do that, we will return to Zanuck's comparison with newspaper headlines. As newspaper sales decline, perhaps TV is turning to alternative rival media such as social media networks. What is trending on Twitter perhaps (though by the time you read this it may be a different social media platform)? The key is the sense of what kinds of TV people are discussing when they meet for a 'watercooler moment' or chatting at the hairdresser's. Over the past few years two very different types of television material have been central. One is 'reality programming' and in particular talent programmes or those that bring celebrities and 'ordinary' people together. The first of these to develop a global interest were the variations on the *Big Brother* concept – which may be explored via the global trade in **formats**.

Reality programming creates new celebrities and is often covered in the tabloid press and on social media. It appeals to broad audience groups. Filmed series or **serials,** by contrast, particularly those with complex narrative structures and unusual settings – especially on subscription cable services – appeal to only a segment or niche audience (i.e. who might pay extra for subscription channels). We will discuss serials in terms of the export of Nordic crime fiction and contrast them with the spread of *telenovelas* below.

Video cinema

Thus far, we have discussed films on television. But we could consider a different kind of relationship. Since films are now being made with digital cameras perhaps we are now seeing television at the cinema or perhaps 'video' is simply replacing 'film'? In fact the cinema industry – the exhibition sector – started to explore the projection of television images in cinemas from the 1930s through to the 1950s in the US (Gomery 1985: 54–61). Today cinemas are able to take satellite feeds of all kinds of HD television material and display it on cinema screens (see Chapter 12).

The following are three different examples of how video technology has changed ideas about cinema.

'Straight to video'

When the video cassette rental boom began in the 1980s, the new 'home video' market was relatively open to new ideas. The studios did not immediately see the potential in the market, and new distributors such as Vestron (Wasser 2001: 107) were able to acquire titles and make considerable profits. The studios eventually focused on the market that had already grown to include a very wide range of films, music and other forms of material.

In the US and other Western territories, video was considered a lower status format compared to 'theatrical'. Therefore if a film was deemed not 'good enough' for a cinema release it ended up in the 'straight to video' market. This 'poor-status' profile was unfortunate but not necessarily bad for business. Some film genres that were thought 'not respectable' or unlikely to attract a mass audience in cinemas actually did quite well on video rental – especially horror, violent action, martial arts, soft pornography (including the erotic thriller), etc. The different viewing conditions suited these genres. Video also stimulated the development of cult cinema – films no longer on cinema release were still available on video and other films that featured cult stars/directors could be released direct to video. Certain stars became popular

Format has two meanings in the TV industry. One is concerned with the technical description of the platform or carrier (e.g. DVD or videotape). The other refers to a (very specific) package of elements that make up a programme designed for a particular audience, often to be scheduled at a specific time of day.

The Coronation of Elizabeth II in London in June 1953 was a major landmark in television broadcasting with live television feeds to cinemas and other public venues in the UK. The *Manchester Guardian* (3 June 1953) reported a 'nearly eight-hour' show at the Manchester Gaumont cinema. The same source reports film copies carried to North America by jet aircraft allowing network broadcasts only eight hours after the live event.

because of video releases. In some ways 'straight to video' became the equivalent of the B-movie output of classical Hollywood. Some of the same films that went straight to video in North America and Western Europe may also have been 'dumped' at low prices for distribution in cinemas in Africa and the Middle East.

V-cinema

The Japanese form of video film carries different connotations of quality. V-cinema as it is known has attracted directors of ambition, since it does not carry the same stigma as 'straight to video'. These low-budget productions are designed from the outset to be seen on video, and in the late 1980s and 1990s they attracted new directors who perceived this sector as less restrictive than mainstream cinema production. Takashi Miike is one of the well-known directors to emerge from V-cinema (see Chapter 5). The successful horror franchise *Ju-on* created by Shimizu Takashi began with two V-cinema films before the third film in 2002 gained a theatrical release. This title was exported and then remade as *The Grudge* by Shimizu in the US with Sarah Michelle Gellar in 2004 with further sequels in 2006 and 2009. Since the early 2000s the V-cinema market has declined and more films are getting a release in the new cinemas built since the late 1990s (i.e. rather later than in North America).

Nigerian video films

These are covered in Chapter 8, but here we should just note that the development of video films was a response to production costs and the decaying cinema infrastructure in many African countries. The success of the Nigerian video film (nvf) has spread to other parts of Anglophone Africa and has now begun to appear in Francophone countries as well. What the nvf did was solve the problem in so many relatively poor countries of how to make films that represent local culture when there is no local industrial film production infrastructure. A film industry requires processing laboratories and cinemas, whereas video films could be made for a few thousand US dollars and then shown in any space in which a TV monitor could be installed.

Fig. 9.6
Ito Misaki as Hitomi in *Ju-on* (Japan, 2002).

International TV trade

From our discussion thus far, we have recognised that the US and the UK have had an advantage in selling TV material in the global marketplace. They were first into the marketplace and they both had strong domestic markets in which to develop material that could be exported. In Chapter 4 we noted that when 'commercial TV' was introduced into the UK, what was then the second most valuable film industry went into a steeper decline in admissions. Much of the creativity and resources of that film industry then fed into the development of British television. The BBC and Granada (one of the main suppliers to the ITV network) developed quality brands in several different TV programme categories, including drama, light entertainment, feature documentaries, sports, etc. Each of these has potential export opportunities. We also noted above that the UK independent production companies founded in the 1980s and 1990s – and now in some cases merging with European and Australian independents such as Endemol or Grundy – have also been able to export formats, if not recorded programmes.

One of the reasons why some television exports are successful is that certain local cultural developments are shared across groups of countries in ways that to some extent exclude the possibility of US market domination. The most obvious non-film example is the television coverage of football. English Premier League (EPL) 'product' – games, analysis, interviews, etc. – is watched in 212 territories worldwide via 80 different broadcasters (http://www.premierleague.com). The annual income from TV rights has risen at the end of each three-year period. In 2012 the domestic and overseas rights were sold for £4.42 billion over a three-year period – an annual income comparable to the turnover of the entire UK film exhibition sector – with annual exports of £450 million. European football rights – the UEFA competitions and those of other major European leagues – are also big earners. US sports generate similar TV income in North America but the export potential is reduced because these sports do not have the wide international appeal of football. Alongside cricket with its huge South Asian audiences, European football revenues provide a striking example of a **contra-flow** of TV rights payments. But since much of the football revenue returns to the UK, we need to look further afield for examples of non-European flows.

ESPN, the sports channel owned by Disney, briefly operated a UK business from 2009 to 2013 before withdrawing after losing rights to UK telecoms company BT.

Contra-flows in the international television market

We define contra-flows here as any kind of trade in television programme material that cuts across Anglo-American export flows. Most of the academic studies focusing on these contra-flows have considered them on the basis of interruptions to a 'North–South' exchange dominated by the Anglophone North (i.e. the US/UK). This is problematic, since it equates Japan and China, the second and third largest economies in the world, as 'Southern' producers. It also possibly ignores other European producers who are making an impact in global television in interesting ways. We will focus here on two specific sets of global exports, but also note that in other chapters there are references to trade in Japanese *anime* and Korean television dramas as part of the 'Korean Wave' in East Asia (see Chapter 5).

One of the first indications of the potential for global television trade that didn't involve Anglo-American exports came in the form of the *telenovela* and other similar forms.

Telenovelas: soap, romance and melodrama

As the term implies, *telenovelas* are related to the idea of serialised novels adapted for television (see Thussu 2006: 196). A common saying in the UK is that the popular nineteenth-century novelist Charles Dickens would have written for *Coronation Street* (the longest running soap opera on UK television) if he was alive today. When Dickens wrote novels such as *Oliver Twist* or *Great Expectations*, they were first published in serial form in weekly or monthly magazines – each episode ending with a cliff-hanger.

The *telenovela* began in Latin America and became associated with production companies like TV Globo in Brazil and Televisa in Mexico. Latin America has long had a media ecology dominated by Hollywood product, so the success of the *telenovela* in the domestic markets of the two countries was remarkable, but the astounding export success was something else again.

It is important to be clear first about the narrative structure of the *telenovela*. They are sometimes referred to as 'soaps' but soaps in the Anglo-American sense are continuous serials – i.e. they don't have a narrative resolution; they aren't expected to end (though, for commercial reasons, unsuccessful soaps do have to stop). *Telenovelas* are serial narratives that do end – though they may have 200 'chapters'. Chapters (rather than 'episodes' – see Tufte (2000) on 'The Brazilian *telenovela*', which is the source for much of this section) might be broadcast close together so that a whole *telenovela* might last for six or seven months. However, like soaps, *telenovelas* are a form of 'open' narrative in that once they have been established, writers are in a position to respond to audience reactions and adjust storylines. Chapters are usually broken up into sections in which the first enables the recap and consolidation of events in the previous chapter, the middle sections advance the dramatic narrative and the final section sets up the cliff-hanger. The four sections take into account advertising breaks. *Telenovelas* are primetime shows broadcast in the evening – therefore they can appeal across audience segments rather than being restricted, like daytime soaps in the US, to targeting specific audiences, especially women. Such is the status of the *telenovelas* that two or three different titles may be broadcast on the same evening.

The origins of the *telenovela*

Tufte suggests that in Brazil, the *telenovela* draws on a background of traditional narratives in a matrix comprising three distinct local forms of storytelling. The first is oral storytelling, the second the popular literature known as *cordel* – stories read or sung aloud in peasant villages – and the third the mimes and forms of popular theatre that developed in the circus and travelling shows. These forms all have roots in Iberian culture prior to the colonisation of South America, and they became important in rural Brazil up until the first half of the twentieth century when the *radionovela* took off. At this point the later European cultural developments like the stage melodrama and the *feuilleton* became influential. The French term *feuilleton* has several meanings but here refers to newspaper serials or newspaper gossip and trivia about current events.

What is crucial is the suggestion that the *telenovela* draws heavily on stories from traditional culture that everyone in the society will understand. The Latin American stories are usually grouped into romances, thrillers, historical dramas (set in the colonial or early independent period) and family dramas. Comedy is also an important element in the *telenovela*. Stories often involve two families, perhaps from different social backgrounds. In Chapter 2 we discussed the importance of forms of melodrama across different film cultures, and the strength of the *telenovela* is its appeal both locally and transnationally. Partly this is because it provides a public space in which to discuss issues of modernity – how lives are changing in a society that is getting richer but where there are still newly urbanised communities that have links back to an agrarian past. Unlike Hollywood soaps where the fictional world is idealised, the *telenovela* works with the 'lived' experiences of its audiences.

The earliest *telenovelas* appeared in the 1950s but little scholarly work has been done on this period because videotaping in Brazil didn't arrive until 1960 and there are few or no archive recordings. Tufte suggests that the first phase of *telenovela* production was dominated by romances and historical romantic dramas. Stories and writers often came from Cuba or other Spanish-speaking countries and relied on a shared history. But after 1968 there was a turn to 'realism' and contemporary Brazilian stories, and Tufte recognises the next 20 years as the period of social change in Brazil – the migration of large numbers of people to the cities (different programming emanated from São Paulo and Rio de Janeiro). It was also a period of authoritarian governments. All of this provided rich material for the *telenovela*. After 1986 and the return of democracy, a 'post-realist' phase began and the Brazilian *telenovela* became 'multi-faceted'.

Our interest in the *telenovela* is the way in which it stimulated local audiences with stories that spoke directly to them and how that would eventually be an element in the amazing export success of the form, both in the trade in finished programmes and in the encouragement it gave to similar forms elsewhere. Certain titles have been picked out as particularly successful. Both Tufte and Thussu (2006: 197) mention *Escrava Isaura* (*Isaura the Slave Girl*), a 1977 literary adaptation

Fig 9.7
Angélica Vale as Leticia 'Lety' Padilla Solís in *La fea más Bella* (Mexico, 2006). This 300-episode *telenovela* was a remake of the Colombian *Yo so, Betty la fea* (1999). Perhaps the most adapted of all *telenovelas* worldwide, the story idea also produced *Ugly Betty* (2006–2010), the US weekly series.

that sold in Italy, France, the USSR, and in China where 450 million viewers were claimed.

Brazilian *telenovelas* have a large home market and other potential Lusophone markets in Portugal, Angola and Mozambique. They have also sold dubbed into Spanish, but it is the Spanish-speaking market that provides the export potential for *telenovelas* made elsewhere in Latin America, especially in Mexico. As well as circulating within the region, these have been exported to Hispanic TV stations in the US – a form of 'reverse media imperialism' perhaps.

As well as the markets in the Americas and Western Europe (but not the UK) *telenovelas* also began to sell heavily in Eastern Europe and Southeast Asia. We could argue that some of the reasons why such exports were so successful were:

- because of the scale of production, entire series could be sold at relatively low prices, offering competitive rates comparable to syndicated US shows;
- even when edited and usually dubbed, the narratives were relatively easy to follow;
- their origin in countries like Brazil and Mexico meant that they came from societies closer in socio-economic terms to some of the poorer countries which bought them than programme material from the US or Western Europe – and therefore the issues covered were more accessible.

Havens (2006: 128) uses Hungary as a case study and shows a TV schedule with short (30-minute) chapters of seven different *telenovelas* from Argentina, Mexico and Peru on the same day in 2001. These were all scheduled in the daytime and targeted older women. By the following year, tastes had changed and the number was much reduced.

The figures associated with these exports are impressive – Thussu quotes a figure of 130 countries worldwide which bought TV titles from the Brazilian company **TV Globo**, most of which were *telenovelas*.

All of **TV Globo International**'s programmes, including *telenovelas*, are listed with brief descriptions on http://www. globotvinternational.com.

A good example of the contra-flow between Brazil and South/Southeast Asia is the *telenovela, India – a Love Story* (Brazil, 2009). This production of 103 x 45-minute episodes features a family romance melodrama involving Raj, a young Indian executive who falls for a woman in Brazil, and Maya, a young middle-class Indian woman who has a relationship with a 'well-educated *dalit*'. The families of Raj and Maya won't allow them to marry these 'undesirable' partners. Can Raj and Maya come together in marriage and forget their past experiences?

Shot in India and Brazil, the series won an Emmy in 2009 as a *telenovela* and has subsequently been widely seen in Asia. Announcing the sale of the title to a pay TV channel in Indonesia, Globo TV claimed that audiences of 80 million would watch it in that territory alone (http://www.globotvinternational.com/newsDet. asp?newsId=156). Internet searches around *telenovela* titles like this reveal different controversies and different audience pleasures being discussed in various territories.

Ramadan dramas

The conditions that produced *telenovelas* also exist to a certain extent in North Africa, the Middle East and many parts of Asia. In Chapter 6 we explore the film industries of the Arab world, and in particular Egypt and Lebanon in terms of film production. Egypt has always been the main regional producer and as in

Fig 9.8
Egyptian Ramadan serials
are viewable in cafés
and other public places.
Source: Stephanie Keith.

Latin America the history of melodrama in the cinema combined with the allure of Hollywood, and a long-standing local storytelling tradition has helped to produce serial drama as a television form. In the Arab world and in other Muslim countries such as Indonesia, the biggest television audiences are available to advertisers during the holy month of Ramadan. In Egypt, most families watch television after *iftar*, the evening meal that breaks the day's fast. In 2012, Egyptian television broadcast 50 different series/serials during Ramadan with a combined production cost of nearly US$200 million. (BBC Monitoring, 17 August 2012).

Two factors increased the output of serials in 2012 – the civil war in Syria disrupted production in Egypt's traditional rival as TV exporter to other Arab countries, and the lifting of some aspects of censorship within Egypt following the removal of the Mubarak regime encouraged producers to try new subject matter. For example, one of the most expensive new productions, *Naji Atallah's Crew*, concerns an Egyptian fired from his job in Israel with his bank account frozen because of actions by Israeli security. He plans a bank raid in revenge. The serial effectively critiques the Egyptian–Israeli détente under Mubarak and has been criticised in Israel and by some of Egypt's Arab neighbours – but it achieved the highest ratings according to Egyptian official audience figures (BBC Monitoring, 17 August 2012). Brief descriptions of the 2012 Ramadan serials are given on: http://www.albawaba.com/entertainment/ramadan-2012-tv-shows-434873.

Gümüş and Noor

The Turkish TV serial *Gümüş* (100 x 90 minutes) was first broadcast in 2005 without generating special interest in its domestic market. In 2008, MBC (the satellite broadcaster based in Dubai) purchased rights to *Gümüş* and renamed it *Noor*. The serial was dubbed into colloquial Syrian Arabic and scheduled as an afternoon soap. *Noor* is a romance in which a young woman, Noor, marries into a wealthy family. Although it wasn't the first Turkish serial on MBC, it seemed to grab the audience more strongly than earlier offerings and was soon moved into a

Fig 9.9
Noor merchandising on sale in Ramallah on the West Bank. Source: Press Association.

Turkish melodrama serials have similar content to *telenovelas*. According to the MBC website (http://www. mbc.net/en.html) its 2012 offer includes *Ezel*, based on the classic Alexandre Dumas story, *The Count of Monte Cristo*.

See Chapter 6 on Turkish cinema.

Since this chapter was written, events in both Syria and Turkey have raised doubts about both Turkish 'liberalism' and the reception of Turkish cultural exports. But the long-term trend is likely to see further developments in a regional television drama culture.

primetime evening slot. By the end of its run it was estimated that some 85 million viewers across the whole Arab world were following the story – 50 million of them women (figures from Médiamétrie, quoted in Buccianti 2010).

Noor was attractive for Arab viewers because it showed an Islamic world in which women could be treated as equals (Noor's husband Mohannad supports her aspirations to become a fashion designer) and where social conventions appear more relaxed. Although criticised by some Muslim clerics, the serial has been argued to be socially liberating in representing a more 'modern' marriage that was in fact arranged in a traditional way. The effects of the serial have been reported as an increase in tourism from Arab countries to Istanbul, new fashion trends based on the serial's costume design, and the appearance of the names 'Noor' and 'Mohannad' in maternity hospitals in various Arab countries. The importance of dubbing into colloquial rather than formal Arabic (which had been used for imported Mexican *telenovelas*) was seen as important and this practice has spread to other programming.

The success of Turkish TV serials is now being explored in terms of Turkish cinema and may be seen as an important element in Turkey's **soft power** in the region. This in turn raises the question of a 'post-colonial relationship'. Although it is nearly a century since the Ottoman Empire was finally expelled from Palestine and Syria at the end of the 1914 to 1918 war, there are still resonances, positive and negative, within the region. It is also worth noting that *Gümüş* was exported to the Balkans, playing in Bulgaria, Macedonia and Albania (as well as other parts of Eastern Europe). Again, some of these countries have Muslim communities and were once part of the Ottoman Empire. This is another example of how cultural links across a region and/or through historical ties can create a contra-flow.

Research and Explore 9.3

Imagine that you are trying to explain the attraction of a *telenovela* or a Ramadan serial drama to someone who has never seen one. What would you want to emphasise in your explanation?

Nordic crime fiction

The extraordinary success of Swedish and Danish TV series and serials in Europe, North America, Australia and worldwide since 2007/2008 is part of a wider success for Nordic Cinema and, most importantly, Nordic crime fiction novels – the stimulus for the whole movement. Literary crime fiction has always been popular in Northern European countries and the first indication of the potential export possibilities of Swedish TV crime came in the 1970s with German adaptations of the 'Martin Beck' novels by the Swedish writers Maj Sjöwall and Per Wahlöö. The key features of these stories were:

- a focus on police procedures, often in a realist mode emphasising the routine drudgery of police work;
- a distinctive political edge to the stories dealing with the social context of crime – the writing couple were both Marxists.

The 1990s heir to this early success was Henning Mankell, who saw himself as continuing a tradition and who felt an urgent need to explore contemporary Swedish society through the medium of crime fiction. He recognised that what had once been seen as a settled, stable, social democracy was now changing, mainly through the impact of economic globalisation and global politics as Sweden's economy was changing and greater demands were being made on its social welfare provision. Mankell's stories also focus on the impact of feminism and a strong equal opportunities culture. These various traits are also evident in the more directly political work of Stieg Larsson, whose Millennium Trilogy of crime thrillers featuring the investigators Mikael Blomqvist and Lisbeth Salander, published posthumously during 2005/2008, had sold 65 million copies around the world by the end of 2011.

This section should be read in conjunction with the case study on Nordic national cinema in Chapter 4.

The assassination of the Swedish Prime Minister Olaf Palme in 1986 has been cited by Mankell as a key moment in his thinking about crime fiction.

Crime fiction and its readers

The link between popular novels and television drama has not perhaps received the amount of attention in film and media studies that it should. Readership of crime fiction literature is clearly gendered. Women are far more likely to read all kinds of fiction than men and this includes crime fiction. One of the (possibly) surprising aspects of this is that some of the most violent crime fiction is written by women – and also some of the most interesting in terms of relationships, both domestic and work-related, of police officers. Whether crime stories are written by men or women, gender is often important as an ingredient in story structure. Television watching is also gendered, with women more likely to watch soap opera forms and long-form drama generally.

'Cop shows' are a staple of television drama in many countries, and especially in the UK and US. However, most of those shows have been developed either as 50 to 60-minute episodes for a series or more recently as 100 to 120-minute episodes for a short series or 'mini-series'. There have been variations such as the soap-like scheduling of *The Bill* (UK, 1984–2010) and other experiments, but rarely have the pleasures of 'long-form' narrative crime fiction been explored as persuasively as in the recent Nordic TV productions.

Long-form narratives allow writers to explore the backstories of an array of characters and to create a complex weaving of separate narrative strands. They allow 'readers' to engage with characters and to recognise the development of long-running discourses about social issues. The Anglo-American 'series' with its single episode structure creates a 'narrative arc' over a season of episodes, in the US culminating in a big season finale. But single episodes are constrained by the need to tell a story in as little as 45 minutes in a show like those in the *CSI* franchise. Long-form narratives such as *The Sopranos*, *The Wire* and *Mad Men* have screened successfully on cable channels such as HBO, Showtime and AMC. Those American shows were certainly an inspiration for Nordic producers – especially in terms of their more cinematic visual style and complex narratives. In Sweden and Denmark long-form narrative productions have aired on public service television, capturing a larger popular audience (i.e. as a proportion of the national TV audience) than the US cable shows. The original *Wallander* films were made with SVT, the Swedish PSB channel. As we noted in Chapter 4, these films highlighted the close cooperation between TV and film companies in Sweden and the integrated release patterns of films designed from the outset to be 'theatrical' *and* DVD/broadcast products. This is one element of 'Nordic Crime Fiction TV' that has proved attractive worldwide – encouraging other broadcasters to schedule longer and more complex crime fiction films.

In the UK, the success of *Wallander* encouraged BBC4 to import *Inspector Montalbano* from Italy (TV films from the Italian PSB RAI based on crime novels by Andrea Camilleri). The Italian series of 115-minute films was produced between 1999 and 2011 in a co-production with SVT. BBC4 had previously imported the French crime serial *Spiral* (*Engrenages*, France, 2005–2012), featuring a female police commander, and the growing popularity of subtitled crime fiction meant that *Spiral* Seasons 2 and 3 were shown in 2009 and 2011 and Season 4 in France in 2012. Although *Spiral* is perhaps closer to US series such as *The Wire*, it fits in with the overall contra-flow of non-English-language TV material with a global reach. In July 2012 *Spiral* became the first foreign-language/subtitled pick-up by the US VOD provider Netflix. All four seasons are scheduled for screening in the US with Netflix becoming one of 72 networks worldwide taking the show (www.variety.com/article/VR1118057090/).

Danish serials

The single most dramatic impact of Nordic crime fiction on global television was made by *The Killing* (*Forbrydelsen*, Denmark, 2007–2012). Made by the Danish PSB, DR (Danmarks Radio) as a co-production with SVT and other Norwegian and Danish partners as a serial (20 x 55 minutes), *The Killing* was notable for two features:

1   The length of the single narrative – just over 18 hours for the first serial.
2   The focus on three parallel narrative strands involving the death of a single character: the police 'procedural'; the impact on the victim's family; the political turmoil surrounding a prime suspect, a candidate for election as Mayor of Copenhagen.

In addition, it is worth emphasising two other factors that have been important (and which have also been important in the US and possibly to a lesser extent in the UK):

1   The guarantee of creative control given to the writer(s), ahead of directors or producers/managers.
2   The high quality of acting talent and crews prepared to work in theatre, film and television without concerns about 'status'.

Broadcast in the UK in 2011 by BBC4 in double episodes, 110 minutes each week for 10 weeks, the serial became a sensation in the niche market of viewers for subtitled European TV. Audiences rose across the 10 weeks to 600,000 and the start of the second serial (with the central character Inspector Sarah Lund retained for a new story) saw a peak of 1.2 million. These figures may seem modest but they represent far larger audiences than those for most foreign-language cinema releases in the UK.

The appetite for this kind of TV has been sustained worldwide with the subsequent export of two further serials from DR: *Borgen* (Denmark, 2010–2013) and *The Bridge* (*Bron/Broen*, Sweden/Denmark/Norway, 2011). At least as many people (over one million) saw *The Bridge* in the UK as in Denmark or Sweden.

The success of Nordic crime fiction television has been in a solid local/regional performance for co-produced drama and a much more unexpected export success (although that success was certainly a target for Nordic producers). It is worth pointing out here that television distribution (including VOD and DVD box sets) has been able to build audiences for this kind of drama far more quickly than the traditional international distribution of feature films – and this in turn has increased interest from newspapers, magazines and social media. However, just as with feature films, all the successful Nordic crime serials have been 'acquired' as remake material in the US or UK.

An insightful comparison of the Danish serial *Forbrydelsen* and the US remake shown on AMC: http://www.nytimes.com/2012/04/01/arts/television/comparing-the-killing-to-the-show-forbrydelsen.html

The BBC episode guide: http://www.bbc.co.uk/programmes/b017h7m1/episodes/guide

Borgen (Serial 1) is arguably a melodrama of politics and family but it is similar in format to *The Killing* and features two women and one man as central characters with 'personal' narratives intertwined with the central political narrative.

Fig 9.10
Sidse Babett Knudsen as Prime Minister Birgitte Nyborg in the second series of *Borgen*. This still emphasises the melodrama elements of the serial. The woman in the background is the current partner of Birgitte's husband from whom she is separated.
Source: DR TV.

In a final example, we will consider the industrial/institutional factors in that success and the possible final stage in the process of exporting 'Nordic Noir'.

Case study 9.2: Yellow Bird (http://www.yellowbird.se)

Much of Mankell's considerable income from the novels goes on the community theatre he runs in Mozambique and on actions like his participation in attempts to break the Israeli naval blockade of Gaza.

Yellow Bird was formed in 2002 as a partnership between **Henning Mankell**, his agent Lars Björkman and film and TV producer Ole Søndberg. Their sole aim was to exploit the popularity of Mankell's books – mostly crime fiction stories – and the characters he created. Since all but one of the Wallander books had already been adapted for Swedish TV, the company's initial project was to adapt the remaining novel and create a TV series around it with 12 new stories based on Mankell's ideas.

The Yellow Bird plan was familiar for a new company in a globalised media environment. Søndberg knew from experience that in Sweden it was difficult to sustain production with one-off projects that relied solely on cinema and video (DVD) distribution. Television series in partnership with more than one broadcaster are far more viable. Initially, Yellow Bird was a 'brand' built on the high profile achieved by Mankell's novels, not just in Sweden but across the Nordic region and crucially in Germany – a far larger market. It is ironic that the international socialist Mankell should so adeptly exploit his own intellectual properties by using the business model of globalised capitalism. Once he had established the possibility of controlling the adaptations of his novels, Mankell effectively withdrew and Yellow Bird was bought in 2007 by the second largest Scandinavian media group Zodiak Entertainment. In 2010 Zodiak was merged with the UK independent TV company RDF under the ownership of the Italian media conglomerate De Agostini.

By 2012 Zodiak Media was a powerful independent TV and film producer with bases in the UK and US as well as in the Nordic Region, Germany and parts of Eastern Europe. The larger De Agostini Group is involved in publishing, lotteries and television in France and Spain.

Fig 9.11
Krister Henriksson and Johanna Sällström as father and daughter in 'Before the Frost' from the Yellow Bird series *Wallander* (Sweden/ Germany, 2005). Source: Yellow Bird.

In the midst of all these acquisitions and developments, Yellow Bird continued to focus on crime fiction. As well as *Wallander* and the Millennium Trilogy from Stieg Larsson it was also involved in adaptations of crime fiction novels by Helen Tursten, Liza Marklund and Anne Holt. In 2008 Yellow Bird worked with Left Bank Pictures in the UK to produce the British *Wallander* series shown on BBC2 and subsequently shown on TV in Sweden and Norway, and released on DVD throughout the Nordic region.

The *Wallander* success at home and abroad (with sales of the British series to 14 countries) encouraged Yellow Bird to become even more ambitious. In 2011 the company was a production partner on *Headhunters*, the biggest-selling Norwegian film for many years (see Chapter 4 on Nordic cinema). Yellow Bird will work with Summit (US independent distributor of the *Twilight* series) on the US version – following the partnership with Scott Rudin on the David Fincher version of *The Girl With the Dragon Tattoo*.

Marianne Gray, the Yellow Bird producer involved with the US project, was interviewed in *Screendaily* (Geoffrey Macnab, 19 October 2011). She reiterates that the Yellow Bird model is to develop mini-franchises based on books, not to make one-off movies. She speaks about plans to produce more crime fiction TV films and to work further with authors like Jo Nesbø. Co-productions with Germany and Norway are already underway but intriguingly she also mentions a plan to recruit American writers for crime thrillers made in the US using European money. Although this has to some extent already been tried by the UK production company Working Title when it produced the Coen Brothers' *Fargo* in 1996, the implication is that Yellow Bird would seek more input and control.

A UK crime fiction 'single play' offered the opportunity for a director from *The Killing*, Birger Larsen, to create a Nordic *noir* in Nottingham – *Murder* (UK, 2012).

Research and Explore 9.4

Look up the various blogs and newspaper reports referring to the fashion for 'Nordic Noir' or 'Scandi drama' in the UK and US (or other countries outside the Nordic region). What explanations are given for the success of Nordic TV crime fiction (or a serial like *Borgen*)? Which aspects of Nordic culture appear to have an international appeal?

Summary

This chapter has tried to demonstrate that though the global television market initially developed with a built-in Anglo-American domination, contra-flows of programme material have become a regular feature of international television trade. This has enabled regional exchanges and also exchanges between regions as well as some export opportunities to North America. Unlike the relatively small audiences for subtitled/dubbed cinema from outside North America, imported *telenovelas* and other similar drama forms generate audiences in the hundreds of millions worldwide. We should be aware, however, that there are still parts of the world where local TV production is difficult to sustain, never mind the possibility of exports. In parts of Africa cheap syndicated US TV material vies with Bollywood and Hong Kong films, often on pirated video copies, for the attention of audiences. In Chapter 8 we considered how the less formalised distribution of Nigerian video films might impact on these audiences.

References and further reading

Altman, Rick (1999) *Film/Genre*, London: BFI.

Anderson, Benedict (1983, rev. 1991) *Imagined Communities: Reflections on the Origin and Spread of Nationalism*, London and New York: Verso.

Balio, Tino (2002) '"A Major Presence in All the World's Major Markets": The Globalisation of Hollywood in the 1990s', in Graeme Turner (ed.) *The Film Cultures Reader*, London: Routledge.

Branston, Gill and Stafford, Roy (2006) *The Media Student's Book* (4th edn), Abingdon: Routledge.

Buccianti, Alexandra (2010) 'Turkish Soap Operas in the Arab World: Social Liberation or Cultural Alienation?' *Arab Media & Society* 10 (spring). Available at http://www.arabmediasociety.com/?article=735.

Gomery, Douglas (1985) 'Theatre Television: The Missing Link of Technological Change in the US Motion Picture Industry', *The Velvet Light Trap* 21 (summer): 54–61.

Hall, Sheldon and Neale, Steve (2010) *Epics, Spectacles, and Blockbusters: A Hollywood History*, Detroit: Wayne State University Press.

Havens, Timothy (2006) *Global Television Marketplace*, London: BFI.

Mann, David (2012) 'Epicurean Disdain and the Rhetoric of Defiance: *Colonel March of Scotland Yard*', *Scope* 11 (February). Available at http://www.scope. nottingham.ac.uk/article.php?issue=11&id=1021.

Mellencamp, Patricia (2003) 'Lucille Ball and the Regime of Domiculture', in Frank Krutnik (ed.) *Hollywood Comedians: The Film Reader*, London: Routledge.

Mitchell, Wendy (2012) 'Target Audience'. Available at www.screendaily.com (31 January).

Moran, Albert (1998) *Copycat TV: Globalisation, Program Formats and Cultural Identity*, Luton: University of Luton Press.

Noble, Peter (1954) 'British Films You Don't See', in F. Maurice Speed (ed.) *Film Review 1953–4*, London: Macdonald.

Thussu, Daya Kishan (2006) *International Communication: Continuity and Change* (2nd edn), London: Hodder Education.

Thussu, Daya Kishan (ed.) (2007) *Media on the Move: Global Flow and Contra-flow*, London: Routledge.

Tufte, Thomas (2000) *Living with the Rubbish Queen: Telenovelas, Culture and Modernity in Brazil*, Luton: University of Luton Press.

Wasser, Frederick (2001) *Veni, Vidi, Video: The Hollywood Empire and the VCR*, Austin: University of Texas Press.

Weddle, David (1996) *Sam Peckinpah 'If They Move … Kill 'Em'*, London: Faber and Faber.

For a fascinating glimpse into the importance of filmed material on early American television from *Television* magazine go to: http://www.americanradiohistory.com/Archive-Television-Magazine/Television-1952-Jul.pdf·

Further viewing

Most of the European serial dramas mentioned in the text are available on Region 2 DVD box sets subtitled in English. (Scandinavian productions are nearly always subtitled in English, but check those produced in other European languages.)

Subtitled (and dubbed) versions of popular Hispanic *telenovelas* are available on Region 1 DVDs. (Region 2 DVDs for the Spanish market may not have English subtitles.)

YesAsia.com sells Region 1 box sets of South Korean TV serials with English subtitles. These dramas, often romances, have been very successfully exported and have been a major component of the 'Korean Wave' (see Chapter 5).

CHAPTER 10

Diverse Indian cinemas

- Outline history of film in India
- Language diversity
- Hindi cinema
- Bollywood examined
- Bollywood and 'Indian popular cinema'
- Changing audiences for Bollywood
- Statistics and the Indian film industries
- The corporatisation of Indian media
- Nationalism, sectarianism and 'India Shining'
- ☐ Case study 10.1: *3 Idiots*
- ☐ Case study 10.2: *Endhiran*
- Bengali cinema, art and politics
- New Indian cinema and parallel cinema
- Indian diaspora filmmakers
- New Bengali cinema and the parallel legacy
- ☐ Case study 10.3: *15 Park Avenue*
- 'New Bollywood'?
- ☐ Case study 10.4: *Anurag Kashyap and 'independent' Indian films*
- Summary
- References and further reading
- Further viewing

In an online poll for BBC News in 1999, the Indian film star and former politician **Amitabh Bachchan** came first in a vote for the 'greatest star of stage or screen of the Millennium'. In 1994, the future daughter-in-law of Amitabh Bachchan had been crowned Miss World. **Aishwarya Rai** went on to become the best-known Indian face across the globe, not only as an Indian film star but also as a 'brand ambassador' for L'Oréal cosmetics and a regular guest on American TV talk shows, and appearances on the covers of major magazines. The high profile of these two celebrity figures demonstrates the potential spread of Indian film culture on a global scale. Amitabh Bachchan – the 'Big B' – is a tall, handsome man exuding authority and the capacity for action. Aishwarya Rai is beautiful, hard-working and multi-talented. But arguably the most successful film star in India is virtually unknown in Europe and North America.

Fig 10.1
Amitabh Bachchan in a promotional image from *Bunty Aur Babli* (India, 2005). Source: The Kobal Collection/www.picture-desk.com.

Fig 10.2
Rajnikanth in London in 2012 during the shoot for *Kochadaiyaan* (India, 2013). Source: Miguel Medina/AFP/Getty Images.

Fig 10.3
Aishwarya Rai with Abhishek Bachchan in *Guru* (India, 2007). Source: The Kobal Collection/www. picture-desk.com.

Fig 10.4
A poster for an A.R. Rahman concert in Kolkata in 2009.

Rajnikanth (Shivaji Rao Gaekwad) has appeared in 150 films, mostly produced in Tamil cinema. Although born in the same state (Karnataka) as Aishwarya Rai, Rajnikanth's looks and personality are more like those of an 'ordinary Indian' and his superstar status is more appreciated within Asia than in Europe or North America (apart from within the South Indian diaspora). One of the defining features of Indian cinema is its diversity. Rajnikanth and Amitabh Bachchan represent different language cinemas in India. A fourth celebrity figure with a lower personal profile but increasingly a high level of name recognition globally is **A.R. Rahman,** the musical composer whose work moves easily between Tamil, Hindi and English-language cinema.

Film in India has tended to be both highly visible to the rest of the world yet somehow 'disconnected' from the practices of the international film industry. Famously producing more films for larger audiences than any other film-producing country, India's several film industries have only begun to interact in a formal way with industries elsewhere during the past 20 years. What is true for the film industry in India is also to some extent true for film studies. Although there is an international community of film scholars that includes many scholars in India, there is still a widespread ignorance about Indian cinemas within film studies generally, characterised by misunderstandings surrounding the concept of 'Bollywood'. This has several implications that we need to explore.

Outline history of film in India

Indian cinema developed in a colonial context. A Lumière Brothers *opérateur* showed films in Bombay in 1896 and screenings in Madras and Calcutta soon followed. Indian producers were quick to see the potential of the new entertainment medium and were soon producing short 'topicals' and narrative fictions alongside those made by Europeans. *Raja Harishchandra*, written and directed by Dadasaheb

Phalke, appeared in 1913, running at around 48 minutes, and it has generally been accepted as marking the beginning of the Indian film industry. By the early 1930s cinema was well established as popular entertainment in India with local films gradually beginning to compete with imports, especially as the growing number of cinemas attracted new audiences with an increasing appetite for seeing their own cultures on screen. Sound was gradually introduced during the early 1930s. Bombay Talkies was founded in 1934, joining the existing New Theatres in Calcutta, active from 1931 and making films in Bengali, and the Prabhat Film Company, founded in 1929 and in Pune from 1933 making films in Marathi and Hindi. These three studios produced films with wide circulation through dubbing into other languages and thus India had a form of 'studio system', although Bombay Talkies was the only limited company. Film companies were also established in South India but their films had less opportunity to travel nationwide. However, as Valentina Vitali has pointed out (2006: 262–273), it is misleading to focus too much on the studios as producers in India in the twentieth century. The industry was driven more by strong local demand that encouraged financier-distributors to fund individual productions, using an array of often untraceable investment monies.

'100 Years of Indian Cinema' was celebrated in 2013 with a website produced by the National Film Archive of India at: http://indiancinema100.in.

Because of the flourishing film culture before independence in 1947, the 'colonial legacy' in India was quite different to that in much of British Africa (see Chapter 8). In the post-independence context, the colonial legacy of partition had a profound effect with the relocation of producers in Lahore to Bombay, strengthening Bombay as the main production centre while creating divisions in local language film cultures in Bengal and Punjab. Policies to promote Indian nationalist ideologies were a feature of the new film environment, and economic and social policies that emphasised non-alignment and barriers to entry by Hollywood into the Indian market were established. But tensions began to develop in the new state with Hindi as the national language and popular films from the South began to challenge the domination of the North in terms of politics and culture. Madras (Chennai) eventually became the centre of production for many of the 'regional language' cinemas of India and by 1970 had become the biggest production centre in the country.

For reasons of space – and because the films are not easily accessible – this chapter does not cover the histories of the film industries of Pakistan and Bangladesh (or Burma, which was part of colonial India until 1937).

The roots of a **postcolonialist discourse** are partly to be found in the discussions about Indian cultural life that developed in the post-independence period. Important too was the combination of factors that helped to produce a 'parallel' or 'middle cinema' in India discussed later in this chapter. This development needs to be seen as complementary in some ways to concepts such as **imperfect cinema** and **Third Cinema**. But first we need to sort out the structural properties of the Indian film industries.

See Chapter 8 for discussion of postcolonialism, Third Cinema and imperfect cinema.

Language diversity

India is not the only country with more than one official language, nor the only country with several different language populations of significant size. However, no other country can match the scale of linguistic diversity in the subcontinent. There is no agreement on how many separate languages there might be in India, but it runs into hundreds. Even restricting classifications to languages with a million or more speakers leaves 16 separate languages (http://www.ethnologue.com/country/IN/status). Films have been made in many of these languages, but the best indication of language diversity comes from the Central Board of Film Classification

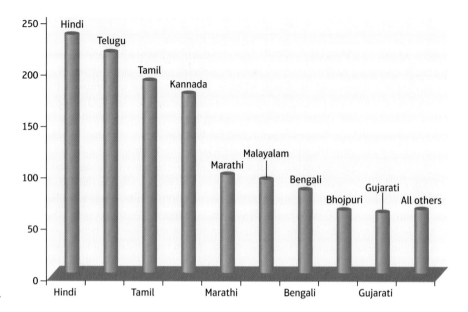

(http://cbfcindia.gov.in/) and its annual statistics on the number of feature films
certificated in each language. In 2009, 1,288 Indian productions in 24 different
languages were given certificates. The breakdown of numbers of films for each major
language is shown in Fig 10.5.

These different language groups (with the exception of Hindi and English which
are classed as 'official languages' of the Union of India) are deemed to be 'regional'.
The term 'regional cinema' is often used to describe Tamil and other language
cinemas. In terms of global cinema this is quite misleading. There are more than 60
million Tamil speakers in India and a **diaspora** population of around 10 million. This
makes Tamil cinema potentially one of the biggest language cinemas in the world
– with a population matching those of the largest European countries and feature
film production of more than 150 titles per year. Reliable audience figures for Tamil
films are not easy to compile, but even if Tamil cinema took only 5 per cent of the
Indian box office there would be 150 million admissions per year, placing Tamil
cinema in the top ten global film markets for audience size. What is true for Tamil
cinema is also true for Telugu (the language of Andhra Pradesh) and slightly less
so for Malayalam (Kerala) and Kannada (Karnataka). In 2009 more than half the
films made in India were made in one of these four South Indian languages. But in
much of the general public commentary (and sometimes academic studies) on Indian
cinema only Bollywood is mentioned. Either Bollywood is taken as a description of
all Indian films or it is assumed that films are only made in Bombay (Mumbai). How
does this happen?

Bengali and Marathi are
both larger language
populations than Tamil.

Hindi cinema

Bollywood is a category in Hindi-language cinema. In some ways, Hindi is an
'artificial' language, created for administration and communication purposes. All
the Indo-Aryan language groups of Northern India and Pakistan draw on the same
language roots (which include Sanskrit, Persian and Arabic). Modern Hindi was

developed from the dialects of the Delhi region. Under the British, English was increasingly used in official discourse and Hindi began to include some English words. After 1947, the Indian government began to standardise Hindi as an official language and it is estimated that 40 per cent of Indians can understand and speak the language. Although the majority of people in Northern India can understand Hindi, in the South it is only the more highly educated who will learn Hindi (i.e. school provision is primarily offered in the language of the state such as Telugu, Tamil, Malayalam, etc.). In Pakistan, the pre-1947 'Hindustani' language has been formalised as Urdu – which differs in written presentation but still shares a spoken vocabulary – so Hindi films are accessible to Urdu speakers in Pakistan and its diaspora.

Cinema, alongside radio and cricket, has been one of the cultural unifiers across the subcontinent. In the 1930s the 'All India' Radio service and the wide distribution of Hindi films contributed to the development of a popular form of Hindi that could be widely understood. This simpler form of language was one of the factors in creating Bollywood. So, what is Bollywood?

Bollywood examined

Bollywood is a Hindi-language film institution producing around 150 films per year. These are entertainment films aiming increasingly for a middle-class Indian audience at home and overseas (the so-called NRI or Non-Resident Indian audience). The term 'Bollywood' ('Bombay/Hollywood') is a relatively recent invention, perhaps growing in usage since the 1990s by which time the old-style 'Hindi popular cinema' had been transformed by the success of larger scale pictures emphasising romance and music alongside comedy and action – and handsome, dashing heroes. Nitin Govil (2007: 85–87) offers a useful discussion of Bollywood's emergence as a 'relatively new culture industry' spread over several different forms of media entertainment, including fashion, music, sports promotion, fast food and soft drink advertising, etc. Bollywood is to some extent comparable with Hollywood in institutional terms. The two institutions have similar features:

NRI officially refers to Indian citizens living abroad, but the term is used loosely in the film industry to refer to the whole diaspora audience, i.e. including those born into Indian families overseas.

- annual production of around 150 films;
- a star system;
- a limited number of large multinational companies dominating distribution;
- relatively high production budgets (i.e. compared to other forms of Indian or American filmmaking);
- an interest in overseas markets;
- an emphasis on institutional promotion via awards ceremonies, etc. and a developed infrastructure for national and international promotion of its products;
- a powerful lobbying function.

Hollywood and Bollywood are successful because they make a limited number of larger budget films (i.e. compared to 'independent' producers). In an Indian context it is important to recognise the following points:

- not all Hindi-language films are Bollywood films;
- Mumbai (Bombay) is the centre of Bollywood production, but Chennai (Madras) makes more Indian films (across a range of language cinemas);

- Mumbai is in Maharashtra state which also houses a Marathi regional language film industry;
- Because Bollywood budgets are higher, it doesn't follow automatically that Bollywood stars are the most popular or best paid (see the example of Rajnikanth above).

Perhaps the most important sense of the distinctiveness of Bollywood is its appeal to a contradictory notion of 'Indian-ness'. The settings for many of the biggest Bollywood successes such as *Kuch, Kuch Hota Hai* (India, 1998) are a kind of upper-middle-class fantasy world but with firm foundations in the concept of an idealised traditional Indian family. In this sense Bollywood seeks to represent 'All-India' without in any way suggesting 'authenticity' in the images it creates. This fantasy is also concretely rooted in the materialism of American **modernity** – so much so that the arrival of MTV in India in 1996 was seen as one of the factors in the emergence of contemporary Bollywood. *Kuch, Kuch Hota Hai* combines a love story, comedy and a family melodrama with settings including college life and work in television for the male lead played by Shahrukh Khan. Karan Johar, the young director (son of producer Yash Johar) brought Western fashion labels and Western pop music into Indian settings and the film became one of the first overseas hits (in the UK Top 10) as well as being very successful at home.

Bollywood and 'Indian popular cinema'

'A rambling tale of personal woe, narrated episodically in unsuitably pretty Technicolor' – the verdict of James Green in the *Observer*, 26 March 1961, on *Mother India* (1957), one of the most widely seen films worldwide (quoted in Thomas 1985).

Naseeb (*Destiny*), directed by Manmohan Desai and starring Amitabh Bachchan, was a major hit film, remade in both Telugu and Tamil versions.

'Indian Cinema: Pleasures and Popularity' (1985) by Rosie Thomas is a key text in introducing what would later become Bollywood to Western film scholars. In this polemical piece, Thomas exposes the condescension and ignorance of Western newspaper reviewers and film commentators. She argues that they use the prism of critical ideas applied to Hollywood and its conventions of narrative, character and realism to denigrate a different popular film culture. She suggests that concepts from Western film studies *can* be useful in raising questions, but only if they recognise the different conventions of Indian popular films. Using *Naseeb*, a popular Hindi film from 1981, as a case study, Thomas suggests a number of key features that define an Indian popular film of the period and which we can use to define the basis for the Bollywood films of the 1990s:

- long films (180 minutes, with a 10-minute interval built into the film's structure);
- interaction with the audience who respond (clap, cheer, join in) to lines of dialogue or songs;
- repeat viewings of popular films – long runs for films in cinemas across India;
- six to 12 song-and dance-sequences – songs by well-known 'playback singers' and soundtrack music released before the film, becoming the mainstay of Indian radio and its music industry;
- song-and-dance sequences not necessarily plot-driven – but can develop other aspects of the narrative (such as the emotional state of the characters);
- stars (*Naseeb* includes a 'roster' of stars in cameo appearances);
- mix of melodrama, musical, comedy, romance and action;
- other categories – 'stunts', 'devotionals', 'social dramas', 'family socials', etc.;
- themes – 'lost' parents and children, male friendships, revenge;
- high levels of emotion communicated to the audience;

- a mixture of social realism and fantasy;
- narratives spanning generations of the same family, links to traditional village stories and the great mythological epics of Indian literature – the *Ramayana* and the *Mahabharata*;
- spectacular locations (since the 1990s often overseas);
- 'borrowings' from other cinemas, especially Hollywood.

These conventions, developed from the 1930s onwards, were important in creating stars and film titles that made Indian films extremely attractive in Africa, the Caribbean, the Middle East, Eastern Europe and Russia (and then China) in the 1950s and 1960s – before the rise of diaspora viewing in the UK. It is important to note the inclusion of the 'social drama' and elements of realism, still evident in the 1980s films. These elements link Hindi cinema to the neo-realist tradition (see Chapter 3) and to the development of melodrama (see Chapter 2). Such links may seem odd but they are important in understanding the appeal of Hindi cinema.

Ravi Vasudevan (1995, 2000) has written extensively about what he terms the 'Bombay social' film. He points out that the nineteenth-century theatrical melodramas from Europe had a significant impact on the development of 'modern' forms of Indian theatre and thus in turn on Indian film drama. In Chapter 2 we discuss the idea that melodrama is a useful form for exploring the social issues faced by families experiencing the change from traditional to modern modes of living. Melodrama offers us the use of coincidence and the stress on good/bad family relations and the sometimes extreme behaviour of family members which stimulate compelling and emotional narratives. In an Indian context three developments are important:

1   The focus on 'social issues' enabled Hindi cinema to be seen as part of a 'National address' soon after independence when this was a crucial aim.
2   The overall success of Hindi cinema in the period 1940 to 1960 enabled India to have a 'national space' for film culture unimpeded by the domination of Hollywood (see Chapter 8 on debates about Third Cinema for the importance of this). But although Hindi cinema did borrow ideas from Hollywood, its interaction with audiences was quite different, as noted above.
3   The social drama elements (as well as the songs and the spectacle) were important attractions for Bombay films in overseas markets in Africa and the Middle East, etc. The social situations in the Indian films and the experience of the transition to modernity were much closer to these audiences than Hollywood fictions.

Vasudevan points out that the Bombay social films (and the 'devotionals') were seen by the studios in the 1930s as more suitable for middle-class audiences – with 'stunts' and 'mythologicals' for the lower class audiences. But by the 1950s producers were beginning to think about a mass audience and the possibility of combining elements.

The industry was boosted in the mid-1970s by the emergence of 'angry young men' like Amitabh Bachchan and the importation of new action styles from Japan, Hong Kong and the 'spaghetti westerns' of Sergio Leone, most famously in *Sholay* (India, 1975) – see Chapter 2. The films that followed still retained social elements but eventually their representation was transformed within the spectacle of the *masala* film.

One of the most popular stars of 'stunt films' in Bombay in the 1930s was Mary Evans, an Australian woman known as 'Fearless Nadia'.

'Devotional films' focus primarily on Hindu religious figures. India has many religions and 'devotional' elements, including music and dance feature in other genre films.

Masala is an Urdu word commonly used to describe a mixture of spices – thus a film mixing genre repertoires. *Masala* films are found in Hindi, Tamil and Telugu cinema.

Research and Explore 10.1

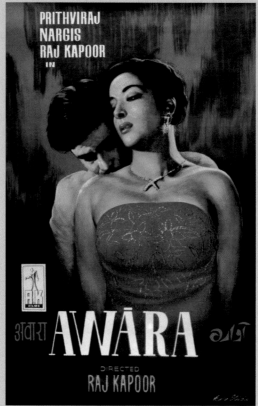

Fig 10.6
A lobby card for *Awaara*. Source: The Kobal Collection/www.picture-desk.com.

To get a full sense of the global impact of popular Hindi cinema, research the career of Raj Kapoor and the international popularity of his film *Awaara* (1951). Dina Iordanova suggests it may be 'the most popular film of all times' (Iordanova and Eleftheriotis 2006).

Changing audiences for Bollywood

Most of the conventional features explored by Thomas in 1985 were still evident in *Kuch, Kuch Hota Hai* in 1998, although now MTV had arrived in India and 'Bollywood' as it was now known had begun to release films in UK and US multiplexes. By the 1990s the regional cinemas were also challenging the 'national' reach of Hindi popular cinema. Some aspects of the original Hindi popular film began to disappear over the next ten years and by 2008, when many Bollywood releases flopped, the central contradiction of appealing to very different audiences via the same idealised stories had begun to fragment the industry.

For poorer cinema-goers the big-budget film showing in a multiplex in a 'metro city' and often shot overseas has started to lose its appeal. For middle-class (see definition below) Indian audiences, Hollywood animations and action pictures are

There are several definitions of 'metropolitan' or metro in India but eight city regions have a population of over five million.

gradually gaining in appeal. At the same time, the more highly educated audience in India is starting to reject popular Bollywood films in favour of more art-orientated cinema from both Hollywood and the international art market – and potentially from independent productions from a range of Indian filmmakers. Although such films are only available in a handful of cinemas in the major cities, television and DVD distribution of international arthouse cinema has been established in India. Meanwhile, the NRI audience appears to be behaving in one of two ways. Some second-generation NRIs brought up in the diaspora communities are attracted to Hollywood releases, while older NRIs may be nostalgic for more traditional stories and resistant to 'new' ideas from India.

The Indian 'middle class'

One of the problems for scholars of global film is that some important concepts from Western sociology are not equally applicable across different film audiences. For instance, in the UK the film industry tends only to use what are in reality quite outdated socio-economic classifications in analysing audiences. The UK audience is now deemed to be primarily 'middle class', as represented by the advertising industry's classification of 'AB/C1' consumers. The UK split in 2009 was AB/C1: 54 per cent and C2/DE 46 per cent. The largest single group is C1 (higher skilled clerical and manual workers).

In India, the definition of middle-class is much more contentious. It ranges from households with just a little more than a subsistence wage up to households with significant spending power. The 'upper-middle class' in India is extremely wealthy by Indian standards and enjoys a lifestyle comparable with the wealthy of Europe and North America. On the other hand, an Indian middle-class family may be so classified simply because it can afford to buy some of the staple goods advertised on television. Taking account of these huge disparities, we may argue that between 200 million and 300 million Indians could usefully be described as 'middle class'. This represents a significant 'new' international market – but it also prompts the question of what kind of approach should the film industry take to the far larger group of poor Indians (800 million or more) who cannot afford a multiplex seat but who still hope to spend a few rupees on a cinema ticket? A 2010 report from the Asian Development Bank suggested that the majority of the new middle class had daily spending power of only $2 to $4 per day and that they were vulnerable to any form of economic downturn.

(http://economictimes.indiatimes.com/news/economy/indicators/Indian-middle-class-booming-but-still-vulnerable-ADB/articleshow/6350893.cms)

One consequence of these socio-economic and demographic changes is that Bollywood is itself becoming less monolithic. There are various forms of 'New Bollywood' or 'New Wave Bollywood' films being made to cater for younger educated audiences and some of the poorer sections of the audience are being drawn away to cheaper seats for productions in Punjabi or Bhojpuri (the language of Bihar and eastern Uttar Pradesh – and also much of the diaspora audience in Mauritius and the Caribbean). These films may be much closer to the experiences of the audience.

Statistics and the Indian film industries

The lack of easily available and reliable data on film in India is a big problem. It is one of the reasons why it is difficult to include discussion of Indian cinema in an international or global context. Instead of data compiled on a regular basis by an official national agency, researchers are reliant on a variety of more partial sources.

Focus is a global film industry survey published by a European Union cultural agency to coincide with the annual Cannes Film Market in May. Its single-page report on India in the 2012 edition published only the Top 10 Hindi language films – presumably this is because its researchers found the Bollywood data to be the most reliable. Yet its sources (such as IBOS Network and the Internet Movie Database) would not usually satisfy professional researchers. Its overall commentary on production, distribution and exhibition drew on sources more likely to be recognised by the international film industry – *Screen International*, *Variety* and *Screen Digest*, and the FCCI (Federation of Chambers of Commerce of India).

Research and Explore 10.2: *What's playing where?*

The diversity of films playing in India is evident from the online cinema listings. The following site offers listings of films in all languages playing in India's major cities:

http://entertainment.oneindia.in/movie_listings

Search by 'City' and by 'Language' and make sure you contrast Mumbai with cities in the South like Chennai, Bangalore, Ernakulam or Hyderabad, and those in the North like Ahmedabad or Delhi, or East, like Kolkata or Bhubaneshwar.

- What do your findings suggest about the popularity and availability of Bollywood vs. Hollywood vs. Other Language films? Check carefully whether Hollywood films are dubbed into other languages.

The corporatisation of Indian media

The lack of reliable data is one of the problems standing in the way of the complete corporatisation of Indian 'filmed entertainment' (film, television, DVD/online, etc.). Up until the 1990s, most of the commercial film production in India was financed on an *ad hoc* basis. Literally hundreds of small producers would borrow money from businesses with spare capital and the accounting practices made any kind of industry data difficult to collect. Rumours about money from illegal trading and falsified reports of cinema takings, etc. were rife. But apart from the relatively small sums of public money invested by the National Film Development Corporation, there were no other sources of finance after the Hindi cinema studio system declined in the 1950s.

The National Film Development Corporation (http://www.nfdcindia.com) was set up in 1975, continuing the work of the Film Finance Corporation set up in 1960.

Things changed in the 1990s when the Indian government moved towards a more market-driven economic policy and deregulated many business practices. The market was reopened to overseas companies wanting to distribute films in India, and film was finally recognised as an 'industry' by the Indian state in 1998. Gradually Indian media companies emerged which were able to develop film entertainment business models along American lines. By 2010 a group of such media conglomerates had established film divisions which, working with smaller production companies (including those owned by some of the major stars such as Sharukh Khan and Aamir Khan), could each distribute a significant number of features theatrically every year. For a more detailed background on these Indian media majors see www.globalfilmstudies.com. Here we note some of the defining characteristics of the ecology of the Indian film business over the past few years.

Most of the new companies have, thus far, decided to focus on the traditional Indian markets (i.e. within India and the 'overseas' group of around 18 territories) and they have done so through the establishment of offices in the UK and North America as well as in the Gulf and sometimes in Southeast Asia. In 2012, the British Film Institute *Statistical Yearbook* listed the following five UK distributors in its Top 10 foreign-language film distributors for 2011 (the five released a total of 42 features with an average of 33 prints for each release):

Eros International
Reliance Big Pictures
UTV
Yash Raj Films
B4U Networks

In addition, Ayngaran (majority owned by Eros) released 17 Tamil films on 10 prints or fewer (there were also other South Asian films released by smaller distributors in the UK in 2011).

The list above looks slightly different in other overseas markets. There is still something of a North/South split in the Indian media environment (partly because of the language difference) but there is a significant shift in the policies of some companies towards investment in all three forms of film production in India (Bollywood, regional, parallel/specialised – see below).

The link to the television industry, both in India and in the diaspora, is increasingly important in the development of filmed entertainment. B4U Networks began as a cable and satellite provider for the UK South Asian diaspora before moving into India and also branching out into film distribution and production. In the case studies below we consider a major film from Sun Networks, the main television provider in South India. Studio 18 (which has previously distributed films in the UK) is one of the companies now in a partnership involving the Hollywood major Viacom and the Indian group Network 18 – facilitating the sale of films to TV channels such as Colors, the Hindi entertainment brand available in the UK and North America as well as in India.

This corporatisation process has provoked frantic buying and selling of companies and movement of personnel in the process known in the international industry as 'consolidation' of the sector. In India this has involved other major players as well. For instance, the big infrastructure issue for film in India is the relatively small number of cinema screens per head of population and the large percentage of run-down single-screen cinemas in smaller towns and cities (i.e. the 'B' and 'C' circuit houses). This has led to interest from new multiplex cinema companies led by PVR which began building cinemas in 1997 in conjunction with Village Roadshow, the Australian company that partnered Warner Bros. for several years. PVR has now moved into production and distribution partnerships.

See also the plans
of Mexican multiplex
operator Cinepolis
in India (www.
cinepolisindia.com) –
and the discussion of
E-cinema in Chapter 12.

The flipside of the 'under-screened' Indian exhibition sector is a weak 'ancillary sector', so that whereas in North America, theatrical distribution only generates around 35 per cent of revenue for the studios, in India it is still around 70 per cent. One company that has seen the opportunities here is Moser Bauer, the 'second largest manufacturer of optical media in the world'. Moser Bauer has launched very low-cost DVDs in many Indian languages in order to drive the ancillary market. Two points to consider here are the very low levels of income of many potential DVD buyers (and would-be cinema-goers) and the high levels of physical and online piracy in India. The Indian filmed entertainment market offers many opportunities – and many pitfalls for both new entrants and established players.

Viacom's partnership with Network 18 is only one of several tie-ups between the new Indian media majors and the Hollywood majors. UTV has developed strong ties with Disney, and Reliance Big Pictures is a major stakeholder in the relaunch of DreamWorks. The other Hollywood majors have also entered the Indian market with Sony and Fox (Star in India) able to work with their own Indian subsidiaries, both important television operators, and Universal investing in NDTV.

Nationalism, sectarianism and 'India Shining'

Before we consider a couple of contemporary mainstream Indian films, we should recognise some of the contentious aspects of the Bollywood films of the late 1990s and into the 2000s which feature NRIs. At one time, Indian characters who travelled overseas were marked as 'corrupted' in some way but after 1991 this began to change and they became admired figures who were part of modernisation. Bollywood came to be identified with what some commentators saw as a dominant North Indian patriarchal Hindu culture which was presented as the national image.

> Ethnic nationalism and pan-Indianism gained currency during the 1990s while the country's economy was being opened up after the first liberalisation measures in 1991, which benefited most the middle classes and the Hindu nationalist Bharatiya Janata Party (BJP). The party's slogan 'India Shining', a paean to urban, yuppie, capitalist growth embodied by the IT sector, symbolised this period.
>
> (Therwath 2010)

This development ties in with the growth of the NRI market in the diaspora and also reflects the benefits of Bollywood's high profile worldwide in terms of Indian 'soft power'. But its corollary at home is opposition from audience groups alienated or excluded by such claims for 'national' status. It is ironic that two films from the 1990s directed by Mani Ratnam that were widely seen as important in debates about national identity/security and about sectarian conflict were in fact Tamil films dubbed into Hindi – *Roja* (India, 1993) and *Bombay* (1995). Some of the 'New Bollywood' films described later in this chapter are reacting against this conception of the 'India Shining' figure.

Case study 10.1: *3 Idiots* (India, 2009 – Hindi)

3 Idiots was claimed as the most successful Indian film at box offices across the world on its initial release. The film's success is related to several important factors that could be seen as associated with a globalising trend in India:

- a star cast headed by Aamir Khan;
- based on a best-selling novel by the leading writer of English language fiction in India, Chetan Bhagat;
- comedy – slapstick/romantic comedy – 'universal' genre repertoires;
- a theme exploring the educational philosophy of élite schools in Asia;
- setting – in a prestigious graduate school with young men competing for their passport to well-paid jobs at home or overseas; spectacular scenery in Shimla.

Plot outline

(There are no spoilers here and you need to watch the film to get the most benefit from this case study.)

Three young men enter a famous graduate engineering school, knowing that if they succeed in their course work and exams they will be first in line for top jobs. Hari comes from a comfortable middle-class background but Raju's parents have struggled to support his education. Rancho gives little away about his wealthy background but he seems the most confident of the three and has a flair for inventions. The school has a charismatic but eccentric head of faculty, Professor Viru Sahastrebuddhe (nicknamed

Fig 10.7
(From left) Madhavan, Aamir Khan and Sharman Joshi in *3 Idiots*. Source: The Kobal Collection/ www.picture-desk.com.

'ViruS'). The trio soon get into his bad books. They also fall out with the 'swot' in the class and Rancho develops a relationship with the ViruS's daughter Pia, a medical student.

The events over the academic course are conventional for a college-based comedy but *3 Idiots* is largely constructed as a flashback to '10 years ago' and the film's coda comprises Hari and Ranju discovering what has happened to Rancho and why his past was so mysterious. There is also a resolution concerning Rancho's relationship with Pia.

Global distribution

3 Idiots conformed to the release pattern of a contemporary major Bollywood film. It is a Hindi-language film with one of Bollywood's A List stars who uses his own quite specific star image to promote his films. He starred in the biggest Bollywood film of 2008, *Ghajini*. Producer Vinod Chopra has a strong track record, and with the Chetan Bhagat connection it isn't surprising that the film was picked up by Reliance Big Pictures for release in India and worldwide.

On its release in Christmas week of 2009 it claimed No. 6 in *Screendaily*'s International Chart and US$15.4 million for the opening weekend (including North America). At the end of its run that figure had risen to more than US$60 million. Compared to Hollywood blockbusters grossing US$400 million or more worldwide, this may not seem a particularly impressive figure. However, given the lower ticket prices in India, the numbers seeing the film were significant. In addition, even a high-profile Bollywood release like *3 Idiots* is distributed initially to only the traditional Indian diaspora territories. Hollywood films regularly reach 50 or more territories. To become truly 'global' in its reach, a film like *3 Idiots* needs a wider distribution.

Hindi films need to be either dubbed or subtitled if they are to reach beyond the Hindi/Urdu-speaking diaspora audience. In the UK and North America/Australasia Indian films are now subtitled in English. But popular audiences who might be expected to enjoy a film like this aren't generally attracted by subtitles. Dubbing between the three main Indian film languages is common and Hollywood films are also dubbed in India. But dubbing Hindi films into languages other than Indian regional languages is not usually feasible on a large scale. Individual titles are dubbed into other languages but there isn't yet the infrastructure for routine dubbing into German, French, Spanish, etc., and therefore one-off projects are relatively expensive. But there is a second problem: those conventions of Bollywood cinema are still 'other' for many audiences. The song-and-dance choreography is possibly over-emphasised as a problem, but coupled with the length of the films (*3 Idiots* is 170 minutes), the usual six or seven song sequences may seem excessive for audiences not used to the format. Indian comedy is sometimes very broad and some of the other aspects of a film like *3 Idiots* can seem strange. For instance, Aamir Khan playing Rancho as a grad student involved in conventional student romances and practical jokes does seem odd when you consider that the actor was aged 44 when the film was released. Khan is a serious filmmaker, an excellent actor and a big star but imagine if *3 Idiots* were a Hollywood film and Rancho was played by an actor of similar stature such as Brad Pitt (born two years before Khan). What would the reaction be in most film territories where Hollywood rather than Bollywood conventions are dominant? Khan also played a student in an earlier major film *Rang De Basanti* (2006) and there is a greater tolerance for such casting in the rather artificial world created in most Bollywood films.

The story elements such as the prestige college for high achievers, cheating in exams, family pressure to do well, etc. are likely to be of interest to audiences across East

Asia as well as Europe and North America, but Bollywood has not yet achieved regular distribution in Japan, South Korea, China, etc. However, *3 Idiots* did eventually secure a release in China and Hindi films are beginning to get releases in South Korea. In Hong Kong, *3 Idiots* grossed US$3 million to finish at No. 14 in the annual chart in 2011.

> Edko Films released it nearly two years after its Indian release, as they were waiting for the film to pass censorship in mainland China. Edko's Audrey Lee says it was *3 Idiots*' humour and subject matter, especially the storyline about the pressures of the education system, that struck a chord with local audiences. It remains difficult to release most Bollywood films in Hong Kong. 'We polished the subtitles to help Hong Kong people understand the references,' explains Lee. 'It catered to a wide audience, professionals, parents and retirees, and it's been a long time since we've seen people in the cinema laugh so frequently.'
>
> (*Screendaily*, 12 August 2012)

On the other hand, the same elements are not necessarily attractive in the poorer districts of India where fantasy action and escapism may play better. Some of these issues are worth considering in a similarly successful film from South India.

3 Idiots was remade by S. Shankar as a Tamil blockbuster titled *Nanban* (*Friend*) in 2012 with Vijay in the Aamir Khan role.

Case study 10.2: *Endhiran (Robot*, India, 2010 – Tamil)

Proclaimed as 'the most expensive Indian film to date', *Endhiran* is the product of a triumvirate of star names in Tamil cinema. Director S. Shankar and composer A.R. Rahman are major names in both Hindi and Tamil cinema (and Rahman has a global reputation). The real star though is Rajnikanth, announced in the credits simply as 'Superstar Rajni'. How successful the film might have been is difficult to judge – primarily because box office figures for Tamil films are not published officially. In addition, it is difficult to assess its global impact because it exists in three separate versions with three different titles. The Tamil title is *Endhiran* (or *Enthiran*), in Hindi it is *Robot* and in Telugu it is *Robo*. Most press reports have suggested that *Endhiran* has outgrossed every other modern Indian film (and carried the biggest production and marketing budget). Some reports suggest that it generated an international box office of Rs61 crores (US$11.8 million) from the Tamil and Telugu prints in the first week.

Indian counting systems use lakhs – 100,000 – and crores – 10 million. 100 Rs = approx US$1.8 (but the rate fluctuates). The new official symbol for the Indian rupee is ₹.

Plot outline
Rajnikanth plays two roles – a scientist who develops an android robot and the robot itself. The scientist wants the robot to become an intelligent weapon for the Indian Army but the military chiefs require him to attempt to teach the robot human emotions. This causes complications – the robot develops a romantic relationship with the scientist's girlfriend. At the same time the robot is reprogrammed by the scientist's unscrupulous boss and turned into a deadly killer (as well as learning how to reproduce itself endlessly). This leads to a major showdown between the robot(s) and their creator.

North and South
Endhiran both helps to explain the difference between Hindi cinema and the industries of the South, and at the same time to show how close they could become. For a non-Indian

'Kollywood' refers to the
Tamil film industry in
the Kodambakkam area
of Chennai. 'Tollywood',
originally referring to
Calcutta's Tollygunge
studios, now also refers
to Telugu cinema.

Remakes of films from
another Indian-language
cinema are very common
in India – across Hindi,
Tamil, Telugu, Malayalam
and Kannada cinemas.

audience *Endhiran* may well be a Bollywood film, especially as in the UK outside London the print on offer is likely to have been dubbed into Hindi and Rajni's co-star is Aishwarya Rai, usually referred to as a Bollywood star (though she comes from the South and has also appeared previously in Tamil films). Although 'regional films' usually have lower budgets, this film was more expensive than any Bollywood feature, much of the budget going on SFX, created in partnership with Hollywood (the Stan Winston Studio) and Hong Kong. Finally, the film is very much a *masala* picture in the mode of both Bollywood and Kollywood – a mix of comedy, romance, action, science fiction, drama, animation and music.

The big difference is the star and his fanbase. Film stars in North India are celebrities, but also élite players who have to some extent lost the devotion of the 'little person'. In the South, Rajni is not just a star, he is a demi-god who at 60 in a wig is believable as an action hero. During the opening days of *Endhiran*'s run in cinemas in Tamil Nadu, newspapers and websites were full of descriptions of fans making offerings to cardboard cutouts of Rajni. Cinemas opened at 4.30 a.m. to accommodate the crowds and tickets changed hands for hundreds of rupees. The maximum set price in Tamil Nadu is 50 rupees for a single screen and 120 for a multiplex cinema (FICCI-KPMG Report 2013).

The film was expected to do well in the South but, to the surprise of many commentators, although it opened more slowly on the Hindi dubbed prints, *Robot* also did well in the North. Perhaps audiences appreciated the more old-fashioned appeal of Rajni. However, this does raise questions about Rajni's appeal outside India. Rajni's fans have strong expectations of their hero – curt dialogue and then violent action. Although his initial appearance in *Endhiran* is restrained, he does perform in the expected way via the antics of the robot. Some of the behaviour of the scientist (towards the robot and towards his girlfriend) could seem oddly churlish and unnecessarily violent to Western audiences.

Various commentators (e.g. Velayutham 2008: 185–186) have noted the success of Rajnikanth's films in Japan where dubbed Japanese prints have run successfully. It is

Fig 10.8
Aishwarya Rai
and Rajnikanth in
Endhiran. Source:
The Kobal Collection/
www.picture-desk.com.

worth pointing out here that there are many Rajni fanclubs in Tamil Nadu, in South India generally and in many parts of the Tamil diaspora. The history of Tamil cinema is closely linked to the state's politics and this has raised questions about how the fanclubs for Tamil stars have influenced political careers. Something similar is found in the history of fanclubs in the Telugu cinema of Andhra Pradesh (see Srinivas 2000).

Endhiran was fully financed by the films arm of Sun Networks, the media major which dominates TV in the South. Its successful launch of *Endhiran* in the international market (in conjunction with Ayngaran) looks like it will raise the stakes for Tamil cinema both domestically and internationally. Even so, for the moment, Tamil cinema will remain 'regional' as far as most international and Bollywood companies are concerned. Perhaps the success of *Endhiran* and other blockbusters will push Tamil production and distribution companies towards a more open business model, more aligned to international practice.

Besides the prolific and fiercely commercial Tamil and Telugu industries there are several other significant language cinemas in India, and the next section considers one such industry which has also been strongly associated with the concept of **parallel cinema**.

Bengali cinema, art and politics

Film is taken very seriously as an art form in West Bengal. It is also a commercial proposition and Bengali films compete with Bollywood in cinemas in West Bengal but that isn't our focus in this section. Every year the state government funds the Kolkata International Film Festival, showing a wide range of films from around the world to an audience boosted by subsidised places for 500 or more local students and filmmakers. Kolkata (Calcutta) played an important part in the development of Indian cinema with the establishment of a studio in the suburb of Tollygunge (thus the term 'Tollywood' is sometimes used for current productions in the city).

Bimal Roy was a prominent Bengali filmmaker who became a leader in Hindi cinema from the late 1940s into the 1960s – when Hindi production had settled decisively in Mumbai (Bombay). Roy was an innovator within a mainstream film industry but a later trio of writer-directors were locally celebrated for making very different kinds of films, largely in Bengali. Satyajit Ray, Ritwik Ghatak and Mrinal Sen pursued, in their very different ways, ambitions to make films as art, political statement and cultural intervention. Bengalis have long believed that Kolkata is the 'cultural capital' of India – the centre of intellectual debate and cultural experimentation – and the continued local support for film culture is an important factor in maintaining the diversity of Indian cinema.

Satyajit Ray (1921–1992) was a middle-class Bengali from a well-known family who had studied fine art before starting work in an advertising agency. He started work on his first film in 1952 and it took three difficult years to complete. He used up his own savings to finance the film, which was eventually completed with the help of some government funding. *Pather Panchali* was based on a 1920s novel about the family of an impoverished priest in rural Bengal. It used a mix of theatre and film actors, non-actors and location shooting, and broke many of the conventions of contemporary Indian filmmaking, with Ray working closely with his novice

One of the most memorable shots of *Pather Panchali* is of the children watching a train travelling across the fields. Trains are very important in Indian film narratives, signalling journeys both functional and metaphorical.

cinematographer Subrata Mitra. There were no song sequences and no attempts to create escapist fantasies. Instead, the film resembled the realist works developed first by Jean Renoir in 1930s France and then by Visconti and Rossellini in Italy during the 1940s (see the discussion of neo-realism in Chapter 3).

Steeped in the traditions of Bengali literature, art and music, and open to European ideas, Ray found himself in a similar situation to the Japanese director Kurosawa Akira (see Chapter 5) whose prize at Venice in 1951 marked the acceptance of some of the major directors of Japanese cinema into international distribution in the emerging art cinema market in Europe and North America. The main difference between Ray and Kurosawa was that the Bengali director had no Indian film industry connections, whereas Kurosawa had come up through the ranks at the major studio, Toho. However, the two directors shared a background that bridged 'East' and 'West', 'national' and 'global'. They would both find themselves successful abroad but sometimes criticised at home – and they became admirers of each other's work.

From 1956 onwards Ray began to win prizes at Cannes, Venice and other major international film festivals – but nothing in India until 1967. These early films were seen by overseas film buyers as exploring the 'humanism' which dominated much of what would later be termed 'World Cinema'. (See Chapter 3 on humanism.) Ray chose to remain an 'artisanal' filmmaker, funded locally for his low-budget films, and he went on to complete a trilogy of films about Apu, the small boy in *Pather Panchali*, which have since become central to the canon of international art cinema. He declined several opportunities to make films in Hindi that would open throughout India because he didn't want to be constrained by the conventions of Hindi cinema. For the next 30 years Satyajit Ray became one of the leading figures of international art cinema – but for a long time he remained unknown in most of India. Before the 1990s success of certain Bollywood films in Europe and North America, most of the art cinema audience in the West would only know about Indian cinema through the Bengali films of Satyajit Ray – films completely at odds with the Hindi mainstream.

In contemporary Indian film culture Ray's work is now properly appreciated, not just in West Bengal but across India. However, it is worth noting:

In 1991 Satyajit Ray became only the second Asian filmmaker (following Kurosawa in 1989) to receive the 'Honorary Award' Oscar for services to cinema.

- the importance of the international audience for his work;
- the role of political support and funding at various stages of his career;
- the decision to stay with the Bengali language for the majority of his films;
- the refusal to include conventional 'entertainment' elements from popular Indian films.

Research and Explore 10.3

Try to watch one of the films from Ray's *Apu Trilogy* and one from his later 1960s or 1970s films with their more marked critiques of contemporary social conditions and their use of modernist devices (e.g. *Days and Nights in the Forest* (1969), *The Adversary* (1970) or *Company Limited* (1971)).

Are the two films very different in their style and overall approach? Why do you think Ray's later films were less successful in the international market?

Fig 10.9
Sharmila Tagore and Barun Chanda at the racetrack in *Company Limited*.

Ritwik Ghatak (1925–1976) was driven by rather different desires – perhaps 'demons' might be a better word. He was motivated by anger about the partition of Bengal in 1947. The British divided the territory of Bengal into a Hindu majority West Bengal and a Muslim majority East Bengal. The latter became first East Pakistan and then, following the war of 1971, the independent state of Bangladesh. Ghatak was born in East Bengal but found himself in Calcutta when partition took place. Partition became like a dream or nightmare that ran through many of his films. Ghatak produced some eight features over the course of 25 years, as well as a number of screenplays, short films, documentaries and uncompleted projects. He also directed and acted in plays, and wrote short stories, plays and two books on cinema. Ghatak's work was political, cultural and art-orientated.

In 1948 Ghatak began work with the Indian People's Theatre Association, a leftist organisation associated with political theatre, and for the next few years theatre was his focus. Later he had a commercial success with the script for the Hindi studio picture *Madhumati* directed by Bimal Roy in 1958 and starring Dilip Kumar. *Madhumati* is one of the 'Golden Greats' of Hindi cinema, but Ghatak's own films as writer-director were unlike anything else in the Indian cinema of the time. The most celebrated of his films comprised a trilogy set within the East Bengal refugee community in India: *The Cloud-Capped Star* (1960), *Komal Gandhar (E-Flat)* (1961) and *Subarnarekha (Golden Line)* (1962). These films use music and theatre, camerawork that is partly realist but also at times strikingly expressionistic, and narrative devices that draw on melodrama traditions, not just from India but from around the world. It may be argued that Ghatak was working as an **exilic**

filmmaker at this time and towards the end of his life he 'returned' to make a film in
Bangladesh, *A River Called Titas* (1973).

Unfortunately, Ghatak's films were not commercial successes in Bengali cinema
and they didn't travel. (They have become celebrated mainly since his death.) In
the mid-1960s he became a teacher at the recently established Film and Television
Institute of India (FTII) in Pune. Here he was able to influence an important group
of young filmmakers from different parts of India, both through direct contact
and through his writings on cinema. The students of this period, including **John
Abraham**, Mani Kaul and Kumar Shahini, were among the leaders of the 'New
Cinema' movement from the end of the 1960s. Today, Ritwik Ghatak is probably
better known by Indian filmmakers than he was during his lifetime.

Mrinal Sen (b. 1923) also left East Bengal for Calcutta and became interested
in the cultural work of socialist and communist groups, but he eventually gained
employment in a commercial Bengali film studio. Sen's career has seen him use his
commercial experience to develop a more consistent career in making political films
that have been central to the development of a **parallel cinema**.

New Indian cinema and parallel cinema

Mrinal Sen's *Bhuvan Shome* and Mani Kaul's *Uski Roti* are often quoted as
signalling the beginning of New Indian cinema in 1969 (Rajadhyaksha and Willemen
1994). The crucial factors here are the establishment of the FTII in Pune and the
emergence of a 'cadre' of young filmmakers trained not just in the traditions of
Indian cinema but also exposed to the modernist ideas and avant-garde forms of the
various New Wave cinemas around the world in the 1960s. Added to this was the
national dimension of the school so that the students met like-minded enthusiasts
from other parts of India on an equal footing (rather than following a familiar
pattern of starting in a regional cinema and then moving to Bombay or Madras).
The national perspective was also evoked by the cultural policies of the Indian
government during the 1960s. As Ashish Rajadhyaksha (1998: 536) notes:

> [T]he adoption of official measures to discipline the film industry into adhering
> to new cultural and ideological priorities […] led to the government entering
> film production.

In concrete terms this meant the establishment of the Film Finance Corporation and
it was the FFC that provided the funding for the up until then unsuccessful filmmaker
Mrinal Sen to make *Bhuvan Shome* on a minimal budget. The film on its national
release proved popular. It seemed fresh with its odd story and short running time – and
its lack of stars. Sen was surprised by its success and thought it was misinterpreted by
audiences, but it boosted his career and proved the worth of FFC financing.

Eventually the FFC's (relatively small) production initiative could be seen as
encouraging three rough trends. Satyajit Ray (who was initially sceptical, but whose
own work was much more diverse and aesthetically enterprising than his reputation
has sometimes suggested) represented 'quality art cinema' more easily accessed by
the international market. Kumar Shahini and Mani Kaul were more avant-garde and
their work typified this second rough trend. The most visible trend emerged in the
shape of what Rajadhyaksha (ibid.) has termed 'state realism'. The most prominent
director in this sense was Shyam Benegal whose film *Ankur* (*The Seedling*) appeared

in 1973. Benegal came out of advertising and he tended to explore Indian stories and social issues in a more conventional story structure (at least initially). He had made many documentaries and taught at the FTII before starting a series of features that were both critical and commercial successes. Benegal was always able to find independent funding via his advertising contacts but he was an important figure in promoting the talents that came out of Pune.

The government initiative that established the FTII and FFC had various other aims. One was to support the development of regional cinema, which in one sense was more likely than the rootless Bombay industry to produce films about the 'real' India. Adoor Gopalakrishnan was a prominent FTII graduate and his film *Rat Trap* (*Elippathayam*, India, 1982) is a good example of an Indian film that won international prizes and helped to expand the Malayalam industry in Kerala. The film tells the story of a landowner's family in which the adult son is lazy and uncomprehending. He fails to run the estate or to help his three sisters find husbands and his world gradually disintegrates. The setting of a rat trap by one of his sisters acts as a metaphor for his failure to engage with the world. Gopalakrishnan was initially funded by a filmmakers' cooperative set up by FTII graduates in Kerala and state governments elsewhere also encouraged local production with investments and tax concessions.

The final piece of the jigsaw for New Cinema was the emergence of a new type of cinema hall in the major cities. These were smaller with better seats designed to attract a niche middle-class audience. A further new form of distribution came with television, initially via the monopoly of the state broadcaster Doordarshan which began national broadcasting in 1982 and featured New Cinema films on Sunday afternoons. Later it also funded films and TV drama series.

Fig 10.10
The metaphor of the *Rat Trap*.

What was established in the 1970s and 1980s was in effect a new form of cinema that was distributed 'parallel' to Hindi cinema and the more populist films of the larger regional industries. Some of these parallel films were also described as '**middle cinema**', literally standing between 'the popular cinema and the élite art cinema'. This description comes from Gokulsing and Dissanyake (2004: 91) quoting Raina (1986) on a type of film 'aimed at that section of the middle class audience who are satisfied with their petty-bourgeois lifestyle and like the comforts of moderately high prosperity'.

The parallel films of the 1970s and 1980s thus covered a wide range of films from art/avant-garde and political to relatively 'middle-brow' – but all were distinguishable from the prevailing popular cinema because they:

- tended not to offer the song-and-dance sequences;
- dealt with social issues in a serious way.

They did have stars, notably Smita Patil (who died aged only 31 in 1986). Shabana Azmi, Naseeruddin Shah and Om Puri are still active today, bridging mainstream, parallel and international productions.

Two significant changes in Indian society during the 1970s also had an impact on parallel cinema. First, the political climate changed with widespread unrest culminating in the State of Emergency enforced by Indira Gandhi in 1975. The desire to make more political films coincided with greater reluctance by the FFC to fund potentially controversial films and a general closing down of opposition voices. The re-emergence of such voices in the early 1980s constituted the final period of New Cinema. Also in the mid-1970s, popular Hindi cinema re-invented itself with action films and the 'angry young man' typified by its new superstar, Amitabh Bachchan, in films like *Deewaar* and *Sholay* (both 1975). The distinction between mainstream and parallel became more pronounced.

In 1975 the FFC became the National Film Development Corporation (NFDC) but, as the 1990s approached and the liberalisation and consequent corporatisation of Bollywood gathered pace, publicly funded films struggled. The NFDC invested in some overseas productions such as Richard Attenborough's *Gandhi* (UK/India, 1982) but by the late 1980s the period of New Cinema was over and the future of parallel cinema was in doubt, despite the continued activity of Shyam Benegal and his erstwhile cameraman-turned-director Govind Nihalani.

Nevertheless, the various government initiatives had established several important infrastructure elements – FTII, NFDC, important international film festivals, television and theatrical distribution, support for Indian films at overseas festivals, specialised film markets (film bazaars), etc. Over the past 20 years, the parallel cinema concept has been kept alive partly because of the emergence of **diaspora filmmakers**, some of whom have returned to India to make films featuring both established parallel stars such as Shabana Azmi and newer 'social activist' stars such as Nandita Das and Rahul Bose.

Indian diaspora filmmakers

The most prominent of these diaspora filmmakers are Deepa Mehta (based in Toronto) and Mira Nair (based in New York). Both were trained in North America after leaving India as new graduates. They bring a different aesthetic approach and a different sensibility to their Indian films. Nair's *Salaam Bombay* (1988), *Monsoon Wedding* (2001) and *The Namesake* (2006) have proved successful as specialised films in Europe and North America as well as in India. Deepa Mehta's trilogy of *Fire* (1995), *Earth* (1998) and *Water* (2006) have proved controversial in their subject matter (lesbianism, sectarian violence during Partition and the treatment of widows in

Diaspora audiences

The South Asian *diaspora* (see the extended discussion of the diaspora concept in Chapter 4) has produced specific populations across the world. Although some earlier trading communities overseas were established before the arrival of the British in India, the two main reasons for migration are both associated with the consequences of colonialism. During the nineteenth century Indian workers were used as indentured labour in British colonies across the tropical world. Indenture was a form of low-waged contract labour that began in the 1830s after the abolition of slavery meant that plantation-owners in Fiji, Natal, Burma, Ceylon, Malaya, British Guiana, Jamaica and Trinidad needed to recruit a new workforce. Indians were lured into long-term contracts often with very poor working and living conditions. Gradually female workers became part of the scheme and other Indians with different kinds of skills were recruited. Settled populations of 'East Indians' became established in the Caribbean and other areas. A young lawyer called Mahatma Gandhi who arrived in South Africa in 1893 eventually helped to end the indentured labour system and to establish rights for Indians who remained in the country when their term of indenture was completed. One estimate puts the diaspora population that resulted from indentured labour in the nineteenth century at 2.5 million (http://www.nationalarchives.gov.uk/pathways/blackhistory/india/forced.htm).

The Making of the Mahatma (directed by Shyam Benegal, India, 1996) covers aspects of Ghandi's life in South Africa.

Other forms of South Asian migration included joining the British Indian Army – which was used in other parts of the British Empire (and continues to be an issue today with the recruitment of Ghurkhas) and also, especially for Sikhs, training as police officers. But the main engine of migration following the 1947 partition has been economic – this time mainly to the UK and Canada initially and then to Europe and the US as well as Australia and New Zealand. More recently the Gulf States have attracted large numbers. The diaspora has now become, for the Indian film industry, the NRI or Non-Resident Indian community. However, the diaspora is as diversified in language, religion and culture as India itself. Although in many areas Hindi and Urdu are the languages that may be used to maintain cultural links with 'home', there are also significant communities of Bengalis, Punjabis and Gujaratis (sometimes resulting from a second migration, e.g. from East Africa in the 1970s). Indian films also interest Pakistani and Bangladeshi diaspora communities. In the Gulf, the main community is Malayalee from Kerala in South India, and in Malaysia and Singapore it is Tamil. The diaspora is also diverse in terms of class structure – a Bengali academic in Boston may have relatively little in common with a Malayalee fisherman working as a labourer in the Gulf.

the 1930s). British Asians who have made films in India include Gurinder Chadha (see Chapter 4) and Asif Kapadia, as well as Shekhar Kapur who left India to make films in the UK, but returned to make *Bandit Queen* in 1994 – like several other diaspora films, part financed by Channel 4 in the UK. The films of diaspora filmmakers tend not to attract big audiences in India, but they attract diaspora audiences.

New Bengali cinema and the parallel legacy

Although the Bengali regional industry is smaller than those in the South, it is still producing interesting filmmakers such as Ritaparno Ghosh and, more recently, Aniruddha Roy Chowdhury, both of whom have made urban dramas in Kolkata that may be described as parallel (and which feature several well-known parallel stars). Perhaps the major name, however, is **Aparna Sen**. Sen is in many ways instrumental in creating a kind of dynasty of Bengali parallel filmmaking. She herself appeared as a teenager in Satyajit Ray's *Three Daughters* (1961) and had roles in later Ray films, as well as many others in Bengali cinema (over 50 in total). She is the daughter of the critic Chindananda Das Gupta and her own daughter, Konkona Sen Sharma, is a leading player in her mother's films and in Bollywood. Aparna Sen has completed nine features, one of which is discussed here.

Case study 10.3: *15 Park Avenue* (India, 2006 – English)

'15 Park Avenue' is an address in Kolkata – but does it really exist or is it just a figment of the disturbed mind of Meethi, a young woman suffering from schizophrenia? The film's cast comprises many actors who became well known in Ray's art films or other parallel cinema films.

Story outline
Meethi (Konkona Sen Sharma) is the younger sister of Physics Professor Anjali (Anu – Shabana Azmi), who is divorced and now shares her home with Meethi and their elderly mother (played by the great Hindi cinema star Waheeda Rehman). With only a maid to help, Anu struggles to keep up with a demanding job as well as looking after Meethi and Mother. After another crisis, Anu discusses Meethi's case with a new consultant, and through a series of flashbacks we learn about Meethi's genetic 'propensity' for schizophrenia and depression and the shocking experience that triggered the onset of a chronic illness. Part of the story involves a fiancée (Rahul Bose), who broke off the engagement when Meethi became ill. An important sub-plot covers Anu's long-term relationship with Sanjeev (Kanwaljeet Singh) and how it is affected by the appearance of the new consultant Dr Kunal Barua (Dhritiman Chatterjee).

Commentary
This is a challenging film with an 'open ending'. Its themes (the professional careers of women with responsibilities for the care of the elderly and the mentally ill, the causes of the illness, etc.) are important for middle-class Indians. But the experience of watching the film couldn't be more different than watching most of mainstream cinema.

Once in a while comes along a movie which promises nothing that an average cinemagoer looks for on silver screen. Obviously, such movies are not meant for

Fig 10.11
Konkona Sen Sharma is
Meethi in *15 Park Avenue*.

entertainment, but they leave you numb as they show a reality which only a few directors can transport on the screen. In this context, *15 Park Avenue* needs no introduction other than its director's name.

(*Hindustan Times* review, January 2006)

Some reviewers found the English dialogue stilted but Sen explained that she didn't think she could fund the film in Bengali. Presumably she believed that it would stand more chance internationally in English. She did however allow a Hindi dubbed version to go out on 15 prints. The film was shot on digital video for SPS Telefilms, a local Kolkata company making material for Zee TV, and its audience will have been mostly via TV and DVD.

Aparna Sen's next
film *The Japanese
Wife* (2010) involved
a pen-pal relationship
between a Bengali man
and a Japanese woman
exploring a different kind
of global relationship
compared to the NRI
films of Bollywood.

'New Bollywood'?

Films like *15 Park Avenue* and those of other directors working in regional and parallel cinema have had an impact on commercial Hindi cinema. There are many examples of what might be called New Bollywood with films in more distinct non-musical genres, less concentration on star roles and more use of parallel cinema actors. Some writers and directors have come from completely outside the film industry. Others have moved from regional cinemas to Mumbai.

A good example of the new style of scriptwriter is Jaideep Sahni, who first started work with Ram Gopal Varma, an innovator in the gangster genre, and has since had hits with *Chak De India!* (2007) and *Rocket Singh – Salesman of the Year* (2009). Sahni trained as an engineer and came to films late.

In nearly all the movies he has scripted, there's a strong inclination towards showcasing middle-class and small-town India. And even *Rocket Singh* tells the extraordinary tale of an ordinary salesman. 'I just bring characters to life which people can relate to and don't think of them as people from outer space,' he says.

(Aabhas Sharma, 21 November 2009, www.business-standard.com/india/
news/a-writers-tale/377088/)

In each of his films, Sahni has found a genuine social issue/phenomenon which affects the new breed of middle-class Indian. These are not the traditional Bollywood super-rich, but 'ordinary people' who have been to college or held down a skilled job. 'Rocket Singh' sells computers, but with a seemingly naive integrity with which he overturns corruption. *Chak De India!* showcases women's hockey featuring superstar Sharukh Khan in a restrained role as a coach with something to prove in his attempt to take the team to an international competition final. In *Khosla Ka Ghosla!* (2006), the central character is a minor civil servant who is about to retire to build his dream home on a new plot of land on the edge of Delhi. When he is swindled out of his property, his family rally round to get it back in a social comedy that would have echoes throughout the world if it was considered as an international art film.

None of Sahni's scripts countenance standard Bollywood song-and-dance choreography (although there is music – much as there is in Hollywood). They all feature well-known character actors and sometimes stars (Ranbir Kapoor in *Rocket Singh*). The films do not do massive box office business but at the same time they are not as expensive as the Bollywood blockbusters that are prone to fail disastrously at the box office.

Case study 10.4: Anurag Kashyap and 'independent' Indian films

The release of *Gangs of Wasseypur* in India in 2012 was a calculated move by an unusual filmmaker in partnership with an Indian media major backed by a major Hollywood studio. The press pack for the two-part 320-minute film announces a new initiative by Viacom 18 Motion Pictures called '**Tipping Point**'. This is focused on the 'execution of clutter-breaking concepts'.

'Tipping Point' is a reference to the concept popularised by Malcolm Gladwell in his 2000 book of that title. The implication is that films under this banner represent the start of a significant new trend in Indian film culture.

The independent filmmaker whose work is one of the main elements of 'Tipping Point' is **Anurag Kashyap** and his company AKFPL. In May 2012, Kashyap took both *Gangs* and a second film, *Peddlers*, directed by Vasan Bala, to Cannes. Kashyap is an unusual figure as writer, director, producer and actor, and he has worked his way into a position where he is invited to take his films into the international festival arena as well as into mainstream Indian distribution, revealing his industry nous and grasp of international cinema.

Anurag Kashyap is extremely prolific in terms of writing, direction and producer roles. In 2013 he took more films to Cannes as producer or director. See IMDb to get a sense of his whole output.

Kashyap decided to become a filmmaker after university – yet another director inspired by *Bicycle Thieves* (see Chapter 3) seen at a Delhi film festival in 1993 (*Indian Express*, 14 June 2008). The interest in neo-realism is evident in different ways in most of his films. His first script for *Satya* (India, 1998), a crime film by Ram Gopal Varma, won an award and box office rewards, but his first directorial venture *Paanch* (India, 2003) still remains unreleased in India having been refused certification by the CBFC. The film is loosely based on serial killings in Pune. Kashyap's breakthrough came in 2007 with three films he directed being released in the same year. *Black Friday* (made in 2004) was the film about the Mumbai bombings of 1993 that prompted Danny Boyle to review Kashyap's work in his preparation for *Slumdog Millionaire*. In 2011 Kashyap co-produced Michael Winterbottom's English-language *Trishna* (UK/Sweden, 2011) – set partly in Mumbai – and also appeared in the film as a Mumbai filmmaker with his wife Kalki Koechlin as a celebrity figure.

The year 2007 also saw the release of *No Smoking*, one of the most surprising Bollywood films for many years. A box office flop and a critical failure, *No Smoking* has

Fig 10.12
Kalki Koechlin is *That Girl With Yellow Boots*.

since begun to develop something of a cult status after festival screenings. Loosely based on a Stephen King short story, 'Quitters Inc.', *No Smoking* also has the feel of a Philip K. Dick story in Kashyap's hands. The central character is 'K' (possibly a reference to Franz Kafka's *The Trial*?), a wealthy businessman who chain-smokes and who is persuaded to visit a 'guru' who is guaranteed to stop him smoking. But the guru's methods involve severe and terrifying penalties for any relapse and K's life becomes a nightmare. The film's narrative is 'fractured', and shifts so often between 'reality' and dreams/nightmares that audiences lose any sense of a coherent story. Various interpretations have been offered. Is smoking a metaphor for something else, such as filmmaking?

In 2009 *Dev.D* represented Kashyap's re-working of the *Devdas* story (see Chapter 2) and in 2010 *That Girl With Yellow Boots* was widely praised for its realist portrayal of Mumbai. Kalki Koechlin plays a young Englishwoman searching for her Indian father who disappeared when she was an infant. To earn money during her search she works in a Mumbai massage parlour.

Gangs of Wasseypur is perhaps the film that will get to the biggest international audience as well as being a successful mainstream film in India. It offers a gangster saga set over several decades from the early 1940s to the 'recent past' in the mining region of Jharkhand in Northeastern India. Inevitably the film has been compared to the gangster epics of Coppola and Leone, with a focus on two warring Muslim families and the Sikh family that controls the local industries. But this is a mainstream film that made a profit in Indian cinemas, and it retains some of the familiar elements listed on pages 270–1:

- it is very long (two parts each of nearly 160 minutes) – but without an intermission in the separate films;
- there are many references to Hindi films, including a scene in a cinema screening an Amitabh Bachchan *masala* film;
- there are 14 songs with two diegetic song sequences – other non-diegetic songs sometimes 'comment' on the action;
- violent action is mixed with some comedy and family melodrama;
- familiar themes include revenge and male friendship;
- narrative links three generations – from village to city – and some reviews mention the *Mahabharata*;

'Diegetic' means 'in the fictional world of the film' – in this case two songs are performed by characters in the scene. 'Non-diegetic' means the song is heard over the images with no obvious music source in the scene depicted.

- 'borrowings' from **gangster films** from Hollywood and other cinemas.

This list suggests that the film is close to the Hindi cinema/Bollywood tradition. However, for Indian popular audiences it is still 'strange' because of three factors:

1   The film does not have recognisable Bollywood stars (though the lead actors may be well known and one actor has arguably become a star partly on the basis of this film).
2   The locations are filmed in a realist mode (matched by the acting style) and there is no sense of escapist fantasy.
3   The whole scenario is 'wrong' – there isn't a clear sense of 'hero' or 'villain' or a predictable narrative line with a satisfying resolution.

For these reasons the film may alienate the 'all-India' popular audience – even though it pleases critics, younger metro audiences with knowledge of international cinema, older audiences with knowledge of parallel cinema, etc.

Research and Explore 10.4: *A 'New Bollywood' film?*

Select *one* of the following films:

- *Mumbai Meri Jaan (Mumbai, My Life*, India, 2008 – Hindi)
- *A Wednesday* (India, 2008 – Hindi)
- *That Girl With Yellow Boots* (India, 2010 – English, Hindi, Marathi, Kannada)
- *Delhi Belly* (India, 2011 – English, Hindi)
- *Kai po che* (India, 2013– Hindi)

Research the background of your chosen title and try to watch the film. It should be available on DVD or online.

Apply the list of bullet points above as in *Gangs of Wasseypur*. Check whatever reviews of the film that you can find through internet searches. Make sure you know how a range of critics/bloggers in India received the film. Is your conclusion that the film is significantly 'different' from mainstream Bollywood?

If you were offered the opportunity to release the film in your own country as a 'specialised title' with subtitles, how would you set about selling it to cinema audiences? What kinds of problems would you anticipate?

Summary

In this chapter we have tried to emphasise the diversity of filmmaking and film culture in India. We have traced the development of Hindi cinema from the 1980s through to the present when Bollywood is being challenged in a number of ways. We have also considered the popular films of so-called 'regional cinema' and explored 'parallel films' in a variety of forms. This is by no means all of Indian cinema – powerful documentaries (see the reference to Anand Patwardhan in Chapter 8) and animated films are also important, and the true sense of diversity is not fully accessible because apart from Hindi, Bengali and Tamil films, most of the other Indian-language cinemas are not distributed internationally on DVD.

This chapter has also introduced the corporatisation of Indian cinema. Uneven though this is, it is beginning to change Indian film industries and potentially make them more 'open' to globalisation and forms of exchange. It is important to read the section in Chapter 12 on E-cinema in order to gain a sense of how it is not inevitable that Indian cinema will become increasingly open to Hollywood imports. Equally, global film is unlikely to remain unaffected by developments in the Indian film industries and Indian film culture. Film in India is now over a century old as an indigenous industry with the prospect of future growth based on the world's biggest established film market in terms of regular cinema-goers.

References and further reading

Gokulsing, K. Moti and Dissanyake, Wimal (2004) *Indian Popular Cinema: A Narrative of Cultural Change* (2nd rev. edn), Stoke on Trent: Trentham Books.

Govil, Nitin (2007) 'Bollywood and the Frictions of Global Mobility', in Daya Kishan Thussu (ed.) *Media on the Move*, New York and Abingdon: Routledge.

Iordanova, Dina and Eleftheriotis, Dimitris (2006) 'Indian Cinema Abroad', *South Asian Popular Culture* 4(2): 79–82.

Mukhopadhyay, Dipankar (1995/2009) *Mrinal Sen: Sixty Years in Search of Cinema*, Noida, UP: Harper Collins.

Raina, M.L. (1986) '"I'm Alright Jack" – Packaged Pleasures of the Middle Cinema', *Journal of Popular Culture* 20(2): 131–141.

Rajadhyaksha, Ashish (1998) 'Indian Cinema', in John Hill and Pam Church Gibson (eds) *The Oxford Guide to Film Studies*, Oxford: Oxford University Press.

Rajadhyaksha, Ashish and Willemen, Paul (1994) *Encyclopedia of Indian Cinema*, London: BFI; New Delhi: Oxford University Press.

Robinson, Andrew (2004) *Satyajit Ray: The Inner Eye*, London: I.B. Tauris.

Srinivas, S.V. (2000) 'Devotion and Defiance in Fan Activity', in Vasudevan (op. cit.).

Therwath, Ingrid (2010) ' "Shining Indians": Diaspora and Exemplarity in Bollywood', *South Asia Multidisciplinary Academic Journal* [Online] 4. Available at http://samaj.revues.org/3000.

Thomas, Rosie (1985) 'Indian Cinema: Pleasures and Popularity', *Screen* 26(3–4): 116–131.

Vasudevan, Ravi S. (1995) 'Addressing the Spectator of a "Third World" National Cinema: The Bombay Social Film of the 1940s and 1950s', *Screen* 36(4): 305–324.

Vasudevan, Ravi S. (2000) 'Shifting Codes, Dissolving Identities: The Hindi Social Film of the 1950s as Popular Culture', in Vasudevan (ed.) *Making Meaning in Indian Cinema*, New Delhi: Oxford University Press.

Velayutham, Selvaraj (ed.) (2008) *Tamil Cinema*, New York and Abingdon: Routledge.

Vitali, Valentina (2006) 'Not a Biography of the "Indian Cinema": Historiography and the Question of National Cinema in India', in Valentina Vitali and Paul Willemen (eds) *Theorising National Cinema*, London: BFI.

http://www.youtube.com/user/DoordarshanNational (Search for 'Portrait of a Director' and 'The Story of New Theatres').

Further viewing

Recommendations are restricted by the skewing of Indian films in international distribution being mainly Hindi releases (or dubbed into Hindi). The titles discussed in this chapter give some indication of the availability of Tamil and Bengali titles, as well as examples of 'parallel' or recent 'independent' titles.

The major Indian filmmaker who is mentioned in this chapter but whose films have not been discussed in detail is Mani Ratnam. Several of his earlier films are available from Bollywood distributors in poor transfers dubbed into Hindi. His later titles made in Hindi are easily available. The Ayngaran online shop (eshop.ayngaran.com) lists some of his more recent Tamil films, including *Kannathil Muthamittal* (*A Peck on the Cheek*, 2002), a family melodrama set against the Civil War in Sri Lanka.

Ratnam has also on two occasions shot the same script with different casting for Tamil and Hindi versions; for example, *Yuva* (Hindi, 2004) and *Ayitha Ezhuthu* (Tamil, 2004) opened at the same time in India and offer the opportunity to compare Hindi and Tamil popular cinema. Both films feature a star-studded cast in a film which mixes political thriller, romance and action.

Chinese cinemas

As this book was being written, more than five new cinema screens were opening in China every day. China was adding new cinemas and screens equivalent in number to the total exhibition sector of a medium-sized European country every year. As Kevin Tierney (1983: 115), a British visitor, put it in a discussion about his experience of going to the cinema in China: 'In China, numbers are numbing.'

If we view China from the perspective of someone in the international film business, it must indeed feel that way. The population of China is four times the size of the US but relatively few Chinese currently visit a cinema at all. If the average Chinese person were to develop the modern cinema habit to the extent that they managed two visits per year (half the American frequency of cinema-going), China would become the biggest cinema market (or at least share that title with India). Since current Chinese audiences have shown themselves to be attracted to the limited number of Hollywood blockbusters included in the agreed annual quota of foreign

In the 1980s 70 million people were claimed to be watching films each day in China.

Screen International now refers to its correspondent in 'Greater China'.

imports by the Chinese authorities, it is no wonder that Hollywood is interested in how all those new screens are being used. Most operations in the mainland Chinese film world have to go through the state-controlled China Film Group, including film imports and distribution deals. The State Administration of Radio, Film, and Television (SARFT) is the supervisory body that proscribes certain kinds of films and can prevent the export of mainland films.

It is also tempting to think about how a thriving local market in China could sustain a large-scale film industry that could successfully export films and compete with Hollywood in global markets. However, throughout this book we have argued against this kind of simple binarism. The history of film in China is very different from that of Hollywood and in some ways it is unique. We need to understand why this is so and how those differences may still be important in the future.

In *Chinese National Cinema* (2004) Yingjin Zhang is careful to warn us of the difficulty in even defining what 'Chinese cinema' may be. For nearly 50 years after 1949 there were three separate Chinese film industries in Taiwan, Hong Kong and the People's Republic of China (PRC) on the mainland. Add to this the 'overseas Chinese' communities in Southeast Asia with separate small-scale productions in Singapore and Malaysia (and with a history of importing films from Shanghai going back to the 1930s), as well as individual Chinese diaspora filmmakers in Europe, North America and elsewhere, and the complexity of Chinese film culture becomes even more pronounced. Most Chinese films are now made in Mandarin or Cantonese (and sometimes dubbed into the other language), but other Chinese languages are also used (and films in English are also produced). This in itself is not that unusual, but the institutional differences prompted by very different political systems in each of the Chinese language territories have produced a set of distinctive modes of production. State control over the film industry in the PRC (and also of Taiwan up until 1987) contrasted with commercial freedom in Hong Kong explains only part of the story. We cannot hope to explore the whole variety of Chinese film cultures, but we will try to focus on some key features.

Chinese cinemas viewed from outside China

China has been a major producer, and films in Chinese languages have circulated in the international film market for 50 years. In the 1960s and 1970s most of the globally available Chinese films were relatively low-budget titles from Hong Kong that found ready markets in Southeast Asia. Over the next 30 years these exported films, mostly action films and comedies, were distributed widely in South Asia, the Middle East and Africa. They reached Europe and North America mainly via screenings for diaspora audiences and then through Hollywood's cooption of Hong Kong star Bruce Lee. Films from Taiwan and the PRC began to appear in the 1980s at international film festivals as art films, but it wasn't until the success of *Crouching Tiger, Hidden Dragon* in 2000 and *Hero* in 2003/2004 in the multiplexes of North America and Europe that a slightly different perception of Chinese cinema developed outside of East Asia. Even so, Chinese cinema is still associated (for the mainstream audience) almost completely with 'martial arts' films (contemporary or historical) and the associated popular genre of crime thrillers. What's missing in the international profile is a sense of the broad comedy, the music (traditional and pop) and the variations on melodrama modes that characterise much of the history of popular film in Chinese film culture.

Fig 11.1
Fists of Fury (The Big Boss/Tang shan da xiong, Hong Kong, 1971) was the first of Bruce Lee's Hong Kong films to achieve success in the US. Source: The Kobal Collection/www. picture-desk.com.

The other aspect of Chinese cinema that skews the perception of audiences outside the PRC is the understanding that the Chinese state maintains a controlling position in the film industry. Official policy towards the film industry has changed over time and certainly since the emergence of private investors, but mainstream films still need the censor's approval and the distribution of films is controlled. The outcome of these various developments is that contemporary Chinese filmmakers are faced with a variety of 'models' for Chinese film productions. Dai Jinhua (2009) analyses a number of these, including what she calls the 'Zhang (Yimou)' model of the transnational blockbuster, contrasting it with more domestic models of both blockbuster and lower budget 'independent' production (both also exportable in certain circumstances). These models also relate to what Dai describes as the 'political main theme' film. Yingjin Zhang (2010) helpfully cuts through this complexity and suggests that students might study the 'global' action adventure film (e.g. by Jackie Chan or John Woo) with a 'national' (i.e. for a mainstream Chinese audience) crowd-pleaser from Feng Xiaogang and an independent film about the 'marginal' China from Jia Zhangke. We will explore some of these directors' films in this chapter.

In the next section we will select some specific periods of Chinese production, mainly after 1949, and consider some case studies of directors and stars that will offer ways into debates. The scale and complexity of Chinese film means that this will be a different kind of chapter to others in the book but we will try to make links to other chapters where possible. We will focus on case studies of directors, not necessarily because they are great auteurs but because, as the comments above indicate, they represent different models for film production (and their films tend to be available in most countries).

Early history of cinema in China

Cinema appeared in China during the colonial period when Shanghai was an important 'international city' of the late nineteenth century with concessions held by the major Western powers. Although the new film culture did not penetrate far into the Chinese interior, in Shanghai (and, to a lesser extent, Beijing and other cities) by the 1930s a sophisticated industry had developed, with many production companies/ studios competing for an urban audience. Shanghai film culture boasted stars and film journalism and, though on a relatively small scale, this has been referred to as a 'Golden Age' of Chinese cinema. More than half the films screened were American and these attracted Western residents of Shanghai and wealthier Chinese. The approaching war with Japan and its later transmutation into a civil war meant that until the early 1950s film production became difficult to organise on a national basis. Many of the filmmakers from Shanghai moved to Hong Kong during the 1940s and another movement – of the supporters of the Kuomintang – to Taiwan in the late 1940s led to the development of three different film industries with some common features but different local conditions.

China had become a republic in 1912 but the new government was unable to control local warlords. The Kuomintang or Nationalists were the main political party, eventually gaining control in the 1920s.

Fig 11.2
One of the early stars of Shanghai cinema was Ruan Ling-yu, seen here in *The Peach Girl*, 1931. Later she would be played in a biopic by Maggie Cheung Man-yuk (see Fig 11.12). Source: The Kobal Collection/ www.picture-desk.com.

Cinema in the People's Republic of China (PRC)

In the newly formed People's Republic of China established in 1949, film production was swiftly nationalised and the Communist Party leadership attempted to build a socialist cinema. By 1953 this had become formalised, drawing to some extent on the model of Soviet Cinema after 1930 and the concept of **socialist realism**. Over the next 30 years relatively small numbers of films were produced but they were shown to vast audiences, both in conventional cinemas and in huge factory halls and other communal buildings served by projection teams. Yingjin Zhang (2004: 192) quotes annual attendance at film screenings in the PRC rising from 47 million in 1949 to 1.7 billion in 1957 and a maximum of 27.9 billion in 1979. These numbers were maintained in the early 1980s when there were as many as 180,000 'exhibition outlets' – a small proportion of which were actual cinemas, the majority being organised by projection teams. This massive growth in audiences is partially explained by the work of projection teams in rural areas where cinema had previously been unknown. In major cities full-time commercial cinemas ran alongside workplace cinemas with two or three screenings a week – all the screenings being very well attended.

Screening films 'in the community' outside the conventional cinema circuit has been a common practice in many countries at various times. Usually, attendances at such events are not recorded in industry figures, but the situation in China from the 1960s to the 1980s was unique in scale and importance.

Fig 11.3
A village projectionist in a 1966 poster 'Down with imperialism!' Source: International Institute of Social History, The Netherlands.

The Chinese Communist Party (CCP) faced a range of problems in the early 1950s. Not least were the economic problems in a large country with a very high population – how to feed the population adequately and how to encourage economic growth with little industrial infrastructure after more than 30 years of war. But control of the economy was only possible once complete political control had been achieved and that was in turn dependent to some extent on the CCP developing a cultural **hegemony** within China. Although some Chinese intellectuals supported the communist leadership, there was also a perception that many university academics, teachers, scientists, engineers, journalists, artists and writers were part of an élite that associated with the bourgeoisie who had survived the disruptions of the civil war. During the 1950s, the CCP leadership switched between policies encouraging these cultural workers and 'experts' to support the revolution (e.g. through the Hundred Flowers Movement of 1956) and then turning against the same groups as part of the Anti-Rightist Campaign in 1957. It was in this context that socialist realism, imported from the Soviet Union, became part of cultural policy.

Socialist realism

It is important not to confuse this term with the more widely applicable **social realism** (see Chapter 2) that could be used to describe some of the leftist films from Shanghai in the late 1940s. **Socialist realism** refers to the officially approved mode of filmmaking in the Soviet Union introduced under Stalin in the early 1930s to unambiguously support and promote the aims of Soviet communism. This required a focus on working-class characters as the protagonists of stories that were allegories for the advancement of labour under communism.

Often seen in the West as romanticising working-class life, socialist realist films tended to draw their villains (class enemies, landlords, etc.) very broadly and to present heroes as almost monumental (sometimes through low-angle shots of 'noble' working men and women). The films were intended to be easily accessible by mass audiences. One of the reasons why these films have been traduced in the US and elsewhere is perhaps because they reversed the ideological basis of classical Hollywood, validating personal sacrifice for the collective public good rather than the American Dream which suggests that every individual can become successful on his or her own terms. In fact, the socialist realist films employed many of the same Hollywood conventions. Both Hollywood and socialist realism drew upon the narrative structures and characterisation of nineteenth-century realist novels, and Hollywood directors such as John Ford (in a film like *The Grapes of Wrath*, 1940) were consciously used as models by certain Chinese directors (see Case study 11.1 on Xie Jin below).

Zhang (2004: 202) sees socialist realism as an attempt by the state to resolve early problems associated with the takeover of private studios in Shanghai and the encouragement of a 'socialist film culture'. Shanghai studios had been divided during the 1930s and 1940s between those supporting the Nationalists and those supporting the Communists. The 'rightist' filmmakers had mostly left the country but the leftists' conception of a socialist film did not necessarily fit that of the new PRC's leaders.

Building on tradition

We don't have space here to discuss the wide range of filmmaking styles in China up until 1949, but we need to pick out some general points. Chinese storytelling culture is perhaps the oldest and most developed in human history and, as we might expect, there was a wealth of literature and performance works for early filmmakers to draw upon. Chinese opera, whether developed around the Imperial court as Beijing opera or in local popular forms away from the centre, was one source. Popular literature included the 'Four Great Classical Novels' – historical romances with political intrigue and action adventures.

In the 1930s and 1940s, Shanghai filmmakers drew on a similar range of material as in Europe and Hollywood. They used forms of **melodrama** (see Chapter 2) as their main mode or style but also explored realism. Melodrama tends to enable major roles for women, and Chinese cinema in the 1930s produced female stars in roles that have been described as 'suffering women' such as those played by Ruan Ling-yu (see also the comments at the end of this chapter). Zhang (2004: 104) refers to the didacticism of 'political melodramas' and the sense of leading audiences through difficult social problems in the late 1940s. This would be emphasised, and simplified, as part of the move towards socialist realism in the nationalised industry after 1949 and then emphatically 'reduced' to the core message in the few films allowed into production during the Cultural Revolution.

Several Chinese films have been based on stories from *The Romance of the Three Kingdoms* written in the fourteenth century. John Woo's two-part *The Red Cliff* (China, 2008/2009) was a big commercial success in East Asia.

Research and Explore 11.1

Explore the website associated with the documentary film *Morning Sun* (US, 2003) at http://www.morningsun.org. The extensive website offers examples of all kinds of Chinese media materials relating to the background to the Cultural Revolution, including film clips, songs and posters.

- What sense of Chinese society in the 1950s and 1960s do you get from these materials?
- What do you think was the impact of the revolutionary operas and massive public demonstrations on ordinary Chinese citizens?
- How do they compare to the similar media events created within contemporary Western consumer culture?

From the mid-1960s up until the late 1970s film production was severely curtailed by the impact of the Cultural Revolution and its aftermath, and during this period Chinese film culture was effectively 'closed' to the outside world.

The Great Proletarian Cultural Revolution (1966–1976) was the major policy initiative with which the CCP under Mao Zedong attempted to resolve the problem of confirming cultural hegemony. It was to be a sustained attack on the experts and cultural élites both within the party and more broadly in Chinese society. Schools and universities were particularly hard hit with arrests of professors and teachers and official encouragement of students to challenge their teachers and what was taught. The revolution quickly veered out of control, with estimates of deaths from suicides, street violence and forced labour of half a million or more. (This followed the deaths of millions from starvation and economic catastrophe in the failed 'Great Leap Forward' of 1959.) Hundreds of thousands of cultural workers of all kinds were sent to the countryside with their families and expected to work in the factories and fields. This included all youths deemed to have been born into bourgeois families. Social disruption occurred on a massive scale and the experiences of the next ten years would become central to the lives of a significant part of the Chinese population – as well as the basis for many film narratives in the following 40 years.

The Chinese film industry was particularly affected with writers, musicians and artists among those exiled to the countryside. Film production was severely restricted and the few films that were sanctioned by the leadership were mainly based on the eight officially approved 'revolutionary model operas' as designated by Jiang Qing, wife of Chairman Mao. The four best known of these were *The Red Lantern, Taking Tiger Mountain by Strategies, Red Detachment of Women* and *White-Haired Girl*. Since these were the only entertainments available in China at the time, the songs from the operas became extremely popular. Foreign imports were also severely restricted. Mao died in 1976 and the Gang of Four leaders (including Jiang Qing) were ousted soon afterwards.

Fig 11.4
Red Detachment of Women, a 'Model Opera' ballet image from the coverage of US President Nixon's visit to China in 1972. Films at this point were modelled on theatre productions like this. Source: John Dominis/Time & Life Pictures/ Getty Images.

The Chinese film industry began to return to a semblance of 'normality' in the late 1970s but the actual number of films produced in the PRC was still relatively small, the maximum reaching 151 in 1986. These figures were not exceeded until the relatively 'free' internal market in the 2000s. Film imports, mostly from other communist countries, made up around one-third of the films screened. Tierney (1983: 116) reports that Roman Polanski's 1979 Franco-British production of *Tess* was a big hit in China. This isn't perhaps that surprising. Thomas Hardy's original novel tells the story of a woman's rebellion in an agrarian setting. Tierney also comments on the absence of American films, suggesting that Hollywood producers were not prepared to accept the trade deals offered by Chinese officials.

The emergence of the Fifth Generation filmmakers

Chinese cinema, because of the social and cultural upheavals outlined above, has come to be categorised to a certain extent by the recognition of different generations of filmmakers (i.e. filmmakers who share the same 'lived experiences' of Chinese social and cultural life and who start their careers at roughly the same time). This description has become problematic because it first began to circulate outside China in the late 1980s with the export of a specific group of films. It then became entangled with ideas about a **New Wave** in China. We will explore the concept carefully.

For many film audiences outside China the first real sense of what a PRC Chinese film might be like (i.e. as distinct from a Hong Kong film) came with the release on to the international arthouse circuit of the first films by the new group of filmmakers who had been the first to graduate from Beijing Film School when it reopened after closure during the Cultural Revolution. The film that introduced this group to international audiences via screenings in Hong Kong in 1985 was *Yellow Earth* (China, 1984) directed by Chen Kaige and photographed by Zhang Yimou. Zhang later became a director himself (see below). The third director to get exposure outside China was Tian Zhuangzhuang, with *The Horse Thief* (China, 1986). Several other directors, writers and cinematographers from the same group made films in China that didn't get the same kind of international circulation.

This Fifth Generation did in some ways represent a 'New Wave' in Chinese filmmaking and that is certainly how distributors, festival programmers and critics received the new films in the West. But this was less because the films were similar in style, genre or content and more because the filmmakers shared a context and a set of constraints:

- they had all experienced the Cultural Revolution as adolescents, having being sent to the countryside;
- in film school they had been exposed to a wide range of filmmaking approaches from around the world;
- they began work mainly in the more remote state-owned studios, far away from the influence of Beijing, and thus gained more leeway in choosing subjects to work on.

The subject matter of the Fifth Generation films varied greatly, but often it was more related to the kind of character study rich in artistic detail familiar from international arthouse films than the more mainstream genres of traditional Chinese cinema. The approach was certainly not restricted by socialist realist dogma. *Yellow Earth* sends a young People's Liberation Army soldier to live with a peasant family in a remote part of Yunan province during the Civil War. His aim is to research the local language and customs and to find folk songs which will help the communists work more effectively with the local people. *The Horse Thief* is a Tibetan bandit whose crimes bring shame upon his community. Films like this were not likely to attract popular audiences seeking entertainment and they were subject to often arbitrary bans and censorship within China. They were not widely seen. During the 1980s, melodramas and martial arts films formed the bulk of mainstream releases in China. However, Zhang Yimou's *Red Sorghum* (China, 1987), adapted from a popular novel by Mo Yan, did reach a much wider audience. As well as the profile created by the novel and its setting (the war against the Japanese in the 1930s) Zhang's film also introduced Gong Li who would go on to appear in several further films by the director and to become a star both in China and on the international art circuit.

One of the consequences of the international success of the Fifth Generation films was that isolated examples of films by earlier Third and Fourth Generation directors also began to appear outside China. These older directors had spent their working lives attempting to second-guess the changes in cultural policies that affected the film industry. They emerged from the period of the Cultural Revolution and returned to making films not unlike those they had made in the 1950s and 1960s. The most celebrated of these directors was Xie Jin (1923–2008) who produced important and popular films in the early 1980s, some of which were seen outside China. *Hibiscus Town* (China, 1986) was a melodrama that provided a contrast to the films of Chen Kaige for Western audiences.

Xie is described in some academic studies as a Third or Fourth Generation director. Although the terms are not generally used we might argue that the 'First Generation' worked in the early Shanghai cinema in the 1920s and the second in the 1930s. The Third and Fourth Generations would then be associated with the 1940s, 1950s and 1960s, though how the two 'generations' are distinguished is not clear. We will explore the differences between Xie and Zhang Yimou in detail below. One thing that should be clear is that the older filmmakers carried on working when the new generations appeared, so Xie and Zhang were still working in the 1990s when a Sixth Generation was being hailed (see below).

Case study 11.1: Xie Jin (1923–2008)

We will use Xie's career to explore some of the issues in PRC cinema between 1949 and 1989. His sixth film, *Woman Basketball Player No. 5* (1957), was his first big popular success. Although suitably didactic in its tale about a basketball team that would eventually represent China overseas, the film also features a romance melodrama. The older male coach of the team identifies one of the young female players as a future star. She turns out to be the daughter of the woman who the coach loved and lost in Shanghai before 1949. But aside from the romance narrative, there is also the story of how the young women become a team – which can travel abroad and represent China with pride.

Outside China, *Two Stage Sisters* (1965) is the best known of Xie's films. The film was ready for release as the Cultural Revolution was about to begin but after criticism during production and post-production it was held back and not seen by the public in China until 1979. Soon after, it was made available for export and highly praised in the West. Zhang (2004: 216) quotes Gina Marchetti's observation that Xie manages to combine four distinct influences into a coherent style:

1 Soviet socialist realism.
2 Hollywood classicism.
3 Shanghai drama.
4 Indigenous Chinese opera forms.

Fig 11.5
The closing sequence of
Two Stage Sisters shows
the two women together
again on tour in the first
few months of the PRC
in 1949.

The story involves a travelling opera group in the 1930s. After one performance a young
woman fleeing persecution pleads to join the troupe and she is welcomed by the
daughter of the troupe's leader. The young women become firm friends but in Shanghai
during the 1940s they become separated in the politically divided city – one marries
a wealthy theatre owner and the other is drawn into socialist theatre. After one of the
women is attacked, a climactic courtroom scene sees the pair reunited and in 1949 they
return to tour a revolutionary play, *The White-Haired Girl*.

Unable to work during the Cultural Revolution Xie returned in the late 1970s to make
films as he had done earlier. *The Legend of Tianyun Mountain* (1981) is a good example of
how Xie was able to tell a human story in the form of a political melodrama and to please
a mass audience. The story is similar to *Two Stage Sisters* but it is contemporary, looking
back via flashbacks to the late 1950s when two young women are part of a development
team in a remote region. One of the women falls in love with a geologist but is then
re-posted elsewhere. In her absence the man is accused of being a rightist and ostracised
by the community. The woman ends up marrying her local political leader. After suffering
herself during the Cultural Revolution and then regaining her political authority, she
learns that her former lover now lives a frugal life with her old friend who has become a
village schoolteacher. She vows to find the couple and reinstate them but is held back by
her jealous husband.

The Legend of Tianyun Mountain is an old-fashioned film for the 1980s but this and
Xie's other later films were hugely popular with audiences, if not with younger film critics.
As well as pleasing audiences with romance and melodrama Xie was able to negotiate
the changes in the 'main theme' of the contemporary politics of China. It is interesting to
compare his approach with that of Zhang Yimou.

Case study 11.2: Zhang Yimou (b. 1951)

Arguably the best-known Chinese director outside China, especially after his direction of the opening ceremony for the Beijing Olympic Games, Zhang Yimou is a filmmaker who has been prolific in completing a wide range of films, from relatively low-budget popular and 'social' films to sumptuous arthouse and extravagant epics. Outside China he was first praised as a rebel but later written off as a conservative apologist. The response inside China has sometimes been different to that outside the country and it is tempting to conclude that Zhang does more or less what he wants, whatever the likely outcome.

Zhang was born into what was seen as a Nationalist or rightist family. Consequently, during the Cultural Revolution he was forced to work in the countryside as a young man before entering the reopened Beijing Film Academy from where he graduated in 1982. Appearing first as an actor in *Old Well* (China, 1982) he then worked as cinematographer for his classmate Chen Kaige on *Yellow Earth* and *The Big Parade* (China, 1986) before completing his own first feature *Red Sorghum* (China, 1987). Since then Zhang has completed 18 further features as well as other works, including opera productions. His international profile has been built around the reception of such contrasting films as the historical melodrama *Raise the Red Lantern* (1991) and the spectacular *wuxia* epics, *Hero* and *House of Flying Daggers*. Less well-known titles, sometimes only available on DVD in the West, include comedy-dramas (*Happy Times*, 2000 and *A Woman, a Gun and a Noodle Shop*, 2009) or realist dramas such as *Not One Less* (1999) or *Riding Alone for Thousands of Miles* (2005).

The early Zhang films were introduced at international film festivals and became arthouse hits on the international circuit, winning prizes and attracting significant audiences. Apart from *Red Sorghum*, Zhang's films did not immediately reach large audiences in China. Part of the problem was the attitude of the Chinese authorities in valuing the prestige the films won abroad but also finding them too potentially 'subversive' for a home audience.

Wu xia or *wuxia* combines 'martial' with 'chivalry' and describes a broad genre/category of martial arts action narratives set in historical China.

Fig 11.6
Gong Li (centre) plays Songlian, the 'fourth mistress' of the household in *Raise the Red Lantern*, standing outside her quarters here with her maid Yan'er (Kong Lin) as the 'red lantern' is placed before her door.

The decisions of the state-controlled film industry in China had an impact on the ways in which Zhang's films were viewed abroad, especially in the US. Overseas reviewers who were drawn to films 'banned' in China were equally prepared to condemn Zhang if his films seemed to support the government line in some way. Zhang has always shown a talent for display and for attracting audiences. An example of this was his presentation of a young Gong Li in the central role for his first seven films. Later an equally young Zhang Ziyi featured in three films. Zhang Yimou was praised for his use of colour and set design but also attacked for **self-orientalising**. Feminist film scholars differed in their responses to the early films featuring Gong Li. We will consider one title in more detail.

Raise the Red Lantern (Taiwan/Hong Kong/China, 1991) is an early example of a co-production across the 'Three Chinas' before the Hong Kong handover and it was exec-produced by Hou Hsiao-hsien from Taiwan (see below). Based on a novel, it is set in the 1920s with Gong Li playing a young woman forced to become the fourth wife/concubine of a rich man. She finds herself battling against the other three wives to build and protect her own position in the very traditional household. Red was the dominant colour of Zhang's first three films. The 'red lantern' of the title is lit and hung over the door of whichever wife has been chosen for the rich man's bed that evening.

Zhang avoided direct political discourse by choosing a historical subject from before the foundation of the PRC; but this didn't prevent critics and academics from interpreting the film in terms of metaphor. Verina Glaessner (1992) suggests that the patriarchal power of the rich man is a metaphor for the Communist leadership at the time of the Tiananmen Square protests in 1989. She sees the colour red as less about passion and more about status. The people in the traditional household find their lives subsumed by the unchanging traditions of the house and the rich man himself, who likes things to be 'bright and formal', as representing the dead hand of socialist realism in the face of the sophisticated visual sense of the Fifth Generation.

Meanwhile, Andrew Grossman (2002) and Mary Farquhar (2002) disagree about Zhang's treatment of the women played by Gong Li in the three 'red' films (*Red Sorghum*, *Ju Dou* (1990) and *Red Lantern*). Grossman, like several other critics, sees the Gong Li character in terms of Zhang's self-orientalism – constructing the image of the woman for the Western orientalist gaze – and the discourse of the 'suffering woman' in Chinese culture. Farquhar sees the trilogy as Zhang's 'masterpiece':

Ju Dou is set in a dye works and vibrant colours (including red) are integral to its *mise en scène*.

> Its visual power rests on female sexuality as onscreen spectacle.
>   Its narrative power rests on reworking the early 20th century debate on Chinese patriarchy, liberation and modernity. [...] Old men personify a system that never relinquishes power. Freedom only comes from real or symbolic patricide that is carried out by the son but instigated by female desire. Women have agency.
>
> (Farquhar 2002)

Mary Farquhar's 'Senses of Cinema' entry includes a range of resources and critical texts on Zhang's early career. A detailed narrative analysis of Zhang's *Hero* (China/Hong Kong, 2002) may be found at www.globalfilmstudies.com.

The Sixth Generation

The next major group of Chinese filmmakers to graduate from film schools was inevitably dubbed the Sixth Generation when they began to produce films from the late 1990s onwards. Several of the individuals concerned rejected the description but it has stuck to a certain extent and has become a useful shorthand term to describe the considerable differences in approach adopted by the younger group in contrast to the Fifth Generation. Partly this is because the context of production in China had changed significantly by the late 1990s:

- The new generation were born around the time of the Cultural Revolution and as such carried no memories of the events as adults – although some had childhood memories of a disrupted family life.
- When they came to make films they discovered a new ecology of Chinese media with openings (and potential investors) in television and the music industry.
- The cinema audience had largely disappeared during the 1990s, partly because of piracy, and traditional studios were not funding new kinds of films – but deals with overseas producers were possible.
- New technologies such as digital video allowed access to filming without official approval.

Fig 11.7
Much as in *Bicycle Thieves* (see Chapter 3), a young man from the country is distraught when his bicycle, which he needs for his job, is stolen and he searches for it in *Beijing Bicycle* (*Shiqi sui de dan che*, France/Taiwan/China, 2001), directed by Wang Xiaoshuai, one of the 'Sixth Generation'.

Some of the important figures in this new generation are Jia Zhangke (b. 1970) who features in our case studies, Wang Xiaoshuai (b. 1966), Zhang Yuan (b. 1963) and Lou Ye (b. 1965). Since the emergence of this group, the use of the 'generation' tag seems to have been dropped in discussion of more recent entrants into the Chinese industry. To some extent the films of this group of filmmakers were produced and distributed in an almost underground way – Jia's early films circulating as pirate DVDs. Sixth Generation films began to appear in the PRC at the time when Hong Kong filmmakers were increasingly looking at what the 'return' to China after 1997 might mean.

Hong Kong cinema: Chinese cinema as commercial cinema

Film production in Hong Kong, then a British colony, did not begin in a significant way until 1930 and it was 1935 before Cantonese sound films began to be produced. At that point most of the local audience was Cantonese speaking but the industry links were to Shanghai (Mandarin or local Shanghainese dialect). The brief flurry of local production was then ended by the Japanese invasion in December 1941. When production began again in 1946 it was influenced by the various migrations between China and Hong Kong that occurred between 1937 and 1949 as people moved after the Japanese invasion and again after the establishment of the PRC.

Popular cinema in Hong Kong has at different times been dominated by Cantonese- or Mandarin-language films. Subtitling and dubbing have allowed a form of mixed language economy. Cantonese was widely spoken among the Chinese diaspora in Europe and the Americas as well as in Southeast Asia, but now the Mandarin-speaking diaspora is growing. This is a function of Chinese migration patterns but it has been important in the circulation of Hong Kong films in the international market.

Hong Kong's status as a British colonial possession up until the handover to the PRC in 1997 had an impact on the Hong Kong film industry in several ways. In industrial and commercial terms it placed the colony in an important position regarding international trade and Anglo-American business investment as well as helping relations with other Southeast Asian countries and also India and Japan. Hong Kong's film industry has always been strictly commercial in operation. In the 1960s the arrival of the Shaw Brothers and Cathay from Singapore began a period of Mandarin production with an increase in exports to Taiwan (see the sections on Taiwan and Malaysia and Singapore below). As first Cathay declined and then Shaw Brothers began to turn to television (TVB) in the 1970s, new players emerged. Raymond Chow and Leonard Ho had been executives at Shaw Brothers and in 1970 they set up Golden Harvest, an operation that involved a more open structure with opportunities for independent producers and an approach to Western markets. Bruce Lee and – at the start of the 1980s – Jackie Chan allowed the company to build a strong presence overseas. Two other studios with similar models, Cinema City and D & B Films, helped to sustain what has been seen as the peak period of Hong Kong studio production from 1980 through to 1995 (see Leung 2008: 71–73).

For 15 years, Hong Kong was a genuine competitor in the international film industry, exporting films, mostly action and comedy, and growing a strong local film culture that saw cinemas (mostly owned by the same three studio interests) filled with audiences eager for domestic product. A territory of only five million people produced 150 films per year and in 1992 the Top 10 films of the year in Hong Kong were all local productions. Leung points out that this was a relatively low-budget industry making 'homogeneous' films which were not seen as market-specific (and which in Hong Kong terms were apolitical) – export business was so strong that pre-sales of new titles in major export markets such as Taiwan sometimes covered the cost of production.

This industrial system developed under very specific local conditions. The ease of production based on local funding and export sales meant that directors and stars were constantly in work, honing their skills, but at the same time production standards could be sloppy without proper preparation of scripts. Films became more formula-based and producers copied ideas from their most successful competitors.

The bubble was bound to burst at some point and Leung argues that the expansion in the number of screens in multiplex cinemas at the end of the 1980s created the opportunity for Hollywood product to gain more exposure. This became increasingly important in conjunction with other factors during the 1990s.

Hong Kong producers, like those in Mainland China and Taiwan – and indeed around the whole region – lost income through the rise of video/VCD viewing and the rapid spread of piracy. More low-budget films were made on digital video and distributed on video. Theatrical admissions began to fall, and those that remained increasingly wanted the special effects and spectacular action offered by Hollywood. The economic crisis across the 'tiger economies' of Southeast Asia in 1997 was another blow and when other local industries such as South Korea began to recover strongly around 1999, it was at the expense of Hong Kong.

The handover of Hong Kong

Hong Kong was officially 'returned' to China on 1 July 1997 but the handover planning was based on the Sino-British Declaration of 1984. Hong Kong residents had no direct say in the negotiations. The UK government then changed the status of Hong Kong residents in 1986. The most visible effects of the process (i.e. including the years of preparation and the aftermath of the change in status) were changes to migration patterns and uncertainty as to what the change would mean. Some critics have argued that Hong Kong films of the 1990s use metaphor and allegory to express anxiety about what might happen (e.g. in a film like Fruit Chan's *Made in Hong Kong* (Hong Kong, 1997)). One of the enduring themes of the work of Hong Kong auteur Wong Kar-wai is a discourse about migration and a sense of nostalgia (e.g. in films like *Days of Being Wild* (Hong Kong, 1990) and *In the Mood For Love* (Hong Kong, 2000)).

The decline of the 1980s Hong Kong industry model was marked by a reduction in the number of production starts and a shift to much more expensive local blockbusters which could compete with Hollywood titles. Leung's 2008 paper picks out the *Infernal Affairs* trilogy (Hong Kong, 2002/2003) and *Kung Fu Hustle* (China/Hong Kong, 2004). Both titles reprise successful Hong Kong genres, the crime film for *Infernal Affairs* and the kung fu comedy for *Kung Fu Hustle*. Both also feature major Hong Kong stars with international appeal – Andy Lau and Tony Leung in *Infernal Affairs* and writer-director Stephen Chow in *Kung Fu Hustle* – as well as a host of Hong Kong character actors and local stars. Both films were big local box office hits but *Kung Fu Hustle* was also a major international hit, making US$92 million outside Hong Kong, recapturing all the former Hong Kong export markets in East Asia as well as in North America and Europe. However, the film was a co-production by the Chinese major Huayi Brothers and the state-owned studios in China. This leads us into a consideration of the new Hong Kong–Chinese relationship in film production (see below). First, though, we will give a little more insight into the 'separate development' of Hong Kong cinema and a case study of one successful Hong Kong director.

Case study 11.3: Ann Hui: from the Hong Kong New Wave to mainland productions

Perhaps the leading female director in Chinese cinema, Ann Hui was born to Chinese-Japanese parents in Manchuria in 1947 but moved to Hong Kong aged 5. After completing a Masters degree in Hong Kong, she spent two years at the London International Film School and on her return to Hong Kong worked for the TV company TVB in the late 1970s. She became part of the **New Wave** in Hong Kong cinema at the end of the 1970s alongside Allen Fong, Tsui Hark, Patrick Tam, Yim Ho and Alex Cheung (Teo 1998: 553).

Hong Kong thus had its own 'new' cinema in the early 1980s, roughly at the same time as the Fifth Generation in China and the Taiwanese New Cinema. In Hong Kong the changes brought about by filmmakers with experience overseas and a willingness to experiment included the following:

- a move towards Cantonese popular cinema;
- more focus on the realities of Hong Kong daily life;
- three new studios to replace the older Mandarin studios;
- the introduction of techniques and technologies from Europe and Hollywood;
- the development of new popular stars through a close relationship with Cantonese language television and pop music.

As in other New Waves, the films made by this group were diverse in style and thematic content. Tsui Hark became well known as a director and producer who was a major innovator in terms of commercial genres. Allen Fong trained as a journalist and then switched to filmmaking and worked for the government broadcaster RTHK on documentaries before producing the semi-autobiographical social realist *Father and Son* (Hong Kong, 1981). Ann Hui has moved between commercial genre pictures and more specialised films throughout her career. Early critical successes included her loose trilogy of films about Vietnamese refugees which began with a documentary for RTHK and then two features, *The Story of Woo Viet* (1981) and *Boat People* (1982). In the small-scale but intense production environment of Hong Kong's film and TV industry in the 1980s it is notable that future international stars Chow Yun-fat and Andy Lau appeared in these two films (one in each). Hui herself had been an assistant director for King Hu (see the Taiwanese section of this chapter below) and one of her assistants was Stanley Kwan, who later became a director.

Hui tended to focus on character-driven stories during the 1990s but her output also featured action, crime, romance and comedy with major stars as well as further documentary work. Three of her more recent films bring together these different elements of her career in co-productions – all of which feature central performances for female stars.

Goddess of Mercy (Hong Kong/China, 2003) is a romance thriller with a complex narrative involving a woman who works as an undercover police officer for a drugs squad. She discovers that her relationships with three different men each challenge her emotional responses and her sense of justice and duty. The story, based on a novel, is set in mainland China and stars Vicki Zhao, one of the four young women recognised as major stars of Chinese film, TV and music early in the twenty-first century. Playing opposite her is Hong Kong star Nicholas Tse. In the action episodes of the narrative Vicki Zhao's character recalls the action roles of Hong Kong stars, including Brigitte Lin and Michelle Yeoh.

The London Film School (as it is now called) is, unlike many similar schools, truly 'international' in its recruitment and therefore not seen as creating 'British filmmakers' as such (see http://www.lfs.org.uk).

The close ties of film, TV and pop music are a feature across East Asian cinemas generally. Andy Lau is an example of a major Hong Kong film star with a long career as a Cantopop idol starting in the 1980s. Mandopop (Mandarin) and later K-pop (South Korea) have similar **synergy** with film and television.

Postmodern Life of My Aunt (Hong Kong/China, 2006) is an unusual film that explores several different facets of contemporary Chinese film culture. The title itself is intriguing, promising to comment in some way on the 'new China'. The story concerns a middle-aged woman, Ye Rutang (played by mainland actress Siqin Gaowa) who lives alone in an apartment in an old part of Shanghai (which in the late 1990s was often described as the ultimate postmodern city of skyscrapers in concrete and glass – a city that seemed like a hybrid of its international past in the 1930s and its equally international future as the face of modern China). As the title implies, she has a young nephew whose arrival on a short holiday at the beginning of the narrative introduces us to the daily life of a woman who is seemingly 'out of place' in the modern world. She is an educated woman with a clear sense of personal morality but Shanghai is a 'fast' city and even her own nephew tries to trick her.

Later in the narrative, Rutang meets the charming Zhichang singing opera in the park. Played with a real sense of mischief by the star of Hong Kong action cinema, Chow Yun-fat, Zhichang is a conman who cruelly attempts to steal Rutang's heart and relieve her of her savings. In the final part of the narrative, Rutang has an accident that brings her estranged daughter (Vicki Zhao again) to Shanghai from Northeast China – where Rutang eventually goes to see if she should return to her working-class husband. The appearance of her family suggests that Rutang was an educated young woman who was sent to the Northeast during the Cultural Revolution and that she entered into an unfortunate marriage before returning to Shanghai.

This brief description describes a film that is in itself a hybrid of comedy and drama – an uncomfortable mixture that speaks more of an attempt to reach an arthouse audience than a popular audience. This uncertain genre classification is compounded by having the popular Chow Yun-fat play against type. The title may refer to this generic hybridity or to the representation of Shanghai and the uncomfortable position in which the aunt finds herself. In one telling episode, Rutang is not accepted as a teacher of English on the

Fig 11.8
Chow Yun-fat, often considered an 'action hero', plays a charming conman in *Postmodern Life of My Aunt*.

grounds that the English she speaks (very well) is British English rather than American English. This may be read in a number of ways. British English may be seen as an unfortunate reminder of colonial Hong Kong/pre-communist China. Alternatively it may be simply that American English is seen as 'modern' – either way it seems like a form of continued repression of the pre-Cultural Revolution intellectual tradition.

The Postmodern Life of My Aunt won several prizes in China and Hong Kong but also baffled some audiences – perhaps because of the promotional material that seemed to promise a more straightforward comedy or because of misconceptions about a film co-starring Chow Yun-fat. Perhaps the film is best seen as a 'personal film'. The Northeastern city to which the aunt returns is also the city that Ann Hui left as a child and the character is roughly the director's age. Comments in some Western reviews suggest that the film is 'too Chinese' to travel. It is worth noting, however, that the score for the film is by Japanese composer Joe Hisaishi and the cinematography is shared by Hui's earlier collaborator Kwan Pung Leung and her 'next' collaborator Yu Lik Wai, the regular cinematographer for Jia Zhangke, suggesting that it has the credentials for a pan-Asian release.

A Simple Life (Tao Jie, Hong Kong, 2011)

Yu Lik Wai is also responsible for photographing this carefully judged melodrama about a middle-class, middle-aged man in Hong Kong who finds himself responsible for the care of his old *amah* Ah Tao – the family servant who acted as his nanny when he was a child and has been his housekeeper ever since – now that the rest of the family has emigrated to the US. Roger (Andy Lau) is a film production accountant travelling between the mainland and his Hong Kong base and after she has had a stroke Ah Tao (Deanie Ip) asks to move into a care home. Roger organises everything and visits regularly. Ann Hui uses her documentary experience to represent a carefully selected district of Hong Kong and the daily life of the care home. Andy Lau gives a restrained performance and the star is Deanie Ip, a veteran of 1980s Hong Kong cinema and a major Cantopop star. The film also features three of Ann Hui's colleagues from the 1980s, Tsui Hark, Stanley Kwan and Sammo Hung in cameo appearances.

A Simple Life won major prizes across Asia and in European film festivals, becoming one of the most honoured Asian films of recent years. Although as an art film its audience has not been as large as those for Chinese blockbusters, it was a significant hit in Hong Kong and also attracted audiences on the mainland. Its success with critics is important in changing the perception of Chinese films in international distribution with a realist drama/melodrama rather than a spectacular *wuxia* or 'self-orientalising' costume melodrama.

Cinema in Taiwan

When Edison's kinetoscope was first demonstrated in Taiwan in 1896 it was a Japanese merchant who organised the event (Zhang 2004: 114). The island had been ceded to Japan by China after the First Sino-Japanese War a year earlier. For the next 50 years the island was a colony of Imperial Japan. When film production began it was dominated by Japanese companies. Japanese settlement meant that audiences too were majority Japanese and hundreds of Japanese films were imported each year. Although some Taiwanese production was possible it was not until 1945 that full control of a local industry making films in Mandarin or local Taiwanese languages was possible. To a certain extent, the Taiwanese situation was similar to that in the Japanese puppet state of Manchuko (Manchuria) after 1931 when a Japanese industry was set up (see Chapter 5).

Production in Taiwan did not however take off properly until ten years later. In the meantime Taiwanese audiences, deprived of Japanese films at first, turned to Hollywood and European productions and to old features from Shanghai. The Kuomintang (KMT) government set up in Taipei in 1949 and then banned the import of films from the mainland and any Hong Kong productions associated with PRC sympathisers. At various times the ban on Japanese film imports was lifted and the imports were again successful. Hong Kong producers found ways around their ban and Taiwan found itself importing films from its smaller neighbour as well as Hollywood and Japan.

The KMT sanctioned a number of anti-communist features but the popular audience turned towards Taiwanese-dialect films which began to be produced on a large scale. It was not until the 1960s that Mandarin production in Taiwan evolved a new cycle of popular genre films, based on Hong Kong models, that was able to get past the scrutiny of KMT censors. In the late 1960s and early 1970s this finally saw the emergence of successful films for export to Asian markets (since box office revenues from Taiwanese audiences alone could not sustain production budgets). King Hu's *Dragon Gate Inn* (1967) and *A Touch of Zen* (1970) were hugely popular *wuxia*. *A Touch of Zen* was shown at the Cannes Film Festival in 1975. But despite these successes Taiwanese audiences increasingly turned to Hong Kong and Hollywood.

When the KMT leader Chiang Kai-shek died in 1975 and the US set up diplomatic relations with China in 1979, something clearly had to change in terms of KMT attitudes towards film. The mood among artists and elements of the local audience was for more focus on Taiwanese 'national' issues. Taiwan was set up to experience a form of 'New Cinema' in a similar way to both the PRC and Hong Kong. Taiwanese New Cinema (TNC) is defined strictly by Chen Kuan-Hsing (1998: 557) as an 'alternative cinematic movement' which started with *In Our Time* (Taiwan, 1982), a film co-directed by four of a new generation of filmmakers, including Edward Yang who would go on to become an internationally known director over the next 20 years. Chen dates the conclusion of this movement as 1986 when *All for Tomorrow*, a film produced to promote a military school, was completed by two TNC directors. How could a film financed within the state system be deemed alternative? One of the two directors of this film was Hou Hsiao-hsien, now considered a key figure in TNC alongside Yang. We will use Hou as a focus to explore more about this 'New Wave'.

Case study 11.4: Hou Hsiao-hsien (b. 1947)

Hou was born in Guangdong in Southeast China but his family moved to Taiwan when he was still an infant. Unlike Edward Yang and Ang Lee, Hou did not have experience of living and working in the US. Instead, after graduating from the Taiwan School of Arts, he gradually worked his way up through the local film industry and was an experienced assistant director and screenwriter by the late 1970s.

The striking innovation of the TNC was the break away from the traditional genres and what the KMT policy had promoted as 'healthy realism' (i.e. stories that did not delve into the social and political realities of life in Taiwan). TNC films did deal with these subjects and Hou at first tended towards investigating rural life in Taiwan, mainly by looking back at the (relatively recent) past. Bingham (2003) suggests that Hou was asking: 'What does it really mean to be a modern Taiwanese?' With limited budgets and a desire to represent 'real lives', TNC turned to approaches to filmmaking such as location shooting, use of non-actors, etc. – the kinds of techniques used in **social realism**, **neo-realism**, etc. Hou adopted certain techniques that have stayed with him for over 30 years. He has said that he began to use long takes and long shot sizes in order to keep his distance from non-professional actors. This has remained a feature of his work, even though he now uses both film stars and other 'performers'.

Hou has not been 'political' as such and during the TNC period film production was still dependent on state funding via the Central Motion Picture Corporation. The KMT also provided the framework for a new film journal and a film festival to promote Taiwanese film culture. Hou's aim was to explore Taiwanese social history through personal stories and to focus on ordinary families. In 1989 he made a film about a family in Taiwan in 1947 – before his own family arrived on the island. *A City of Sadness* touched a raw nerve in Taiwan, since it dealt with events associated with the uprising against the imposed Chinese Nationalist regime during which thousands of Taiwanese were killed by KMT troops from the mainland. For 40 years the memory of the event had been repressed by the KMT with martial law only being lifted in 1987.

A City of Sadness, a film using the local Hokkien dialect, won the Golden Lion at Venice in 1989, demonstrating again that the best locally focused films often play well to international audiences. Hou joined Fifth Generation PRC directors such as Zhang Yimou and Chen Kaige as Chinese directors able to get exposure and distribution deals via international film festivals in the 1990s. Edward Yang and the younger Taiwanese director Tsai Ming-Liang also became part of this group. Tsai was born in Sarawak (now part of Malaysia) and moved to Taiwan aged 20 in the late 1970s. He became part of the 'Second New Wave' in Taiwan during the 1990s.

One of the leading roles in *A City of Sadness* went to the Hong Kong actor Tony Leung who could speak neither Japanese nor Taiwanese and played the part as a deaf mute.

Hou continued to make films through the 1990s and in 2000 with *Millennium Mambo*, set ten years into the future in Taiwan, and in Japan he began to locate some stories outside Taiwan. Along with the other Taiwanese directors listed here he has operated within a complex formulation of local and global, and also post-colonial and corporate. At the same time his films have moved further towards what we might call a cinephile niche in the international market. Highly praised by critics, his films risk alienating mainstream audiences. Since Hou represents such an important transnational filmmaker and we can link one of his films directly to one of our other case studies it is worth exploring *Café Lumière* in detail.

Café Lumière (Japan/Taiwan, 2003)

Like the Claire Denis film *35 rhums* discussed in Chapter 7, *Café Lumière* is a conscious reflection on the work of the classical Japanese director Ozu Yasujiro. The film was commissioned by Shochiku, the studio that employed Ozu in the 1950s and early 1960s, to celebrate the centenary of the director's birth.

Hou had not actually studied Ozu's films to any great extent but now he watched them closely and expressed his interest in the most famous title, *Tokyo Story* (Japan

In August 2012, *Tokyo Story* was announced as the No. 3 'Best film of all time' in the *Sight and Sound* magazine poll of critics (held every 10 years) and No. 1 in the directors' poll. *Late Spring* was No. 15.

1953) as well as *Late Spring* (1949) and *Early Summer* (1951). Hou recognised that Ozu 'understood Japanese families' – many of his films tell very similar stories from different perspectives. Working with his long-time collaborators, scriptwriter Chu T'ien-wen and cinematographer Mark Lee Ping-bin, Hou constructed a film around one of Ozu's familiar story ideas located mainly in Tokyo with iconic images of railways and suburban streets. He cast a non-actor but known performer, the pop singer Hitoto Yo (herself from a Taiwanese-Japanese family), as Yoko, a young single woman working as a freelance writer. She is researching a Taiwanese musician Jiang Ewn-Ye (1910–1983) and has just returned from Taiwan. We see her visiting her father and stepmother who live in Takasaki, a city 100km from Tokyo and then observe her travelling around Tokyo and meeting her friend Hajime played by a leading Japanese film star Asano Tadanobu. He clearly loves her but she seems to prefer just his friendship. There is very little plot in the film but at one point Yoko tells her parents that she is pregnant. In the final part of the film the parents visit Yoko in Tokyo, puzzled by her rather laid-back attitude towards motherhood – she tells them that she doesn't want to marry her Taiwanese boyfriend.

In Chapter 3 we explored possible approaches to reading films from other film cultures – and other forms of cinema. *Café Lumière* is in some ways a challenging film, but only because of what it *doesn't* do. It is easy to watch and many audiences find it beautiful as well as calm and relaxing. But it is slow with many static compositions – the camera is locked in position looking into a room through a door, down a corridor, round a corner, etc. as characters talk or simply sit in silence. At other times it follows Yoko in long shot as she walks through streets or travels by train. You may feel frustrated that so little happens. The film seems designed to contradict the way in which mainstream popular films build narrative flow through what Bordwell and Thompson (2010) refer to as a cause-and-effect chain of events. When Yoko does something it is not necessarily going to have an 'effect' later on, but since we are so used to reading films in this way we may disengage from the narrative because of our frustration. On the other hand, 'real life'

Fig 11.9
A typical composition by Hou Hsaio-hsien in *Café Lumière* shows a family group of father, daughter and stepmother but Hou shows them sitting separately via a camera which seems to be peering around a doorway. This is the sequence in the film that contains a direct *hommage* to Ozu's *Tokyo Story*.

does not proceed via a neat process of cause and effect. Hou presents us with the chance to observe characters in a social context and leaves it up to us to reflect on what we see.

What we are left with is an experience in which we can perceive a **postmodern** narrative, one in which references are made to other 'texts' on several levels. The situation of the unmarried daughter and her parents' concern features in both *Late Spring* and *Early Summer*, and one scene is very close to that in *Tokyo Story* when the parents visit their widowed daughter-in-law who has to borrow something from a neighbour in order to offer them hospitality. Hou doesn't attempt to copy Ozu's compositions directly but he achieves something of the same tone. The obsession with Tokyo's railways emerges not just through Hajime's actions as a character but also the camera's seeming obsession in almost fetishising train images as if exaggerating Ozu's occasional glimpses of trains simply for effect. Yet railways also act as triggers for memory – Yoko spots the station cat which she remembers from her childhood in Takasaki when she took the train to school. It is also interesting that she lives on a tram route in Tokyo, one of the last two remaining from Ozu's Tokyo. None of these references will mean much to audiences unaware of either Ozu or Taiwanese-Japanese history, but this is the nature of film art for a cinephile audience.

The little details that emerge about the Taiwanese boyfriend and from Yoko's meeting with Jiang Ewn-Ye's widow and daughter point us towards a **discourse** about the personal and cultural history that brings together China, Taiwan and Japan over the past century and which is mirrored in the histories of the film industries in these countries (and which also involves Hong Kong). We could extend these connections and point out that the cinematographer Mark Lee also shot Wong Kar-wai's *In the Mood For Love* (2000) in Hong Kong (and would later shoot *Norwegian Wood* in Japan – see Chapter 5). These connections emphasise the **transnational** nature of the work of this group of filmmakers. Nicholas Villiers (2011) discusses Hou's work in Paris and Tokyo and reports that in both places, local critics and filmmakers were impressed with Hou's grasp of local culture.

In 2007 Hou made another film overseas, *Le voyage du ballon rouge* in France. This was a reflection on an earlier film, the classic short film by Albert Lamorisse, *La ballon rouge* (France, 1956). Hou's film stars Juliette Binoche and **Song Fang**, a young Chinese filmmaker who studied in Belgium. Binoche plays a woman who works as a voiceover artist for a Chinese puppet theatre in Paris. She hires Fang to look after her small son Simon. The boy has adventures with a red balloon – including a train trip. Hou's choice of projects turns us back to Zhang's comments at the beginning of this chapter about what makes a film 'Chinese'.

The comments on Hou's approach in *Café Lumière* could also be applied to much of Ozu's work.

Villiers discusses *Metro Lumière*, a French promotional film for Hou's Japanese venture. It has the witty tagline: 'Made in Taiwan, Assembled in France, Big in Japan'.

Song Fang's first film, *Memories Look at Me* (China, 2012), displays the influence of both Jia Zhangke (her producer) and Hou Hsiao-hsien.

Research and Explore 11.2

Try to watch similar scenes from *35 rhums*, *Café Lumière* and Ozu's *Late Spring* or *Tokyo Story* (e.g. scenes between father and daughter).

Is there a similar feel to these scenes? If so, how is it created?

What are the other common features between the three films? What do you think we learn from the three films – are Denis and Hou simply copying or have they discovered something?

Chinese diaspora cinema in Southeast Asia

Chinese film interests in Malaysia and Singapore began in the 1920s with the establishment of cinemas and later studio facilities as a form of Shanghai 'inward investment'. The Shaw Brothers, Runme and Run Run bought, leased and then built local cinemas and imported American, British and Chinese films. They also set up a studio in Singapore in 1937. Film production had not really developed fully before the Japanese occupied British Malaya in 1941 but when the studio reopened after the war the Shaw Brothers became major producers as well.

British Malaya with its unique cultural mix of Malay, Chinese and Indian communities proved an excellent base from which Shaw Brothers could build a chain of cinemas and other entertainment facilities across Thailand, Borneo and Indonesia as well as Singapore and Malaya. The company mainly made films in Malay with Indian technicians and Chinese administrators. By the mid-1960s, the Malaysian cinema market was in decline and Shaw Brothers moved production to Hong Kong, becoming major players in the commercial success of Hong Kong cinema during the 1970s. They were then able to import their own Mandarin-language films back into Malaysia.

Research and Explore 11.3

Investigate the extensive Shaw Brothers Organisation history as set out on http://www.shaw.sg/sw_about.aspx.

- Sketch out the ways in which Shaw Brothers is a good example of a vertically integrated filmed entertainment company.
- To what extent do you think Shaw Brothers is a pan-Asian company or a global company?

Shaw Brothers' success in Singapore and Malaya attracted competition in the form of Cathay, a company founded in the mid-1930s and emulating Shaw Brothers in terms of local production and in the regional spread of its cinema chain before the 1980s collapse of the business. Cathay moved earlier into Hong Kong production and like Shaw Brothers now finds itself with a valuable library of Mandarin, Cantonese and Malay film titles as well as a revived cinema exhibition business in Malaysia (see http://www.cathay.com.sg/corporate_history.html).

Recently, local Chinese independent producers in Singapore and Malaysia have successfully competed with Chinese imports in releasing local Chinese New Year films. (See Chapter 12 for a discussion of the potential for Singapore-Malaysian production.)

Mainland Chinese cinema since the 1990s

The current expansionist period for the mainland industry started during the 1990s with China's gradual engagement with international markets. Co-production deals with Hong Kong had begun before the handover. What would once have been seen as a 'mainland production' now often became a joint venture with Hong Kong for the domestic Chinese market with directors, crews and star performers from previously separate industries working together. Chen Kaige's *Farewell My Concubine* (1993) was a China/Hong Kong production with the Hong Kong star

Leslie Cheung heading a cast of mainland stars, including Gong Li. Zhang Yimou's *Shanghai Triad* (1995) was a Chinese/French co-production.

Several factors have come together in the development of the new ecology of Chinese cinema over the 20 years since *Farewell My Concubine*. As noted above, the Hong Kong industry began to decline as 1997 approached. Cooperation with the mainland offered:

- employment/exploitation of Hong Kong's human (stars and creative talents) and technical resources;
- greater access to the mainland audience;
- opportunities for mainland producers to get better access to international deals via Hong Kong networks.

Potential drawbacks included, first, the possibility that production would be disrupted by PRC officials, and second, the practical requirement to transfer some working practices to mainland studios. Hong Kong stars were mainly Cantonese speakers entering a Mandarin industry. Two alternative models for contemporary Chinese cinema are represented through the work of Feng Xiaogang and Jia Zhangke.

Case study 11.5: Feng Xiaogang (b. 1958)

Kong (2009) opens her discussion of contemporary commercial genre pictures in China with a lengthy quote from a speech by **Feng Xiaogang**, the most consistently successful commercial Chinese director of the past 20 years. Feng develops a metaphor that is helpful in understanding contemporary Chinese cinema. He suggests that Chinese film culture is like a 'sacred hall', which after 1949 was taken over by the Third and Fourth Generations of trained professional directors. Then the Fifth Generation broke in through the windows and the Sixth Generation tunnelled their way in from underneath. These two new groups occupied different parts of the hall which was now very crowded. When it came to his turn, Feng (who didn't train at the Beijing film school) found the hall was full and built himself an outhouse. He found it to his taste and now some of the others want to share his space.

Feng actually began work in television as a designer and then a scriptwriter. When he emerged as a director in the mid-1990s he quickly established a reputation for popular films released during the Chinese New Year season. With regular star Ge You, Feng produced box office hits and appeared to have developed a new model for Chinese popular film. However, Feng has refused to remain trapped within a single mode of film production. In some ways his work may be compared with that of certain Bollywood producers. *Be There or Be Square* (*Bu jian bu san*, China, 1998) is a romantic comedy about two Chinese migrants living in Los Angeles. *Big Shot's Funeral* (*Da Wan*, China/Hong Kong, 2001) stars Donald Sutherland as a US TV director on location in China. These are films that might have been made by the Hong Kong industry of the early 1990s.

Feng's **main melody** films include *Assembly* (Hong Kong/China/S. Korea, 2007), a war film set in the late 1940s and early 1950s, and *Aftershock* (China, 2010), dealing with the aftermath of the Tangshen earthquake in 1976. These films deal with major historical events and address issues about representing 'ordinary Chinese' in terms of the national

Since the late 1980s those Chinese films that appear to have been sanctioned or highly praised by government have been known as **main melody** films. *The Founding of the Republic* (China, 2009) is an obvious example, celebrating 60 years of the PRC (see http://shaoyis.wordpress.com/2010/04/01/trends-in-chinese-cinema-part-ii/).

Fig 11.10
The death of Mao Zedong
in 1976 was a major event
in China and in *Aftershock*
it is marked by the white
flowers everyone must
wear for the funeral
parades.

An interesting analysis of
Aftershock is offered by
Wang Rujie on: http://
mclc.osu.edu/rc/pubs/
wangrujie.htm.

story. *Aftershock* marries an effective blockbuster opening with CGI effects for the earthquake but then develops the personal story of 6-year-old twins separated during the disaster. The boy is saved with his mother but the girl is found later and adopted by a PLA soldier couple and the twins' lives then work out differently. The story comes up to date and it is noticeable that the narrative begins with the purchase of a humble electric fan and ends up more than 30 years later in a world of shopping malls, BMWs and product placements.

A World Without Thieves (*Tiānxià Wú Zéi*, China/Hong Kong, 2004) is an action-comedy-drama that gives several clues as to why Feng's films are so popular in China. Hong Kong star Andy Lau and Taiwanese star Rene Liu play a feuding couple who are both con artists. He wants to continue with this line of work but she is looking to have a family. They find themselves in the far west of China selling a BMW and using the train to return east. She visits a monastery and becomes protective of a naive young man travelling with all his savings. Also on the train is a gang of thieves (led by Ge You) – and a plain-clothes detective. A four-way tussle for the Andy Lau character provides the action on the train. He is torn between stealing the young man's money and thwarting his partner as well as defeating the thieves and evading the police. The film offers Chinese audiences comedy and action, as well as romance and the spectacle of a train travelling across the desert (the achievement of Chinese technology). It also points to a social issue – theft on the train – that concerns many ordinary Chinese. Feng is interested in the materialism of contemporary China. The conflicts between the various characters perhaps refer to his own position caught between commerce and art.

But while Feng seemingly has this popular model worked out, he is also attracted by the prospect of competing with Hollywood (*Variety* has called him the Chinese Spielberg). *The Banquet* (China, 2006), a historical drama loosely based on *Hamlet* and starring Zhang Ziyi, Ge You, Daniel Wu and Zhou Xun, was seen by some critics as an attempt to match the Zhang Yimou epics, looking more towards Western markets. Zhang's similar film *The Curse of the Golden Flower* (Hong Kong/China, 2006) with Gong Li and Chow Yun-fat was released the same year.

Research and Explore 11.4

Search for information on Dynamic Marketing Group (DMG) Entertainment and their film directed by and starring **Xu Jinglei**, the romantic comedy *Go LaLa Go!* (*Du Lala sheng zhi ji*, China, 2010).

What does this production suggest about the possibilities of US/Chinese co-productions? What other films have DMG been involved in? Why is co-production especially attractive to Hollywood in China?

Xu Jinglei and Vicki Zhao are two of the four female stars picked out as important in contemporary Chinese cinemas. The other two are Zhang Ziyi (a Zhang Yimou protégé) and Zhou Xun (initially known for her roles in Sixth Generation films).

Case study 11.6: Jia Zhangke (b. 1970)

Of all the Sixth Generation directors, Jia is the one who has made an equal impact inside and outside China and who also provides us with links to other aspects of Chinese film culture and industrial practice. He left Beijing Film Academy in the mid-1990s and his first three films were made outside the Chinese film studios on relatively low budgets. All are located in Jia's home province of Shanxi in Northeast China and they deal with the lives of young people in urban areas representative of smaller industrial cities away from Beijing and Shanghai. The 'Hometown Trilogy' – *Xiao Wu* (Hong Kong/China, 1998), *Platform* (Hong Kong/China, Japan, France, 2000) and *Unknown Pleasures* (Japan, South Korea, France, China, 2002) – offer us a glimpse into the lives of young people during China's periods of transition. *Platform*, the most ambitious in narrative terms, covers the period after the Cultural Revolution during the 1980s when a group of young people involved in popular music are struggling with China's slow emergence into modernity. *Xiao Wu* (*Pickpocket*) is a realist portrayal of the everyday life of a petty criminal – leading to comparisons with Robert Bresson's *Pickpocket* (France, 1959). *Unknown Pleasures* is a mournful but strangely beautiful film shot on digital video. Two young unemployed men drift through their days in a once busy mining town, trying to enjoy the diversions

Fig 11.11
Zhao Tao as the singer and Wu Qiong as the young man who pursues her in Jia Zhangke's *Unknown Pleasures*.

offered by contemporary electronics-based entertainments. A young woman who seeks her fortune as a singer enters a talent contest organised by a beer company.

The three films reveal a contradictory figure in the sense that Jia's achievement is to bring realism back into Chinese cinema in a way that had been lost by the Fifth Generation. His early films were independent of state support, effectively 'underground' in China with funding coming from outside the country in the form, for example, of Japanese director Kitano Takeshi's company or the Busan Film Festival in South Korea. More than the other members of the Sixth Generation, Jia seems on the one hand 'connected' to forms of youth culture, especially through his use of popular music, and on the other revered by the international cinephile community for whom he has become one of the world's leading auteurs.

Thus, the contradiction is that the director most associated with representing the 'real China' on screen is discussed not in terms of his relationship to Chinese cinema, but instead his relationship to other auteurs outside China such as Ozu Yasujiro or Hou Hsiao-hsien (see above). Lee (2003) lists these two names as being mentioned by Jia himself, as well as Bresson, Fellini and Vittorio De Sica (see Chapter 6 on neo-realism) in interviews. Jia's early films circulated on bootleg DVDs (like those traded by the young men in *Unknown Pleasures*). Since 2004, he has been recognised by the state and now his frequent presence at international film festivals and awards events brings prestige to China.

Jia's trademarks include a camera style reminiscent of several of those directors listed above with long takes and characters wandering through and out of shot. Jia's regular collaborator on camera is Yu Lik-wai (who also works with Ann Hui, above) and he has consistently worked with the same actors, especially Wang Hongwei and Zhao Tao. What also marks Jia out is, as Kevin Lee puts it:

> his acute sense of how the local occurrences that appear onscreen are shaped by immense, unfathomable global forces emanating from sources well off-screen. Jia's importance on the global cinematic stage is inextricably tied to his depiction of contemporary China, if only because Jia's China reflects global conditions and trends that affect us all.
>
> (Lee 2003)

Many examples of this 'sense' are apparent in *24 City* (China/Japan/France, 2008). The film could be described as a 'poetic documentary', but it is a hybrid form that involves witness statements and actors playing the roles of real people with their statements ('memories') drawn from a mass of documentary records. '24 City' is a new commercial development being built on the site of a former secret aircraft factory located in the city of Chengdu in southwest China. The factory was moved there from northeast China in the 1950s for strategic reasons. Around 4,000 workers found themselves transported thousands of miles and then somehow kept 'separate' from the rest of the city. Yu's camera records the final days of the factory and presents several individual stories from all the generations of people associated with the community forged around the aircraft work. Once again, Jia's use of popular music proves both affecting and provocative with Taiwanese pop music, the local popularity of a Japanese TV series *Blood Suspect* in the 1980s, when its young characters became popular role models for local youth, and a group of older women workers singing the 'Internationale'.

Specific references from other films appear in several of Jia's titles, ranging from the Hindi film classic *Awaara* (India, 1951) to *Pulp Fiction* (US, 1994).

Action men and suffering women?

The final section of this long chapter offers a brief look at a different starting place for studying Chinese cinemas – the gendered nature of many Chinese film narratives. In much of the analysis above there has been an emphasis on 'suffering women' in traditional Chinese melodramas: Xie Jin's social realist melodramas, Zhang Yimou's 'Red Trilogy' and all the way through to Ann Hui's *Postmodern Aunt*. We have noted how the difficult lives of these different women have been associated with a wide range of social changes in China, but also how they have been, as in criticism of Zhang Yimou's use of Gong Li, potentially 'prettified' accounts of suffering for an orientalist gaze. Gary G. Xu (2007: 154) criticises Mark Cousins (in an article in *Prospect* 4, November 2004) for applying an orientalist perspective in supporting East Asian cinema. Xu sees Cousins as explaining the attraction to Western audiences of films like Zhang Yimou's *House of Flying Daggers* and Wong Kar-wai's *2046* (both 2004) as based on a collective 'Asian aesthetic' that is exotic, erotic, feminine, seductive and decorative. Xu wants to argue that Asian cinema is

Fig 11.12
Maggie Cheung plays the 1930s star Ruan Ling-yu in *Centre Stage* (see also Fig 11.2). Source: The Kobal Collection/www.picture-desk.com.

not 'exclusively feminine' and quotes the work of director John Woo, actor Chow Yun-fat and others.

It is perhaps the case that our examples in this chapter have tended more towards female-centred narratives than male ones. Xu's point is well made and there are many male-centred action narratives in Chinese cinemas. Yet what is distinctive about Chinese cinemas is the presence of female action stars. Some of these are the female stars of a popular cinema who are asked to play action roles alongside the melodrama/romance roles for which they have sometimes become more well known. A good example would be Maggie Cheung Man-yuk, known for a number of roles in which action is important but perhaps more so for roles in melodramas and romances (e.g. as Wong Kar-wai's Su Li-zhen character in *Days of Being Wild*, *In the Mood For Love* and *2046*).

Perhaps Cheung's key performance is in Stanley Kwan's *Centre Stage* (*Actress*, Hong Kong, 1992). This unusual film is an 'experimental biopic' that explores the 'real life' story of Ruan Ling-yu, the great star of the Shanghai cinema of the 1930s. Ruan was a victim of salacious gossip about her private life that drove her to commit suicide aged 25 at the height of her success. Kwan chose to present several different representations of this iconic figure of Shanghai cinema. Some of the films Ruan made have survived, so Kwan was able to use clips from them alongside photographs from the period. He edited these with sequences showing Maggie Cheung playing Ruan in re-creations of some of the scenes as she would in a conventional historical biopic. Finally, Kwan cut between the re-created 1930s and interviews on set with Cheung and some of the survivors from the 1930s industry. Cheung won the Silver Bear at Berlin as well as other major prizes for her performance.

Maggie Cheung has also acted in *wuxia* films and alongside Jackie Chan in *Police Story* (Hong Kong, 1985), performing in sword fights and action sequences, but she isn't trained in martial arts and that's where some other female stars shine.

Fig 11.13
Michelle Yeoh as the eponymous heroine Yim Wing-Chun easily defeats a male challenger in the key action film *Wing Chun* (Hong Kong, 1994). The contest requires her to protect a tray of tofu. She wins if her challenger cannot damage the tray.

Fig 11.14
Brigitte Lin as *The Bride With White Hair* (Hong Kong, 1993), a martial arts film with supernatural elements.

Research and Explore 11.5

Brigitte Lin and Michelle Yeoh have been two of the most important female action stars in Hong Kong cinema. Research their backgrounds and the films in which they have starred. How do their stories fit into the developments in Chinese cinema over the past 30 years outlined in this chapter and what makes them distinctive as female stars?

Summary

Chinese film industries and film culture are changing rapidly, and much of this chapter has been taken up by attempts to explain the historical background to contemporary production. There is no doubt that Chinese cinemas will be at the centre of developments in global film over the next few years – whether it is the increasing number of Chinese films in the International Box Office Chart, the co-productions with Hollywood or simply the size of the Chinese-language market and its position as the second most valuable market in global film.

References and further reading

Berry, Chris (ed.) (2003) *Chinese Films in Focus: 25 New Takes*, London: BFI.

Berry, Mike (2009) *Jia Zhangke's 'Hometown Trilogy'*: Xiao Wu, Platform, Unknown Pleasures, London: BFI.

Bingham, Adam (2003) 'Cinema of Sadness: Hou Hsiao-hsien and "New Taiwanese Film"', Cinetext: film and philosophy. Available at http://cinetext.philo.at/magazine/bingham/cinema_of_sadness.html.

Bordwell, David (2000) *Planet Hong Kong*, Cambridge, MA: Harvard University Press.

Bordwell, David and Thompson, Kristin (2010) *Film Art: An Introduction* (9th edn), New York: McGraw-Hill.

Chen Kuan-Hsing (1998) 'Taiwanese New Cinema', in John Hill and Pamela Church Gibson (eds) *The Oxford Guide to Film Studies*, Oxford: Oxford University Press.

Dai Jinhua (2009) 'Celebratory Screens: Chinese Cinema in the New Millennium', in Khoo and Metzger (eds) (op. cit.).

Farquhar, Mary (2002) 'Zhang Yimou'. Available at http://sensesofcinema.com/2002/great-directors/zhang/#senses.

Glaessner, Verina (1992) Review of *Raise the Red Lantern*, *Sight and Sound* February: 41.

Grossman, Andrew (2002) 'Better Beauty Through Technology: Chinese Transnational Feminism and the Cinema of Suffering', *Bright Lights* 35. Available at http://www.brightlightsfilm.com/35/chinesefeminism1.html.

Hunt, Leon and Leung Wing-Fai (eds) (2008) *East Asian Cinemas: Exploring Transnational Connections on Film*, London: I.B. Tauris.

Khoo, Olivia and Metzger, Sean (eds) (2009) *Futures of Chinese Cinema: Technologies and Temporalities in Chinese Screen Culture*, Bristol: Intellect.

Kong, Shuyu (2009) 'Genre Film, Media Corporations and the Commercialisation of the Chinese Film Industry: The Case of "New Year Comedies"', in Khoo and Metzger (eds) (op. cit.).

Lee, Kevin (2003) 'Jia Zhangke'. Available at http://sensesofcinema.com/2003/great-directors/jia/ (plus other useful resources via links).

Leung Wing-Fai (2008) '*Infernal Affairs* and *Kung Fu Hustle*: Panacea, Placebo and Hong Kong Cinema', in Hunt and Leung (eds) (op. cit.).

Reynaud, Bérénice (2003) '*Centre Stage*: A Shadow in Reverse', in Chris Berry (ed.) *Chinese Films in Focus: 25 New Takes*, London: BFI.

Silbergeld, Jerome (1999) *China into Film: Frames of Reference in Contemporary Chinese Cinema*, London: Reaktion Books.

Teo, Stephen (1998) 'Hong Kong Cinema', in John Hill and Pamela Church-Gibson (eds) *The Oxford Guide to Film Studies*, Oxford: Oxford University Press.

Tierney, Kevin (1983) 'Saturday Night at the Movies', *Sight and Sound* 52(2), spring.

Villiers, Nicholas (2011) '"Chinese Cheers": Hou Hsiao-hsien and Transnational Homage', *Senses of Cinema* 58 (March). Available at http://sensesofcinema.com/2011/feature-articles/"chinese-cheers"-hou-hsiao-hsien-and-transnational-homage/.

Xu, Gary G. (2007) *Sinascape: Contemporary Chinese Cinema*, Lanham, MA: Rowman & Littlefield.

Zhang, Rui (2008) *The Cinema of Feng Xiaogang: Commercialization and Censorship in Chinese Cinema after 1989*, Hong Kong: Hong Kong University Press.

Zhang, Yingjin (2004) *Chinese National Cinema*, London: Routledge.

Zhang, Yingjin (2010) 'Chinese Cinema and Transnational Film Studies', in Durovicova and Newman (eds) *World Cinemas, Transnational Perspectives*, New York: Routledge.

Further viewing

As with Chapter 10, recommendations are restricted to a certain extent by the availability of titles. yesasia.com does provide some access to Taiwanese popular cinema, including titles such as *You Are the Apple of My Eye* (Taiwan, 2011, dir. Ko Giddens), a blockbuster hit as a 'coming-of-age' comedy romance. *Cape No.7* (Taiwan, 2008, dir. Wei Te-Sheng) is a love story with an even stronger sense of nostalgia. *Monga* (Taiwan, 2010, dir. Doze Niu) is a **gangster film** set in the 1980s. (DVDs are usually available in editions for China, Taiwan or Hong Kong – please check subtitles and Region codes.)

Johnnie To's two *Election* films (Hong Kong, 2005, 2006) are examples of the gangster genre in the territory. Successful at home, they have also been distributed internationally.

Chinese blockbusters are now moving towards the franchise model. *Painted Skin* (Hong Kong/China, 2008, dir. Gordon Chan) is an action-romance-fantasy, deemed successful enough for a sequel in 2011 and a third film announced in 2013. *Lost in Thailand* (China, 2012, dir. Xu Zeng) is a relatively low-budget comedy that proved to be the most popular film of the year.

CHAPTER 12

Looking to the future

- New markets: Southeast Asia
- Case study 12.1: Eric Khoo and Zhao Wei Films
- Will Hollywood's hegemony last?
- The potential of the BRICs and MIKT
- The gaming industry
- Digital cinema and cultural policy
- Winners and losers in digital cinema?
- E-cinema and digital diversity
- Online film
- Summary: the bigger picture
- References and further reading

The future of filmed entertainment is as uncertain in 2014 as it was in 1994 when 'new media technologies' were first beginning to change every aspect of the film industries. The rapid development of the internet and social media, and the shift from film to digital sound and image technologies have occurred within a global framework that has seen audiences (and revenues) increase in many parts of the international market, especially in Asia. Mature markets in North America and Europe have been more uncertain. Yet projections suggest that North America will remain the biggest market for some time to come and Hollywood, because of its global reach, will similarly remain the biggest revenue earner. Beyond these very broad observations it is dangerous to speculate about which developments will turn out to be 'game changers' and which will simply be recorded as 'of the moment'. In this final chapter we will look at some trends and explore possibilities as well as raise questions.

In summer 2012 James Cameron, a cheerleader for many forms of technological innovation in the film industry, announced a move for the Cameron Pace Group into China with the establishment of a new facility in Tianjin in partnership with two local studios (*Screendaily*, 8 August 2012). The facility is designed to provide a full range of services dealing with 3D technologies. This announcement appears to make sense for several reasons. China has a rapidly developing digital screen network and Chinese government policy changed in 2012 to increase the quota for foreign imports – as long as they are 3D or IMAX films that will feed the new exhibition sector. James Cameron's films *Avatar* and the refurbished *Titanic*, both in 3D, were in 2012 the two biggest box office titles in Chinese cinema history. But in the UK Cameron's announcement was met with some scepticism during a summer season when audiences seemed to be clamouring for the 2D versions of the big blockbusters and avoiding paying extra to watch 3D. Also in summer 2012, while the Olympic Games was offered as 3D programming on TV, a new 'Super Hi-Vision' form of television Olympics broadcast was being demonstrated in Japan, the UK and the US – a format promising much higher definition and 'total immersion' compared to current 3D formats.

Whatever the outcome of Cameron's move, we can reasonably confidently argue that:

- development of new 'film' and 'cinema' technologies has been a feature of commercial filmmaking for more than a century and will continue to be so;
- China and India, as the countries with the largest populations in the world as well as important histories of film culture, must be important players in any future developments.

The attachment of all communities to the pleasures of stories goes much further back than cinema or indeed forms of organised drama. We can predict that audiences will still want to access stories in future but what format for filmed entertainment will they prefer and what price will they be prepared to pay? As yet, new digital platforms and associated new business models have not been proven in the global marketplace. But alongside the globalising push of these technological and industrial factors there has also been a growth in interest in *local* stories. Although filmed entertainment is driven in the main by profit-seeking organisations, significant parts of the industry, especially in Europe, are subsidised by public money and underpinned by local, national and supranational policies that recognise both the cultural and the economic importance of film. These policies will seek to harness new developments for their own purposes, and in doing so may help shape the forward plans of the commercial industry.

New markets: Southeast Asia

The global film industry is dynamic. We have noted that 'Global Hollywood' remains the dominant player across international markets, but also that local producers have shown the potential to grow and to establish themselves in local (domestic) and regional markets and compete with Hollywood. Sometimes this local growth is not sustainable over more than a few years, but there are signs that this may change.

The development of the filmed entertainment business in South Korea and the impact of the 'Korean Wave' in East Asia (see Chapter 5) is a model that might be emulated elsewhere. Southeast Asia looks like a possibility. Thailand, Malaysia/ Singapore, Indonesia and the Philippines have a combined population of 435 million – more than North America or Europe. The basic data about the film industry in each country are shown in Fig 12.1.

In the three most populous countries there are relatively few cinema screens and they show very low rates of cinema attendance, with Indonesia registering only 0.2 visits per head per year. By contrast, Singapore shows over 4 visits per head. Singapore is one of the richest countries in the world with per capita GDP of over US$50,000, whereas Indonesia, the Philippines and Thailand are all under US$6,000.

Super Hi-Vision also known as UHDTV (Ultra High Definition) gives an image that is 16 times the quality of HD with an 8K resolution of 7,680 x 4,320 pixels.

	Pop. (millions)	Films produced	Admissions (millions)	Box Office (US $ millions)	Local % share of B.O.
Indonesia	241	84	52	127	–
Malaysia	29	49	60	197	22
Philippines	96	78	48	153	26
Singapore	5	13	22	151	5
Thailand	64	49	28	125	38
Total	435	273	210	753	n.a.

Fig 12.1 Film industry data for Southeast Asia. Most data is for 2011 (some figures for Indonesia, Philippines and Thailand are for 2010, 2009 or 2008). All figures are rounded. Source: *Focus 2012*, European Audio-visual Observatory.

Malaysia has a per capita GDP closer to US$9,000 – comparable with several countries in Latin America and Southeastern Europe. But for the film industry, per capita GDP per head is not necessarily relevant. More important is the size of the 'middle-class' market. As we saw in India, the number of customers able to buy a multiplex ticket is what drives global Hollywood and the international film trade (China's per capita GDP is roughly the same as Thailand and India's is lower than Indonesia).

It is not difficult to see the potential for expansion of the film industry in this region. But if it does expand, who will benefit? Singapore's wealthy audience goes to see mainly imported films and local features attract only 5 per cent. The Philippines has a local share of 26 per cent but there is a strong attachment to Hollywood (with the US as the ex-colonial power). What is the possibility that growth in the region may mean more local production or more trade between the five territories? If they do expand exhibition will it be Hollywood or the major Asian producers (India, China, Japan and South Korea) who benefit?

The international film trade press is starting to report on Indonesia in some detail. In 2012 this was prompted by the international success of *The Raid*, an action film made by the Welsh director Gareth Evans who is based in Indonesia. The film features a distinctive form of martial arts – leading to comparisons with similar films from Thailand such as *Ong Bak* (2003). *Screendaily* (22 August 2012) reports some familiar developments: international film festivals are accepting individual Indonesian films and Asian festivals have started to showcase Indonesian output. There are some signs that the Indonesian government is beginning to recognise the value of supporting the local industry and suggestions that Korean film companies are interested in opening cinemas in Indonesia. Given the geography of Indonesia (a group of islands large and small), another possibility may be that Indian systems of the digital distribution of films (see below) may be a useful model in the region.

But considering the current situation in the region, the most likely hub for immediate expansion is Singapore/Malaysia. As the data in Fig 12.1 show, the numbers currently make most sense in these two territories. Both have a history of local production (see Chapter 11) and a healthy exhibition sector. They also have other potential advantages:

- Singapore and Malaysia are unique as mixed societies of Malay, Chinese and Indian, and therefore a mix of religions, cultural practices and languages.

- Singapore rose to prominence as an *entrepôt* – a trading post for imports and exports in a global trading system: perhaps it can become a hub for the global film trade?
- Malaysia has borders with both Thailand and Indonesia, and Singapore is only a few miles by sea from Indonesia.

The recent increase in co-productions between Singapore and Malaysia seems to be a sensible move. The Singapore domestic market is not big enough to support a large-scale commercial film industry, although TV comedian Jack Neo has developed a career as a film director. But Singapore does have internationally known auteurs such as Royston Tan and Eric Khoo.

Malaysia has a growing film and television sector that includes film production for both the Chinese market and the Indian (Tamil) market alongside production in Malay. In co-productions with Singapore, Malaysian producers are able to enter into genre production and potentially sell to Thailand, Indonesia and beyond.

Case study 12.1: Eric Khoo and Zhao Wei Films

Eric Khoo has had several of his independently produced films shown at major festivals, including Cannes, and has seen limited international releases for them. His film *Tatsumi* (Singapore, 2011) is interesting in two ways. First, its story is a form of biopic about a well-known Japanese *mangaka* – a writer and artist creating *manga*. Tatsumi Yoshihiro first used the term *gekiga* in 1957 to describe his work – a form of graphic novel with much more downbeat and realist stories and imagery than mainstream *manga*. The film uses Tatsumi's own autobiography and combines it with some of the stories he wrote. Eric Khoo, himself originally a graphic artist, demonstrates his interest and respect for Tatsumi's work – and, in passing, the interest in Japanese story traditions. *Tatsumi* the film is a 'drawn animation' using a simple, rough style based on that of Tatsumi's own drawings. It was produced by Khoo's own company Zhao Wei Films, with the animation work completed at the Indonesian studios of Infinite Frameworks (http://www.kinema.

Fig 12.2
A still from *Tatsumi*.
Source: The
Kobal Collection/
www.picture-desk.com.

frameworks-studios.com/). The studios (only 45 minutes from Singapore by sea) work on major international productions as well as local Indonesian and Singaporean productions. A short 'making of' documentary for *Tatsumi* was posted on YouTube: http://www.youtube.com/watch?v=Ke7Nf2_EwOc.

Zhao Wei Films (http://www.zhaowei.com/) also produces genre films and Eric Khoo executive-produced *2359* (Singapore/Malaysia, 2011). This is a horror film, one of the most popular regional genres, in which a young national service soldier goes missing at precisely 23:59 one night in the seventh lunar month when 'spirits roam' according to local Chinese folklore. Made in a mixture of Chinese and 'Singlish' (Singapore English) and with three Malaysian-Chinese pop singers as the young soldiers, the film is designed to appeal to its local audience (http://www.filmbiz.asia/reviews/2359).

Horror films from both Thailand and Indonesia are shown in Malaysia, and *2359* marks an attempt to exploit the market opportunity. Following the success of the film in both Malaysia and Singapore, director Gilbert Chan made *Inside the Urn*, another horror film about a *toyol* – a small child spirit – in 2012. The Singapore–Malaysia connection is showing real signs of development. At one time, Hong Kong would have provided the model for enterprising filmmakers locally, but now it appears that South Korea may be the most important major player through the impact of aspects of the Korean Wave such as K-pop (see Chapter 5). Eric Khoo also made a film about an Indian performer and his son in Singapore, *My Magic* (Singapore, 2008). This film was made mostly in Tamil and it did receive a limited release in India, though this was difficult to organise. The Tamil film industry in Malaysia does have direct links with India but so far these are mostly concerned with access to post-production. Even so, there is potential in such links and Singapore–Malaysia as a hub demonstrates that local production in Southeast Asia is a future development that could create new contra-flows of film exports.

Will Hollywood's hegemony last?

In Chapters 1 and 2 we outlined the ways in which the Hollywood studios began to exert their hegemonic power over international markets from the 1920s onwards. The studios' strength has always been their large domestic market, enabling them to maintain a high level of production/distribution of big-budget titles. This has made it difficult for any overseas competitor to compete – either through distribution in North America or in other international markets. This doesn't mean that film producers elsewhere haven't posed a threat. So far, however, none have been successful. Let us remind ourselves of some of those challenges.

In the 1920s the giant Ufa studio in Berlin produced several films on a scale to challenge Hollywood and it targeted the biggest film markets in France, the UK and the US as well as its own domestic market. But such production was not sustainable in the economic and political context of Weimar Germany and the rise of the Nazis in the early 1930s. Coupled with the problems associated with multiple-language productions the challenge faded – but Hollywood had in any case begun to draw away creative talent, technical expertise and the ideas for films themselves. The Hollywood studio system of the 1930s and 1940s featured many talents who had begun at Ufa or other German studios, including Ernst Lubitsch, F.W. Murnau (who died in 1931 with his Hollywood career already established), Fritz Lang, Joseph von Sternberg, Marlene Dietrich, Billy Wilder and many, many more.

In the late 1940s, with the British film industry at its height, the largest player, Rank (owner of two cinema chains and a clutch of British studios), made a concerted effort to distribute films in North America as well as other English-speaking territories. This challenge failed, as did several more over the next 30 to 40 years. The problem for British producers has been that it is seemingly impossible to straddle the line between being distinctively British and therefore 'foreign' in North America and being 'American' enough to compete in the North American domestic market. No British 'studio' has had the resources to sustain production along the lines of a Hollywood major and one major flop has been enough to halt the rise of Goldcrest in 1986, Palace Pictures in 1992 and Film 4 International in 2002. Polygram Filmed Entertainment, beginning as part of the Dutch multinational Philips, eventually grew to be a UK-based producer poised to become a 'major' capable of North American distribution, but was then taken over by Universal. All of these UK-based companies worked with Hollywood money at some point and the identity of many British films is often lost in the international marketplace. In 2012 *Skyfall* became the most successful James Bond film at the international box office. In Europe the film was 'British' because its success proved the ability of European cinemas to sell tickets for 'European' films as required by various cultural policies, but elsewhere the film is usually seen as American. The same was true of the wholly British-funded *Slumdog Millionaire* (UK, 2008).

British properties and creative talent have been effectively 'absorbed' by Hollywood. Hollywood's other major period of European-based production during the 1950s and 1960s in Italy and the associated emergence of Italian-German-Spanish popular genre filmmaking (e.g. 'sword and sandal' films, 'spaghetti westerns') was also eventually absorbed with the most prominent filmmaker, Sergio Leone, making films in North America. In the late 1990s the cycle of remakes of Japanese and South Korean titles began in Hollywood (and among American independent producers) – carrying on the tradition of remaking titles that previously featured European and especially French hit films. In other words, although Hollywood has certainly drawn upon other film industries for ideas and talent, there has not been a sustained challenge to the studios' hegemonic position. Will this change with the development of the Indian and Chinese industries?

The establishment of Studio Canal (www.studiocanal.com/en), with French, British and German bases and a huge library of titles, is the latest European contender for 'major' status.

eOne Entertainment (entertainmentonegroup.com) is a big player in independent film, TV and music. Initially Canadian, the company has acquired interests in the US, UK and several European countries.

The potential of the BRICs and MIKT

One single factor governs the *potential* size of an individual national film market and a domestic film industry: the disposable income of an urban middle class. We noted above that although the average GDP of India or China might be low, the sheer size of the population means that there is a sufficiently large middle class to sustain the development of cinema building and investment in digital film technologies and relatively big-budget film productions. The development of higher education and associated forms of cultural production are also indicators.

Over the past ten years, groups of economists and business consultants have attempted to predict which economies will grow. At the same time, national governments have looked for potential partners and supporters among countries with similarly sized economies at roughly the same stage of development. New groupings have thus been formed in order to strengthen negotiating positions with the developed countries of North America, Europe and Japan. We shouldn't be surprised that the various groupings include countries with long-established film

These various groupings have changing members and overlaps so that the G7 group of advanced economies became the G8 with Russia and is likely to become the G20+ at some point.

industries, some of which will become more noticeable as international players in film markets as their economies grow and social structures develop. For example, the 'MIKT' countries include Indonesia, discussed earlier in this chapter. The other three MIKT countries are Mexico, South Korea (see Chapter 5) and Turkey (Chapter 6), each recognised as have rising cinema admissions and, in the case of South Korea and Turkey, significant domestic film production and growing overseas sales.

Mexican producers to some extent face the same problem as British and English-speaking Canadian producers – sharing a language and a border with the US. The growing Hispanic population of the US represents a potential export market for Mexican films but so far the full potential of Hispanic-language films in North America has not been realised (see Chapter 3). Chapter 9 discusses the phenomenon of the *telenovela* as a major export for both Mexico and Brazil but as yet Latin America hasn't seen the same level of 'exchanges' of regional filmed entertainment as East Asia, nor the coordination of public funding and industry support seen in Europe.

The BRICs (Brazil, Russia, India and China) have been identified as the four major economies poised to overtake most of those of the original G7 members (e.g. the UK, France, Germany, Italy, Canada and Japan) and perhaps even the US. Brazil and Russia have relatively large populations, but their pre-eminence is also based on natural resources. In the case of all four countries, the future of their filmed entertainment industries is to some extent dependent upon their relationships with Hollywood. India has such a strong domestic market share – of such a large market – that Hollywood can be approached as a potential partner rather than as a dominating presence. Similarly in China, genuine partnerships appear possible because of the strong domestic share – and the control of the industry by the Chinese government.

Like China, Russia has a long history of extensive local film production. Up until 1989 the Soviet Union recorded admissions of close to four billion annually, mainly for locally produced features (Vincendeau 1995). The breakup of the Soviet Union halved the Russian population, and although the Russian film industry has revived in the past ten years, the rate of growth has been much lower than in China with admissions at 168 million in 2012. Crucially, though, only 64 Russian films were completed in 2011 and only 15 per cent of admissions were for Russian films. The Russian government has started a publicly funded Cinema Fund and has joined Eurimages. With the pursuit of various co-production deals, Russia in 2013 appears to be vying for No. 3 in Europe as its immediate target (data from *Focus 2012* and European Audiovisual Observatory February 2013).

Brazilian film offers a similar story. The local film market has grown significantly over the past few years with more screens and higher ticket prices (especially for digital 3D). Admissions rose to 149 million in 2012 and box office by 15 per cent but this growth largely served Hollywood. Less than 10 per cent of box office was for Brazilian films (data from *ScreenDaily*). With a local population heading towards 200 million and potential Lusophone markets in Portugal and Africa, there is a great deal of potential for local films. At a 2012 conference on film finance, Brazil was recognised as offering a successful model with public support and 'reasonable budgets by Latin American standards' for 80-plus local productions per year (*Screendaily*, 1 December 2012). Part of the problem, however, is that admission rates are still low. Mexico with half the Brazilian population attracts 33 per cent more admissions. Brazil needs to expand admissions further but also to improve the box office performance of local films.

The gaming industry

For some time now, commentators on the videogames industry – and academics wanting to change the focus of their work – have pointed out that the international videogames industry is 'bigger than Hollywood'. In practice it is difficult to compare the two industries directly but Price Waterhouse Coopers' *Global entertainment and media outlook: 2012–2016* predicts that global spend on filmed entertainment will be worth US$99.7 billion by 2016, whereas the videogame spend will be US$86 billion (the figure for TV licence fees and subscriptions is US$290.6 billion).

The comparison of the two industries is nevertheless useful for several reasons:

- they both now appear on the same platforms – as physical products (discs), online and on mobile devices – but:
- the games industry has migrated much more quickly to online distribution;
- the forecast **synergies** arising from the sharing of the same content across both industries are still being explored but haven't yet been demonstrated to produce revenues meeting earlier expectations;
- although North American producers and consumers are important in the videogames industry, they do not dominate the global market as they do in filmed entertainment – Asia/Pacific and Europe/Middle East/Africa are equally important as producers and consumer markets.

These figures suggest that the rise of gaming has not seriously damaged the global filmed entertainment market as yet. It may be that gaming is becoming a more mature market (i.e. it is now not growing so quickly with companies beginning to consolidate what they hold). Perhaps film industries will now take gaming more seriously. There is much to learn. Gaming has moved into online delivery and 'play'

Synergy refers to the potential 'cross-fertilisation' of ideas and products between two different media, especially if the rights are owned by the same parent organisation.

China is already the biggest market for online gaming and by 2016 is expected to represent 45 per cent of the global market.

Fig 12.3
Scott Pilgrim vs. the World (US/Canada/UK/Japan, 2010) was first a comic and then a film adaptation that used the conventions of videogaming in its presentation of a 'battle of the bands'. Subsequently it became a videogame title as well. Given the importance of music in the film, Edgar Wright's ambitious film combined elements of four different media. Source: The Kobal Collection/www.picture-desk.com.

more quickly than film. It offers some gamers a much richer experience (certainly a longer experience) of engagement with a single game title than with a blockbuster film. Major games and films represent the same investment in development time, production budget and promotion, so perhaps there is a challenge here to change the experience of watching a film, not simply in terms of 'immersion' in the film narrative in a theatre for two hours but some form of interactive engagement with the film as a 'text' that might last for several hours. Perhaps we will finally move towards alternative endings for film narratives or different forms of identification with different characters. Fig 12.3 shows an example of film and gaming 'coming together'.

There isn't space here to even begin to explore gaming as a global activity or to look closely at what future developments may bring. If you are a videogames fan you will have your own ideas about the possible relationship between films and games.

Research and Explore 12.1

UK Market Research suggests that videogaming is a 'mainstream' leisure activity (see the summary of the report 'Gaming Britain' on the Internet Advertising Bureau website – www.iabuk.net). It is also an activity enjoyed by male and female, young and old.

How much impact does the growth of gaming have on the filmed entertainment sector?

- Conduct some research among your friends and family. How much *time* do they spend on gaming compared to going to the cinema, watching films on TV/computers, etc. How much of their income do they spend on games and on films?
- What conclusions do you draw?

Digital cinema and cultural policy

What does the impact of the switch to digital mean for most film audiences? At the beginning of this chapter we suggested that the early 1990s was the time when several separate developments began to change aspects of film culture. Audiences experienced a new level of special effects in Hollywood blockbusters, DVDs began to improve the quality of 'home entertainment' and the internet gradually began to become a platform for fan discussions. Production technologies and home entertainment have continued to develop, and the internet has become the focus for marketing, retail, booking tickets and both legal and illegal ways of viewing films, but the changes to the actual experience of sitting in an auditorium with an audience to watch filmed entertainment are more recent.

'Digital cinema' first referred to the use of digital technologies as an 'acquisition format' – replacing celluloid film in cameras – and as an editing and post-production process. Editing moved quite quickly to digital because the advantages of simulating the physical process of splicing, trimming, etc. clips on a computer screen were obvious. The choice of film or digital acquisition or 'capture' is not so clear-cut and in 2013 three of the main five contenders for major cinematography awards chose film over digital formats. This isn't really an issue, since both film and digital footage enter the same digital editing process. The real crunch comes in distribution and exhibition.

It is worth reflecting on the amazing longevity of 35mm film as the basis for cinema operation, lasting 100 years from the time when it was first standardised on a global scale through to its replacement in many territories by 2013. The coming of sound, colour and widescreen prompted various upgrades in cinemas over time, but the basic process of delivering several reels of film to individual cinemas remained in situ. New cinemas are now being built for digital projection and the main cinema chains are converting their screens so that by 2014 most Hollywood studio pictures shown in a multiplex anywhere in the world are likely to be projected not from reels of film but from a **DCP** or 'Digital Cinema Package'.

Winners and losers in digital cinema?

As we might expect, the Hollywood studios, as the biggest earners (and the biggest spenders) in global film, have attempted to preserve their dominant position by imposing a technological standard on the projection of their films. Hollywood has always tried to set standards. Most film and video equipment has been manufactured to standards set down by SMPTE (Society of Motion Picture and Television Engineers) since 1916 (see www.smpte.org). SMPTE is an internationally based organisation, but its leadership is mainly in the US and most of its members look to Hollywood as the industry leader.

When digital projection began to appear as a viable option, the six major Hollywood studios moved swiftly to set up the Digital Cinemas Initiative (DCI) in 2002 (www.dcimovies.com/). This in turned produced very detailed specifications for processing a DCP. In simple terms a 'film' is now completed post-production as a 'master' – a collection of computer files. From this the distributor can then create a range of digital products to suit different platforms – a broadcast TV version, a DVD or a Blu-ray disc, a digital download and a DCP for cinemas. Cinemas must install 'DCI-compliant' projectors (the current standard is moving towards '4K' – a reference to the number of 'vertical lines' in the projected image – but 2K projectors were still common in 2012). When the DCP arrives in the cinema (as a digital hard drive or as a broadband download) the projectionist must go through a process of loading and decoding the DCP so that it can be placed in a screening programme. Projection is authorised via a Digital Key system (KDM). The operation of digital cinema in a multiplex theatre is organised by Theatre Management System (TMS) software. The whole process is known as **D-cinema**.

D-cinema does not come cheap. Projectors are expensive to install and like most modern technologies will probably become obsolete in a few years' time. There are big savings to distributors who can now avoid the high cost of physical film prints that last only a limited number of plays through a projector as well as heavy transport costs. Changes in exhibition practice require the exhibitors to be convinced that they should make a big investment. The business solution was a **VPF** (Virtual Print Fee) scheme that attempted to spread the load of new expenditure between distributor and exhibitor, charging the distributor a fee per screening. The fee was managed by a third party that installed the technology on a lease-purchase arrangement with the exhibitor. The large cinema chains and the studio-distributors seemingly agreed on how to do this, but the situation with smaller, single-screen cinemas and smaller, specialised distributors is more complicated. Some small distributors cannot afford the fee and some small cinemas cannot see how they can afford to make the switch.

At the UK Digital Cinema Conference in 2013 David Hancock, head of film and cinema at IHS *Screen Digest*, announced: 'By the end of 2015, 35mm will no longer exist in cinemas.'

35mm film prints cost around US$1,000 for each copy of a film. 'Digital prints' are much cheaper to reproduce in large numbers. Since blockbuster films can be on 5,000 screens across the world at any one time, the cost of prints is an important issue.

Sweden was one of the first countries to try to ensure that smaller community cinemas were able to make an early move to digital.

Norway, where most cinemas were municipally owned, was the first territory to complete 100 per cent conversion to digital in 2011 (www. kino.no). Oslo's cinemas were sold to Danish company Nordisk in 2013.

In several European countries, governments concerned to make sure that smaller, local cinemas survive have subsidised the acquisition of digital equipment. In China the recent extensive cinema-building programme means that there is a high proportion of digital screens, but in India the majority of cinemas are still single screens. A two-tier system is developing. In Europe and North America, the studios will probably stop distributing film prints in 2013 or soon after. Cinemas which haven't 'converted' will be faced with exclusion from first-run studio product. One response may be to opt for various forms of **E-cinema**.

E-cinema and digital diversity

Given the definition of D-cinema as 'DCI-compliant', E-cinema has been defined as all other forms of digital projection, i.e. not using the DCI standard. In theatrical terms, E-cinema is most important in India. In 2011 there were just over 10,000 cinema screens in India; 543 of these were DCI-compliant but over 5,000 were classified as E-cinema with digital projectors and systems provided by UFO Moviez and Qube (Real Image). Since Hollywood accounts for only 10 per cent of the Indian market, the future of digital cinema in India depends on the majority of single-screen cinemas showing Bollywood and regional cinema films (*Focus* 2012).

The business model used by UFO Moviez and Qube has meant programming a chain of digital screens in hundreds of privately owned single-screen cinemas in small-town India. This has allowed national brand advertising back into cinemas (when it had mostly gone to TV) and the revenue has subsidised the cost of re-equipping. (The business model also has less demanding VPF-style fees than for D-cinema.) Qube argues that this new virtual circuit served by satellite network delivery has already had an impact on the kinds of films being made and the problem

Fig 12.4
UFO is a major Indian distributor of both E-cinema and D-cinema across the subcontinent. Source: UFO Digital Cinema.

of 'metro India' versus the 'all-India' audience. The E-cinema image quality is argued to be lower than D-cinema (1.3K to 1.9K) but still superior to the quality traditionally achieved by 35mm in these small-town cinemas (www.qcn.in). Both UFO Moviez (www.ufomoviez.com) and Qube also offer D-cinema solutions, but their successful E-cinema solutions may also be attractive in other large countries with a wide spread of cinema audiences – Brazil and parts of China, for instance.

If Indian cinemas represent the high-profile E-cinema outlets, there are many more 'alternative' cinema venues all over the world in different territories. The D-cinema/E-cinema divide does mean the end of one aspect of Hollywood's domination. What constitutes a 'film' – and for that matter a 'cinema' – is no longer fixed. Cinemas in village halls, schools, hospitals, 'pop-ups' in all kinds of buildings or open spaces, giant public screens in squares, etc. can show anything that is available in a digital format – on DVD or Blu-ray, Digibeta tape or HDCAM/DVCPRO. This may include Hollywood films alongside locally made material (professional and amateur), but the problem for the studios will be how to protect their copyright and how to maintain their quality standards. Multiplexes were meant to offer audiences more choice, but mostly this has been 'more of the same'. Perhaps the various E-cinema outlets will just recycle the same, mainly Hollywood, films – but some will experiment and there is much more material available on DVD/Blu-ray than on DCP.

Alternative *content* is increasingly available for both D-cinema and E-cinema. Sport, opera, live theatre and live music have all been successfully presented via satellite for a number of years. Such screenings have one important social/cultural benefit in that audiences for whom travel and expensive seating costs make attendance at live events impossible are now able to access performances in a local cinema. There is a range of questions about how different the experience of watching, for example, live theatre broadcast to a cinema screen might be. A research report 'Beyond Live: Digital Innovation in the Performing Arts' by NESTA (National Endowment for Science, Technology and the Arts) in the UK in 2010 surveyed audiences for two 'National Theatre Live' theatrical performances. It found that:

> Cinema audiences report even higher levels of emotional engagement with the production than audiences at the theatre.

As far as the cinemas are concerned, the high demand for seats for these live broadcasts is very attractive and for some venues such as specialised cinemas and community cinemas the revenue (including the food and drink theatre audiences might expect to buy) may be very welcome. However, for the specialised cinema audience there could be two disadvantages. First, 'alternative content' takes up programme slots that would otherwise be available for film screenings; and second, the expanding audience for theatre/opera, etc. acts to confirm the higher status conferred upon these art forms at the expense of cinema. It may be that this is only an issue in the UK but more research is needed into who attends 'live broadcasts' in cinemas. In India, for instance, what is the impact of live Indian Premier League cricket on 400 E-cinema screens?

Digital downsides

There are two big social disadvantages so far identified for digital cinema of all kinds. One is that it 'deskills' the job of the projectionist – and severely reduces the employment prospects in film exhibition. In an extreme example, a large multiplex

Qube Cinema is part of Real Image Media Technologies which provides hardware and software digital cinema solutions for major clients, including the Hollywood studios.

Satellite distribution in India and remote programming in cinemas has two distinct benefits in terms of reliability of transport and security from piracy.

Through the MPAA the Hollywood studios (and other film industries) are able to 'police' cinema screenings via their relationships with distributors and exhibitors in what is a 'self-regulating' industry.

An actor in London's West End featuring in a live satellite broadcast might discover that her relatives in Los Angeles are able to watch the performance – and tweet their responses.

The NESTA research shows that the cinema audience for theatre in the research sample already had as much knowledge of theatre as the National Theatre audience.

cinema might now hire only a couple of projectionists to oversee what is almost an automated process. When something goes wrong, an outside contractor (the equipment supplier) may have to be summoned. The knowledge of how to project celluloid will gradually disappear. Associated with this disappearance is the whole question of archiving digital film. When digital formats change every few years, which formats should be used for archive prints? Celluloid film, in the form of safety stock, has lasted 60 years (and earlier nitrate film is still salvageable by expert restorers). Digital film prints offer consistent quality but film festivals are now faced with a plethora of digital formats, some of which are not really designed for big-screen operation. Festivals now sometimes show prints of far lower quality than 35mm film.

Research and Explore 12.2

How do you feel about digital cinema?

In your experience:

- Is digital projection consistently better than film in terms of image and sound?
- Are there more venues, pop-up events, clubs, etc. using digital to show a wider range of films than before in your area?
- Do you worry about the narrowing skill base for projectionists and the quandary for archivists – why not go and ask some of them what is happening locally?

Online film

If E-cinema threatens to be less 'controllable' by Hollywood, online film distribution/ exhibition via VOD services offers a different set of questions. VOD is available in most territories from a range of providers including forms of free 'catchup' or 'timeshift' of TV broadcast programming to Pay-TV film services and dedicated VOD providers. In Europe alone there are hundreds of VOD services. The EU may claim a 'single market' but in reality there are 27 national markets with many TV services that are 'geo-blocked' (i.e. not available by internet access outside the host nation).

The global home entertainment market is dominated by the US and Europe, but the latter lags behind US developments with the UK as the only market where VOD was showing signs of significant potential growth (*Variety*, 7 May 2012). This lack of development means that US providers have a head start in recruiting subscribers and making deals to acquire content. The studios have at various times attempted to develop their own online services but they are now having to make deals with new players, Apple with iTunes, Netflix and Amazon. The other US player is Google/ YouTube which announced 60 TV channels for Europe in 2012. Amazon has also announced its own TV channels to complement its VOD service, which includes LoveFilm in Europe. However, the most significant move may have come from Netflix which in 2013 launched its own TV drama serial – a remake of the BBC serial *House of Cards* (UK, 1990) – with a Hollywood-size budget for its 13 x 50-minute episodes and Hollywood director David Fincher as an executive producer and director of the first two episodes. The key to the strategy was that all 13 episodes were available immediately to subscribers in the US and Europe, exclusively via a Netflix subscription and an internet-connected TV.

Hulu is an online service with joint ownership by NBC/Universal, Fox and Disney - in 2013 it is only available in the US and Japan.

The Netflix strategy is both a challenge to cable TV channels such as HBO and DVD suppliers of box sets of TV material and to the conventional nature of TV programming. We need to be careful here because industry executives are prone to announce innovations as 'changing everything' when in practice it is very difficult to shift entrenched positions. Netflix and Amazon are not Hollywood studios. They acquire 'content' from a range of sources (including the studios) but they have business models that are more suitable for digital development and they approach the expansion of their services into other parts of the global market without the backing of the MPAA and a long history of global operations.

While the moves of the big US players make most of the headlines, it is important to remember that digital distribution and exhibition open up opportunities for specialised films as well as local initiatives for short films, artists' films and community productions. Specialised films have been stuck in a business model that is largely driven by the mainstream industry. A new art film/documentary, etc. opens in key cities on a few screens hoping to benefit from reviews, etc. timed for the opening weekend. But specialised cinema audiences are not so tied to the 'first weekend'. Does it really matter if you don't see the film until a few weeks later? Or consider the restoration of classic films on Blu-ray releases. In the new digital ecology, a community cinema, a film society or even a few friends who meet socially could organise a screening at any time.

The business model issue here is the exclusive **window** built into film release schedules – the period in which the initial cinema release is guaranteed a free run before competition from what used to be called 'ancillary markets'. These, too, have usually had a hierarchy of DVD/Blu-ray, Pay TV, subscription TV, terrestrial 'Free-to-air', etc. VOD challenges the old system. Where should it come in the chain? Why should the system remain in place at all? For several years there have been one-off experiments in releasing films across all these platforms at the same time. An important move was made in 2012 when the UK's main arthouse distributor, Artificial Eye, decided to start a day-and-date VOD service with differential pricing, following a similar model in the US set up by IFC and Magnolia. The difference here is that whereas the US companies are primarily distributors, Artificial Eye is also a significant exhibitor with the three major Curzon arthouse venues in Central London and another nine full-time and part-time venues. Releasing its own titles in cinemas and on VOD simultaneously means that not only does the opening week promotion bring a higher return, but films that build through 'word of mouth' are then much more widely available over the next few weeks.

Artificial Eye's Philip Knatchbull believes he can offer what *Variety* has described as 'a viable niche as a boutique serving a cinephile audience with a carefully curated supply of films' – and indeed Curzon has offered 'seasons' curated by well-known figures. But he also emphasises the importance of the cinemas: 'What's great about physical venues is that you're more connected to your community' (*Variety*, 21 April 2012).

Google has found, like Hollywood, that operating in China requires negotiation with the Chinese authorities who have a history of blocking internet access.

France has also seen attempts to use the **'cultural exception'** policy (see Chapter 4) to prevent local media producers from suffering unfair competition in the digital environment

Artificial Eye's VOD is called Curzon On Demand (www. curzoncinemas.com/ film_on_demand/).

IFC (www.ifcfilms.com/) and Magnolia (www. magpictures.com/ ondemand/).

Summary: the bigger picture

What happens in Europe and other places where arthouse cinemas and 'niche' distributors survive will have an impact on the diversity of films available worldwide, but let us end this book with the major question about how the future looks from six major producing territories for film. How will they interact and what will that

	Population (millions)	Films produced 2011	Cinema Admissions (mill)	No of screens per million	Cinema admissions per head	GDP $ billion	GDP per capita $	Domestic share % of box office
US	315	817	1,285	130	4.1	15,610	49,601	91
China	1,350	588	624	8	0.3	12,382	9,146	48
India	1,210	1,274	2,700	13	2.2	4,457	3,693	89
Nigeria	170	1,000	–	–	–	413	2,800	95
South Korea	50	216	195	40	3.8	1,622	32,431	58
Mexico	112	73	205	45	1.8	1,743	15,177	6.8

Fig 12.5 Comparison of six major film territories in 2012. (Population figures based on most recent official estimates, film industry data from *Focus 2012* and *Screen International*. Nigerian film industry figures are estimates or are not available.)

interaction mean for the rest of us? Fig 12.5 pulls together data from some of the fastest growing major film industry territories and displays it alongside data for the US.

Fig 12.5 shows some remarkable disparities and illustrates very clearly certain sets of relationships explored in this book. Note first that wealth disparities have an impact on the number of cinema screens available. The strength of the North American domestic market lies in the sheer number of screens available to play popular films. South Korea's remarkable performance in 2012, when it grew its local box office by 22 per cent, was possible because of the relatively high number of screens per million of population. This observation also points towards the recent entry of the Mexican cinema chain Cinépolis into the Indian market. Mexico has triple the screen ratio of India, and Mexican companies have some experience of growing the cinema habit in communities outside Europe and North America. The phenomenal growth of the cinema box office in China has followed an extensive cinema-building programme and there is a lot more to come – China would need to increase the number of screens by a factor of five to reach Korean levels.

The availability of screens doesn't automatically lead to a strong domestic film industry – so Mexico suffers very badly from domination by Hollywood whereas South Korea has consistently achieved around 50 per cent of box office for domestic productions. In China, the surge of admissions and box office has, despite quota restrictions, seen Hollywood benefit. South Korea managed the process of halving its own 'protective quota' (the number of days when cinemas have to screen domestic titles) very well, so that local production has competed successfully with US imports. However, it remains a struggle and 2012 was a good year for South Korea following a dip between 2007 and 2010. South Korea spends the highest proportion of its GDP on the 'entertainment and media' business sector, followed by the UK (*PWC Entertainment and Media Outlook* 2012).

It is unfortunate that the lack of reliable up-to-date statistics means that it is impossible to make any meaningful comparisons between the six territories. It is no surprise that the two poorest countries, India and Nigeria, have the main problem in business reporting. On the figures presented here, India looks to be doing well by international standards. But in fact the number of admissions has been falling because multiplex screens are not attracting enough new audiences to replace those lost by the slowly decreasing number of single screens. The FICCI-KPMG *Media and Entertainment Report 2013* suggests that 2012 was a good year in increasing revenue – but that this came from audiences paying higher prices for bigger budget films, both Indian and Hollywood.

Both India and Nigeria are attempting to increase film exports and to raise the domestic industry's profile in international markets. This is being pursued in two ways. Indian producers are becoming involved in co-productions and are also directly investing in the American filmed entertainment business. Nigerian producers are also looking for overseas partners, but the main source of growth for companies may be within Africa. Producers in both countries are also trying to change perceptions about the kinds of films they could produce. More 'independent' Indian films are appearing at international festivals and some Nigerian producers are attempting to produce 'cinema' rather than 'video' films. Again Mexico seems to be in an odd position. In 2012 Mexico overtook Brazil in the value of the local box office. It has long had the most screens and the biggest admission figures in Latin America. But local production starts are still fewer than 100. Both Mexico and Brazil have a strong local TV drama industry (see Chapter 9). What are the chances of better support from television for film production (so important in Europe)?

For most of the last 100 years, the international film industry has seen a fairly consistent pattern of large-scale production matched in numbers of films produced between North America and Europe, with audiences favouring American over domestic titles to actually watch in cinemas. American films have also dominated Latin America and parts of Africa and Asia. India and China up until the 1990s were 'outside' the international market. In 2013 the international marketplace looks rather different. East Asia in the form of 'the three Chinas' (PRC, Taiwan and Hong Kong) as well as Japan and South Korea now matches Europe in production and admissions – and there is some evidence that Asian governments are moving towards cooperation in filmed entertainment production and film culture. A new equilibrium is beginning to emerge that sees North America and Europe with slow or nil growth having to accept the emergence of East Asia. Hollywood leadership of the international market will in future depend more and more on its relationship with the growing markets of Asia and the ambitions of domestic industries to collaborate and to exchange films regionally.

The health and vitality of film industry and culture in any territory depends on a mix of factors. We have identified the following in different parts of this book:

- the size of population and its growth rate;
- the wealth of the country overall, and the proportion affluent enough to buy a cinema ticket (which apart from India and most parts of Africa is usually in the range of US$5 to $10);
- the infrastructure of cinemas and production facilities;
- a significant number of domestic film productions with local content;
- a high level of broadband internet penetration for online film.

We might add to this list:

- high levels of literacy and general education – high status for forms of cultural production;
- central and local government policies with incentives for local production and distribution of a diverse range of films;

- a developed business culture to support local participation in the international competition for attracting audiences;
- less quantifiable factors such as creativity, entrepreneurship, cultural traditions, innovation, etc.

There is no single territory that has all of these factors in the perfect balance. Hollywood has had certain advantages and has been the leader in the international film market. But as the range of factors suggests, there is nothing 'natural' about this and the likelihood is that over time that leadership will be challenged or, more likely, circumvented so that the future equilibrium in global film looks different.

In one week in early 2013, The International Top 40 films chart showed 21 US titles and 19 from Europe and Asia. Six were from China (during the Chinese New Year season), two of them children's films. A few weeks later (12/13 March), Filmbiz Asia (www.filmbiz.asia/) carried two important news stories. First, the Japanese major distributor Nikkatsu announced a plan to screen four major Bollywood hits in Japan and to promote the package with an aim to develop Japanese audiences for Indian films. One of the four films was *3 Idiots* (see Chapter 10). This demonstrates a commitment to a new contra-flow with delegations of industry personnel from India and Japan travelling to the other country.

The second story was about a new policy announced by Disney. The US major announced that it would no longer treat India and China as standard export markets for films and other media. Instead it would develop separate new strategies for each of the two major markets, reflecting local differences. In India, plans were announced for four different 'Indian Disney' businesses looking after film, television, digital media and consumer products. The film business will be branded as UTV, the identity of Disney's Indian partner. In China, Disney reported that it was less hopeful of developing film distribution via imports from the US because of Chinese government controls and was therefore investing more in its theme park and merchandising efforts. Its second theme park in Asia, in Hong Kong, had finally moved into profit after seven years of losses. Disney opens a new theme park in Shanghai in 2015.

The developments at Disney do seem to signal a shift in global film, if only to emphasise that Hollywood hegemony does face challenges and that the major studios have started to think about what the rise of Asian media corporations means for the ways in which they conduct business in what may become the biggest regional market for filmed entertainment.

Thanks to Eric Khoo for discussing Tatsumi *and his ideas about Singapore/ Malaysia co-productions.*

Indian producer Yash Raj Films started production of English-language films from its Hollywood base in 2012. In 2013 it announced that the Weinstein Company would release *Grace of Monaco* with Nicole Kidman for the US Christmas and Oscar awards season.

References and further reading

Enders Analysis (2012) *Digital Europe: Diversity and Opportunity*, available to download from: www.letsgoconnected.eu/files/Lets_go_connected-Full_report.pdf.

FICCI-KPMG (2013) *The Power of a Billion: Realising the Indian Dream*, Indian Media and Entertainment Industry Report, available to download from: www.ficci.com/spdocument/20217/FICCI-KPMG-Report-13-FRAMES.pdf.

NESTA (2010) *Beyond Live: Digital Innovation in the Performing Arts*, Research Briefing, February, available to download from: www.nesta.org.uk/library/documents/Beyond-Live-report.pdf.

Price Waterhouse Coopers (2012) *Global Entertainment and Media Outlook: 2012–2016*, available to download from: www.pwc.com/gx/en/entertainment-media/index.jhtml.

Shackleton, Liz (2012) 'Indonesia Spreads its Wings', *Screendaily* 22 August. Available at http://www.screendaily.com/reports/in-focus/indonesia-spreads-its-wings/5045560.article.

Vincendeau, Ginette (ed.) (1995) *Encyclopedia of European Cinema*, London: BFI/Cassell.

Glossary of key terms

These are brief definitions of how key terms in global film are used in this book.

art cinema/arthouse – descriptions of both a category of cinema and the theatres that show such films

art film – originally a film with high art content, later a film dealing with characters, themes and the expressive ideas of the filmmakers rather than as mainstream entertainment

artisanal – referring to filmmaking that is treated more as a 'craft' than an industry, used to distinguish certain kinds of specialised films

artists' films – a category of films defined by the status of the filmmaker as already established as a fine artist whose work appears in galleries: artists' films may appear in both galleries and cinemas, and some have 'crossed over' into more conventional specialised cinema distribution

auteur/auteurism – the concept of the filmmaker as 'author' (cf. novelist), particularly important in terms of 'world cinema', since auteur films are more likely to circulate via film festivals and international art cinema

avance sur recettes – the French form of public funding support for filmmakers, an advance on receipts/box office

awards films – films released and promoted by studios to have the best chance of winning major prizes (Oscars, Golden Globes, BAFTAs, etc. or Cannes, Venice, Berlin prizes)

back catalogue – the film library owned by a studio or other major distributor which provides an income flow to offset losses on current productions

bilateral agreement – a co-production agreement between two film-producing countries, allowing co-produced films to receive public funding

binarisms – opposite values used to define the relationship between two different agencies or sets of ideas, such as Hollywood vs. 'Not Hollywood'

blockbuster – in Hollywood, a high-budget film released wide with heavy promotion, often part of a franchise; definitions vary in other film industries

BRIC – acronym for the 'emerging' economies of Brazil, Russia, India and China

business model – the various film business practices, assumptions about audiences and profitability, etc. that make up the conventional ways of distributing and exhibiting films in the international market: business models for local films may vary in specific territories

cinephile – someone with a passionate interest in films and film culture

classical (cinema/film) – one of the key debates in film studies focuses on the definition of the Hollywood studio period of 1930 to 1960 as 'classical cinema', reaching a form of perfection and acting as a model to be followed or reacted against; other forms of studio filmmaking in other film-producing nations could also be described as classical, thus challenging such a definition

coloniser–colonised – the **binarism** that describes the power relationship underpinning colonialism

contra-flow – the flow of film and TV (or other media) exports that runs 'against' or 'across' the usual flow *from* Hollywood *to* the rest of the world

co-production – a film officially recognised as having a shared national ownership and therefore eligible for funding support from both partner countries

creolisation – the process of 'mixing' elements of two different cultures (e.g. languages, music, cuisine, etc.) to produce a new form; see also **hybridity**

cultural cinema/cultural production – films made or distributed in order to advance cultural aims

cultural exception – French public policies designed to protect the 'difference' of French media production in the face of Hollywood imports

cultural imperialism – the domination of cultural activity in other countries by a powerful media producer such as Hollywood

cultural test – a schedule of requirements to determine the nationality of a film and therefore whether it is eligible for support

cycle – in genre study, the identification of a group of films, produced over a short period of time, which share the same combination of genre elements: a cycle sometimes starts with the unexpected success of a relatively low-budget film that is then remade and given a sequel and prequel

D-cinema — digital cinema distribution and exhibition compliant with the DCI protocols set down by the Hollywood studios

DCI – Digital Cinema Initiative of the Hollywood studios

DCP – Digital Cinema Package, the collection of computer files comprising the data needed to project a DCI-compliant digital film

demographics – in the film and television industries, the attempt to identify a specific segment of the population and to target that segment with different types of films or programme material. Blockbuster films aim for 'all four quadrants' of the population: young and old, male and female.

diaspora – describes both the process of migration or 'dispersal' of large numbers of people from one country/region to another and the community of immigrants in the new host country

differential pricing – the practice of charging different prices to buyers in different countries, especially re US filmed TV series

discourse – any regulated system of statements or language use which operates with conventional and social assumptions, excluding or marginalising some participants and generally being subject to power relations

distributor – a company that has acquired the rights to distribute a film in specific territories (and on specific platforms)

Dogme – a term for films and filmmaking using ideas derived from the Dogme manifesto proclaimed by Lars von Trier and Thomas Vinterberg in 1995

domestic – used to describe the 'home' market for any film industry, in North America, the US and Canadian markets combined

dubbing – in general use the replacement of one film soundtrack (or one element of the soundtrack) with another, one of three ways of dealing with 'foreign-language' film imports

E-cinema – any form of digital cinema distribution and exhibition that is not DCI compliant (i.e. not D-cinema)

early cinema – the first 10 to 15 years of cinema, before the institutional structures were fully established

eurocentric – the adoption of a perspective on issues which is solely European (usually taken to include North America and Australia/New Zealand)

exilic filmmakers – filmmakers who are in exile for political or personal cultural reasons but who continue to make films about their homeland from their new base

externalities – in economics the various forms of the impact of an economic activity, some of which may be difficult to measure

extreme film – a film which goes beyond Hollywood conventions in its representations of sex, violence and social behaviour, seen as derogatory in categorising films from specific countries

facilities house – a company offering post-production facilities: provision of facilities locally is attractive to film producers from outside the region who want to use local locations

festival film – a film seen as targeting a film festival audience and unlikely to achieve a wide commercial distribution

film commission – an organisation (usually publicly funded) set up to attract potential film productions to a specific country/region/city with support to find locations, gain permissions, etc.

film culture – usually distinguished from film industry and referring to how audiences respond to films, how films are promoted and discussed in other media, film criticism and film scholarship

film format – for celluloid film, the selection of different sizes of film stock for capture and for projection

film industry – preparation, production, post-production and distribution/exhibition of films

film movement – creation by film marketeers and journalists/critics of a group identity for new filmmakers with a similar approach or focus on specific themes, often associated with a national cinema

filmed entertainment – the overall market for film-related products, including 'theatrical' exhibition, digital online/streaming, Blu-ray/DVD and television

format – (1) referring to different types of media carrier such as videotapes, discs, etc.; (2) a package of production ideas for a certain type of television programme, often for a particular audience or schedule slot, that may be sold/franchised to other broadcasters; (3) different sizes of filmstock for capture or projection along with different associated technologies; (4) simply another term for 'genre' or 'category': is 'documentary' a genre or a format?

fragmenting – the process by which modern audiences for film and television are increasingly splitting into more specialised audiences for specific categories of films

franchise – the creation of a package of ingredients making up a successful film based on a central character and situation, the production of sequels and prequels and 're-boots' of a highly successful film title or the successive adaptation of book titles by the same author (e.g. the Harry Potter series)

gangster film – a genre defined, in retrospect, to describe Hollywood films focusing on the development of 'organised crime', initially in the early 1930s, and subsequently recognised as a suitable description for films with similar content from many other industries, including France, UK, Italy, Hong Kong, Japan, India, etc.

gatekeepers – term from media studies to describe the key individuals/companies who control access to films (e.g. distributors, certification bodies, cultural agencies, etc.)

gendaigeki – a broad genre category in Japan referring to contemporary films

genre repertoires – an emphasis on the fluid and dynamic nature of genre as a category comprising groupings of elements

globalisation – the process by which local markets and local cultures become part of global markets and global cultures with both the possibilities of greater economic/cultural activity, but also less local control over that activity

global television – the concept of television that has an audience beyond national boundaries, including television **formats** that can be developed for different national audiences

government cultural policies – film is covered by various forms of public policy initiatives in many countries, usually designed to encourage interest in local stories, to project national cultural ideals or to encourage forms of diversity

hegemony – the concept of dominance by consent, stressing culture as a form of power

Hollywood – an industrial presence through the six major studios, a physical location and a social institution creating the internationally recognised concept of an entertainment film

humanist film – usually refers in cinema to a film which attempts to present a range of characters, each of whom displays 'human characteristics' rather than conforming to conventions of 'hero' and 'villain' and other typical roles, or to conventions of happy endings, etc.

hybridity – the product of 'mixing' cultures or genres to produce something new (see also **creolisation**)

imagined community – the concept suggested by Benedict Anderson to represent the 'nation': since it is impossible for all members of a nation state to meet and know each other, they must instead relate to a socially constructed community sharing similar ideas but not necessarily bound by economic, geographical or political boundaries

imperfect cinema – the concept associated with the Cuban filmmaker and theorist Julio García Espinosa, referring to a filmmaking practice which attempts to engage the popular audience, asking them to work *with* the film in order to produce meaning rather than to simply 'consume' a commercial product

independent – a film company which is not associated with a major studio and/or which produces films with lower budgets, focusing on stories or themes or treatments that would not be found in mainstream films of that country

international – in distribution terms, the 'rest of the world' outside North America; as a description of a film, one intended for an international audience (as opposed to a specific **local** audience)

inward investment – usually refers to Hollywood productions made in a country outside the US as described by the country with the production base

jidaigeki – broad genre category in Japan referring to historical films

letterboxing – the black bars above and below a wide film image as presented on a television screen; when bars appear on the sides of the image (e.g. showing a 1.37:1 film image on a 16:9 TV set), known as pillar-boxing

local – referring to films produced in a specific country or region intended for local audiences (as opposed to **international**)

magic realism – a literary style in which realist detail is applied to a fantasy situation

main melody – in mainland Chinese cinema, referring to a theme which is in tune with state policies on development

mainstream – Hollywood studio films or their equivalent in other territories

melodrama – in nineteenth-century theatre, a spectacular show emphasising music, costumes and sets; in cinema, first a genre of spectacle and action, later a genre of relationships with meanings expressed through an excessive *mise en scène* (colour, lighting, costumes, décor, etc.)

micro-budget – a film with a very low budget, in the UK under £250,000 (approximately US$375,000)

middle cinema – in Indian cinema, a type of film falling between 'popular' and 'art cinema', mostly now subsumed under the broader term **parallel cinema**

mode (vs. genre) – a broad category or repertoire that informs other, more specific genres

modern/modernity – referring to aspects of everyday culture associated with the use of new technologies, and new modes of living and forms of social behaviour

modernist/modernism – the art movement of the early twentieth century which challenged the conventions of the classical; in cinema, films of a later period, mainly in the 1950s and 1960s

MPAA – the Motion Pictures Association of America, the trade association formed by the six major Hollywood studios

multiple-version production – the practice of shooting two or more language versions of the same basic script at about the same time, usually with different actors

multiplex – a purpose-built cinema with three or more screens (usually 6 to 20 screens)

national cinema – a disputed term with several possible meanings because of the international nature of film production: possibly based on (1) production base and funding; (2) specific national themes or stories; (3) distinct aesthetic decisions developed through art cinema; (4) film culture as expressed via audience choices, critical writing

national-popular – derived from the writings of Antonio Gramsci, the concept of promoting a nationalist narrative via popular rather than élite culture

neo-colonialism – the continuation of a form of colonial relationship after the formal end of colonial rule, usually expressed through unequal terms of trade and business practices which work against the former colony

neo-realism – the filmmaking mode developed 'on the streets' among the ruins of the Italian film industry after 1945 that became highly influential in many other countries lacking filmmaking resources over the next 20 years and more

new media – the new media forms which became possible following the switch from analogue to digital media technologies

New Wave – the concept of a significant group of filmmakers producing new kinds of films over a relatively short time period, usually as a reaction to prevailing ideas about cinema

Nollywood – the popular term for the video film industry of Nigeria (and Ghana), now also covering films intended for cinema release

orientalist – the tendency to view non-Western cultures as imagined by the Western spectator rather than in terms of their local conditions

other – the identification of the non-Western as 'other', 'not Hollywood', is at the centre of studies of power relationships between coloniser–colonised and relationships associated with gender, sexual orientation, social class etc.

pan-African – 'across Africa' has a specific meaning in the history of African politics and African cinema, referring to the movement, after decolonisation in the 1960s, to develop African cultures in a collaborative manner: FESPACO, the Ouagadougou film festival, is one of the legacies of this cultural movement

pan and scan – the telecine technique which presents a film image with reduced width as 'full screen' on a television set; cf. **letterboxing**

parallel cinema – in Indian cinema, a type of filmmaking that deliberately avoids the use of Indian popular cinema conventions and focuses more on social issues, but also uses stars, many of whom also appear in popular cinema: a loosely defined term that in the 1970s became associated with 'new cinema' and **middle cinema**

periphery – one of the binarisms of the colonial relationship is the metropolitan centre vs. the 'periphery'

platform – (1) similar to the use of **format** to describe different types of 'carrier' for a media product such as VOD, DVD, etc.; (2) a film distribution strategy that sees screenings in a limited number of cinemas in major cities used to develop audience interest before wider distribution

polar – the French popular genre that combines aspects of the crime film, action thriller, *film policier* and *film noir*

polycentric – an approach to film scholarship which assumes 'many different perspectives' and is explicitly opposed to the **eurocentric**

portmanteau film – a film comprising several short films (linked by a theme or location) by different directors, useful as an outlet for talented filmmakers who find it difficult to raise funding for a solo feature (e.g. in countries without an established industrial base)

post-colonial – pertaining to the period following de-colonisation

postcolonialism – the set of ideas related to conditions in society following de-colonisation

postmodernist/postmodernism – the uncertain 'state of the world' following the end of the Cold War and in post-industrial society where 'meta-narratives' no longer apply; a movement across the arts; specific modes associated with hybridity, uncertainty, intertextuality, etc.

product placement – income for film producers based on appearances of products in feature films, increasingly important in Chinese and Indian productions

PSB – public service broadcasting, usually referring to a public sector broadcaster funded at least partially by a licence fee

public funding – any investment or grant available to film producers from national or local government agencies or from other public sector organisations such as television companies funded by licence fees

quality film – an institutional category referring to films (or television material) with relatively high budgets and high levels of technical skill, but often quite conservative aesthetics or narrative content; sometimes, however, such films or television programmes may be innovative (e.g. some series/serials produced for US cable television)

quota system – various countries have attempted to protect their domestic film industries by requiring distributors and exhibitors to show a set proportion of local titles or to restrict the import of foreign (usually Hollywood) titles

realisms – different aesthetics and production modes designed to create a realism effect

regional support funds – incentives offered to film producers to locate at least part of a film's production in a specific region, especially common in Europe, Australia and North America

remake – a new film made from a script that has already been used to create an earlier film: rights to allow remakes may be bought and sold

rights – ownership of rights to a film title allows a distributor to profit from exploitation of the film, usually in a specified territory and on specified formats for a set period; rights may be bought and sold

second run – cinemas in a national distribution system that screen films after they have been shown in first-run cinemas (or they screen low-budget films or re-releases): the 'B' and 'C' circuits in India represent the same form of stratification

segmenting – a term often used in television to describe the splitting of the mass market according to age, gender, social class, etc.

self-orientalism – the process whereby filmmakers from East Asia create work that appeals to a Western sense of the 'exotic Orient'

serial narrative – a television form with a single narrative thread and an eventual resolution, distinguishable from a series or a continuous serial (e.g. a soap opera)

short film – a film less than 60 minutes in length: in practice it is difficult to achieve theatrical distribution for films under 80 minutes

social realism – a form of realism that involves a focus on social issues and use of 'authentic' locations, speech, costume, etc. to represent social life

socialist realism – the 'official' approach to filmmaking (and other arts) as developed in the USSR in the 1930s

soft money – loans or grants from public funds provided to encourage film production in specific territories

soft power – the negotiating power available to governments as a result of the status of the cultural output of the country (i.e. via commercial success or winning prizes, critical acclaim, etc.)

specialised film – a general term to distinguish films which are not seen as **mainstream** in audience appeal

stars – actors who have an image that circulates beyond the films in which they appear and which gives them marketing status

studio – usually accepted as an established film production company also involved in distribution (see **vertical integration**), often now reserved for the six major Hollywood studios

studio model – an economic or financial model based on studio production

studio production – as distinct from 'independent' production

studio system – the fully integrated studio operations (i.e. including exhibition) that featured in the UK and Japan as well as Hollywood in the 1930s to 1960s

subtitling – the practice of translations of dialogue as text on screen as an alternative to dubbing, sometimes in more than one language

syndication – a general term in media industries to refer to the sale of rights in print material or television or radio productions through distribution deals, often to 'affiliates' in a network; the basis for the hegemony of US media in international markets

synergy – the concept of two media forms (usually owned by the same organisation) sharing the rights to the same property and therefore creating greater profit owing to shared expenditure

tax incentive – forms of tax allowance offered to film companies that fulfil official criteria for a 'national' production in a particular country

telecine – the process of scanning a film image for broadcast on television, no longer needed in the world of digital film

telefilm – a film designed to be shown primarily on television rather than in cinemas

telenovela – a form of long serial drama (e.g. 100 'chapters') originating in Latin American radio and television

tentpole – a major film release that is meant to act as a 'banker' for a distributor

territory – a geographical area in which a film distributor has the rights to screen a film to the public on a particular platform

theatrical – used in the film industry to refer to the rights to screen a film in public cinemas

Third Cinema – a polemical/campaigning term to describe cinema that is not 'Hollywood-style entertainment' or 'European-style art cinema'

transnational – used as a term to challenge both 'national' and 'international', it suggests that the production of films and the meanings that films produce are not bounded by national definitions; films may be both local and global and the impetus for using the term comes from outside Hollywood (which has long made international films from an American perspective)

transparency – the concept associated with Hollywood continuity editing which is 'invisible' and avoids attention to the process of editing

universal genres – those genres with basic repertoires found in the production schedules of most major film industries

V-cinema – the Japanese concept of films made on video for distribution on video

vertical integration – the ownership of each stage of the film production/distribution/exhibition process that characterises the major studios during the studio production era

VPF – the Virtual Print Fee paid by distributors for each screening of a digital film as a contribution to the investment in digital projection equipment

[the] western – a genre referring directly to aspects of the history of the American West between 1865 and the closing of the frontier in the 1890s; genres with similar repertoires of landscape, lawlessness, frontier, etc. in many different territories

window – in film distribution, the practice of granting an exclusive time period when one format will have the market to itself for a new film release

world cinema – term used in marketing films, referring broadly to any film outside Hollywood, but tending towards specialised rather than popular entertainment cinema

worldwide – in the international film business, the total film market comprising 'domestic' (North America) and 'international'

Indices

Items discussed at length are signalled in **bold**, margin entries with (m) and illustrations by *italic numbers*.

Names

Prominent filmmakers, film industry figures, theorists and academics.

Selected key terms

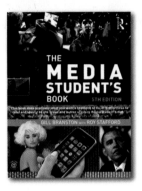